*Dr. John A. Weber*

# Sales Growth Secrets

How to Realize Continuous Sales
Growth for Your Company

*Dr. John A. Weber*

Dr. John A. Weber (weber.1@nd.edu)
Mendoza College of Business
University of Notre Dame
Notre Dame, IN 46560
www.linkedin.com/in/johnweberphd/

Book Layout ©2023 Book Design Templates & https://usedtotech.com

Sales Growth Secrets – How to Realize Continuous Sales Growth for Your Company / Dr. John A. Weber —2nd ed.
**ISBN**: *TBD*

# Reactions to the Sales Growth Secrets Book

Become the next sales superstar in your company! Blow away your sales targets. Be your boss's 'go to' sales pro. See some of the hundreds of 5* reviews below - from sales pros who have successfully started or totally re-launched their careers using this innovative, proven selling process.

# What sales professionals are saying about the Sales Growth Secrets book

- **Essential Reading for Sales Professionals**
- **Easy to Understand and Retain**
- **A Logical Process**
- **A Fun Read, Full of Real World Examples**

## Essential Reading for Sales Professionals

- **A must-have for marketing & sales professionals.** "This book is as well-organized as it is insightful. Crucial information is integrated and neatly packed into brief sections that capture one's attention with clear examples, observations and caveats. Professionals in any field can benefit from this book, but for marketing/sales professionals this book is a must-have!"
  Greg G.
- **A treasure trove of great information.** "I've been finding a treasure trove of GREAT information in this book. I feel like I'm getting a business degree in selling just by reading this book."
  David L.
- **This book has turned around my sales career!** "This book has become my 'how-to' guide – literally turning around my sales career. The process explained has been particularly helpful when I'm pursuing big ticket sales opportunities."
  M. Murphy
- **My 'go-to-source' for selling success.** "Having recently embarked on a career in sales, I can say unequivocally that the detailed approach presented so clearly in this book has been a difference maker for me for both preparing for my interviews and now as my 'go-to-source' for my selling success."

Barbara B

- **A must read for anyone in the marketing world.** "This book is a 'must read' for anyone in the marketing world seeking new perspectives and insights for growing their sales."
  Danielle P.


## Easy to Understand and Retain

- **Well-organized, easy to follow.** "This book is all well-organized and closely linked - offering a clear, concise outline at the beginning of each book, which make it easier to follow along the different stages of the selling process. A great read for anyone wanting to learn to sell more effectively!"
  Sofia S.
- **Short chapters.** The short chapters make it easy to pay attention, as they break down the information into specific smaller steps. This helps to understand, rather than be overwhelmed by the logical selling process presented."
  Jane E.
- **Bring the selling process to life**. "Whereas most sales books get bogged down with verbose conceptual descriptions, this book bring to life the selling process in a simple, engaging manner – highly recommended for any veteran or aspiring sales professional."
  Jeff A.
- **A quick read, easily digestible**. "This book is a quick read and are easily digestible for anyone looking to improve their selling skills – whether new to sales or a professional sales veteran."
  Mark C.


## A Logical Process

- **A logical checklist for planning any selling effort.** "This book provides a clear and thorough step-by-step process for tackling and closing on any prospective sale."
  J. Agar
- **Clear structure and supporting diagrams.** "The selling process detailed in this book is ideal for anyone favoring clear, unambiguous structure, presented with easy-to-understand supporting diagrams and examples."
  A.C

- **An integrated approach.** "Rather than presenting a bunch of theories and terms scattered about overwhelmingly long chapters, this book present a logical, integrated approach - neatly packed in brief chapters that use clear examples throughout to capture and hold one's attention."

  G. Garner.

- **Clearly laid out tools – for immediate use.** "I cannot say enough good things about this book. The book provides a clear, proven way for successful selling -- full of easy-to-use tools one can use immediately in the real world to enhance sales!"

  T. Redman

## A Fun Read, Full of Real World Examples

- **Fun and engaging.** "What a refreshing change from the typical book about selling! Reading this book was fun and engaging, as it includes tons of pictures, cartoons, amusing characters, and insightful charts and exhibits."

  Darin C.

- **Very enjoyable reading.** "I never thought I'd actually enjoy learning about sales. But this book has totally changed my opinion. It makes the whole selling process come alive with cogent, often times humorous characters, dialog and examples."

  Adam S.

- **The book is a joy to read.** "The Sales Growth Secrets book is a real joy to read, as it is not only super-logical, but is also filled with straightforward clarifying illustrations, humorous characters and anecdotes, and extensive dialogues clarifying key points."

  E. Reilly

# About the Author

John A. Weber (Ph.D., University of Wisconsin), is Emeritus Professor of Marketing at the University of Notre Dame where he taught for decades, only recently retiring. He has published over seventy articles, monographs, books, and computers programs on planning corporate growth.

John has worked with hundreds of major firms - among them more than thirty Fortune 500 companies - helping them to identify and pursue new sales and profit growth opportunities. Corporate clients have included General Electric, AT&T, IBM, 3M, Xerox, Bristol-Myers, International Paper, Bell South, Miles Labs, Pioneer Seed, Honeywell, Mastic, Nekoosa, Bradley, Thomaston Mills, Kellogg, Certainteed, Uniroyal, Whirlpool, American Greetings, Square D, Cabot, Richards Medical, Continental Can (JSC/CCA), Camshaft Machine, Adria Labs, Jeld-Wen, Dukane, Gould, Hammermill, Sears, Federal Express, and many other companies manufacturing and marketing a wide range of industrial and consumer products and services.

Professor Weber is a certified instructor of Solution Selling®. In addition to his own extensive material on planning corporate growth, the Sales Growth Secrets Book integrates his interpretation & expansion of the Solution Selling® system - with SPI's approval, but without SPI's carte blanche endorsement of all the specifics of his professional interpretation and expansion.

# Acknowledgements

All of the young professionals below made significant contributions to the development, drafting, and editing of this work. Thank you all!

Back: *Colleen MacDonald, John Weber, Collin Erker, Phil Anderson, Sam Dettman, Will Ivancic, Ozzy Rocha, Chris Jacques, Rob Kirk, Eric Chyriwski, Erin Laughlin.* Middle: *Chris Davis, Amanda Walter, Kate Albertini, Morgan Walsh, Katie Adams, Maya Pillai,* Front: *Alejandra Barrios, Teresa Keeney, Alexa Wilson.*

**Special acknowledgement** to **Jack Clarke** for his help with proofing and to the enthusiastic individuals shown below for their similar extraordinary dedication and contributions. Thank you!

Catherine Russell     Michael Nokes     Mike Donnelly     Leo Dipiero     Laura Taylor

Kate Albertini     Chris Jacques     Kristina Hamilton     Kirsten Bescher     Elizabeth Linnemanstons

# Sales Growth Secrets

----

# Outline

Part 1 – Preparing for Sales Growth

Part 2 – Preparing Your Account Marketing Plan

Part 3 – Implementing Your Account Marketing Plan: Making the Individual Sale (4 Steps)

Part 4 – Ensuring Continuous Sales Growth

# Introduction & Overview

The Sales Growth Secrets book is written to help companies realize continuous, aggressive growth of sales and profits. *All materials presented in the book have been tested countless times through the author's own growth planning consulting experiences with scores of major firms*. (Refer to the Author profile.)

The book is fast-moving and easy to read, featuring short, single-concept chapters, accompanied by many cartoons and clear exhibits that bring to life the principles as they are presented. To build and maintain interest, the various concepts and processes detailed throughout the book are presented in an actual Account Marketing scenario that includes a cast of fun characters introduced and followed along the way, providing a lively and entertaining storyline.

The book begins (*Part 1: Preparing for Sales Growth*) by reviewing key concepts, frameworks and practical planning perspectives that provide the base necessary for any firm desiring to achieve consistent growth of both sales & profit.

The coverage then moves on (*Parts 2: Building your Account Marketing Plan* to pursue the commonsense notion that sales and profit growth are achieved one profitable sale at a time. The chapters in this section provide a hands-on review of how to develop a thorough Account Marketing Plan for capturing sales from any target customer. *While the examples used throughout the book focus on selling high value, complex, long sales cycle products & services, the principles detailed are equally applicable for targeting and selling virtually any business to business or consumer product or service.*

The book then (*Parts 3: Making the Individual Sale – 4 Steps*) uses a single, detailed practical example to demonstrate how to effectively implement all dimensions of the thoroughly developed Account Marketing Plan outlined in Part 2 – right on through negotiation, closing, implementing and follow up.

The final chapters of the book (*Part 4: Ensuring Continuous Sales Growth*) offer a proven approach for monitoring and integrating the selling efforts of the entire salesforce to virtually ensure continuous growth of sales and profits

The latter three parts of the book draw heavily on Solution Selling® -- an ultra-effective selling system used for training more than a million sales professionals in large and small companies around the globe. The Solution Selling® coverage is detailed with the author's own interpretation and extensions.

# Part 1
# *Preparing for Sales Growth*

CHAPTER 1

# Growth is King

| Introduction: Growth is King | | |
|---|---|---|
| Ch | 1 | Growth is King! |

"Fat, drunk and stupid is no way to go through life, son." This sound observation came from Dean Wormer while chastising Flounder in the movie classic, *Animal House*.

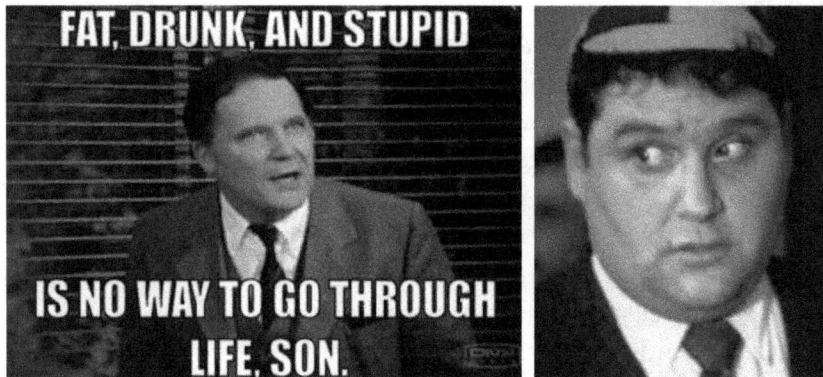

Although Dean Wormer was referencing the crazy college life that Flounder was experiencing, a similar observation can be made in reference to the corporate world: *Constantly struggling to meet quarterly profit projections through cost cutting and massaging the numbers is no way to run a business! It's not fun either* ☹ *!*

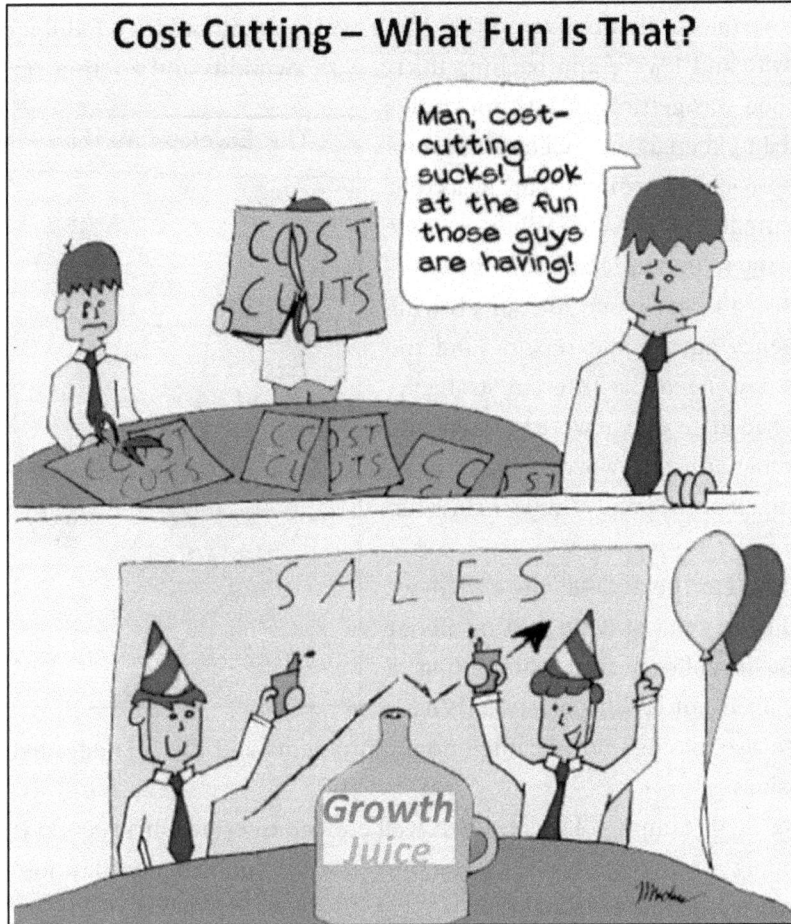

## The 'Envelope Method'

The envelope method consists of cashing your check each month (or week), paying all fixed monthly or weekly bills, divvying up the remaining proceeds into separate envelopes for identified, budgeted items (food, baby sitter, entertainment, automobile expenses, household maintenance, etc.) – and then pulling cash out of envelopes as expenses occur. Finally, and inevitably, as the next payday approaches, you start raiding any envelopes with money remaining in order to cover expenses where the envelopes are 'mysteriously' empty.

Years ago, our young family discovered that the 'envelope method' (See Exhibit) is no fun. By the time my wife and I were approaching thirty, with two kids and another on the way, the envelope method was getting old! Although this method worked to keep us on budget for several years, the approach just didn't cut it as our household continued to expand. When it came time to cover larger, 'unpredictable' costs such as school expenses, a larger home for our growing family, emergency automobile repairs, and the like, we realized we needed a different strategy.

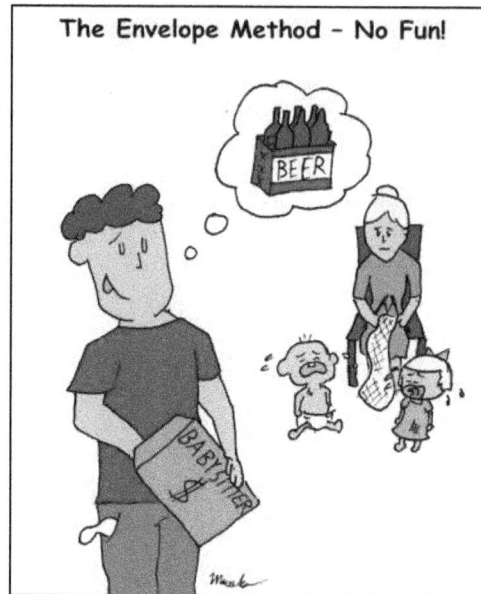

The Envelope Method - No Fun!

Something had to give if we were to move into the future without constant worries, quick fixes, and spending squabbles. Sound familiar? How fun is that?

Happy ending. For the decades since then, we have managed to stay out of debt, putting all our children through college and maintaining a comfortable - albeit not lavish - lifestyle. What's more, we have also avoided both 'panic' money problems and the related, never-fun 'family money discussions.'

How did we do it? Simple – I was trained well enough to establish a second income stream through providing consulting services, which eventually doubled my 'day job' salary. *More income trumps cost cutting every time!*

## Steady Top Line Revenue Growth is Key!

Increased revenue solves existing problems and helps avoid new ones. Not having to worry about paying the bills made our family life much less stressful and much more enjoyable! Who doesn't like that? Increased revenue enabled us to focus on opportunities ahead rather than on budget cutting and its subsequent negatives.

Well-planned revenue growth can do the same thing for a corporation as it does for a family. In fact, if there existed a list of 'magic elixirs' for corporate problems, then steady revenue growth would certainly be THE number one item on that list!

*Of course, you say... but... much, much easier said than done. You bet. That's the motivation for this book and its exact purpose: to help your company achieve more regular, profitable revenue growth.*

## Growing Companies
## Are 'Happy' Companies

Few complaints are heard at companies where 'home-grown' organic revenues and profits consistently grow 5-10% per year. Outside players such as stockholders, distributors, and suppliers are pleased, as are insiders, ranging from C-level players (e.g., CEO, CFO, COO, CMO, etc.) to operating players (like those involved in supply chain management, manufacturing, finance, and marketing).

Instead of trouble-shooting the problems associated with a lack of foresight, vision, and planning, these companies can devote much more time to finding and pursuing new, creative growth opportunities.

## Grow or Go

One insightful study[1] uncovered a very interesting phenomenon: the expected tenure of a new Chief Marketing Officer (CMO) is less than half that of a newly minted CEO (23 months vs. 54 months). Why do CMOs get fired so often? Usually, it is due to faltering top line revenue growth. For, without top line growth, the bottom line inevitably fades, resulting in pressures to blame someone. The most obvious and likely scapegoat is the officer in charge of revenue growth, that is, the CMO. Thus, the key to a long and successful tenure as a Marketing Executive is to keep top line revenue growing – year after year after year!

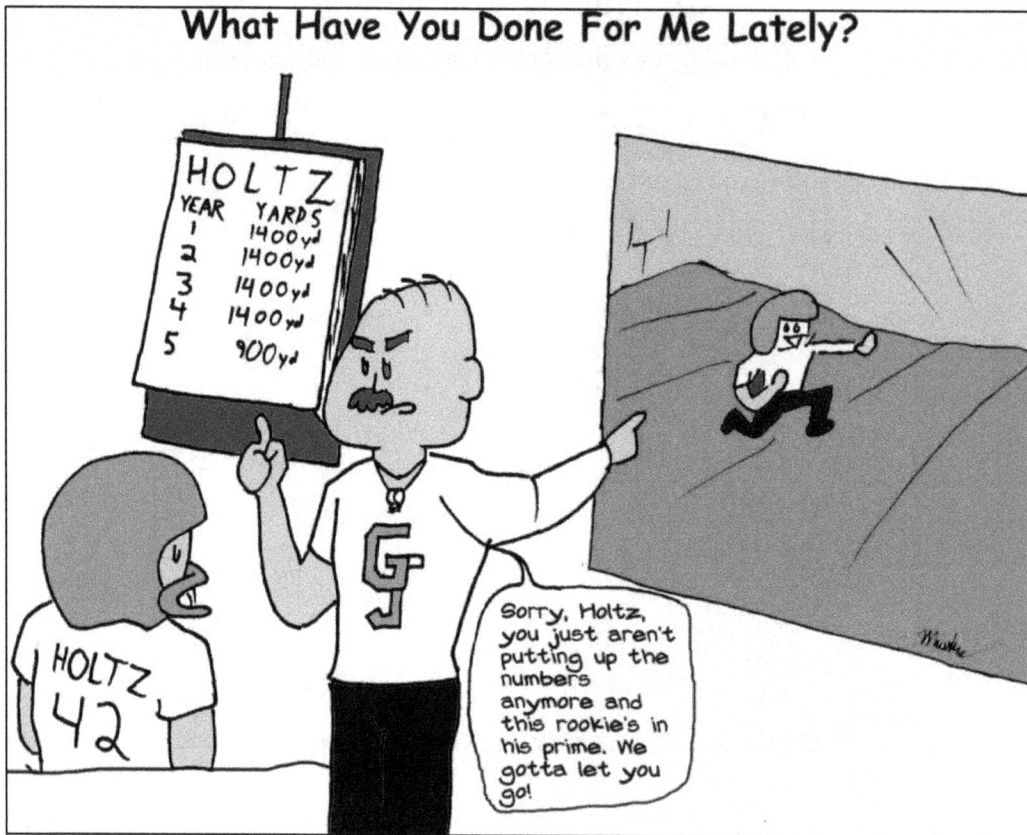

## Can Your Company Achieve
## Steady Top Line Revenue Growth? Sure, You Can!

Certainly, steady growth is easier said than done in today's increasingly competitive environment. The truism 'nothing worthwhile is easy' seems appropriate. But fear not - steady growth is possible. The first step to achieving regular growth is to recognize the reasons why so many companies fail to meet the growth challenge. In the following chapters, we discuss the primary causes of faltering revenue growth. We will then provide practical perspectives and tools for successfully addressing the challenge of achieving steady and profitable top line growth.

In the next several chapters we discuss the hurdles that inhibit steady, profitable growth in today's markets. *Then we move on to the important stuff – "How to Grow Consistently & Profitably!"*

CHAPTER 2

# What Business Are You Really In?

| Why is Steady Growth so Difficult to Achieve? | | |
|-----|---|----------------------------------------------------------------|
| Ch | 2 | **What Business Are You Really In?** |
| Ch | 3 | You Need the Best _Overall_ Solution Value (Not the Best Core Solution) |
| Ch | 4 | You Cannot Stop Commodity Drift |

In this chapter, we will begin the discussion of why steady, profitable growth is so difficult to achieve in today's markets.

Growth starts when you first recognize your company's true business. You can do this by asking what set of fundamental needs your company is trying to address with its current primary product or service. Focus on identifying those underlying needs. Thinking of your business as providing solutions rather than specific products or services can open entirely new avenues of potential growth.

You already know your customers and their needs related to your current products and services. Who better than you to seek out new product and service areas that more adequately satisfy those needs? If you don't, your competitors will – taking away your customers, your sales, and your growth.

## Brick & Mortar Book Stores Example

Take Blockbuster for example. Blockbuster was late in recognizing the industry trend towards video streaming. Netflix CEO and co-founder Reed Hastings approached Blockbuster CEO John Antioco in 2011 seeking a partnership between the two rental services, but Antioco declined. You can thank Blockbuster's short-sightedness for your new neighborhood eyesore. Michael Brush of MSN Money observes that "Video rental icon Blockbuster is a great example of how technological change can crush winners that fail to keep up. First, Blockbuster got hammered as video rentals began moving to mail distribution pioneered by Netflix. ... Now, video distribution is shifting to the Internet, and Blockbuster is lagging again. The amount of content you can download directly will make Blockbuster obsolete." Building off that sentiment, Strata Capital's Scott Stevens states "It seems to me, though, that technology has doomed Blockbuster as we know it. But at least we can all say goodbye to late fees forever."[2]

Like Blockbuster, Borders was also a victim of technological change. So, what went wrong with Borders? First came the Internet, which brought aggressive price competition from Amazon.com. Then, Walmart's tendency to slash prices on bestsellers and Amazon's ability to match those price cuts brought more competition for Borders. Then, Amazon's Kindle and other e-book readers gained popularity. More and more readers could simply download digital books at lower prices than print versions. All these trends reduced the need Border's brick-and-mortar stores, driving the company to bankruptcy because of their high inventory and store-related costs.[3]

## Stand-Alone GPS Units Example

Magellan, the former leader in GPS, is another once-great company that was doomed. GPS, the technology plotting your location via satellite, served as Magellan's relatively unique advantage for years, but soon became available just about everywhere. Besides dashboard GPS devices in cars, consumers could soon access GPS services on their smart phones & cameras. This was a natural progression in technology. Over time, consumers had few reasons to buy stand-alone GPS devices from Magellan because software on their phone performs an identical service.

To better understand how GPS was increasingly commoditized, consider the intense price competition in this category. On Black Friday in 2011, vendors like Magellan were offering generic GPS devices as low as $69. This price was $21 below the cost of materials in each device, but Magellan offered such a low price in order to try to maintain their current shelf space. You know a business appears doomed when it has to sell below costs, even temporarily, just to stay in the game.[4]

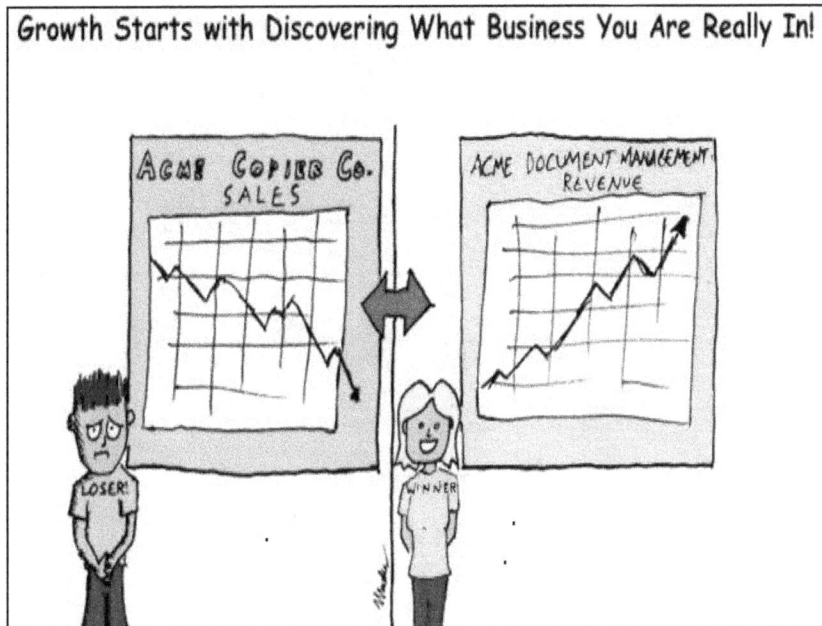

Growth Starts with Discovering What Business You Are Really In!

## Try This

Here's an exercise in discovering new growth opportunities. Consider the multiple "Current Products or Services" listed in Column 1 of the upcoming exhibit. Ask yourself, what fundamental, underlying need is each product or service providing? For example, Column 3 suggests some options or possibilities for identifying 'what business' the listed companies are actually in. Column 4 asks the question: what new 'solutions' might be the future for that industry? To succeed, a company must understand who their real competitors are - today and in years ahead. The company that does this the best typically wins the game. Those who lack foresight and fail to adapt will lose out. ***What is your company's primary product or service? What business is your company actually in?*** Consider these examples. Focus on Columns 3 & 4 of the Exhibits.

**What is your company's primary product or service?  What business is your company actually in?  Consider these examples.  Focus on Columns 3 & 4 of the Exhibit.**

| 1 Current Product or Service | 2 Company Examples | 3 What Business Are You Really In? | 4 Potential Products or Services to Consider? |
|---|---|---|---|
| Automobile leasing | Wheels, Corporate Fleet Services, Enterprise | Convenient, economical transportation business | Short-term car rental (i.e. Zipcar) |
| Bookstores | Barnes & Noble, Books-A-Million, Borders, B. Dalton | Personal leisure and education | E-commerce bookstore and Kindles |
| Computer aided design software | Autodesk, Avid Technology, ANSYS | Virtual product and building design | Software configuration management software |
| Computer hard-drives | Seagate, IBM, Fujitsu, Hitachi, Maxtor | Information storage business | Data storage in the cloud |
| Copiers | Xerox, Canon, Toshiba | Document management business | Document management software & Data Integration |
| ERP Systems | Best Software, Sage, Microsoft, Oracle | Company management & control business | CRM software |
| Fragrances | Sentient, CPL Aromas, Quest Int'l, International Flavors & | Business of making the human body, animals, objects or living | Longer lasting, dynamic fragrances.  Substitutes for |
| Fractional Airline Service | NetJets, Marquis Jets, Flexjet, Avant Air | Travel convenience business | C2C Internet Service that matches renters and lenders |
| Newspaper media | NY Times, Tribune Company, Washington Post | Information delivery business | Online news media |
| Office furniture | Steelcase, Inscape, Commercial Furniture Group | Office design & productivity | Interior design |
| Office leasing | Intelligent Office, Regus, Your Office Management | Office reach and productivity | Short-term office rental |
| Relocation companies | Cort | Relocation services | Relocation software (analyzes and compares potential new |
| Retail self checkout Machines | Fujitsu (U-Scan), IBM, NCR, Pan-Oston, | Retail productivity services | Digital touch-and-go payment services |
| Radio Frequency Identification systems (RFID) | Texas Instruments, Sun Microsystems, HP, MIT | Manufacturing, Inventory & Distribution productivity | More advanced ID technologies – e.g., Micro-sizing sensors |
| Sales Force Automation Systems | Salesforce.com, Sage (Sales Logix), Oracle (Siebel CRM) | Sales force productivity | Project management software |
| Security Services | ADT, Bosch Security Systems, Protection One | Safety & Loss prevention services | More automated & sensitive security systems |
| Signs | Daktronics, Lamar, 3M Digital Signage, LSI Industries | Visual communications / promotion | Digital signage |
| Supply chain management systems | Sirva, UPS, Federal Express, Kronos, IBM | Increasing the efficiency & productivity of Inbound & | Private US Postal Service |
| Temporary Help | Manpower, Kelly, Insperity | Human resource services | Recruiting software |
| Tracking technology | Garmin, Hewlett-Packard, Trimble Navigation | Location & Navigation efficiency & productivity | Retail location analysis |

| 1 | 2 | 3 | 4 |
|---|---|---|---|
| Current Product or Service | Company Examples | What Business Are You Really In? | Potential Products or Services to Consider? |
| Translation services | L-3 Communications, Lionbridge Technologies, SDL International | Global communications productivity | Real-time Automated translation software |
| Travel Agency | American Express, Travelocity, Expedia, American Automobile Assn | Travel management services + related substitutes & complements | Go to Meeting |
| Uniforms | Cintas, Unifirst, Superior Uniform Group | Better look, higher efficiency & productivity of uniform related | Cross-company imaging |
| Web-Analytics | Google Analytics, Omniture, Coremetrics, Visistat | Helping customers develop and execute more efficient and productive web promotions | Social media |
| Web-based Meetings | Web-Ex, Go to Meeting | Improving efficiency & productivity of meetings | Virtual Office? |
| Web-based phone service | Vonage, Phone power, ViaTalk, ITP, Lingo | More efficient audio communication | other web-based communications services |

**What is your company's primary product or service? What business is your company actually in? Consider these examples. Focus on Columns 3 & 4 of the Exhibit.**

---

# Visionary Exercise

Pull up this YouTube video called "A Day Made of Glass" by Corning "Glass" – or is it "Glass?"
http://www.youtube.com/watch_popup?v=6Cf7IL_eZ38&vq=medium;                              then
https://www.mandatory.com/living/945283-cornings-day-made-glass-finally-became-reality

Watch this video.

Now, ask yourself, what business is Corning Glass in?

Then use that visionary perspective to ask yourself, ***what business is your company in?***

CHAPTER 3

# You Need the Best <u>OVERALL</u> Market Solution

| Why is Steady Growth so Difficult to Achieve? | | |
|---|---|---|
| Ch | 2 | What Business Are You Really In? |
| **Ch** | **3** | **You Need the Best Overall Market Solution** |
| Ch | 4 | You Cannot Stop Commodity Drift |

In this chapter, we continue to discuss the important reasons why steady, profitable growth is so difficult to achieve in today's markets.

Firms' failure to explicitly recognize that they are each selling a 'total market solution' rather than a specific product or service often leads to constant struggles in trying to achieve steady, profitable growth. This chapter emphasizes that the company with the best solution will grow most steadily over the long term.

This notion that 'you need the best solution' is not as obvious as it may seem. To start, what do we mean by the 'best solution?' The best solution is *the solution that has the highest overall net value for the target customer*. Several concepts make up that statement.

First, when we talk of the 'best solution,' we are talking about much more than the 'core' or 'naked' solution. We are talking about the *overall* solution. A company's overall market solution includes a core product or service surrounded by a whole bundle of potential auxiliary attributes and related benefits. A wide range of attributes might be relevant – for example, cutting-edge technology, superior customer service, data integration, support services for the customer, etc. Consider the examples in the expanded exhibit entitled "Flexible Market Solution".[5] These examples illustrate just a few of the many potential ways to enhance a core solution. The enhancements that are most valued and appropriate will vary by target customer segment and from one customer to the next.

A company's overall solution does not have to be 'perfect' in order to be the best overall solution in the industry. It just has to be better than the primary competitor's overall solution.

# Definition: "Flexible Market Solution"

A Flexible Market Solution Consists of the Core
Solution Plus Many Potential Enhancements

## Examples of Potential Enhancements

Quality & Innovation Related Enhancements

**Examples -- Helping Customer with:**
- Innovations
- New or refined applications
- Application design assistance
- Enhanced quality & durability, etc.

Customer Relationship Enhancements

**Examples -- Helping Customer with:**
- Sharing data
- Helping customer get into new markets, improved people relationships
- Cooperative arrangements to enhance customer product development, distribution, inventory planning, sales innovations, etc.

Cost Efficiency Related Enhancements

**Examples -- Helping Customer with:**
- Efficiency enhancements in production
- Improved efficiencies in distribution, inventory planning & delivery
- Enhanced efficiency of Service, etc

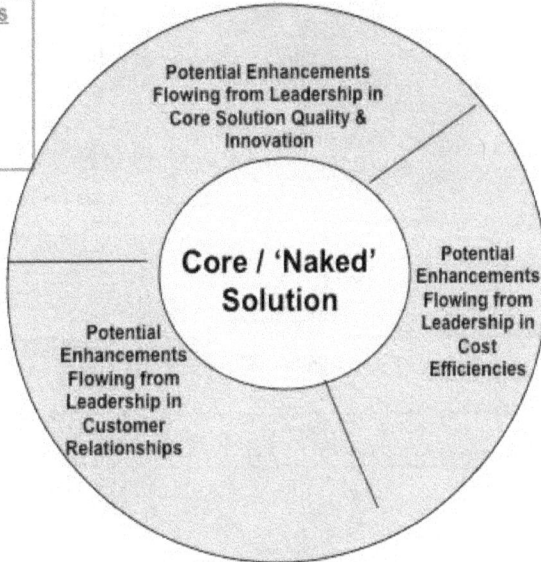

Potential Enhancements
Flowing from Leadership in
Core Solution Quality &
Innovation

**Core / 'Naked' Solution**

Potential Enhancements Flowing from Leadership in Cost Efficiencies

Potential Enhancements Flowing from Leadership in Customer Relationships

Why is this the case? How can a company with an adequate yet competitively inferior core solution beat out a competitor that has a clearly superior core solution? The winning company simply does a better job of listening to the customer, constantly taking the target customers' pulse and regularly adjusting its overall solution to best match dynamic customer needs and expectations. Competitors that continually dump resources into improving already adequate core solutions often falter. Meanwhile, competitors that spend more resources on listening to their target customer ultimately succeed over the longer term – assuming they respond to the needs of the client by surrounding an adequate solution with specific customer-valued attributes.

## You Don't Have to Be Perfect, Just Better Than the Competition

## Listen to the Customers, Not the Engineers

The Company with the Best Overall Solution Wins Even if Its Core Solution Is Inferior to Its Competitors

## Social Media's Role in Enhancing Market Solutions

As markets, customer demands, and competition change more rapidly, it becomes more important each year for firms to continually seek customer input and to respond to changes in customers' wants and concerns. Through using comprehensive Social Media Programs, firms today can do just that.

These programs make it easier and more efficient to monitor and learn about customers' relevant concerns with existing market solutions and to identify what specific new features or services are desired. This information can, in turn, be immediately fed to product development, customer service, IT, or other relevant departments for their consideration - which often leads to the development of better overall market solutions. Customers can then more readily and effectively be informed of new features or corrective actions through prominent updates on the company's website and in one or more of the company's specialty blogs. (More on this in the *Social Media Strategies* chapter).

## Online Surveys.

Today any company can use low cost or even free online survey capabilities to monitor its customer community. These surveys can engage actual and potential customers in meaningful discussions to improve the company's products and support services (i.e., overall market solutions). This easy, fast, and relatively inexpensive survey capability can also be used to generate quick and useful answers to pressing questions that a company may have regarding any actual or prospective dimension of its overall market solutions.

CHAPTER 4

# You Cannot Stop Commodity Drift

| Why is Steady Growth so Difficult to Achieve? | | |
|---|---|---|
| Ch | 2 | What Business Are You Really In? |
| Ch | 3 | You Need the Best *Overall* Solution Value (Not the Best Core Solution) |
| **Ch** | **4** | **You Cannot Stop Commodity Drift** |

In this chapter we discuss yet more reasons why steady, profitable growth is so difficult to achieve in today's markets.

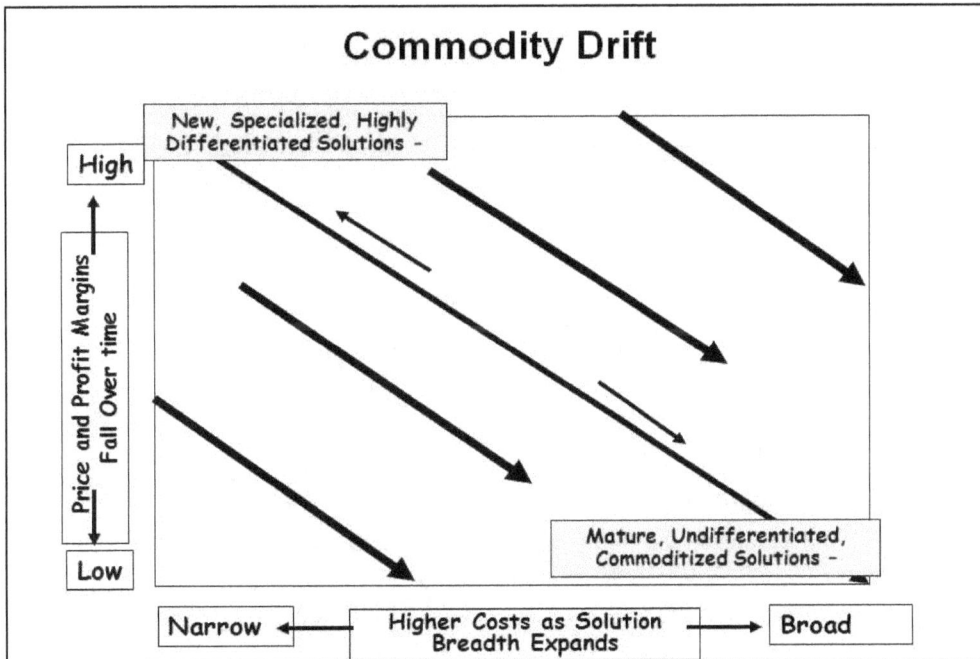

## Commodity Drift

New, Specialized, Highly
Differentiated Solutions –

High

Price and Profit Margins
Fall Over time

Low

Mature, Undifferentiated,
Commoditized Solutions –

Narrow ← Higher Costs as Solution
Breadth Expands → Broad

Bet on this: The attractiveness of every overall market solution for every relevant segment declines over time, reflecting the inevitable drift toward commodity status - with squeezed profit margins. *This drift can be slowed down but cannot be stopped.* Therefore, in order to consistently expand sales and profits, *a company must constantly seek out new market segments for current market solutions and continuously add entirely new market solutions to its portfolio.*

## You Cannot Stop Commodity Drift

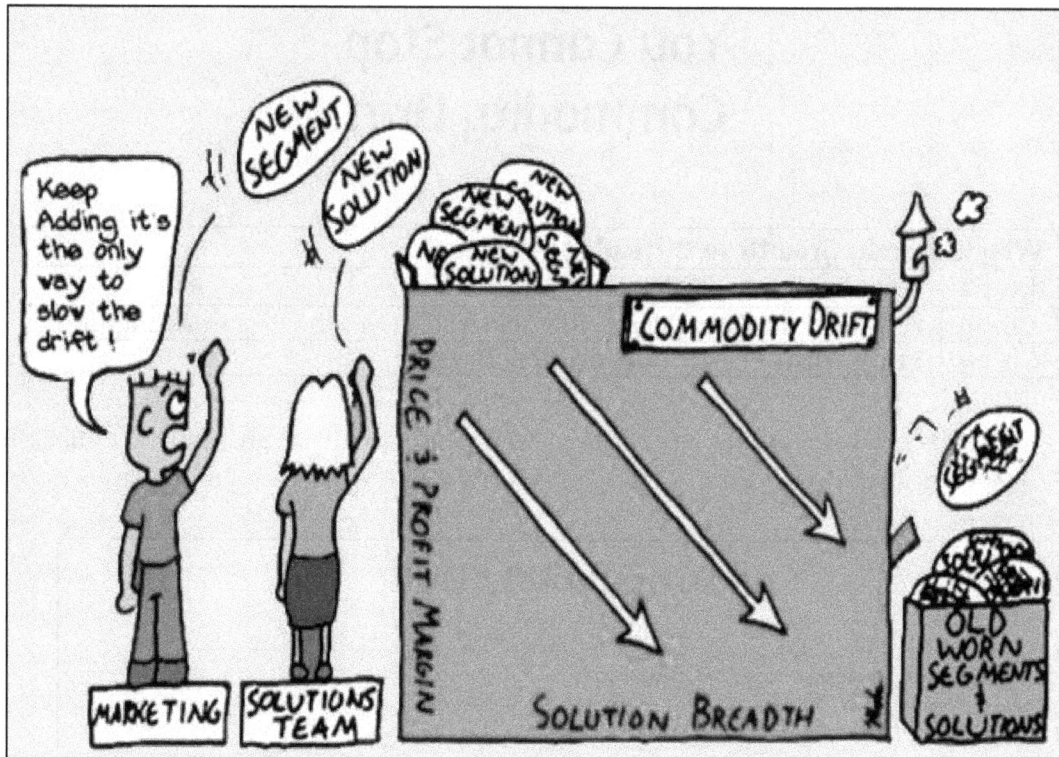

## What is 'Commodity Drift?'[6]

Commodity Drift is the gradual, but continuous power shift from suppliers to buyers for virtually any market solution. Initially, the market solution is an innovative, yet relatively simple core solution that can support a high price because it is unique and lacks competition. In this introductory, innovative stage, the solution requires few costly add-ons (refer back to the concept of a 'total market solution') to attract initial customers, often referred to as the 'innovator customer segment.' Thus, with high price and low costs, the profit margin is high during this introductory stage.

The next stage is undesirable, but inevitable. The high profit margin reaped by the original solution innovator immediately attracts competitors. These competitors gain access to the new market by offering the same fundamental core innovation at a lower price, while also often adding new features and services. The higher cost of these additional features and services coupled with the lower price both quickly drive down profit margin for all competitors, including the original innovator. This process continues over time until the once-attractive market reaches commodity status. Commodity status is characterized by low prices, high supplier costs, and miniscule profit margins. This phenomenon is known as *Commodity Drift*. Although this profit-sapping drift may be slowed (through strategies considered in the following chapters), it is inevitable for virtually every market segment and every solution.

---

## Why Is Commodity Drift So Inevitable?

# Why Does Commodity Drift Occur ?

**Power Axis**

- *Competitive* **Dynamics**
    - **More competitors (domestic and foreign)**
    - **More sophisticated & specialized competitors –**
      competitors are more carefully studying (technology enabled) & catering to narrower Customer Value Segments
    - *More Responsive & Aggressive Competitors* -
      improved ability (technology enabled) & willingness to respond more quickly to changing customer requirements & desires
    - As a result, **Solution Breadth Continues to Expand**
      (horizontal axis of Commodity Drift matrix)

| Narrow ← | Minimum Effective<br>Solution Breadth | → Broad |

---

## Competitors

The high profits from innovative new solutions quickly attract global competitors. These new players enter the market using alternative approaches to try to establish themselves and capture a share of the growing market segment. Some new competitors simply lower their prices, while others maintain the current dominant price but add any number of costly frills to their product or service. Still other companies both lower prices and add frills in the effort to grab market share. Inevitably, this flood of competitors drives down prices, increases costs, and causes once-high profit margins to disintegrate.

## Ever-rising Customer Expectations

Rising customer expectations further accelerate Commodity Drift as customers demand lower prices and new and improved features. Naturally, these demands lead to even faster declining profit margins. More competitors and more intense competition give target customers more choices and more leverage to continually demand 'more for less.' This happens incessantly for the broad cross-section of market solutions and segments.

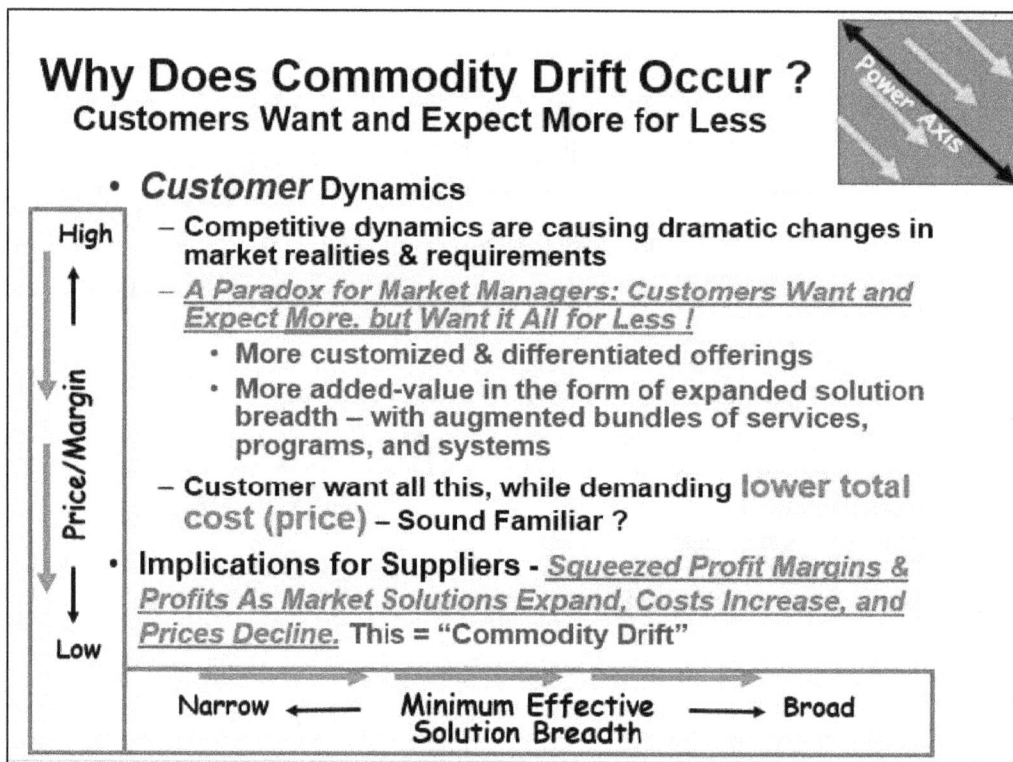

Thus, Commodity Drift causes a market to shift away from attractive, highly differentiated core solutions with high profit margins, towards lower-priced, frilled, higher cost solutions with lower-profit margins.

## Social Media Accelerates Commodity Drift, but also Provides Vehicles to Help Slow the Drift

The proliferation of social media platforms and the ever-expanding use of social media are twin forces that accelerate Commodity Drift in both consumer and business-to-business markets.

Actual and potential customers now have the capability to learn about new competitive offerings almost instantaneously, which enables them to pressure suppliers into matching or even surpassing their competitors' market offers or face the risk of losing out. In turn, this incredibly fast pace of competitive responses leads consumers to continue to set expectations of receiving 'more and more for less and less.'

Fortunately, sellers can also use social media to help cope with Commodity Drift. More specifically, various social media have enhanced the ways that sellers can listen to, engage, and build relationships with existing and potential customers. For example, sellers can monitor and learn what product-specific focused interest groups, blogs and white papers are saying about them and their primary brand competitors, as well as what specific new features and services actual and potential customers are demanding. This regular monitoring of social media by sellers does not slow down the Commodity Drift but can help guide strategy development toward reducing the negative impacts of the inevitable drift on the bottom line.

**

In the next chapter we consider additional potential marketing strategies to employ in order to counter Commodity Drift, *including the need to think innovatively and to regularly pursue new segments.*

CHAPTER 5

# Common Sense Strategies to Counter Commodity Drift

| Requirements for Growth (i.e., Success in Selling) | | |
|---|---|---|
| Ch | 5 | **Common Sense Marketing Strategies to Counter Commodity Drift** |
| Ch | 6 | Focus on Value |
| Ch | 7 | Importance of Having *Sustainable* Advantages (Differentiators) |
| Ch | 8 | Beware of Pricing Traps |
| Ch | 9 | Be Prepared – Know Your Solution & Your Customer |
| Ch | 10 | Other Requirements for Growth (Selling Success) |

In the previous chapters, we considered reasons why steady growth is so difficult for most firms to achieve. Now we consider some requirements for achieving steady growth – i.e., selling success. **We will cover these growth prerequisites in the next six chapters.**

In this chapter, we address two types of 'Common Sense Marketing Strategies' that enable firms to counter Commodity Drift and maintain profitable growth. The first set of strategies - 'pro-active' Commodity Drift strategies - attempts to delay Commodity Drift for current market solutions and current target customers. The second set of strategies -'re-active' Commodity Drift strategies -attempts to salvage profitable growth after significant Commodity Drift has already occurred.

## Pro-Active Marketing Strategies to Delay Commodity Drift

What can a company do to delay Commodity Drift for its current market solutions and target customers? First, we look at solutions and target customers that are still in the attractive position - the upper-left portion of the Commodity Drift diagram. In this situation, prices and profit margins are still appealing. Forward-looking firms design and implement pro-active strategies to delay the inevitable downward drift toward commoditization. Think of pro-active strategies like exercising and eating right to stay 'young.' Eventually you will age, and your physical condition will deteriorate, but you can delay that drifting by working-out, eating right, and making healthy decisions.

How can we delay the inevitable? Several pro-active strategies can possibly slow Commodity Drift—including the following.

## Cut Selective Feature & Service Costs

Identify which current features and services are unvalued or undervalued by the specific target customer, and subsequently cut such services for the target customer in order to reduce costs and increase profit margins.

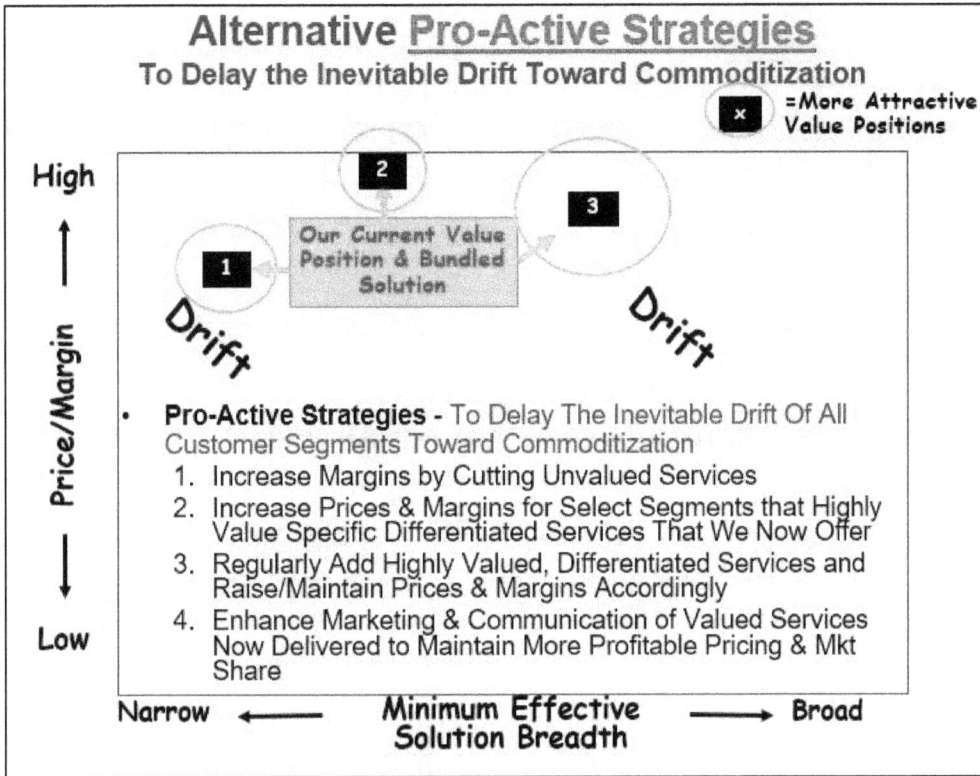

**Alternative Pro-Active Strategies**
To Delay the Inevitable Drift Toward Commoditization

- **Pro-Active Strategies -** To Delay The Inevitable Drift Of All Customer Segments Toward Commoditization
  1. Increase Margins by Cutting Unvalued Services
  2. Increase Prices & Margins for Select Segments that Highly Value Specific Differentiated Services That We Now Offer
  3. Regularly Add Highly Valued, Differentiated Services and Raise/Maintain Prices & Margins Accordingly
  4. Enhance Marketing & Communication of Valued Services Now Delivered to Maintain More Profitable Pricing & Mkt Share

## Cut Selective Feature & Service Costs

Identify which current features and services are unvalued or undervalued by the specific target customer, and subsequently cut such services for the target customer in order to reduce costs and increase profit margins.

## Raise Prices for Selected Features & Services

Identify features and services that the specific target customer values significantly more than the price currently charged. Then increase the prices and margins for those services, while still leaving a transparent price incentive for the customer.

## Innovate with New Features & Services

Use customer feedback, surveys of customers and distributors, and brainstorming to identify brand new, highly valued, differentiated features and services desired by the target customer. Add those where the customer's perceived value is greater than your costs for providing those features and services. Then you can charge more profitable prices for these new features and services.

## Enhance Communications of Highly Valued Features & Services

Enhance the marketing and communications of currently offered features and services that are highly valued by target customers. This helps to maintain higher, more profitable pricing and thus slows Commodity Drift.

Consider these potential pro-active strategies in the context of the Commodity Drift diagram.

# Re-Active Strategies to
# Counter Commodity Drift that has Already Occurred

Re-active strategies address Commodity Drift that has already occurred. Such strategies seek to rebuild commodity offerings into more valued and customized market solutions for selected target customers. If these re-active strategies prove successful, results can include modest price increases, cost reductions, and enhanced profit margins. The success of these strategies may be short-lived because market deterioration has already occurred, but they represent efforts to make the best of an already bad market situation.

To expand on the health example mentioned earlier, think of re-active Commodity Drift strategies like working-out and eating right to improve significantly deteriorated health. You have aged and are now at a different stage of life than when you were using pro-active strategies.

You search for ways to temporarily reverse or at least slow the continuing downward drift in health by working-out, eating right, etc.

How can you employ a re-active strategy? The re-active strategies nearly duplicate the pro-active strategies, but from a different, much less attractive position on the Commodity Drift grid. The goal of the re-active strategies is to try to slow the downward pressures on profit margins. Re-active Commodity Drift strategies might include any of the following.

## Cut Selective Feature & Service Costs

Selectively cut features and services now offered that are unvalued or undervalued by the specific target customers. This will reduce costs and increase profit margins.

## Raise Prices for Selected Features & Services

Increase prices and margins for features and services that are still highly valued by the specific target customers, while still leaving a transparent price incentive for the customer and increasing profit margins for the supplier.

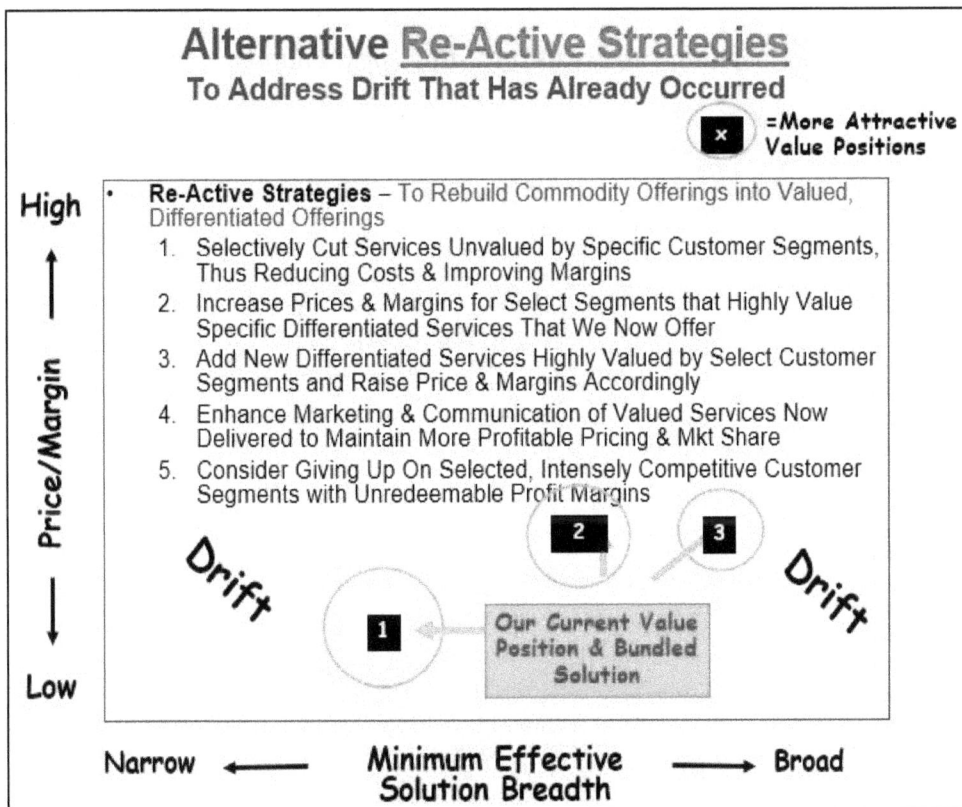

**Alternative Re-Active Strategies**
To Address Drift That Has Already Occurred

[x] =More Attractive Value Positions

- **Re-Active Strategies** – To Rebuild Commodity Offerings into Valued, Differentiated Offerings
  1. Selectively Cut Services Unvalued by Specific Customer Segments, Thus Reducing Costs & Improving Margins
  2. Increase Prices & Margins for Select Segments that Highly Value Specific Differentiated Services That We Now Offer
  3. Add New Differentiated Services Highly Valued by Select Customer Segments and Raise Price & Margins Accordingly
  4. Enhance Marketing & Communication of Valued Services Now Delivered to Maintain More Profitable Pricing & Mkt Share
  5. Consider Giving Up On Selected, Intensely Competitive Customer Segments with Unredeemable Profit Margins

High ↑ Price/Margin ↓ Low

Drift      Drift

[1]   Our Current Value Position & Bundled Solution   [2]   [3]

Narrow ← **Minimum Effective Solution Breadth** → Broad

## Innovate with New Features & Services

Carefully research customers to identify new potential differentiated features and services that would be highly valued by specific target customers. Then add such differentiators – and charge more profitable prices, while promoting these specific new features and services.

## Enhance Communications of Highly Valued Features & Services

Enhance the marketing and communications of currently offered features and services that are highly valued by target customers. This will help to maintain higher, more profitable pricing while simultaneously slowing Commodity Drift.

## Bailing Out

Finally, bailing out from participation in marketing to certain segments is also an option. Before choosing this strategy, however, be sure to assess the potential negative impact (on customers and distributors) of no longer being viewed as a 'full line' supplier.

Consider these potential re-active strategies in the context of the Commodity Drift diagram.

The next growth prerequisite is to *Focus on Value (next chapter).*

CHAPTER 6

# Focus on Value

| Requirements for Growth (i.e., Success in Selling) | | |
|---|---|---|
| Ch | 5 | Common Sense Marketing Strategies to Counter Commodity Drift |
| **Ch** | **6** | **Focus on Value** |
| Ch | 7 | Importance of Having **Sustainable** Advantages (Differentiators) |
| Ch | 8 | Beware of Pricing Traps |
| Ch | 9 | Be Prepared – Know Your Solution & Your Customer |
| Ch | 10 | Other Requirements for Growth (Selling Success) |

In this chapter we continue our discussion on how to achieve steady growth of sales and profits over the long haul.

In the previous chapter we identified strategies for delaying or reversing the price and profit pressures that come with Commodity Drift. A quick referral back to that chapter reveals the *'value focus'* of each potential strategy used to counter Commodity Drift. Given the *value focus* of these strategies, we need to define what *value is and how we can identify which dimensions of our market solution our target customers do indeed 'value.'*

## What is Value and How Do We Identify What Target Customers Value? Consider This Scenario.7

### Customer 'Requirements.

A supplier of closures and terminals for copper and fiber optic cables lost a multimillion dollar customer to a renegade "bare bones" competitor. The customer had been an account for over 15 years and the supplier thought that it completely understood the customer's requirements. When the time came to renew the contract, its sales personnel had visited the customer's plant and asked, 'What would you like from us?' (i.e., what are the Advantages or 'Value Drivers' you want?). The sales personnel came away with a list of detailed product specifications and service requests. In response, the supplier developed and offered a premium-priced "full service" package that it felt would completely meet the customer's stated requirements.

## Result

Supplier managers were shocked when they learned that they had lost the account to a new competitor offering a low-priced "no frills" package. Not only did this competitor's offer contain no support services but the products included also fell slightly below the customer's stated specifications. When asked why they had switched to the new vendor, customer managers replied that the competitor's quote was so low, that even if the products failed, the firm would have enough funds available from the cost difference to readily pay for the products to be fixed.

---

# The Lessons of This Scenario

If the sales force spent *more time asking about what specs and services the customer truly valued and was willing to pay for*, then the company could have likely avoided losing this sizable account and could have maybe even increased its profit margins for this account.

For example, the careful query to discover *what this target customer truly valued and was willing to pay for* could have guided the design of each of the Commodity Drift strategies reviewed earlier. More specifically, that exploration could have revealed several opportunities such as the following.

---

## Unvalued Current Services

Are any currently offered services unvalued or undervalued by this target customer? The supplier could subsequently cut such services for this customer, thus reducing costs, and increasing profit margins.

---

## More Highly Valued Current Services

Does the target customer value any currently offered services valued significantly more than the price currently charged for such services? The supplier could increase those prices & margins accordingly, while still leaving a transparent price incentive for the customer.

---

## New Potential Services.

Are there any highly valued, differentiated services desired by, but not yet offered to, the target customer? The supplier could subsequently add those particular new services where the customer's perceived value is greater than the supplier's incremental cost of adding such services - thus providing a higher overall profit margin.

---

In the next chapter we will consider the importance of having "sustainable advantages" (Differentiators)

CHAPTER 7

# Importance of Having _Sustainable_ Advantages (Differentiators)

| Requirements for Growth (i.e., Success in Selling) | | |
|---|---|---|
| Ch | 5 | Common Sense Marketing Strategies to Counter Commodity Drift |
| Ch | 6 | Focus on Value |
| **Ch** | **7** | **Importance of Having _Sustainable_ Advantages (Differentiators)** |
| Ch | 8 | Beware of Pricing Traps |
| Ch | 9 | Be Prepared – Know Your Solution & Your Customer |
| Ch | 10 | Other Requirements for Growth (Selling Success) |

In this chapter, we continue discussing various requirements for achieving steady, profitable growth.

There's no faster way to collapse profit margins than to haphazardly add new features and services. As seen in the "Adding Unsustainable Advantages" cartoon below, rather than slowing Commodity Drift, Kick's has increased the speed of the drift by adding costly features and services, which were then quickly duplicated by Happy Feet, its primary competitor.

## Consider Another Example.[8]

### Trying to Increase Market Share by Adding New Differentiators.

With a goal of grabbing market in a flat commodity market, a textile producer volunteered to store its products "on consignment" at the plants of a major apparel-producing customer. In addition to keeping the inventory on its own books until used, the textile producer also agreed to:

- Lease warehouse space in the customer's plant to store the inventory
- Furnish an optical scanner and computer system to monitor textile consumption
- Pay for insurance against inventory damage, theft, or loss

Not surprisingly, the customer immediately jumped at the opportunity to implement this innovative program.

## Result

What came as a shock to the textile producer was that, within one week, all three of its major competitors had duplicated the program for the apparel producer. Additionally, after a short-term increase in its share of that customer's business, the textile producer saw its market share and those of its competitors return to their preprogram levels. Soon other apparel producers began to demand the same service.

Taking stock at the end of the year, the textile producer discovered that the consignment program had resulted in an overall loss of several million dollars in operating profits. Its managers assumed the same was the case for its competitors. The textile producer took little solace in the fact that its customer satisfaction ratings from the apparel producer had soared to an all-time high.

# The Lessons of This Scenario

The lesson from this example is clear. Those who added the new and costly unsustainable advantages were largely responsible for eroding the profits for the entire industry. This occurred because competitors quickly and easily duplicated the costly new features and services added for customers.

After a brief sales spurt, the company that added the unsustainable advantages saw its market share return to its former level. Because competitors were forced to add similar costly features and services, their costs also increased substantially, and profits plummeted across the industry. The various competitors had literally given away previously attractive profit margins for this industry segment. Customers were obviously delighted!

## What New Features & Services Should a Company Add to Stimulate Growth without Compromising Profits?

What new features and services can a company add to stimulate growth without compromising profits? Good question!

First, let's recognize that different market segments typically value the same core solution, but vary in terms of features and services. *Value is the first guideline.* The challenge is to identify which specific features and services are highly valued by each segment. The supplier then pursues ideas for new features and services where its own costs would be substantially less than the true value for the target customer – i.e., less than the price that relevant target customers are willing to pay. Not surprisingly, the supplier discards ideas where its own costs would be greater than the price that its target customers would be willing to pay.

This clearly isn't enough, as shown in the textile example. In that case study, arbitrarily adding even highly valued new features and services had disastrous profit consequences - not only for one segment, but for the whole industry! *Sustainability is the second guideline* to use when evaluating which highly valued new features and services one can safely add without compromising segment and industry profits. The key is to add only those unique differentiators that cannot be quickly or easily duplicated by primary competitors.

# Potential Sources of Sustainability

Sustainability can come from a variety of sources. For example.

### Technological Advantages
- Legally Protected Technology / Patents
- High Complexity and Related Skill Requirement
- Professional Expertise (Number and Quality of Experts)
- Dynamic Technology
- Research and Development (R & D) Budget
- Technology Partnerships and Related Synergistic Benefits

### Cost Advantages
- High Initial Investment Requirement
- High Supporting Infrastructure Required
- Operating Cost Efficiency Leader

### Scale & Experience Advantages
- Critical Mass / Economy of Scale
- Learning Curve Advantages

### Supply Control Advantages
- Control of Critical Supply Source

### Market Position Advantage
- Control of Distribution Channels
- Brand Recognition, Image and Loyalty
- Marketing Partnerships and Related Synergistic Benefits
- Superior Customer Relationship Management System

## The Bottom Line on Sustainability

*The bottom line for the growth planner is this.* When attempting to grow sales, market share, and profits through adding new advantages or differentiators, *add only those that are uniquely sustainable – regardless of the source of that sustainability.* Without sustainability, competitors will quickly duplicate any temporarily successful advantages, which will cause both prices and market shares to regress to previous levels. The new costs associated with the added advantages will squeeze profits for all competitors involved. Who wants that? No one - neither you nor your competitors.

CHAPTER 8

# Beware of Pricing Traps

### Traps you can set for yourself - with a focus on pricing dangers & opportunities for industry leaders

| Requirements for Growth (i.e., Success in Selling) | | |
|---|---|---|
| Ch | 5 | Common Sense Marketing Strategies to Counter Commodity Drift |
| Ch | 6 | Focus on Value |
| Ch | 7 | Importance of Having **Sustainable** Advantages (Differentiators) |
| **Ch** | **8** | **Beware of Pricing Traps** |
| Ch | 9 | Be Prepared – Know Your Solution & Your Customer |
| Ch | 10 | Other Requirements for Growth (Selling Success) |

In this chapter, we continue to discuss a series of requirements for achieving steady, profitable growth.

Earlier we examined how Commodity Drift inevitably compresses prices and margins over time. Here we consider some *strategies and related phenomena that can delay the inevitable price and profit crunch, thus contributing to Steady, Profitable Growth!* Such strategies are highly recommended for companies that *can prove* the overall value advantage of their market solution to target customers. In later chapters we will address 'how to prove value advantages.'

## Image as a Sustainable Differentiator: The Price Umbrella

Dropping prices is the easiest way to enter a market. Unless aggressive pricing (i.e., lower prices) is based upon unique, sustainable cost advantages, however, it is generally not an attractive growth strategy. If most firms in the relevant industry have similar cost structures, once one competitor begins to make sales and market share inroads through aggressive pricing, others will follow - accelerating the shift in Commodity Drift for all. Any competitor that significantly lowers price without real, sustainable cost advantages can be considered guilty of killing industry-wide profits. That is *not* good marketing!

## The Industry Leader Should Provide a Price Umbrella

Well-respected firms that have an image as industry leaders can provide a 'price umbrella' for the industry. Providing a price umbrella means resisting lowering prices in order to help all firms in the industry maintain relatively high profit margins for as long as possible. A leading company can do this without compromising its own sales and market share *because its image as the industry innovator and leader is itself a highly valued, sustainable differentiator* for many target customers.

The price umbrella (i.e., a relatively high price) provided by the leading company or companies reduces the temptation for other competitors to lower their prices and destroy industry profit margins. Thus, a price umbrella provides more time for all competitors to receive higher prices and profit margins. When 'price umbrella leadership' is not present for any specific market solution, the prices and profits are destined to quickly slide down the Commodity Drift drain.

## Reaction Threshold

Assume that the primary competitor, Company B, offers a price of $100. Assume also that the industry leader, Company A, can prove to target customers that it has a $20 perceived value advantage over Company B. What price should Company A charge in order to still have a perceived value advantage over Company B?

The logical answer is anything less than $120. But that assumes the customer will shift suppliers whenever there is a perceived value advantage. In the 'real world,' Company A might be able to retain its customers while charging even more than $120. Why? This is because personal and corporate life is difficult enough without re-evaluating brand choices each time one re-buys a product or service. Thus, corporate customers, like regular consumers, establish brand-loyalties to make life simpler by reducing the number of decisions that need to be made each day.

*Enter the 'Reaction Threshold.'* The reaction threshold is the price at which a company's 'loyal customers' will decide to re-evaluate their brand purchasing habits. Say this threshold for a certain customer is $130 in the example above. If Company A charged $135, the customer might change to Company B's brand and with that change, form a new brand-loyalty. Company A, when realizing it lost that customer, might return with a new offer – say $120, $115, or even less – only to be turned down by that formerly brand-loyal customer. You already know why: as mentioned before, the trouble of re-evaluating brands *yet again* is not worth the potential financial gain.

We bring this up now because when pricing for brand-loyal customers, a company can get a price premium because of the hesitancy of customers to continually re-evaluate their satisfactory brand choices of the past.

## The Lesson

A company must know what its brand-loyal customer's 'reaction threshold' is before charging a price higher than the perceived value, before reducing service levels, or before compromising any other dimension of its overall market solution.

Beware of Crossing the Reaction Threshold

CHAPTER 9

# Know Your Customers, Your Competitors & Your Market Solution

| Requirements for Growth (i.e., Success in Selling) | | |
|---|---|---|
| Ch | 5 | Common Sense Marketing Strategies to Counter Commodity Drift |
| Ch | 6 | Focus on Value |
| Ch | 7 | Importance of Having **Sustainable** Advantages (Differentiators) |
| Ch | 8 | Beware of Pricing Traps |
| Ch | 9 | **Be Prepared – Know Your Solution & Your Customer** |
| Ch | 10 | Other Requirements for Growth (Selling Success) |

In this chapter, we continue to discuss a series of requirements for achieving steady, profitable growth.

## Know Your Customers and Competitors

It should come as no surprise that companies with more successful growth records are also more committed to regularly monitoring customers and competitors. After all, customers' expectations and competitors' initiatives are the primary forces that drive Commodity Drift.

## How the Internet and Social Media have Changed the Game

In the not-too-distant past, before the proliferation of Internet access and social media platforms, many firms were content with casual monitoring of customers and competitors. In fact, as unbelievable as it may seem in today's 'instant information world,' according to a study in the late 1990s, approximately 40% of companies paid little attention to either customers or competitors and fewer than 20% closely monitored both.[9] This lack of external awareness may have been a primary driving force behind the disappointing growth records of many companies during this time.

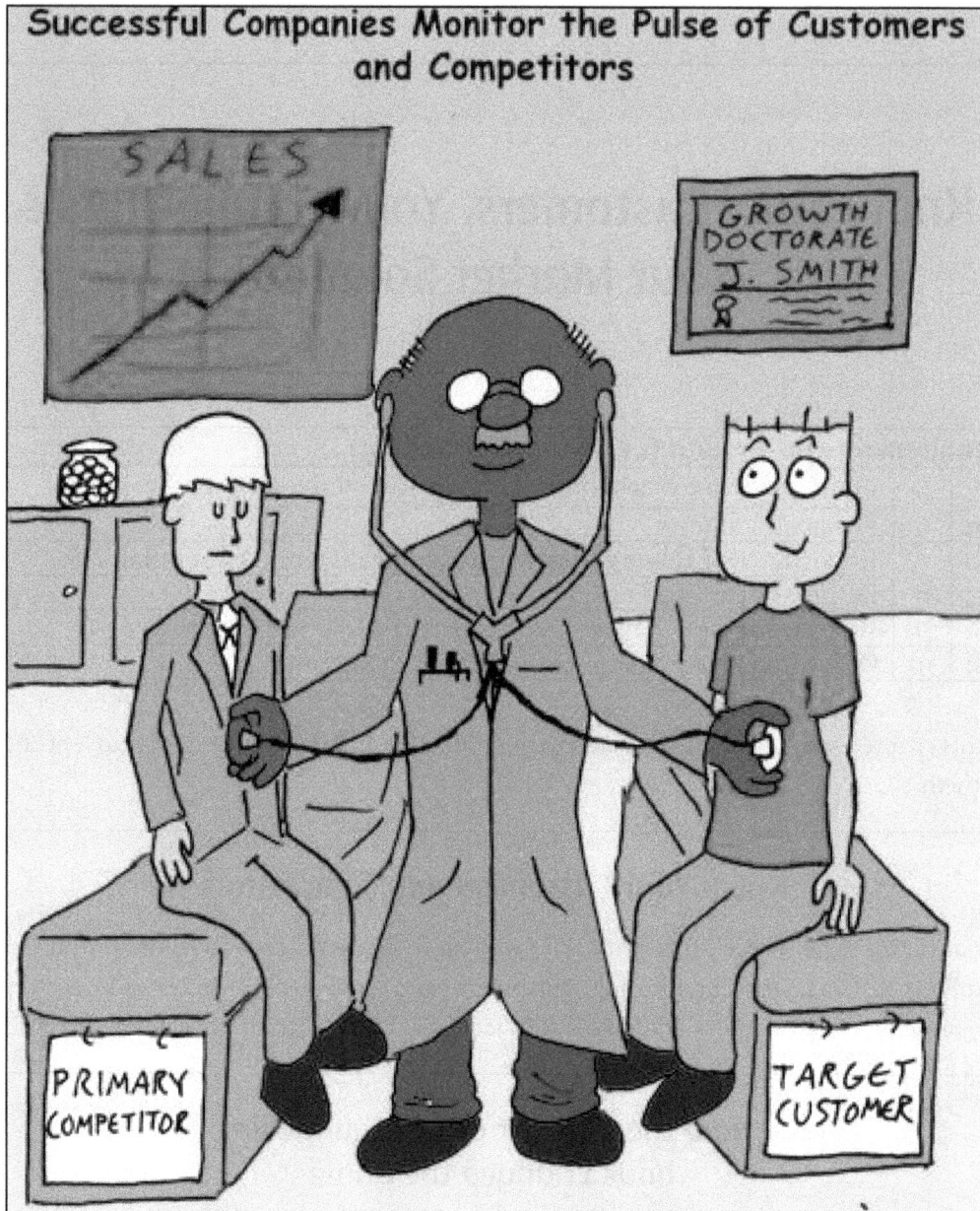

**Successful Companies Monitor the Pulse of Customers and Competitors**

***But that was then, and this is now.*** The proliferation of Internet access and customers' escalating participation in social media platforms[10] have created new, informed customers.

Today, these customers' expectations for nearly all market solutions are becoming more dynamic and demanding each year. And companies had better listen if they want to succeed.

Furthermore, more global competitors are entering the game each year. These are smart players that are *leveraging social media* to succeed in both monitoring and responding to dynamic, heightened customer expectations.

Weak players that do not keep up current trends and have not developed substantive social media strategies to monitor and respond to both dynamic customers' expectations and competitors' offerings are destined to lose their footing on their way down the slippery slope of Commodity Drift.

---

## Know Your *Overall* Market Solution

What could be more important for sales professionals than knowing their overall market solutions inside and out? Nothing, right? If they don't thoroughly understand their solutions, how could anyone expect them to communicate the value of the solutions to a customer?

Yet ask yourself the following question. **How many times has your company failed to capture a new target customer because your sales folks were not adequately familiar with your overall market solution? Or didn't know what benefits are most highly valued by the target customer?**

How foolish can a company be in this day and age when the relative value of different features and benefits can change so rapidly, reflecting the ever-more dynamic competition and customer expectations?

This underlines the importance of thorough initial training and periodic re-training to help the sales folks - both new and old - keep up to date with:

- *All the ins and outs of the market solution being offered;*
- *Each market solution's specific values for target customers today; and*
- *Primary competitors' new initiatives in the marketplace.*

This also highlights the importance of having a well-designed, consistent mentoring program for any new person joining the sales team.

CHAPTER **10**

# Importance of Leadership and Teamwork

| Requirements for Growth (i.e., Success in Selling) | | |
|---|---|---|
| Ch | 5 | Common Sense Marketing Strategies to Counter Commodity Drift |
| Ch | 6 | Focus on Value |
| Ch | 7 | Importance of Having **Sustainable** Advantages (Differentiators) |
| Ch | 8 | Beware of Pricing Traps |
| Ch | 9 | Be Prepared – Know Your Solution & Your Customer |
| **Ch** | **10** | **Other Requirements for Growth (Selling Success)** |

In this chapter, we discuss two additional important requirements for achieving steady, profitable growth – Leadership and Teamwork.

## Leadership and Teamwork

Most would agree that Peyton Manning and Tom Brady are (or were) outstanding quarterbacks. In fact, they both led their teams, the Colts and Patriots, to the NFL's highest winning percentages (72% and 70%, respectively) during their tenures.

But what if either Manning or Brady had played for the hapless Detroit Lions during that same period – when the Lions won only 26% of their games? Would we still think of him as a great quarterback? Would either have been able to lead the Lions to win 70% of their games? *No way!* Outstanding quarterbacking is much more likely to occur when:

- The quarterback is surrounded by other pro-bowl caliber players;

- The coaching staff develops offensive and defensive schemes that cater to the strengths and weaknesses of individual players; and when
- The coaches and front office draft and make astute trades to address key offensive and defensive player weaknesses.

Yes, 'great quarterbacking' starts with raw talent, but talent alone is not enough to make a great quarterback or 'create a great quarterback image.' That image can only be created when one can successfully leverage initial raw talent with creative and effective teamwork and leadership.

## What Does It Take to be a Sales Superstar?

The theme of this Sales Growth Secrets book is that a company's long-term success depends upon its ability to continually expand the top line sales. Firms that do so invariably have some key 'rain makers,' who set the sales growth bar for the entire sales force. Analogous to a quarterback's raw talent, these top tier sales pros also have basic talent – which typically involves good people skills, magnetic personalities, the drive to succeed, and endless energy to make sales happen. Those qualities alone can enable any sales pro to succeed for a quarter or two and maybe a bit longer. But those qualities are *not enough* to ensure long-term selling success for any would-be sales superstar.

Sales pros who are top performers *year after year* leverage natural selling talents with several other critical characteristics. ***First, they are prepared***. As considered earlier, they continually monitor dynamic customer needs and expectations as well as strategic initiatives of primary competitors. They also keep themselves right up to date on all features and services of each of the different market solutions they may be selling.

## Who's He?

JOEY HARRINGTON     TIM COUCH     DAVID CARR

Each of the following quarterbacks had solid raw talent, but no one considers them to have been great NFL quarterbacks.

**Joey Harrington #3 overall draft pick** (Detroit Lions) in 2002. Who's he? Lions won only 26% of their games between 2000 and 2010.[11]

**Tim Couch #1 overall draft pick** (Cleveland Browns) in 1999. Who's he? Browns won only 36% of their games between 2000 and 2010.

**David Carr #1 overall draft pick** (Houston Texans) in 2002. Who's he? Texans won only 38% of their games between 2000 and 2010.

*But there's more!* Top sales pros **_also have enlightened leaders_**, who know the dangers of static market solutions in dynamic markets. Such leaders provide vibrant market solutions that respond to both ever-changing customer expectations and to evermore threatening competitive initiatives. Successful sales pros *also* **_team with company experts_** whose jobs include monitoring the pulse of target customers and primary competitors.

---

## Star 'Rainmakers' Are Made, Not Born

Different members of the sales team possess varying levels of natural selling talent.

*Can a sales pro with non-optimal natural selling skills turn into a sales superstar? You bet!* In fact, some of your own key rainmakers have likely done just that, by successfully overlaying sometimes mediocre natural selling skills with a commitment to superior performance in:

- Keeping up to date on dynamic customer needs and expectations as well as strategic initiatives of primary competitors;
- Keeping up to date on all features and services of each of the different market solutions they may be selling;
- Working closely with leaders in providing advice to help in the development of dynamic market solutions that respond to ever-changing customers and competitive initiatives;
- Teaming with company experts whose jobs include monitoring the pulse of target customers and primary competitors; *and* by
- Becoming intimately familiar with and methodically following the company's single selling 'system.'

## Sales Superstars Leverage Social Media

Your most productive sales professionals today most certainly work very closely with your social media team members, who monitor the pulse of target customers and primary competitors more and more effectively each year. This collaboration enables the most effective sales pros to leverage information flowing from a variety of social media sources in order to enhance their selling performance.

For example, monitoring social media enables them to:

- Obtain more accurate and timely information on dynamic customer needs and expectations as well as on strategic initiatives of primary competitors;

- Follow customer demands and concerns (expressed in interest groups) more closely in order to keep right up to date on dynamic customer demands for new features and services for your self-checkout systems; and to
- Become aware of dynamic customer and competitor market patterns and subsequently relay more accurate and timely information on these patterns to your product development, IT, and customer service and support groups.

CHAPTER 11

# A 'Master Selling Approach' Drives Growth

| A "Master Selling Approach" Drives Growth | | |
|---|---|---|
| Ch | 11 | A "Master Selling Approach Drives Growth |

In this chapter, we discuss the final requirement for achieving steady, profitable growth – **a** 'Master Selling Approach.'

Let's Change Gears for a Moment

As emphasized earlier, Commodity Drift will ultimately destroy the profits for every single solution and segment over time. That's a challenging backdrop for any company hoping for steady, long-term, profitable growth! It is a challenge that requires regularly attacking the marketplace with new solutions, new uses for old solutions, and new segments for both old and new solutions. So that's our starting point: "Any company hoping for steady profitable growth needs to continually pursue new opportunities (solutions, uses, or segments)." Now where do we go from here?

## Consider This

If 'Company A' and 'Company B' are both continually pursuing new opportunities to counter unavoidable Commodity Drift, _**then, how can 'Company A' continually outperform Company B on the bottom line – i.e., achieving better steady, long-term profitable growth?**_

## What's the Secret?

*The 'secret' is this:* <u>**Company A is winning because its sales professionals are much better at capturing the individual sale**</u> *– i.e.,* **winning the deal**. *This variation in the 'close ratios' of the sales forces of the two companies is* <u>**unrelated to**</u> *which specific innovative solutions are introduced and which new segments are being attacked.*

Really?? Yes, Really! *Here's how we're going to try to explain this. We are going to show you one well thought-out selling process. We will explain how consistently and effectively using a single, solid selling process or 'system' will enable sales pros at Company A to consistently outperform their sales pro counterparts at Company B.*

We are not suggesting a 'magic selling elixir' - because, as we all know, there is no fool-proof selling process. In fact, ***there are dozens of different, solid selling processes*** that are helping firms around the globe to achieve steady, profitable sales growth. Just a few of the more popular selling 'systems' (you've likely heard of many if not most of these) include: Holden International (Power Base Selling), Huthwaite (Spin Selling), Miller Heiman (Conceptual Selling), On Target / BRS (Target Account Selling), Sales Performance International (SPI) (Solution Selling®) and Selling Communications (Target Selling).

## A 'Master Selling Approach' Drives the Growth Plan

So, what are we suggesting? The point is this: Company A is more successful than Company B because it invested in and has perfected one single selling process for its entire sales team. The whole team understands and uses the same process. The process has been refined and adapted for the specific solutions that Company A sells. The whole sales team contributes to refining the system over time and participates regularly in training themselves and new sales team members on all dimensions of the system.

## How the Sales Team Benefits from Using a Single, Solid Selling Approach

Using a single, detailed selling process – regardless of which specific system is used - has multiple benefits. Consider how using a single, well-designed selling process or method benefits the whole sales force:

## Benefits of a Single Process for All

The ***first set of benefits*** focuses on *achieving improved close ratios on individual accounts for the whole sales team* **by:**

- **Enabling** *sales rookies* (with considerable live mentoring) **to hit the ground running;**
- **Helping** *grizzled old veterans* **to enhance their sales performance, once they can be convinced to buy into the system** (sometimes a challenging task!);
- **Helping** *solid sales force performers* **become super performers; and**
- **Helping those who are already** *sales superstars* **to generate even better sales and profit growth numbers.**

---

# How the Sales & Marketing Management Team Also Benefit from a Single Selling Approach

A critical *second set of benefits* answers the prayers of sales supervisors, such as Sales Managers, Sales Directors, VPs of Sales, Marketing Directors, Marketing Managers, and the VP of Marketing or CMO.

## Benefits of a Single Process for Sales & Marketing Managers

- **The *second set of benefits* answers the prayers of sales supervisors, such as** Sales Managers, Sales Directors, VPs of Sales, Marketing Directors, Marketing Managers, and the VP of Marketing or CMO.
- **Reaping the relevant benefits for these types of sales supervisors depends upon:**
  - **A rigid commitment to the same** *exact* **selling process by the entire sales force;**
  - **Overlaying the process with technology-enabled live reports from sales folks in the field** [which provide timely updates on progress made (or not made) on every single important sales effort underway.]

---

**Benefits for Sales & Marketing Managers, cont.**

- *Sales supervisors* **at all levels now have potential quantitative bases for:**
  - **More accurately projecting operating period results** *during each operating period* **– rather than awaiting unpredictable numbers at the end of the quarter;**
  - **Stepping in with** *coaching aids during the quarter* **to help individual sales folks stuck in any step of the selling process with important prospective clients;**
  - **Knowing ahead of time when the 'sales hopper' is getting thin at any place – top to bottom – and stepping in to** *generate more new prospects* **(via new solutions, new uses, new target segments, or simply more innovative and aggressive prospecting) as well as to stimulate selective sales efforts already underway.**

---

*Implemented properly, this can ensure steady, long-term, profitable sales growth for the company (The book elaborates on this & other related Sales Management concepts in Part 4).*

---

## Now, What's Next?

So, we see that steady, long-term, profitable growth is driven by a 'Master Selling Approach'[1] for each individual account. Let's repeat that - **steady, long-term, profitable growth is driven by a 'Master Selling Approach' for each individual account.** That is a critical point, as it frames the entire growth planning process that is detailed in the rest of this Sales Growth Secrets book!

Most of the latter Parts of this book focus on the "how to" for capturing the individual sale – for that skill is what will ultimately drive revenue & profit growth. That is, a company cannot expect to grow unless its sales team can consistently turn target customers into actual customers.

After we present the details of one particular selling system (applying it in a single case study), we will return in the latter Parts of the book to emphasize and explain how ongoing, singular sales efforts and successes fit into a larger framework that overlays marketing and sales.

---

[1] *The specific selling system a company chooses does not matter*. *A good sales professional can succeed over the long-term using virtually any well thought out systematic selling process.* The general outline of SPI's "Solution Selling®" system[1] is favored in this book because it is practical, logical, and easily adapted to a broad array of market solutions and segments.

Such an over-encompassing framework, properly designed, implemented and utilized *can virtually ensure continuous company success in profitably selling to customer after customer*.

The closing Parts of the book detail how any company can significantly improve its close ratios for capturing individual sale after sale – and then translating that into continuous, aggressive sales and profit growth.

# Part 1, cont.
# *Preparing for Sales Growth*

---

## *Thoughtfully Segmenting Your Markets*

## *Carefully Identifying Your Competitive Advantages*

# Chapters 12-15

# Thoughtfully Segmenting Your Markets

AS we continue Part 1, we introduce the critical first steps to building an effective Account Marketing Plan (Part 2) for any market solution. These steps involve the inter-related marketing concepts of segmentation (Chs 12-15), competition and key competitive advantages (Chs 16-19).

Reflecting the close inter-relationships among these concepts, Chs 12-19 should be viewed as a unit. As we continue the move forward through these chapters, the inter-relationships among these three marketing concepts (segmentation, competition, and key competitive advantages) will become apparent.

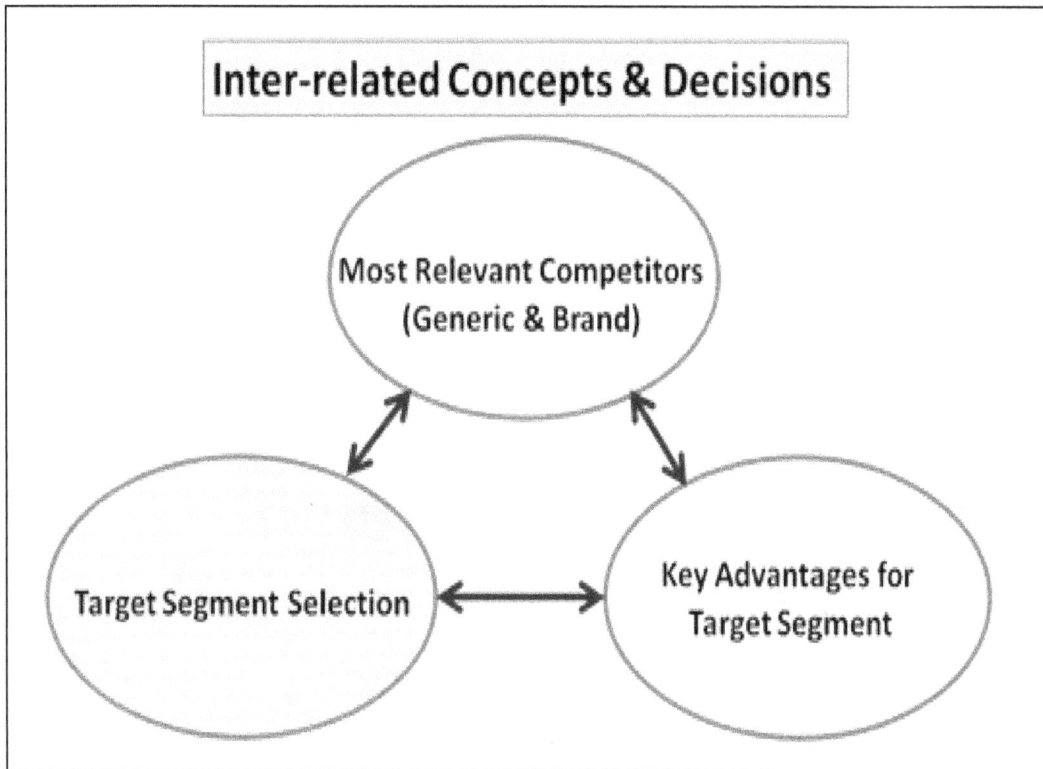

## Inter-related Concepts & Decisions

- Most Relevant Competitors (Generic & Brand)
- Target Segment Selection
- Key Advantages for Target Segment

CHAPTER 12

# Segmentation Basics

| Thoughtfully Segment Your Markets | | |
|------|-----|-------------------------------------------------|
| Ch | 12 | **Segmentation Basics** |
| Ch | 13 | Consider New Potential 'Usage Segments' |
| Ch | 14 | Selecting Appropriate Target Segments |
| Ch | 15 | Focus on Non-User & 'Not looking' Segments |

Segmentation suggests that a firm will most likely grow faster if it targets subsets of the overall marketplace with unique market solutions. Segmentation makes more sense than trying to 'shotgun' the overall market with a single market solution. That is, in today's competitive markets, it is easier to try to capture large portions of smaller market subsets with targeted market solutions than to try to develop a single best market solution for the overall market.

## Defining Segments Too Broadly

Many would-be fast growing companies stifle their potential growth by choosing target segments that are too inclusive. This can easily result in 'one size fits all' market solutions – solutions that, in the long-term, end up fitting no one well.

Companies that stick to this 'shotgun' type approach assume that the best pure product or service wins the game. Not anymore! In fact, trying to please everyone with a single overall market solution is a recipe for disaster and can cause a fast plummet down Profit Crunch Falls.

'One Size Fits All' Solutions Do Not Work in Competitive Markets

Trying to Please Everyone is a One-Way Ticket to Profit Crunch Falls

# Basic Criteria for Segmentation

**Similarities within each Segment.** Within a specific segment all members are similar with respect to what they value in the relevant overall market solution. Ideally, all members of a specific segment demand more or less the same solution quality and price, as well as individual features and add-on services.

**Differences among Segments.** Many alternative potential segments exist for any market solution. Segments within a market are distinct from one another with respect to what they value in the market solution – with each segment assigning different values to the solution quality and price, as well as to individual features and add-on services.

# Importance of Customer Research Enhanced by Social Media in Segmenting Markets

In growing firms, customer researchers are playing an increasingly important role, providing direction not only for the marketing and sales departments but also for the engineers, scientists, and technical folks who design the basic solutions.

The proliferation of social media and the enhanced information available because of it have resulted in more informed buyers **and more informed sellers**. More aggressive and creative companies are shifting significant portions of development resources to **social media dashboards** in order to monitor and analyze customers much more carefully. Customer research findings from both interest groups and tightly focused customer and company blogs can now guide and enable the breakdown of overall markets into much smaller, more tightly-defined segments – each requiring a different, customized market solution. (We'll consider how to select segments in subsequent chapters.) As suggested above, successful companies today are finding that catering to smaller, more carefully chosen segments – even a single customer segment - with unique market solutions is a much more productive way to grow in both new and more traditional markets.

# Many Benefits of Segmentation and Targeting Subsets of the Market

*Overly-broad market segment boundaries* lead to confused growth planning discussions because growth team members are often not on the same page. Growth planning meetings and the resulting plans are muddled with conflicting analyses and conclusions. This confusion occurs due to the growth team's efforts to simultaneously address and respond to the demands and expectations of fundamentally different segments. In this all-too-common 'apples and oranges' scenario, the single market solution typically turns out to be non-optimal and non-competitive for all potential market segments.

Overly *broad market segment boundaries* make it difficult to stimulate distributors. Distributor cooperation and support is vital for successfully implementing growth strategies. Some firms lack confidence in their growth strategies because of overly broad definitions of their target segments. These firms find it difficult to motivate their sales forces. In this situation, a sales force will be less able and less likely to convince overburdened distributors to help the firm effectively implement its planned growth strategies. A company with a well-justified and unified belief in its growth strategies – from top management to the sales force – is able to communicate these strategies to its distributors much more convincingly.

Bigger Segments Are Not Necessarily Better Segments

*Overly broad market segment boundaries* can cause inefficient and ineffective customer research. Customer research is much more efficient and resulting growth strategies are more easily and more convincingly communicated to the sales force and to distributors

*Overly broad market segment boundaries* can cause inefficient and ineffective customer research. Customer research is much more efficient and productive if target market segments are more narrowly defined. Tighter segment definitions generate research questions that are more specific and result in research findings that translate more clearly and directly into effective growth plans. In contrast, more broadly defined target segments require more time and resources to research – with results that are difficult to interpret and hard to translate into clearly defensible growth plans and strategies.

In the next chapter, we consider how to segment markets and how to identify attractive target segments.

CHAPTER 13

# Consider New Potential Usage Segments

| Thoughtfully Segment Your Markets | | |
|---|---|---|
| Ch | 12 | Segmentation Basics |
| **Ch** | **13** | **Consider New Potential 'Usage Segments'** |
| Ch | 14 | Selecting Appropriate Target Segments |
| Ch | 15 | Focus on Non-User & 'Not looking' Segments |

In this chapter, we continue discussing principles for segmenting markets and for selecting segments with the best growth potential.

## New Uses as a Potential Target Segment

In addition to the strategies considered earlier, another potential way to counter commodity drift is to creatively search for whole new segments of prospective users. This can be successful because many market solutions have more than one potential use. Each new use identified can represent a new potential target segment and a new potential growth opportunity. Consider these examples:

- **RFID Chips / Tags.** Consider the many potential uses for RFID (radio-frequency identification) chips or tags, which can be affixed to any object to help track and manage inventory, assets, people, etc. Such chips are now used throughout the supply chain - helping to keep track of production components from suppliers through production, inventory, transportation, distributors, and retailers - right on down to the final user. They can be affixed to cars, computer equipment, books, mobile phones, and a vast array of other items. The healthcare industry has used RFID to reduce counting, searching time and auditing items. Many financial institutions use RFID to track key assets and automate compliance.

- **Programmable Microprocessors.** Programmable microprocessors are now in thousands of items that were traditionally not computer related. These include large and small household appliances, cars, tools and test instruments, toys, light switches and dimmers, smoke alarms, and a wide variety of other uses. More and more products each year now require powerful, low-cost microprocessors for their functionality. 12

- **Multiple Uses for Consumer-Focused Solutions.** Faced with flat sales for specific market solutions, some packaged goods suppliers have uncovered totally new usage segments for their products through creative marketing. Consider the many potential uses now promoted for baking soda (e.g. bath additive, kitchen cleaner, deodorizer, controlling acidity in swimming pools, etc.), vinegar (page long ads in Sunday inserts on all the things one can do with vinegar), baby products (shampoo, oil & powder are promoted to the adult segment), toothpaste (to clean silver and jewelry), Kraft 'salad dressing' (various dinner fare, including meats and vegetables), WD40, duct tape, Clorox bleach, rubbing alcohol, hydrogen peroxide, and the like.

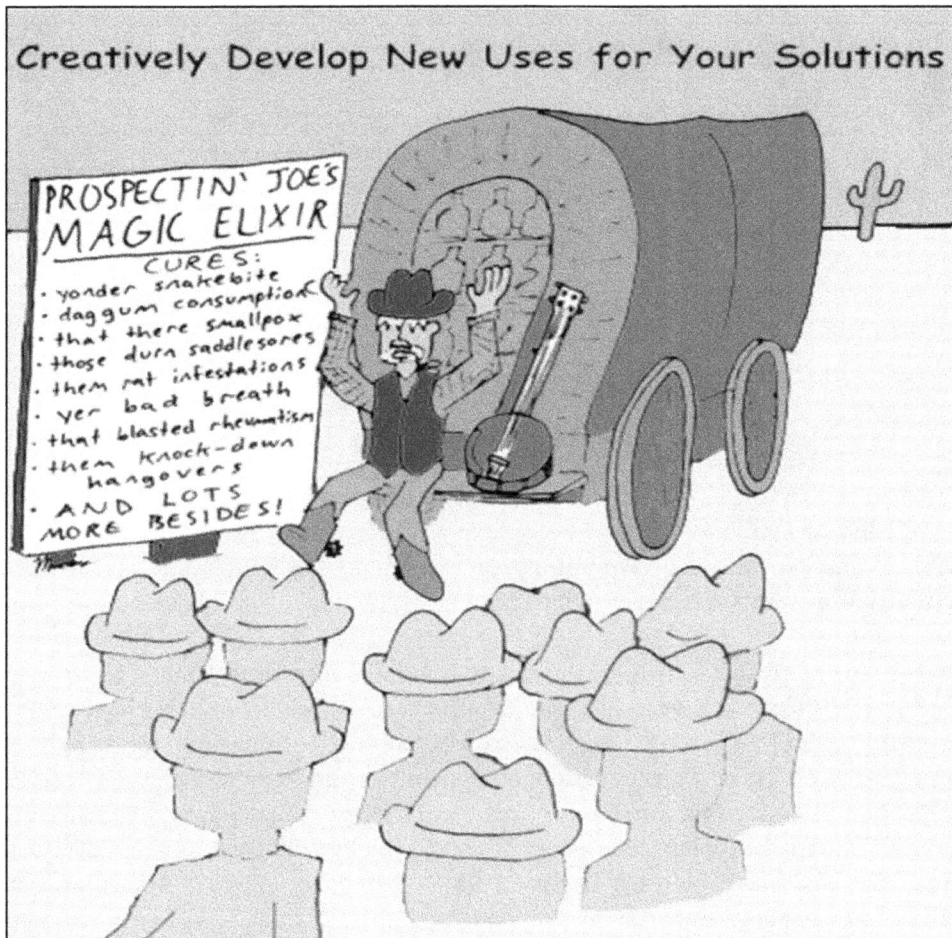

Whether any specific new potential user segment is worth pursuing depends upon certain 'segment selection criteria' that we will consider in the next chapter.

---

# <u>Light Users</u> as a Potential Target Segment

'Light users' provide yet another potential target segment. Overall market potential for any solution is calculated using both the number of potential users and their usage rate.

Using self-checkout systems as an example, one may ask the following questions: what is a realistic estimate of the potential number of self-checkout stations in the type of store being targeted (e.g., grocery, hardware, clothing, sports, super stores, convenience stores, drug stores, or general merchandise stores)? More specifically, what is the target rule of thumb for a grocery store? What proportion of the current cashier checkout stations could be realistically targeted for conversion into self-checkout stations?

Light users would be any store that converts some cashier stations to self-checkout but less than the targeted realistic proportion. That 'light user' segment could be identified as a separate segment, with a targeted marketing program intended to convert these light users into 'full' or heavy users.

Consider a consumer service example to further explore the 'light user' segment concept. What is the market potential for cable TV in a geographic market with 100,000 households that have accessible cable connection and enough income to afford cable TV? The initial target segment would likely be the whole subset of 'non-users' among these 100,000 households – say all 100,000 just prior to cable TV introduction.

As many non-users become users, additional potential 'light user segments' may develop.

- One separate target segment of 'light users' might be the subset of new user households that do have cable but subscribe simply to basic cable with access to only 20 or 30 local TV channels. A cable provider's goal might be to grow that segment by upgrading as many of those 'light users' as possible to enhanced basic cable, which includes a broader set of maybe 100-200 national channels, with a corresponding higher monthly charge.

- Another separate target segment of 'light users' might consist of the subset of cable users already subscribing to enhanced basic cable, with 100-200 national channels, but not subscribing to any 'premium channels' (HBO, Showtime, enhanced sports channels, etc.). A cable provider's goal in this instance might be to grow that segment by upgrading as many of those 'light users' as possible to a broader set of premium channels, with a corresponding higher monthly charge.

- Yet another separate target segment of 'light users' might flow from cable providers' overt recognition that some current cable TV users might be viable candidates for potential conversion into Internet and telephone (VOIP otherwise) users as well – dubbed the 'triple play' by more than one cable provider. This speaks to synergistically leveraging one service with other related services to make them all more attractive. The triple play approach can help raise the 'reaction threshold' for each of the provider's full array of separate but complementary market solutions.

# <u>Light Usage</u> as a Potential Target Segment

For many market solutions, a 'light usage' gap may exist and provide yet another potential target segment. Light usage refers to the amount of a market solution that a customer uses over a fixed period of time – be it a one-time use or usage per week, per month, or per year. Take some examples. A uniform company contracts with a customer to pick up and change over uniforms once a week, instead of the justified goal of every 3 days. A copier / document management company contracts with a user for 20,000 copies a month, rather than a justified goal of 30,000. A consulting company is retained for a maximum of 100 hrs / month rather than a potential need more than doubling that.

A company can specifically identify its subset of 'light usage' customers for any particular market solution and then target those customers with specific creative strategies. Creative packaging is one way to affect usage rates, with some everyday consumer products providing the best examples – think of 16 oz. versus 20 oz. Cokes, 16 oz. versus 24 oz. beers, effervescent cold tablets packaged in sets of two, etc. Tie-in strategies used by business-to-business companies serve as other everyday examples. For instance, companies can address light usage - 30,000 copies / month vs. 20,000 copies / month - by offering volume-related, per-use price incentives or by attractively packaging additional market solutions as incentives for greater use per time period.

## Conclusions on Usage Segments

In the next chapter, we identify some traditional approaches to identifying and selecting target segments. The following chapter then explains that the most attractive segment is often comprised of 'non-users' - that is, potential customers who are currently using some sort of generic substitute for the market solution of interest. The principles reviewed and recommended involve spending more effort and resources on attempting to convert non-users into users. This same recommendation can be relevant for some more mature markets where light user and light usage segments still represent significant growth opportunities. Thus, as the sales lifecycle matures for any market solution, targeting the light user and light usage segments can be an attractive strategy to delay Commodity Drift and the related erosion of both growth and profits.

CHAPTER 14

# Identifying & Selecting Target Segments

| Thoughtfully Segment Your Markets | | |
|---|---|---|
| Ch | 12 | Segmentation Basics |
| Ch | 13 | Consider New Potential 'Usage Segments' |
| **Ch** | **14** | **Selecting Appropriate Target Segments** |
| Ch | 15 | Focus on Non-User & 'Not looking' Segments |

In this chapter, we continue discussing principles for segmenting markets and for selecting segments with the best growth potential.

## Breaking up a Market into Segments
## Step #1: Start with Traditional Splits

Industry traditions generally provide a good foundation for dividing an overall market into specific segments. The primary advantage of starting with industry traditions is that government data, industry trade association data and the company's own internal historical data are likely already divided according to such traditions. Thus, little additional time and fewer financial resources are required to get this '1st cut' data on market breakdowns. Examples of such traditional industry segments include different end use markets, geographic regions, customer size, types of distributors used, etc. Once again, these illustrations often reflect how government and industry trade association research data are reported.

Before jumping into the first segmentation cuts via industry traditions, recall our earlier observation that segments within an overall market should differ from one another with respect to what they specifically value in the overall solution. Each distinct segment should assign different values to important solution dimensions such as quality, price, and other individual features and add-on services. Using these criteria, similarities may exist among two or more traditional segment splits. In such cases, it may be possible to combine two or more traditional segments for targeting purposes. Combining segments like this is more difficult if they are best accessed through different distribution and communication modes.

Consider the example below of traditional market segment breakdowns.

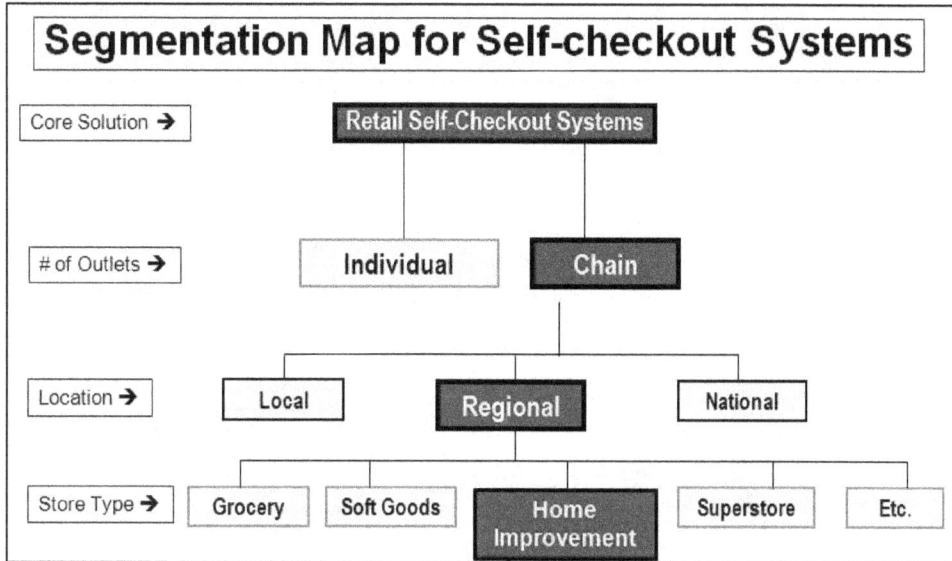

## Segmentation Map for Self-checkout Systems

Core Solution → **Retail Self-Checkout Systems**

\# of Outlets → **Individual**  **Chain**

Location → **Local**  **Regional**  **National**

Store Type → **Grocery**  **Soft Goods**  **Home Improvement**  **Superstore**  **Etc.**

---

# Choosing Target Segments

Once a company builds a traditional segmentation 'map' such as the one for self-checkout systems in this example, you may ask: 'how does the company choose the one target segment that will offer the best growth opportunity?' But this is the wrong question to ask. Any firm with growth aspirations needs to target multiple segments, not just a single segment. The right question is threefold:

1.  Which segments should we target?
2.  Should we pursue all target segments at once?
3.  If not pursuing all target segments at once, which segment or segments should we initially pursue?

Using different 'segment choice criteria' such as the following can help answer the three questions above.

*   **Size.** Critical mass of potential buyers in this segment;
*   **Growth Potential.** Lifecycle for this solution and segment is in 'Fast Growth' Phase (more on this in the 'competition' section);
*   **Profitability.** 'Commodity Drift' is not yet rampant in this segment for this solution;
*   **Availability.** No major competitor 'owns' the segment for this solution;

- **Sustainability.** Good chance to build & hold sustainable advantage in this segment for this solution;
- **Communicability.** Easy to reach this segment without significant waste of promotional $$$.

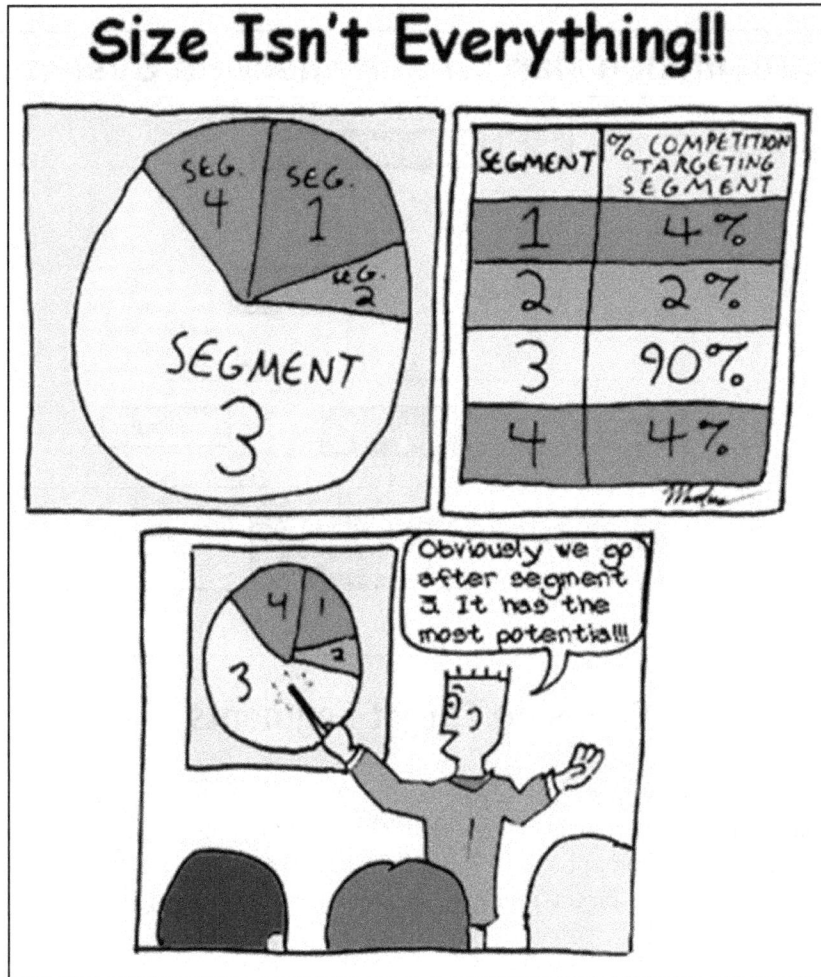

We can apply these six criteria to help prioritize segments for targeting. The exhibit below provides a framework for structuring the selection of a specific target segment from a group of alternative segments. Here, a self-checkout system company is trying to decide whether to target retailers with local, regional, or national coverage. In this instance, applying the criteria suggests that retail chains with national coverage constitute the most attractive target segment for this market solution.

| Why NATIONAL Segment?<br>Using Segmentation Criteria Matrix to Help Make this Decision | | | |
|---|---|---|---|
| **Segment Choice Criteria** | **Local** | **Regional** | **National** |
| Size: Critical Mass of potential buyers in this segment | + | ++ | +++ |
| Growth Potential: Life Cycle for this solution for this segment is in 'Fast Growth' Phase | + | + | ++ |
| Profitability – 'Commodity Drift' Is not yet rampant in this Segment for this solution | +++ | +++ | +++ |
| Availability: No major Competitor has yet targeted & 'owns' the segment for this solution | +++ | +++ | +++ |
| Sustainability: Good chance to build & hold sustainable advantage for this Segment for this solution | ++ | +++ | +++ |
| Communicability: Easy to reach segment without significant waste of promotional $$$ | + | ++ | +++ |

CHAPTER 15

---

# Focus on Non-User and Not Looking Segments

| Thoughtfully Segment Your Markets | | |
|---|---|---|
| Ch | 12 | Segmentation Basics |
| Ch | 13 | Consider New Potential 'Usage Segments' |
| Ch | 14 | Selecting Appropriate Target Segments |
| **Ch** | **15** | **Focus on Non-User & 'Not looking' Segments** |

In this chapter, we continue to review principles for segmenting markets and discuss how to find segments with the best growth potential for your company!

---

## Usage Segmentation

While traditional segmentation is a good starting point, additional layers of segmentation can prove very helpful in positioning a company for aggressive growth. The first of these is 'Usage Segmentation.' Within attractive traditional segments (according to the criteria reviewed earlier), the growth-oriented firm would aim at potential customers that are *not yet using the proposed 'new type' of market solution*. Instead, these target customers are using a more traditional, *generic substitute* for the proposed new market solution.

Continuing the example from the last chapter and adding this new layer of 'usage segmentation,' a company would specifically target 'non-users' that are currently using a more traditional solution – such as those identified in the "Non-Users Using Typical Generic Substitute" table.

| Non-Users Using Typical Generic Substitute | The Proposed New Market Solution | Proposed Target Segment |
|---|---|---|
| **Cashier Checkout** | Self-Checkout System | Regional home improvement store chains currently using only cashier checkout |
| **Travel Meetings** | Online Meetings | Software specialists currently using face to face meetings instead of online meetings |
| **Permanent Employee Specialists** | Temporary Manpower Specialists | Small scientific companies that now depend solely on permanent employees for scientific expertise |
| **Commercial Airlines** | Fractional Airline Ownership / Service | Consultants that currently travel using primarily commercial airlines |
| **Office Leasing** | Virtual Office Space and a la Carte Services | Companies with multiple sales offices that currently use primarily leased office space |

The principal focus in developing, refining and communicating the overall market solutions in these instances would be to sell specifically against the primary generic competitor, rather than focusing on brand competition. We will expand upon this discussion in the 'competition' chapter later and include instances of when targeting 'light users' as well as non-users can represent a significant growth opportunity.

---

# Step #3: Conclude with 'Looking' versus 'Not Looking' Segmentation[13]

The final segmentation cut is to split the 'non-user' target customers into two groups – **Looking Potential Customers & Not Looking Potential Customers.** Thus, the overall segmentation map for a single example (Retail Self-Checkout Systems, in this instance) might look like the splits shown in the next below.

The first group includes those already considering (i.e., 'looking for') a new generic alternative to their traditional way of doing things (e.g., self-checkout system, fractional airline service, online meetings, temporary manpower expertise, etc.). You can bet on this: if your non-user target customer is already looking, then one of your primary brand competitors already has the inside track on this potential sale. That is, the first competitor to reach the customer sets the brand selection criteria in favor of its own brand.

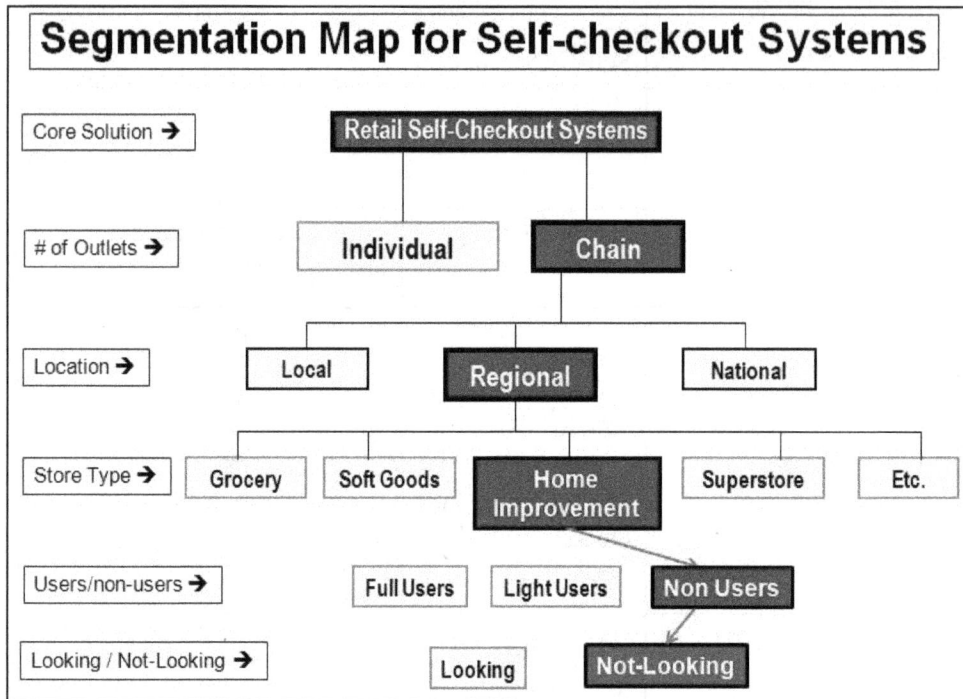

**Segmentation Map for Self-checkout Systems**

That provides an opportunity for your company as well. If you are the first to interest a 'non-user' target customer in considering the new market solution (e.g., online meetings, etc.), then you can set the brand selection criteria in favor of your own brand. That way, **YOU** have the inside track for capturing the eventual sale.

Therefore, for companies striving to grow, the best opportunities lie in targeting potential customers that are **_NOT_** currently considering replacing their traditional way of doing things. These customers include:

- Software specialists exclusively using face-to-face meetings and **_not considering_** online meetings;
- Scientific companies depending solely on permanent employees for scientific expertise and **_not considering_** using temporary manpower for scientific expertise;
- Consultants that currently travel using primarily commercial airlines and **_not considering_** fractional airline services;
- National hardware store chains using only cashier checkout and **_not considering_** self-checkout systems; and
- Companies with multiple sales offices currently using primarily leased office space and **_not considering_** contracting with a virtual office space and service provider.

Competition Is Intense for the 'Looking' Customer– Consider the *Not Looking' Customer*

Therefore, for companies striving to grow, the best opportunities lie in targeting potential customers that are **_NOT_** currently considering replacing their traditional way of doing things. These customers include:

- Software specialists exclusively using face-to-face meetings and **_not considering_** online meetings;
- Scientific companies depending solely on permanent employees for scientific expertise and **_not considering_** using temporary manpower for scientific expertise;
- Consultants that currently travel using primarily commercial airlines and **_not considering_** fractional airline services;

- National hardware store chains using only cashier checkout and ***not considering*** self-checkout systems; and
- Companies with multiple sales offices currently using primarily leased office space and ***not considering*** contracting with a virtual office space and service provider.

# Why Aren't Your Target Customers Looking?

Discovering explicitly why a target customer is not looking for a new generic solution can provide important insight into how to approach that customer and can help you in planning to meet customer objections ahead of time. A target customer might 'not be looking' for several potential reasons.

- **Too Busy**. Maybe a target customer simply has so much on her plate that she does not currently have the time or energy to reconsider what has been a satisfactory way of doing things. The less important the phenomenon addressed by the solution to the target customer, the more likely the customer is to be content with the current solution. This is true even if the customer recognizes that the older way of doing things may not be optimal.
- **A Bad Previous Experience**. Maybe the target customer previously tried an earlier version of this solution and had a bad experience, because the solution did not meet expectations.
- **Ugly Rumors**. Maybe the target customer has not tried the solution itself but has read or heard about any number of horror stories of unsatisfactory experiences with the proposed new solution.
- **Simply Unaware of a Better Alternative**. Maybe the target customer is simply unaware of the 'game-changing' nature of the new generic solution (i.e., totally new way of doing things). Thanks to **social media**, this scenario is less likely in today's age of 'better informed potential customers.'
- **No Interest in Innovating**. Maybe the target customer is comfortable being out of date, with an ingrained preference for the status quo. Fewer and fewer customers are falling into this category of laggards as information about 'the new, better way' now permeates **social media** airwaves, enabling much more informed potential buyers.

It is important for the aggressive growth company to identify the specific reason why a target company is not looking, before attempting to convert the target customer into a 'looking' company. Following customer interest groups and blogs can help in this regard. **Company-initiated interest groups, blogs, and white papers can also play an important role here** because they can enable a supplier to clarify misperceptions that may potentially be the underlying reasons why companies are not looking. Firms can use company-initiated social media such as these to establish themselves as trusted experts and to subsequently gain the inside track as they convert former 'not looking' customers into 'looking' customers.

# Chapters 16-19

# Identifying Your Competitors &

# Your Competitive Advantages

Ｉ*n  Part 1, we are reviewing the critical first steps to building an effective Account Marketing Plan for any market solution..* These steps involve the inter-related marketing concepts of segmentation (Chs 1-4), competition and key competitive advantages (Chs 5-8).

Reflecting the close inter-relationships among these concepts, Chs 1-8 should be viewed as a unit. As we continue the move forward through these chapters, the inter-relationships among these three marketing concepts (segmentation, competition, and key competitive advantages) will become apparent.

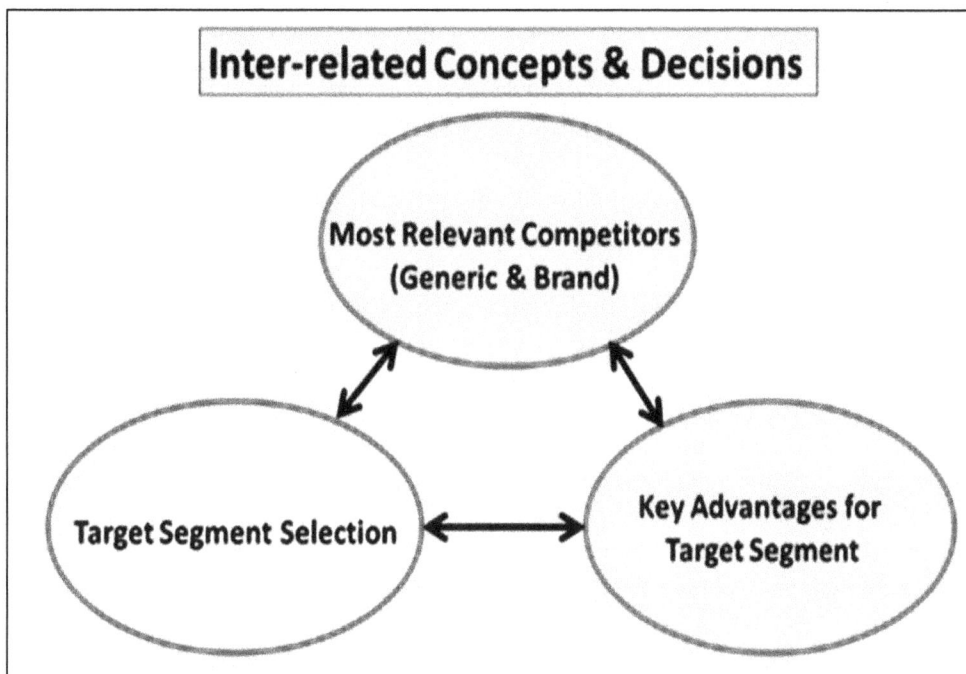

## Inter-related Concepts & Decisions

**Most Relevant Competitors
(Generic & Brand)**

**Target Segment Selection**

**Key Advantages for
Target Segment**

CHAPTER **16**

# Generic & Brand Competitors

| Identify Your Competitors & Your Competitive Advantages | | |
|---|---|---|
| Ch | 16 | **Generic & Brand Competitors** |
| Ch | 17 | Identifying & Focusing on Generic Advantages |
| Ch | 18 | Which Generic Advantages to Emphasize |
| Ch | 19 | Translate Generic Advantages into Operational Benefits |

We start this section by discussing underlying principles for identifying your competitors and your competitive advantages.

## Market Solution Life Cycle

The sales cycles of different market solutions tend to have similar shapes. Sales grow slowly immediately after the innovation hits the market. Recalling the Commodity Drift discussion, prices and profit margins are typically high at this point. Assuming an effective solution, after the initial slow beginning, sales then accelerate rapidly. More competitors soon enter the game, attracted by the fast-growing sales and excellent profit margins. Again, as we saw in the Commodity Drift coverage, the market soon becomes saturated with competitors. Profits plummet as prices fall and costs rise, because customers demand and receive more costly features and add-on services over time. The typical sales and profit curves are shown in the "Market Solution Sales for Target Segment A" exhibit. Note that profits tend to peak well before sales do.

## Market Solution Sales for Target Segment A

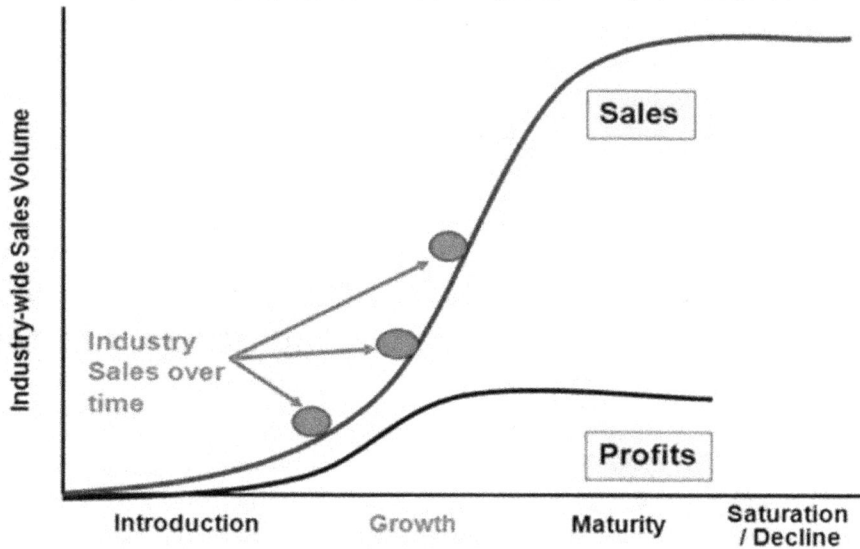

## Commodity Drift

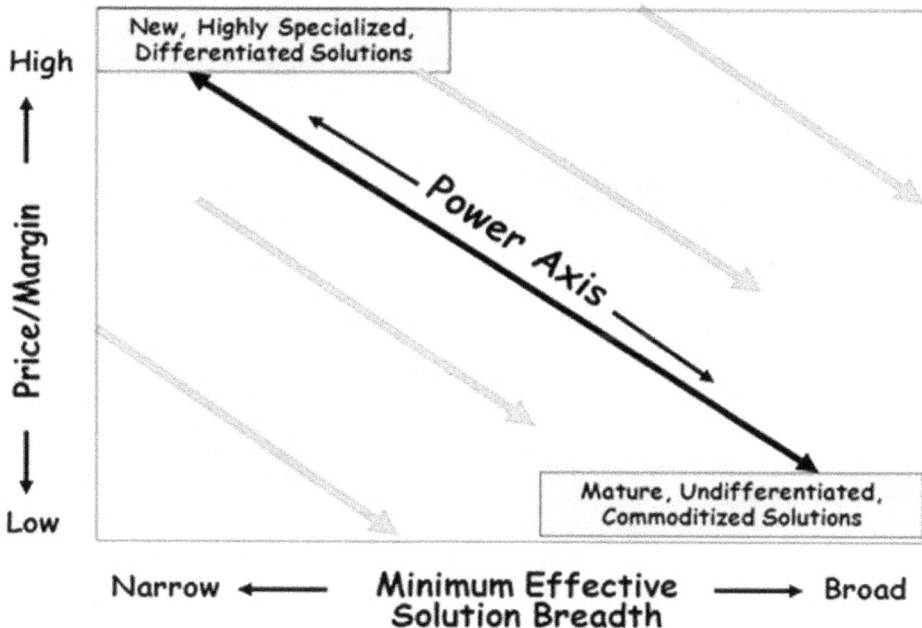

As shown, via the Market Solution and Commodity Drift graphs, this profit crunch transition in the life cycle parallels the commodity drift diagram introduced earlier –profit margins will shrink as a life cycle matures.

An overall market solution life cycle sales curve reflects the sales in many distinct segments. Different segments of the market tend to grow at different paces. Therefore, when a company projects life cycle and commodity drift transitions over time, it should do so on a segment-by-segment basis, since each segment tends to have its own life cycle. For example, consider the market solution, 'Doing business using the Internet.' The capital markets, travel and retail banking industries led the charge to integrate the Internet into their core businesses long before the insurance, agri-business and utilities industries.

---

# Competition Changes over the Segment Life Cycle
## Focus Initially on Generic Competitors and Generic Advantages

The primary challenge in the early stages of any segment life cycle is to convert "non-users" into "users." Non-users are typically using older, more traditional 'generic alternatives' to the proposed new solution. The new solution innovator's initial storyline should focus on communicating 'generic differentiators' to the selected target segment. That is, communicate exactly how the new solution functions better and has greater value than the old solution. For example, consider the primary potential generic advantages of self-service checkout over cashier checkout.

## Generic Advantages

| Self-Checkout | Cashier Checkout |
|---|---|
| **Allows Faster checkout, without waiting in line** | Must wait in potentially long lines for cashiers to become available |
| **Allows one attendant to monitor several checkout points.** | Requires More Cashiers - one Cashier has to monitor each open checkout lane |
| **Allows customers to choose between waiting for a cashier or using self-checkout** | Customers have to wait for help of cashier |
| **Prime floor space opened up for placement of impulse products** | Prime retail space taken up by checkout lanes |
| **Human error is reduced as all cash is stored in machine.** | Cash is handled by employees who may make mistakes |
| **Employees freed to work the floor** | Employees needed to work checkout lanes, taken off the floor. |

Also consider the visual perspective below. This diagram shows an immature market segment, with significant sales potential remaining, represented by the large 'generic competitors' oval. Neither brand competition nor price competition are rampant. The primary sales opportunity in this segment comes from potential customers that are currently using the most common generic substitutes for the innovation.

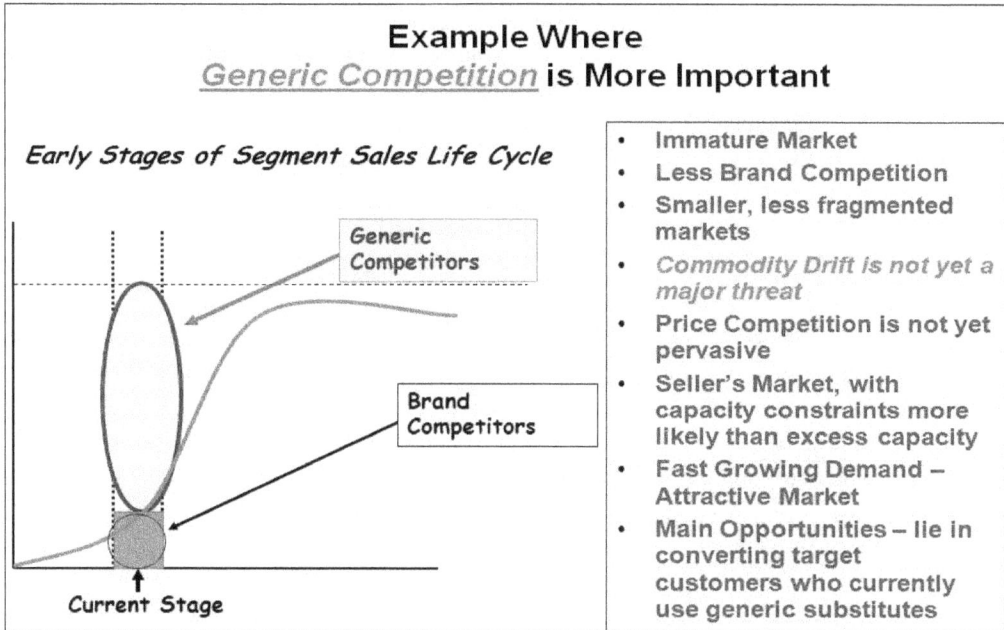

**Example Where**
*Generic Competition* **is More Important**

*Early Stages of Segment Sales Life Cycle*

Generic Competitors

Brand Competitors

Current Stage

- **Immature Market**
- **Less Brand Competition**
- **Smaller, less fragmented markets**
- *Commodity Drift is not yet a major threat*
- **Price Competition is not yet pervasive**
- **Seller's Market, with capacity constraints more likely than excess capacity**
- **Fast Growing Demand – Attractive Market**
- **Main Opportunities – lie in converting target customers who currently use generic substitutes**

## Then Transition to Brand Competitors and Brand Advantages, While Still Emphasizing Generic Advantages

As time passes, direct competitors enter the segment because they are attracted by the segment's growing sales and high profit margins. As each new competitor seeks a unique position in this marketplace, the nature of competition evolves to include both generic advantages ('new' vs. 'old') and individual brand advantages. Different competitors enter the market by focusing on new features, auxiliary services, long-term established customer relationships, or, unfortunately, price. Thus, the slide down the Commodity Drift slope begins.

Consider the visual perspective in the "Brand Competition" exhibit below. This is a rapidly maturing market segment where most non-users are already converted. New sales growth at this point becomes more and more dependent upon stealing customers away from direct brand competitors. Commodity Drift with all of its negative ramifications is running rampant! In the short-to-medium term, the key for the growth planner is to identify, enhance and pursue the company's brand competitive advantages. Consider the example of self-service checkout systems.

In the later stages of the segment sales life cycle - just as in situations where commodity drift has already occurred, any of the *re-active Commodity Drift strategies* introduced earlier might be relevant. These include the following:

- **Cutting Selective Feature & Service Costs.** Selectively cutting features and services now offered that are undervalued or not valued by the specific target customers. This can reduce costs and increase profit margins.

- **Raising Prices for Selected Features & Services.** Increasing prices and margins for features and services that are still highly valued by the specific target customers, while still leaving a transparent price incentive for the customer and increasing profit margins for the supplier. Such price increases can also increase profit margins.
- **Innovating with New Features & Services.** Carefully researching customers' preferences to identify new potential differentiated features and services that would be highly valued by specific target customers, adding these differentiators, and then charging more profitable prices for these specific new features and services. This also can increase overall profit margins.
- **Enhancing Communications of Highly Valued Features & Services.** Enhancing the marketing and communications of currently offered features and services that are highly valued by target customers. This helps to maintain higher, more profitable pricing while slowing commodity drift.
- **Bailing Out.** Finally, bailing out from participation in marketing to certain segments is another way to cut costs.

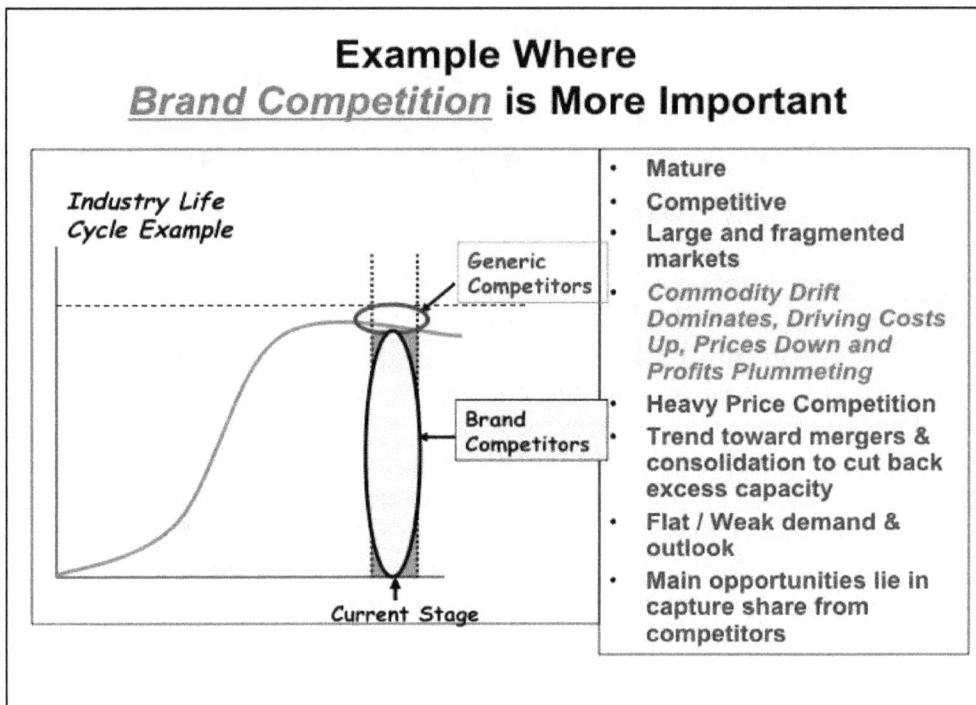

**Example Where**
*Brand Competition* **is More Important**

Cutthroat Competition Prevails for the Meager Spoils Remaining in Mature Market Segments

CHAPTER **17**

# Identifying & Focusing on Generic Advantages

| Identify Your Competitors & Your Competitive Advantages | | |
|---|---|---|
| Ch | **16** | Generic & Brand Competitors |
| **Ch** | 17 | **Identifying & Focusing on Generic Advantages** |
| Ch | 18 | Which Generic Advantages to Emphasize |
| Ch | 19 | Translate Generic Advantages into Operational Benefits |

In this chapter, we continue discussing principles for identifying your competitors and your company's competitive advantages.

## Focus on Market Solutions and Segments with Significant Growth Potential Remaining

In previous chapters, we have emphasized that the key to long-term continuous growth is to concentrate on market solutions and related market segments for which Commodity Drift and related profit erosion have not yet occurred. This means focusing growth initiatives and resources on:

- Identifying attractive 'non-user' segments[14];
- Designing strategies for effectively attacking non-user segments; and then
- Aggressively implementing those strategies to convert non-users into users.

Having already explored how to identify attractive non-user segments, the next challenge is to develop effective strategies for attacking these segments. Let's tackle this in several phases. In this chapter, we identify generic advantages. In the next chapter, we will translate these generic advantages into operational issues and benefits.

# Developing Strategies for Attacking Non-User Segments – 1st: Identify Generic Advantages

By focusing resources on attractive non-user market segments, a company can succeed in and often dominate such segments all the way through the fast growth phase. Through doing so, a smart company can establish a favorable reputation that it can subsequently use to gain traction in other fast growth segments.

## Establish a Beachhead for Future Success on Many Fronts

So, exactly how can a company capture non-user segments? We already know that non-users are using the 'old way generic alternatives' instead of the proposed 'new way solution.' Thus, ***the first challenge for aggressively pursuing attractive non-user segments is to identify the 'generic advantages' of the 'new way' versus the 'old way.'***

## Identifying Generic Advantages in Business Markets

How is the 'new way' better than the 'old way'? The "Generic Advantages" exhibit below highlights the generic advantages of the new way versus the old way using the example of self-checkout systems. Other examples of B2B market solutions are provided in later chapters.

## Generic Advantages

| Self-Checkout | Cashier Checkout |
|---|---|
| Allows Faster checkout, without waiting in line | Must wait in potentially long lines for cashiers to become available |
| Allows one attendant to monitor several checkout points. | Requires More Cashiers - one Cashier has to monitor each open checkout lane |
| Allows customers to choose between waiting for a cashier or using self-checkout | Customers have to wait for help of cashier |
| Prime floor space opened up for placement of impulse products | Prime retail space taken up by checkout lanes |
| Human error is reduced as all cash is stored in machine. | Cash is handled by employees who may make mistakes |
| Employees freed to work the floor | Employees needed to work checkout lanes, taken off the floor. |

## Some Generic Advantages of Self-Checkout Systems

- <u>Faster Checkout</u>. Example: Before SpeedyLane, customers had no option but to wait in the cashier line, no matter what size the purchase. **With SpeedyLane**, customers save time and traffic flow is improved.
- <u>Fewer Employees</u>. Example: Before SpeedyLane, retailers needed one checkout cashier per lane. **With SpeedyLane**, one employee can monitor up to 10 self-checkout units.
- <u>Flexible Customer Checkout Choice.</u> <u>Example</u>: Before SpeedyLane, customers had to go through checkout lanes. **With SpeedyLane**, customers have the option to choose to be helped by a cashier or to use self-checkout.
- <u>Increased Prime Retail Space.</u> Example: Before Speedy-Lane, checkout lanes occupied nearly the entire front of the store, cutting prime retail sale space. **With SpeedyLane**,

more lanes can fit in a smaller area, opening the floor for the sale of more products, specifically impulse products.

- **Theft Reduction.** Example: Before SpeedyLane, self-checkout was impossible due to high security risks. **With SpeedyLane**'s patented security techniques, including a highly advanced weight system, security database, and remote monitoring, theft is now less of an issue.

- **Better Customer Service Is Possible.** Example: Before SpeedyLane, the majority of employees were needed to staff checkout lanes. **With SpeedyLane**, more employees are available on the floor to help customers with problems and to increase customer satisfaction.

---

# Some Generic Advantages of Radio Frequency Identification (RFID)

- **Can change information on RFID tags automatically and instantly**. Example: During the summer the Legacy Stripe Ponytail scarf is $38 and during the winter season, the price changes to $42. With a RFID capability, the imbedded price information can be configured to automatically change the price on any given date.

- **Can be read without line-of-sight; does not require scanner to be present**. Example: A truck load of the new Coach purses needs to be in Macy's in University Park Mall by 8am on Monday November 5th, but because of the time change, the truck driver left the New York warehouse late and does not have time to unload each crate at the checkpoint in Philadelphia. With RFID tag inventory management, the truck load does not need to be unloaded at the checkpoint.

- **Can collect and read real time inventory data**. Example: A local celebrity desperately needs a purse for a charity ball tonight and would like to see if the Bleecker Tattersall Top Handle purse is in stock.

- **Integrates with any inventory system**. Example: Coach already has a pre-existing inventory system that they used with their old bar code scanners yet did not have to make any changes when they started using RFID chips because the chips were compatible with the system.

- **Remotely monitors inventory account balances**. Example: Being nation-wide, Coach has various locations that are constantly producing inventory turnover. RFID allows for communication of the inventory account balances (e.g., when item number 102 gets to the Chicago location, it is added to the Chicago location's account balance) both regionally and nationally.

- **Hold large amounts of data**. Example: Coach has various types of inventory. The RFID chip contains a large amount of information that will tell central management the current stock of purses of each type at each location – by style & color code, arrival date, serial nos., etc., which triggers automatic inventory renewal at company-set efficient order points. Furthermore, if a retailer is looking for a specific purse out of stock locally, he/she can locate it and order it from the closest location.

# There Is a New, Better Way!

---

## What Are the Generic Advantages for Your Company's Primary Market Solution?

What about your company's primary market solution? Ask yourself two questions:

(1) For any remaining attractive non-user segment, what is the primary generic substitute now being used? Then,

(2) What are the generic advantages of your proposed 'new way of doing things' over the old way of doing things? Start considering these two questions now, as you will be asked to identify those advantages in an upcoming chapter.

---

## The Same Generic Advantages for all Players

All direct brand competitors will ultimately be offering similar 'new ways' of doing things by providing the same fundamental generic alternative to the 'old way' of doing things. Therefore, all directly competing brands will have more or less the same generic advantages.

How, then, can a growth planner differentiate its company's own branded solution to take the lead in capturing any attractive, fast growth, non-user segment? This leads us to the next chapter, where we will consider that challenge.

CHAPTER **18**

# Which Generic Advantages to Emphasize

| Identify Your Competitors & Your Competitive Advantages | | |
|---|---|---|
| Ch | 16 | Generic & Brand Competitors |
| Ch | 17 | Identifying & Focusing on Generic Advantages |
| **Ch** | **18** | **Which Generic Advantages to Emphasize** |
| Ch | 19 | Translate Generic Advantages into Operational Benefits |

In this chapter, we continue discussing principles for identifying your competitors and recognizing your competitive advantages.

We begin by considering the growth planner's challenge to design strategies to effectively attract desirable non-user segments to our product or service. As observed in the previous chapter, all potential brand competitors will ultimately be offering pretty much the same 'new way' of doing things – that is, the same fundamental generic alternative to the 'old way' of doing things. Therefore, all competing brands will have pretty much the same generic advantages.

**If all players have the same generic advantages, how can any company differentiate its specific branded solution and secure a leading position in the segment?** A company can do this by simplifying an overall list of generic advantages to a reasonable number. Next, the company should lay out criteria for selecting a subset of generic advantages that are the most significant to the target segment and that also differentiate the company's generic solution from its would-be direct brand competitors.

## How Many Generic Advantages to Recognize?

How many generic advantages might a 'new way' solution have over an 'old way' solution? There might be 4, 6, 8, 10, 15 or even more generic advantages. For example, as shown in an exhibit later in this chapter, a typical Radio Frequency Identification (RFID) solution has more than a dozen generic advantages over bar codes in the 'supplier-to-retail' market segment.

So, how many generic advantages should a company specifically focus on? Certainly, all of the most important generic advantages should be recognized, including those that:

- **Are most transparent to the target non-user segment; and**
- **Promise to bring the most incremental value to that target segment.**

We suggest as a rule of thumb to *focus your growth planning strategy on roughly six of the most important generic advantages.* Previous and subsequent examples in this book follow that general guideline. The logic for focusing on a manageable subset of advantages is twofold:

- This provides a better focus for efforts to design strategies for the target segment; and
- This also provides a better focus for more clearly communicating the advantages of one's market solution to the target segment.

## Selecting the Most Important Generic Advantages

So, what generic advantages should you emphasize? As suggested above, one certainly needs to include those generic advantages that are most obvious and regarded as the most important advantages by the target segment. Monitoring would-be buyer blogs, interest groups and other buyer social media discussions can provide some important insights for identifying those advantages.

For newer innovations, would-be customers may require some education to help them accurately anticipate the most important generic advantages of a totally new solution. One approach is for a seller of the new solution to become an active discussant in customer-initiated interest groups that focus on the new solution. This can be a particularly effective approach for clarifying misperceptions about the nature and benefits of specific potential generic advantages.

A complementary approach is for a seller to initiate its own educational blogs, white papers and other social media communications. Well-planned seller-initiated communications of this sort via social media can establish specific individuals from any specific company as trusted advisors related to the new solution and its primary generic advantages. This 'trusted advisor role' is more likely to emerge if any would-be individual advisor's company affiliation is indicated only incidentally, almost as an afterthought. Ideally, this indirect, subtle mention of an individual's company affiliation can enable direct communications from blog or white paper readers, without coming off as a sales pitch. Not surprisingly, this trusted advisor role, when established effectively, can generate numerous valuable customer-generated leads. (Later chapters will expand on this last point.)

Beyond those few most obvious and important advantages, a growth planner can choose from many additional generic advantages to promote. This provides a chance for a company to differentiate its overall market solution from would-be brand competitors. A company can simultaneously create a built-in bias for its brand during the most critical phases of any segment's development – the takeoff and fast growth phases. A seller can accomplish this by assessing a full range of generic advantages and *then focusing on a subset of those important generic advantages for which one's own brand has a clear, sustainable advantage over would-be primary brand competitors.* A company that has individual experts established as 'trusted advisors' for would-be customers and customer interest groups (through social media) is in a particularly advantageous position to create a built-in bias for its brand.

Consider the following examples of potential sustainable differential advantages that a company might have for market solutions, such as self-checkout systems, online meetings, and fractional airline services.

- Sustainable, clearly differentiated generic advantages ***for self-checkout systems*** might include the following:
  - A company may offer a proven, more flexible, turnkey interface with a wide range of existing database technologies, which facilitates more rapid and trouble-free adoption and integration of self-checkout software with retailers' current systems. This is a sustainable differentiator because it would take considerable time and resources for would-be brand competitors to upgrade their supporting software systems to be as flexible and trouble-free.
  - A company may offer patent-protected technology to more accurately weigh items and a foolproof system to ensure that an industry-low number of items pass through the self-checkout system undetected and unrecorded. This is a sustainable differentiator because of the patented technology and because it would take considerable time and resources for would-be brand competitors to upgrade their detection system to match that accuracy.
- Sustainable, clearly differentiated generic advantages ***for online meetings*** might include the following.
  - A company may boast a clearly superior, proven backbone infrastructure that facilitates connections and uninterrupted service for its clients' online meetings. This is a sustainable advantage because it would take considerable time and resources for would-be brand competitors to match or surpass the effectiveness of that infrastructure.
  - Perhaps a company has an award winning, best-in-market service to trouble-shoot any connection or communication problems that may occur during online meetings. This is a sustainable differentiator because it would take considerable time and resources for would-be brand competitors to match or surpass the effectiveness of that trouble-shooting service.
- Sustainable, clearly differentiated generic advantages ***for fractional airline service*** might include the following.
  - A company may have more planes and more different plane sizes and configurations in their aircraft fleet. This ensures more timely and flexible service for the target segment. This is a sustainable differentiator because of the incremental capital investment (in planes) that would be required by any would-be competitor to match the availability and related air service flexibility.
  - A company may boast a well-established historical interface and connections with a broader network of diversely located smaller airports, as well as larger airports. This is a sustainable differentiator over the short-to-medium term at least because it would take a significant amount of time for any would-be competitor to build a competing network of airport connections.

We saw earlier how a company can use self-initiated blogs, white papers and other methods in order to establish some of its own resident experts as trusted advisors for members of buyer interest groups and the like through *social media*. Once established as advisors, these resident experts are in an ideal position to bias the evaluation of alternative sellers towards the company's own brand. They can do this by focusing buyer attention on the differentiated generic advantages of their own brand.

## Considering Features First Can Help to Identify Generic Advantages for More Complex Market Solutions

The primary generic advantages of the 'new way' versus the 'old way' are evident for the most part, as shown in the examples provided for self-checkout systems and online meetings. In other instances - particularly for more complex, multi-dimensional new solutions - the primary generic advantages may be less obvious. In such instances, it can help to first think about the 'features' of the new solution and then translate those features into generic advantages (essentially operational benefits). For example, consider the features and related generic advantages of RFID chips over bar codes for companies whose primary output is sold through retail channels.

| RFID - Potential for Product Suppliers (as opposed to retailers like WalMart) | |
| --- | --- |
| RF (Radio Frequency) Tracking for Enhanced Inventory Planning & Control at all Levels of the Supply Chain | |
| **Feature** | **Generic Advantage** (over primary generic competitor - bar codes) |
| Ability to read inventory without visual contact (unlike bar codes) | no need to unload & repack inventory at any stage of supply chain to monitor inventory for inventory checking / counting / verifying |
| | reduced manual labor for monitoring inventory (e.g., vs reading bar codes) |
| Ability to remotely monitor / count inventory at long distances (unlike bar codes) | faster inventory monitoring at all levels of the supply chain |
| An RFID chip can hold large amount of data / information - with all data instantly read by RFID monitoring device (e.g., date & place of mfg, serial no., expiration date, shipper(s), transportation & warehousing route, etc.) | broad range of data is instantly available on each inventory item at whatever stage of supply chain the RFID chips are monitored |
| | Out of date merchandise automatically red-flagged for pulling from supply chain |
| Software integrated into or linked to RFID monitoring device facilitates consolidation & analysis of consolidated inventory data for specific needs of each member of the supply chain (more extensive inventory monitoring than possible with bar code monitoring & related backbone software) | Inventory analysis instantly available on consolidated inventory – analysis software customized to specific needs of each member of the supply chain |

| RF (Radio Frequency) Tracking for Enhanced Inventory Planning & Control at all Levels of the Supply Chain | |
|---|---|
| **Feature** | **Generic Advantage** (over primary generic competitor - bar codes) |
| Real time monitoring of inventory location -- i.e., location of product at all times (much more extensive inventory monitoring coverage is now feasible than possible with bar code monitoring & related backbone software) | helps keep production planning more in tune with final consumer / demand needs, while reducing 'dead inventory' in supply chain |
| | more timely monitoring of product inventory during warehousing |
| | more timely monitoring of product inventory during different phases of transportation |
| | more timely monitoring of product inventory at retail level |
| RFID background software can keep track of and alert whole supply chain as to when product goes out the retail door to final customer (more extensive monitoring than possible with bar code monitoring & related backbone software) | improved ability to monitor final sales |
| RFID tags are imbedded and very difficult to detach or become dysfunctional (unlike barcodes that can more easily become detached, torn, or unreadable) | reduce situations where ID on product (e.g., bar code) falls off or becomes unreadable |
| | Reduce theft & other 'lost' product at all levels of supply chain |
| Others ?? | |

# What about Generic Advantages Where One's Own Brand is Inferior?

A company's brand may be inferior to brand competitors on one or more key features that are considered advantages by a target segment. This is not a critical concern, as long as the company can prove to its target segment that the overall value of its solution is superior to that of its brand competitors. Refer back to Chapter 3, where we emphasized the importance of being able to 'live with' specific competitive shortfalls as long as a company can clearly prove that its overall market solution is superior.

Consider another situation where one's brand may be inferior on a specific generic advantage. If one or more segments insist on a competitor's generic advantage that your company cannot match, then avoid that target segment in the short term. Here again we see the interplay between segment selection and the clear recognition of one's competitive advantages (or disadvantages, in this case). Over the longer term, however, if that segment has significant sales and profit potential, a company can strive to overcome the relevant weakness and ultimately compete for that segment during the growth phase – again by focusing on the superior value of its overall market solution.

---

# Importance of Effectively Communicating Key Generic Advantages and Related Benefits

Regardless of the range and degree of the specific operating and financial benefits that are likely to flow from a set of generic advantages, those advantages and their related benefits must be communicated effectively to convert potential customers. Even solid advantages, with substantial operating and financial benefits over more traditional generic alternatives, will not convert non-users unless they are effectively communicated. Later chapters offer a systematic approach for effectively communicating generic advantages and their related benefits.

CHAPTER 19

# Translating Generic Advantages into Operational Benefits

| Identify Your Competitors & Your Competitive Advantages | | |
|---|---|---|
| Ch | 16 | Generic & Brand Competitors |
| Ch | 17 | Identifying & Focusing on Generic Advantages |
| Ch | 18 | Which Generic Advantages to Emphasize |
| **Ch** | **19** | **Translate Generic Advantages into Operational Benefits** |

The previous two chapters covered the first step in designing strategies to effectively attack non-user segments. The challenge was to identify a solid subset of generic advantages promised by the proposed 'new way of doing things.'

This chapter explains how to use these generic advantages as the communications focal point for:

- Capturing the target customer's initial attention and interest;
- Framing an in-depth exploration of the target customer's prospective need for the proposed new solution; and,
- Helping the target customer to visualize how your set of selected generic advantages (i.e., new capabilities) can help to address some of that customer's most pressing operating issues.

To determine how to address each of these communications challenges, the growth planner should answer two questions regarding each recognized generic advantage:

1. What specific operating issue of the target customer is addressed by each prospective new generic advantage / capability? and
2. What specific operating benefit will flow from each prospective new generic advantage / capability?

# Link Each Generic Advantage with an Operating Issue and an Operating Benefit

**Operating Issues: Identify the Primary Operating Issue Addressed by Each Generic Advantage**

The first challenge at hand is to identify what important everyday operating issue ('pain') is addressed by each promised generic advantage. Identifying these specific operating issues serves as the launch pad for the growth planner's systematic approach to communicating with the target customer.

## Operating Benefits: Identify the Primary Operating Benefit Projected from Each Generic Advantage

Once you have identified the link between each operating problem and the promised generic advantage, the next challenge is to extend these connections to show what specific operating benefit will result from each promised generic advantage.

## 3 Examples

Consider the three part linkage (operating issues, promised new capabilities, and – promised operating benefits) for some examples introduced earlier – namely, self-service checkout systems, online meetings, and corporate relocation services.

**Example - Relevant Operating Issues, Promised New Capabilities (Generic Advantages), and Projected Operating Benefits for Self-checkout Service**

| Specific Relevant Operating Issues | New Capabilities (i.e., Generic Advantages) Needed to Resolve Each Relevant Operating Issue | Projected Operating Benefit from Each New Capability (i.e., from each new generic advantage) |
|---|---|---|
| Customer dissatisfaction with long lines leads reduces store loyalty. | Self-checkout (feature) improves traffic flow and customer satisfaction by reducing time spent in line (advantage). | More satisfied customers increases store traffic and customer loyalty. |
| A high number of cashiers is needed. | Remote monitoring (feature) allows one cashier to operate ten lanes, so fewer cashiers are needed (advantage). | Smaller workforce is simpler to maintain. |
| Customer dissatisfaction with long lines reduces store loyalty. | Self-checkout (feature) allows customers the choice between a cashier or using self checkout, increasing customer satisfaction (advantage) | More satisfied customers increases store traffic and reduces walkouts. |
| Too little prime floor space for impulse purchase items. | Compact configuration (feature) opens floor space, allowing more space for the sale of impulse items (advantage). | Saved floor space and faster lines improve traffic flow and provides opportunity for placement of impulse items. |
| Too much theft. | Advanced weight system, security database, and remote monitoring (feature) result in higher security and less theft (advantage). | Increased security reduces customer delinquency and saves retailer time and resources lost handling theft. |
| Not enough employees on the floor reduces customer satisfaction, which leads to fewer customers. | Remote monitoring (feature) allows one cashier to operate ten lanes, so more employees available on floor (advantage). | More employees on the floor means greater customer satisfaction and store loyalty. |

**Example – Relevant Operating Issues, Promised New Capabilities (Generic Advantages), and Projected Operating Benefits for _On-Line Meetings_**

| Specific Relevant Operating Issues | New Capabilities (i.e., Generic Advantages) Needed to Resolve Each Relevant Operating Issue | Projected Operating Benefit from Each New Capability (i.e., from each new generic advantage) |
|---|---|---|
| Long set-up process for meetings (travel arrangements) | Quick and easy meeting set-up | Reduces set up time |
| Difficult to conduct meetings on short notice | Instant meetings capability using instant messaging | Spontaneous meetings are now more possible |
| Clutter and personal files on desktop cause distraction | Reduce clutter on screen during meeting (Screen Clean) | Material absorption rate increases |
| Lack of immediate feedback and engagement in training sessions | Ensure proper training and good communication using shared keyboard and mouse control | Cuts down training time and increases material mastery |
| Disruptive side conversations | Reduce side conversations and distractions during meetings with private chat | Increases meeting efficiency |
| Difficult to keep track of who attends large meetings | Automated attendance reporting | Ensures higher attendance rate |

## Example – Relevant Operating Issues, Promised New Capabilities (Generic Advantages), and Projected Operating Benefits for _Corporate Relocation Services_

| Specific Relevant Operating Issues | New Capabilities (i.e., Generic Advantages) Needed to Resolve Each Relevant Operating Issue | Projected Operating Benefit from Each New Capability (i.e., from each new generic advantage) |
|---|---|---|
| Difficult to manage all relocation processes at once | Service Consolidation | Increases employee efficiency and productivity at all levels of the relocation process. |
| Multiple points of contact cause communication problems | Personal Relocation Agent | Employee satisfaction and productivity increased through dealing with only one Personal Relocation Agent. |
| Difficult to coordinate depending where individual is relocating to and from | Nationwide Services | Increased locations for relocations improve employee satisfaction and productivity. |
| Employees distracted by adjustments at home | Attention to personal needs | Employee satisfaction and productivity increased after family needs are quickly addressed. |
| Limited time to search for new residence | Residential Search | Reduces time spent searching for new housing, thus increasing employee satisfaction and productivity. |
| Lack of information regarding new office and residence makes furnishing difficult | Furniture Specialist | Employee satisfaction and productivity improved as office furniture concerns are addressed by relocation service. |

# Part 2
# *Building the Account Marketing Plan*

## *Linda & SpeedyLane's Account Marketing Plan*

20. Meet Linda, SpeedyLane Salesperson & Brian Wilson, Sales Trainee
21. Linda's Master Selling Plan for House Depot
      ***Identify Players, Issues & Visions Required***
22. Linda's Master Selling Plan for House Depot
      ***Choose Target Sponsor***
23. Linda's Master Selling Plan for House Depot
      ***Choose Target Power Sponsor***
24. Linda's Master Selling Plan for House Depot
      ***Plan for Building Visions for All Important Players***

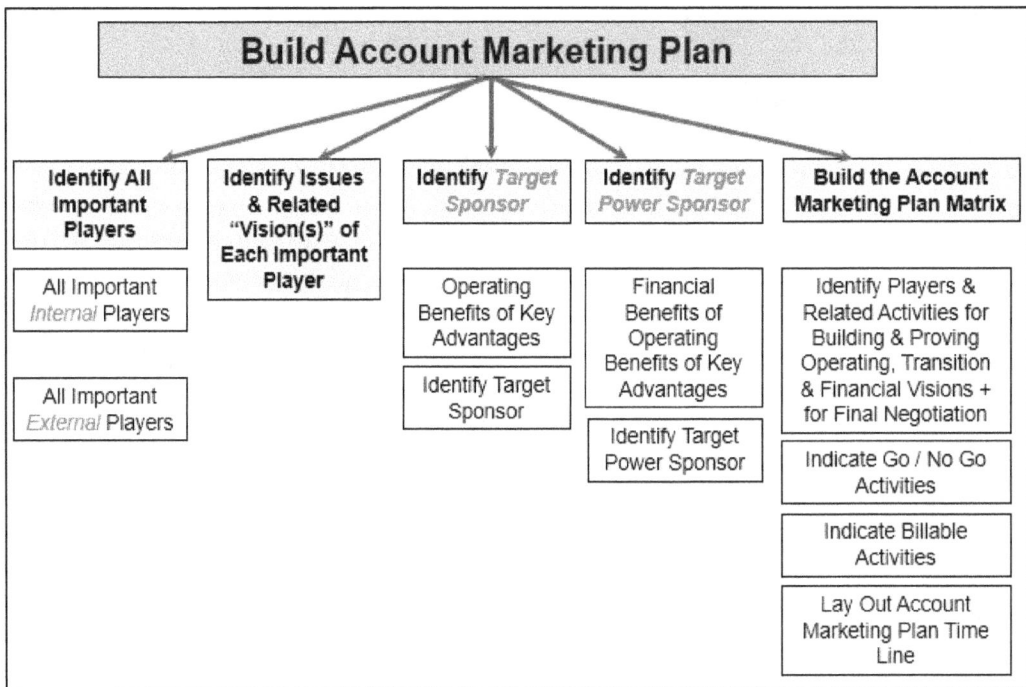

CHAPTER 20

# Meet Linda Brown &
# Brian Wilson

| Linda & SpeedyLane's Master Selling Plan | | |
|---|---|---|
| Ch | 20 | **Meet Salesperson Linda Brown and Sales Trainee Brian Wilson** |
| Ch | 21 | Linda's Master Selling Plan for House Depot (HD), Pt 1. Players & Visions Required |
| Ch | 22 | Linda's Master Selling Plan for House Depot (HD), Pt 2. Choose Target Sponsor |
| Ch | 23 | Linda's Master Selling Plan for House Depot (HD), Pt 3. Choose Target Power Sponsor |
| Ch | 24 | Linda's Master Selling Plan for House Depot (HD), Pt 4. Plan for Building Visions for All Important Players |

At this point, we will change gears a bit to increase the 'fun factor' for your continued reading of the Account Marketing Planning book. To build reader interest, we make the rest of the book a story. This focuses on a fictional, fun young lady named Linda Brown. Linda is a veteran salesperson for SpeedyLane, a self-checkout system solution provider.

The yarn is all about Linda's energetic effort to sell her SpeedyLane Self-checkout System to House Depot. House Depot (HD) is a fictional regional home improvement retailer. HD has been around since the early 1980s, and currently has 225 home improvement centers spread throughout the Southeastern United States. In recent years, HD has significantly increased its growth aspirations -- adding ten to fifteen new stores each year.

For the story, we assume that HD currently uses cashier checkout only and has no plans to change from this traditional checkout system. This will be quite a challenge for Linda, but one that she is anxious to pursue. As you'll see, Linda's selling efforts do not always go smoothly, despite her enthusiasm (sometimes, 'over-enthusiasm') to make this sale and grow SpeedyLane's revenue.

While trying to sell the SpeedyLane Self-checkout System to House Depot, Linda is simultaneously mentoring a new sales trainee – a nice, energetic young fellow named Brian Wilson, whom you will also get to know better as our story moves along.

---

## Meet SpeedyLane Super-Salesperson, Linda Brown

Before we get going, let's meet this Linda character and her protégé, Brian.

**Full name:** Linda Louisa Brown

### Education:

- Graduated from Choctaw High School (Choctaw, OK) in 20xx. Salutatorian in class of 35 students. There were 9 valedictorians, but only 4 salutatorians.
- Received her bachelor's degree in marketing from the Southeastern Oklahoma University - Class of 2009. No GPA indicated on her resume, but she was Chapter President of her Sorority, PI PI PI, the most popular social sorority on campus.

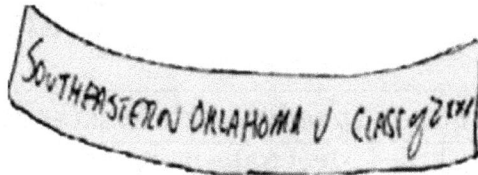

### Personal / Romantic Interest:

- Married right out of college to 'Herby' Dunbar, currently a History teacher and football coach at St. Lucas High School in Atlanta.
- Decided to keep her maiden name (Brown) for her business dealings.
- Happily, has three children, all boys (two, four, and six years old)

### Employment Background:

- Lifeguarded at Choctaw Community Pool every summer during high school and while at Southeastern Oklahoma U.
- Started as a waitress at Big Bud's Burger Joint in Choctaw right after graduating from college. Promoted to Assistant Manager in six months and to Manager within eighteen months.
- Hired by SpeedyLane Self-checkout Systems in 2005.

### Current Position & Company:

- Top tier Sales Rep for SpeedyLane. Based out of SpeedyLane headquarters in Atlanta, where she and her family have lived since 2005.

- Was a member of SpeedyLane's Golden Sales Club for three years running but missed out on it last year. She is determined to win back her club membership this year and has received intense prodding from her family about the situation. Herby and her boys make no secret about being *extremely* disappointed about missing (for the first time in four years) last year's SpeedyLane Holiday Break to Hawaii at year's end for all Golden Sales Club members.

## Hobbies:

- **Jumping rope** -- Linda exercises at 9:00 pm sharp every night to relieve the stresses of work and family life through a rigorous jump roping routine. Jumping since third grade, Linda became city Junior Champion at age 9 in Choctaw, OK (pop. 4,500).
- **Cares for and chats with her pet fish (Whale)** – Linda finds Whale to be a low maintenance, friendly pet, perfect for her already busy life. She has a heart-to-heart chat with Whale most evenings before bedtime. She won't let anyone else - not even her boys - play with Whale. She's currently on Whale IV, with the first three buried in her backyard, where one can find grave markers and a constant supply of fresh flowers.

- **Hangs out with colleagues from work** (SpeedyLane employees and clients) virtually every Thursday night after work. She's ultra-popular with other SpeedyLane sales team members and with previous clients because she is very friendly, smiles easily, is enthusiastic, and radiates a "go get 'em can do" attitude (despite her frequent and well-known sales blunders at SpeedyLane).

## Nickname(s):

- Husband Herby and close friends call her *'Linny'* (nicknamed by her cousin Trudy when they were both four years old).
- As a child, whenever she got in trouble at home, Linda's mother used to call her *'Linda-Lou.'* Linda now uses this same handle when chastising herself for screwing up something – particularly when she repeats one of her many infamous SpeedyLane selling blunders.

## Physical:

- Shoulder-length blonde hair that's straight as a ruler.
- Green eyes
- Longish face
- Average height – **wishes she were taller, like her good friend, Danielle.** Thus, Linda is well practiced at wearing nine-inch heels and is repeatedly asked by new acquaintances whether she plays volleyball or basketball.
- Slender from her vigorous daily jump rope routine
- Feet are slightly too big for the rest of her body (size 9 ½)
- Huge hands – used to crush the hands of male colleagues and clients during introductory handshakes. Most close

male acquaintances are now accustomed to simply saying 'Hello' to Linda as a preferred greeting.

**Vehicle:** Beat-up old VW Polo

- Awfully cramped for her, Herby & the three boys. Would like Herby to get a minivan, so she could get a red BMW convertible, like her friend Danielle.

## Other:

- Gets headaches almost daily. This likely stems from being a workaholic and tending to have too many thoughts running simultaneously through her head. This understandably makes her quite dizzy by the middle of most days. Not surprisingly, Linda is not at all good at multi-tasking.

So, there's one of our stars, Linda Brown. You'll get to know Linda much better as our story moves along. Next, let's meet Linda's protégé, Brian Wilson!

# Meet Sales Trainee, Brian Wilson

Our second fictional character is Brian Wilson, a new sales trainee at SpeedyLane. Let's check out Brian's profile.

**Full name:** Brian Michael Wilson

## Education:

- Recent bachelor's degree in economics & Political Science from Bucknell University in Lewiston, PA - Class of 20xx. Brian's father, mother, and five older siblings also graduated from Bucknell. Brian was an energetic school leader, acting as Associate Editor of the Bucknellian (student newspaper), Founder of the Bucknell Badminton Club, and Social Director of Phi Chi fraternity. There, along with other social contributions, he initiated the annual Polar Bear Plunge – a February dip into the chilly waters of the Susquehanna River. His GPA was 3.71. He's a pretty bright & disciplined guy!

## Personal / Romantic Interests:

- Despite heroic efforts all four years while in Phi Chi at Bucknell, it took Brian until February of his senior year at Bucknell to get his first 'date' ever (at least he counted it as a date) when he somehow talked then
  Sophomore Mary Ellen Fasbender- a popular Bucknell cheerleader, whom Brian talked into joining him in Phi Chi's annual Polar Bear Plunge.
- While it seemed like a fantastic idea at the time, Brian has been trying to break off any continuing relationship with Mary Ellen ever since. However, Mary Ellen is so infatuated with Brian's good looks and his friendly, although somewhat under-developed personality, that she continues to stalk him with daily phone calls, e-mails, and social media pleas of all sorts, even now that he has moved to Atlanta.
- Brian is a nice fellow and doesn't want to hurt Mary Ellen's feelings, but he believes that he's 'just not ready' for a relationship to clutter up his already busy life. He is currently scouring the Internet to find a possible way to change his name and identity to rid himself of Mary Ellen's escalating, unwanted romantic advances. He much prefers the company of several Bucknell frat buddies who have also ventured to Atlanta to either attend law school or start their own careers.

- Brian is a nice fellow and doesn't want to hurt Mary Ellen's feelings, but he believes that he's 'just not ready' for a relationship to clutter up his already busy life. He is currently scouring the Internet to find a possible way to change his name and identity to rid himself of Mary Ellen's escalating, unwanted romantic advances. He much prefers the company of several Bucknell frat buddies who have also ventured to Atlanta to either attend law school or start their own careers.

## Employment Background:
- Coming from a well-to-do family, the only 'job' that Brian ever had was occasionally mowing the lawn at the family estate, located just outside of Lancaster, PA.
- After traveling to Europe with buddies from Bucknell for two months after graduation, Brian's Uncle Harry - a Marketing big-wig at SpeedyLane Self-checkout Systems - managed to wedge Brian into SpeedyLane's Sales Trainee program in Atlanta.

## Current Position & Company:
- Sales Trainee at SpeedyLane Self-checkout Systems based in Atlanta.
- No performance data-to-date. He just started on January 1 this year.

## Hobbies:
- **Would-Be Basketball Star.** Brian was the starting point guard during his junior and senior years at Lancaster Prep, averaging a modest 6.2 points per game, and a not-too-

stellar 1:1 assist to turnover ratio. He was disappointed, but not too surprised, when he was 'dismissed' on day one of walk-on tryouts at Bucknell his freshman year, when his vertical leap was measured at an embarrassing 11.2 inches... Yikes. While Brian still dreams about playing in the NBA someday, he has at least temporarily given up the sport for now in favor of carefully filling out NCAA brackets each March and more aggressively pursuing his badminton passion.

- **Badminton Fanatic.** At age 17, Brian was a nationally ranked Badminton player, having won the PA Jr. State Championship during his senior year of high school at Lancaster Prep. He started a Badminton Club at Bucknell in his freshman year and won the school championship in his first three years. Since moving to Atlanta, he has already joined a Badminton Club and is coordinating the development of a regular league.

- **Would-Be** Fisherman. When he was eight years old, Brian caught a 7 pound, 24 inch largemouth bass while on a fishing trip to Alabama with his dad, his brother Henry, and his Uncle Harry. The fish is mounted in the den at his folks' home in Lancaster. Although he hasn't actually fished since that day, Brian still promotes himself as a 'stellar' fisherman when the opportunity presents itself and is always ready to whip out the well-worn picture of himself with his 'great big bass.'

## Nickname(s):

- His fraternity nickname, *Nite Crawler*, has carried over with him to Atlanta. The nickname has little to do with Brian's 'vague' interest in fishing, but rather with his tendency both in college and now in Atlanta to roam far and wide (now in the Buckhead area of Atlanta) several nights a week. In search of exactly what, he does not know. Hmmm... somewhat strange, no?

- Within three hours of meeting Brian, Linda Brown, Brian's appointed SpeedyLane mentor, nicknamed him *Grasshopper*. This was due to Brian's obvious naiveté, wide-eyed excitement at every new thing, and his obvious eagerness to learn the ins and outs about selling from Linda.

**Physical:**
- 5'10" and about 170 lbs.
- In good shape due to his daily badminton practice, but not exactly ripped
- Looks about 16 years old... Acts about the same age
- Wears his hair in a crew-cut to minimize his prep time for social outings
- Kind of wide-eyed, with a frequent "deer in the headlights" look about him
- Needs major help with his social wardrobe – pretty much limited to worn out jeans and t-shirts with 'funky' sayings on them

# Vehicle: 6 yr old Vespa Scooter

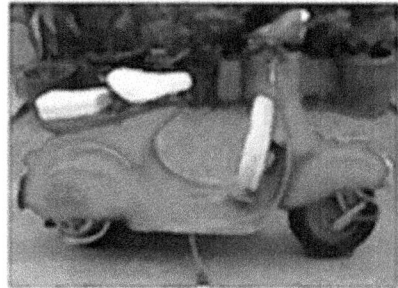

# Other:

- As the youngest of six children, Brian is definitely a 'Mama's boy.' At 23 years old, each Wednesday he and his buddies still anxiously await the weekly box of chocolate chip cookies from Brian's mom – cookies that have been coming like clockwork every Wednesday since Brian's freshman year at Bucknell. Overall, he's a friendly, very popular dude ... at least with the guys. He's well aware that he needs to work on his skills with the ladies, and regularly asks his four sisters and his mom about how he might resolve his social ineptitude with the fairer sex. So far, virtually no progress has been made.

---

So, there's our sales trainee, Brian Wilson. Let's see how this story unfolds for Brian throughout the remaining chapters in this book.

CHAPTER 21

# Players and Visions

| Linda & SpeedyLane's Master Selling Plan | | |
|---|---|---|
| Ch | 20 | Meet Salesperson Linda Brown and Sales Trainee Brian Wilson |
| **Ch** | **21** | **Linda's Master Selling Plan for House Depot (HD), Pt 1. Players & Visions Required** |
| Ch | 22 | Linda's Master Selling Plan for House Depot (HD), Pt 2. Choose Target Sponsor |
| Ch | 23 | Linda's Master Selling Plan for House Depot (HD), Pt 3. Choose Target Power Sponsor |
| Ch | 24 | Linda's Master Selling Plan for House Depot (HD), Pt 4. Plan for Building Visions for All Important Players |

Let's see what plan Linda has up her sleeve for trying to acquire House Depot (HD) as a client for the SpeedyLane Self-checkout system. If she can start her year by capturing this big sale, Linda could jump-start her way toward qualifying the whole family for that Golden Sales Club Hawaii trip at the end of this year. Herby and the three boys would really be pumped about that!

------------

Let's pick up the action with Linda, as she starts mentoring her protégé Brian.

*[Brian, Linda's Protégé]*: "So, Linda, based on what you've been telling me, adding consumer self-checkout would seem to be a real 'game-changing strategy' for HD, right?

When choosing HD as your target customer, you told me that HD falls into the 'non-user,' 'not looking' segment. This means that HD is not even looking for a self-checkout system right now. How on earth will you be able to convince HD to change from having 'no interest' in the system to actually buying and implementing your solution? That is still a mystery to me!"

*[Linda, SpeedyLane Sales & Brian's Mentor]*: "Well, that's why I have this rather involved 'Account Marketing Plan' for HD right here!" She shows Brian a seemingly complex chart full of Xs (shown later in this chapter).

## Linda's 'Account Marketing Plan' for the HD Account

*[Brian]*: "What the heck is an 'Account Marketing Plan? And what is your specific 'Account Marketing Plan' for HD?"

*[Linda]*: "Well, I figured you'd ask that, Brian. My 'Account Marketing Plan' for HD is pretty much exactly the same as my selling plan for other companies facing similar checkout challenges. Simply put, my plan consists of <u>*converting all the HD players who can either affect or will be affected by the prospective adoption and implementation of the proposed SpeedyLane Self-checkout system*</u>."

*[Brian]*: "Wow, that's a mouthful. Can you break it down for me? For example,

- **What 'players' are you talking about?**
- **What do you mean by 'converting'?**
- **How do you know where to start? and**
- **How do you decide where and when to move next, and then where to go from there?**

## What Players are Involved?

*[Linda]*: "Good questions! You're a pretty smart guy to be asking these questions right out of the chute! Well, let's tackle 'em one by one, starting with what specific HD players we'll want to talk to. As I suggested before, we will need to talk with all the HD players who can either affect or will be affected by the prospective adoption and implementation of our proposed self-checkout system.

## Internal Players

*[Linda]*: "Among others, this would include a number of different folks at **HD Corporate Headquarters** – for example:

- Those in charge of store operating efficiency;
- Those controlling the purse strings; and
- Other executives who would be responsible for implementing and integrating the new system into HD's current data and operating systems.

"Different **HD players at the store level** would also get involved with the go / no go decision to invest in the self-checkout system and would also be involved in the implementation of the system at the store level. These would include:

- Store managers & assistant managers,
- Cashiers,
- Customer service folks,
- IT folks, and
- In-store maintenance personnel.

---

# External Players

**"Other players outside of HD** should also be taken into consideration. This includes 'External Players' such as:

- Stockholders
- Customers
- Independent Suppliers
- Retail Labor Unions,
- External IT Support,
- National & Local Business Press
- and others external players may also be affected. I actually have a detailed list of all the players whom we will have to 'convert.' I'll show you that in a minute."

*[Brian]*: "OK, Linda, I think I get this 'player concept'. You identify all the 'players' who, as you said, "would either affect or be affected by the prospective adoption and implementation of our proposed 'game-changing' self-checkout system." That makes sense. *But what about this notion of 'converting' that you mentioned? What does that mean?"*

## Three Types of Visions to Build

*[Linda]:* "Well, different players need different 'visions' if we want them to support the purchase and adoption of self-checkout capabilities at HD. We focus on building three types of visions:

- Operating Visions,
- Transition Visions, and
- Financial Visions.

Let me give you a general overview of each of these three visions by referring you to page 86 of your selling manual. You've got it with you, right, Brian?"

---

### Visions to Build in an Account Marketing Plan

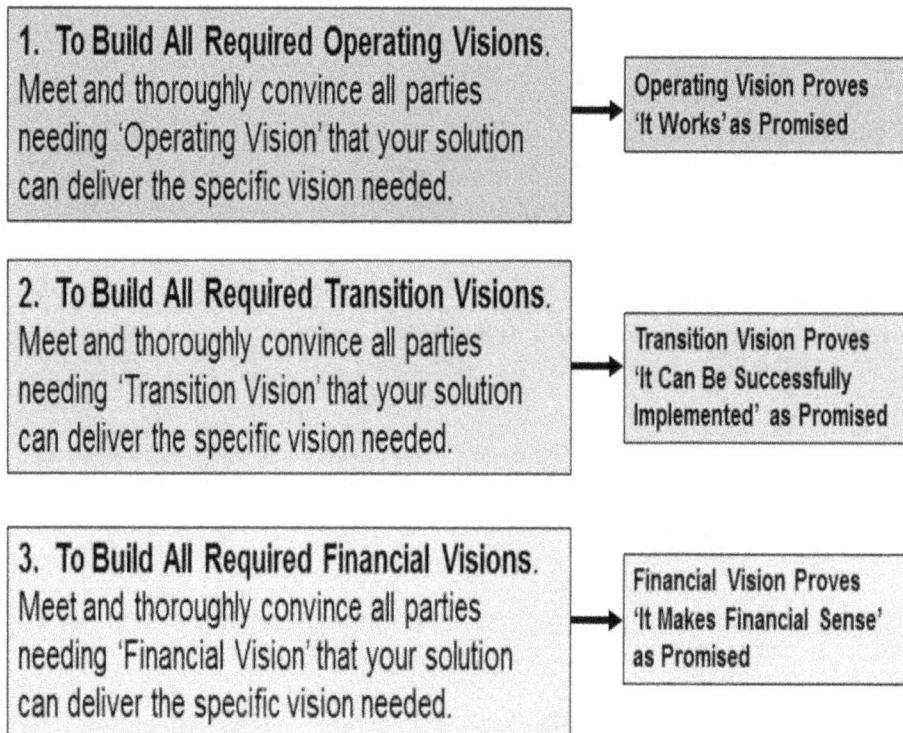

**1. To Build All Required Operating Visions.** Meet and thoroughly convince all parties needing 'Operating Vision' that your solution can deliver the specific vision needed.

→ Operating Vision Proves 'It Works' as Promised

**2. To Build All Required Transition Visions.** Meet and thoroughly convince all parties needing 'Transition Vision' that your solution can deliver the specific vision needed.

→ Transition Vision Proves 'It Can Be Successfully Implemented' as Promised

**3. To Build All Required Financial Visions.** Meet and thoroughly convince all parties needing 'Financial Vision' that your solution can deliver the specific vision needed.

→ Financial Vision Proves 'It Makes Financial Sense' as Promised

---

## What Does 'Converting' Mean?

*[Brian]:* "There are lots of lists here, Linda. No wonder you call it a 'selling system.' But I still don't get what 'converting' means."

*[Linda]:* "The concept of 'converting' the client means working with each relevant internal and external player to help them see how a self-checkout system might benefit them, both as an individual and as a member of HD. At the very least, we need to try our best to alleviate each player's primary concerns about potentially adopting and implementing this prospective new game changing solution.

As shown in the Exhibits (next 2 pages), each internal and external player has different concerns. Many players, particularly some of the more influential internal players, may require multiple visions. For example, the CEO will require an operating vision, a transition vision, and a financial vision."

*[Brian]:* "Golleee! That does seem like quite a challenge! **How would you know where to even start? What players and what visions do you focus on first?**"

*[Linda]:* "Wow, you're full of good questions today. You certainly are going to be fun to work with! But, before I get into this 'where do you start' business, let's take a quick look at the types of 'visions' we'll try to build for each key internal and external player. It's quite a list, as you can see."

"In the end you will see that we might not be able to build all these visions. But the more the better. I'll elaborate on that point as we move along. *[Brian]:* "This is really interesting stuff! Now can you answer my other questions about **_where to start and where to go next_**?"

| Players Internal Players | Operating Vision | Transition Vision | Financial Vision |
|---|---|---|---|
| Board of Directors | efficient operations throughout the corporation | effective, on-time implementation of all decisions | Meet profit expectations |
| Chairman of the Board of Directors | efficient operations throughout the corporation | effective, on-time implementation of all decisions | Meet profit expectations |
| Top Management Buying Committee | efficient operations throughout the corporation | effective, on-time implementation of all decisions | Meet profit expectations |
| CEO | efficient operations throughout the corporation | effective, on-time implementation of all decisions | Meet profit expectations |
| CFO | efficient operations throughout the corporation | low cost vs benefits associated with all system changes | higher revenues, lower costs |
| EXEC VP - OPERATIONS (or COO) | Efficient Operations throughout the corporation | Effective, on-time implementation of all new Operating Strategies | Keep Operating Costs down |
| VP of Marketing | Company Reputation of Customer Service Satisfaction | Smooth Transition for customers, employees | Higher Sales Revenue, lower costs |
| Corporate Director of In-Store Efficiency | efficient corporate-wide in-store operations | smooth transitions in any new in-store systems | keep in-store cost down |
| Corporate Customer Svc Director | develop & monitor customer satisfaction initiatives - keep customers happy! | ensure smooth implementation of any new corporate-wide programs customer satisfaction initiatives | keep customer service manpower costs under control |
| Corporate Director of Merchandising | continuous creative development of in store revenue generating merchandising initiatives | effective implementation of all new merchandising initiatives | continuous creative development of in store revenue generating merchandising initiatives |
| Corporate Director of Human Resources | effective recruitment and handling of all HR decisions | ensure proper training with all new systems | control headcount |
| Corporate Legal Counsel | | avoid potential legal entanglements | avoid costly legal judgments |
| Corporate Director of Information Technology | efficient and productive management of all IT matters | hassle free IT adaptation to all system changes | keep IT costs down |
| IT Managers | manage all IT systems efficiently | ensure seamless integration of all data systems | implement IT efficiency initiatives |
| Store Managers | smooth in-store operations | ensure smooth implementation of corporate in-store initiatives | store level profit responsibility |
| Store Assistant Managers | run smooth operations | implement new systems | efficiently run the store |
| Cashiers | efficiently & courteously checkout customers | learn and effectively implement any new checkout systems | minimize cashier errors |

Visions of Internal Players for Linda to Build in Her Account Marketing Plan for

# Visions of External Players to Build in the Account Marketing Plan

## External Players

| Players | Operating Vision | Transition Vision | Financial Vision |
|---|---|---|---|
| Stockholders | | | Meet profit expectations |
| Customers | know how to use potential new self-checkout system | get in and out of store quickly | pay reasonable price |
| Independent suppliers | efficient interface with retail outlets | seamless adaptation to new systems of stores | high, profitable sales of our products |
| Retail Labor Union(s) | keep retail union members happy & help keep their jobs | help members to adapt to new system requirements | help ensure jobs & favorable wages and benefits for members |
| Nat'l & Local Business press | | announce and publicly evaluate new retail corporate initiatives (e.g., self-checkout) | |

*[Linda]*: "Well, the only place you should be going to is a department store! Really Brian, I cannot take you seriously with those sayings on your t-shirts. We have to schedule a time to talk about your wardrobe."

"OK, now back to your question about '***Where to start and where to go next?***' Let's take a break and then tackle that, OK?"

CHAPTER 22

# Choose Target Sponsor

| Linda & SpeedyLane's Master Selling Plan | | |
|---|---|---|
| Ch | 20 | Meet Salesperson Linda Brown and Sales Trainee Brian Wilson |
| Ch | 21 | Linda's Master Selling Plan for House Depot (HD), Pt 1.  Players & Visions Required |
| **Ch** | **22** | **Linda's Master Selling Plan for House Depot (HD), Pt 2. Choose Target Sponsor** |
| Ch | 23 | Linda's Master Selling Plan for House Depot (HD), Pt 3.  Choose Target Power Sponsor |
| Ch | 24 | Linda's Master Selling Plan for House Depot (HD), Pt 4.  Plan for Building Visions for All Important Players |

## *Brian and Linda pick up their conversation...*

*[Brian]*: "Linda, I forgot where we left off."

*[Linda]*: "Well, so far, we know that the Account Marketing Plan for House Depot (HD) consists of trying to convert all of the HD players who either can affect or will be affected by the proposed purchase and adoption of  SpeedyLane's Self-checkout system. As you can see, it was essential that we identified the many players involved both inside and outside of HD and the likely visions needed by each player before we can expect each to support the adoption of the proposed self-checkout system.

"In sum, therefore, the Account Marketing Plan consists of convincing key players in the target customer company that our SpeedyLane solution provides both operating and financial benefits for HD and can be implemented in a timely and successful manner (i.e., no significant transition barriers).

"Now, if I remember correctly, the next questions you asked:

'How do you know **where to start?**' and

After we start, '**where do we go next**? And next, and next, etc.?'"

*[Brian]:* "How do you remember all this stuff?"

*[Linda]:* "It becomes second nature after a while. You'll see as you begin to get some selling experience yourself."

---

# Where to Start?
# Choose Target Sponsor

*[Linda]:* "So, first you asked, 'How do you know **where to start?**' Well, my first challenge at hand is to get one important person at HD excited about the prospect of adopting and implementing our SpeedyLane Self-checkout system. In the Solution Selling® system[15] we use here at SpeedyLane, we refer to this first critical contact as our "Target Sponsor." If I can get this Target Sponsor on my side, then we could move forward as a team to start building all of the visions necessary for the other key players we previously identified."

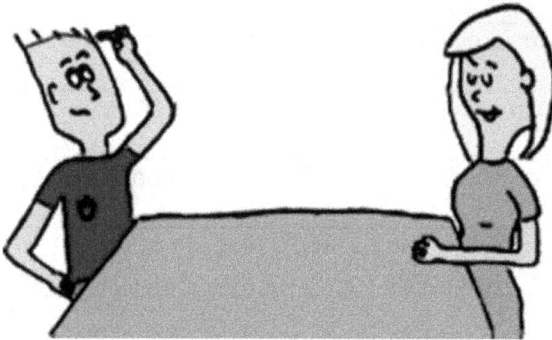

*[Brian]:* "That sounds logical, Linda, just like your earlier descriptions of your Account Marketing Plan. But how do you decide who at HD will be your Target Sponsor?"

*[Linda]:* "OK, let's think about this out loud. What kind of player at HD do you think would benefit most on a daily basis from the capabilities and related operating benefits that our SpeedyLane Self-checkout system promises?"

*[Brian]:* "Well, I suppose that would be someone who lies awake at night thinking about the many operating problems with HD's current checkout system."

*[Linda]:* "Bingo! Exactly! You've been studying the SpeedyLane Sales Manual! I'm glad to see that!

"At any rate, getting back to business, a good Target Sponsor would be someone at HD who does indeed lose sleep thinking about the many operating problems our self-checkout system can address! So, to give you a hint about who would make a good Target Sponsor at HD, I will first review our key capabilities and the problems they address. I've actually done this many times before for other companies, so I have a pretty good idea regarding who to target.

"But let's review those day-to-day problems and related capabilities & benefits anyway – just to walk you through the process. Check out this "Chart of Problems & Related Self-Checkout Capabilities & Benefits" that I use to help identify an acceptable Target Sponsor in almost any company I approach."

## Selecting the Appropriate Target Sponsor for Self-Service Checkout
Relevant Operating Issues, Promised New Capabilities (Generic Advantages), and
Projected Operating Benefits for Self-Service Checkout

| | Specific Relevant Operating Issues | New Capabilities (i.e., Generic Advantages) Needed to Resolve Each Relevant Operating Issue | Projected Operating Benefit from Each New Capability (i.e., from each new generic advantage) |
|---|---|---|---|
| **Target Sponsor = the one who is most concerned on a day to day basis with these primary operating issues & projected operating benefits** | Customer dissatisfaction with long lines leads to reduced store loyalty | Self-checkout (feature) improves traffic flow and customer satisfaction by reducing time spent in line (advantage). | More satisfied customers increases store traffic and customer loyalty. |
| | A high number of cashiers is needed. | Remote monitoring (feature) allows one cashier to operate ten lanes, so fewer cashiers are needed (advantage). | Smaller workforce is simpler to maintain. |
| | Customer dissatisfaction with long lines reduces store loyalty. | Self-checkout (feature) allows customers the choice between a cashier or using self checkout, increasing customer satisfaction (advantage) | More satisfied customers increases store traffic and reduces walkouts. |
| | Too little prime floor space for impulse purchase items. | Compact configuration (feature) opens floor space, allowing more space for the sale of impulse items (advantage). | Saved floor space and faster lines improve traffic flow and provides opportunity for placement of impulse items. |
| | Too much theft. | Advanced weight system, security database, and remote monitoring (feature) result in higher security and less theft (advantage). | Increased security reduces customer delinquency and saves retailer time and resources lost handling theft. |
| | Not enough employees on the floor reduces customer satisfaction, which leads to fewer customers. | Remote monitoring (feature) allows one cashier to operate ten lanes, so more employees available on floor (advantage). | More employees on the floor means greater customer satisfaction and store loyalty. |

*[Linda]:* "Now, when you look back at our list of key players at HD, who do **you** think lies awake at night thinking about the specific operating issues in column 1 and would most benefit from the capabilities and related operating benefits in the other two columns?"

*[Brian]:* "Hmm, let's see that list of key internal players again.
- Chief Executive Officer (CEO)
- Chief Financial Officer (CFO)
- Executive VP of Operations (COO)
- Chief Marketing Officer (CMO)
- Corporate Director of In-Store Efficiency
- Corporate Director of Merchandising

- Corporate Director of Human Resources
- Corporate Legal Counsel
- Corporate Director of Information Technology
- IT Managers
- Store Managers
- Store Assistant Managers
- Cashiers
- In-store Customer Service Reps

*[Brian]:* "I suppose, the higher the better, right?"

*[Linda]:* "When you're targeting a smaller firm with a thin corporate structure or selling incidental or non-game changing solutions to larger companies, that strategy might be appropriate. This is because selling to executives may accelerate the purchase decision in your favor.

"However, when introducing a game-changing strategy that may affect the day-to-day responsibilities of a number of different folks within the target customer company, dictating from the top down might not be such a good idea. The people affected by our solution would all be responsible for making the 'new way' solution work effectively and, unfortunately, force-feeding game-changing solutions down through the corporation can cause all sorts of delays and problems with motivation and implementation. So, it is possible to shoot too high when looking for a target sponsor. It'd be like my husband Herby buying a new house without asking me to participate in the decision. That could result in never-ending squabbles, complaints, and even lasting resentment on my part. So, of course, my dear Herby would certainly make sure that I helped him to evaluate the alternatives and to ultimately make the final decision if we were to be in the market for a new house.

## In Selecting a Target Sponsor, Avoid Starting Too High in the Target Company's Organization

*[Linda]:* "Let me give you a real business example about a time when a friend of mine who runs the IT department over at ACE ran into this type of challenge. In an effort intended to cut down inventory and supply chain costs, her CEO decided overnight - without consulting her or anyone else - to implement RFID (Radio Frequency Identification) for all of their supplies and final products throughout their supply chain. Today, three years later, the RFID system is still not yet operational. This demonstrates the importance of the convincing, learning, and adaptation that must occur before the company can effectively implement their RFID plan. This cartoon in the selling manual (cartoon) says it all!

Top-Down Approach Can Delay and Impact Implementation

"So, the bottom line is this. Since selling to the top, or 'selling high,' can speed the sales process, by all means go for it if you sense that it will not create all sorts of headaches and resentment when it comes time for implementation."

[Brian]: "OK, I understand your point. With real game changing solutions where lots of different folks will be affected by the new solution, it's better to first convert someone lower in the company in order to ease acceptance throughout the ranks, which, in turn, will facilitate faster and more effective implementation once the new solution is adopted."

[Linda]: "Right you are!"

# Also Avoid Starting Too Low in the Company's Organization

[Linda]: "At the same time, however, we don't want to go too low in the company. While ease of access could tempt me to aim low when seeking my HD Target Sponsor, this approach can easily be a waste of time and resources. Why spend all of my time and energy trying to convert a Target Sponsor who can't take me to the next level, which is necessary if we want to make progress on this sales effort. In other words, why aim at someone who does not have access to the influential executives who control the purse strings? Recall the cartoon example in the Sales Manual where the salesperson has wasted time and effort trying to get someone too low in the organization to be his target sponsor."

*[Brian]*: "So, I think I understand your point. When trying to choose a Target Sponsor, I want someone whose primary day-to-day problems can be alleviated by my solution and who has direct access to those higher in the organizational structure."

*[Linda]*: "Exactly! So, when I'm selling the self-checkout system to larger companies like HD, I search for whoever in the corporation has daily responsibility over 'in-store efficiency.' In HD, my Target Sponsor will be **Roger Dunkel, HD's Corporate Director of In-Store Efficiency**, as detailed in the "Important Internal Players" chart. Roger is the one most likely to experience the day-to-day pains that can be addressed with our self-checkout solution.

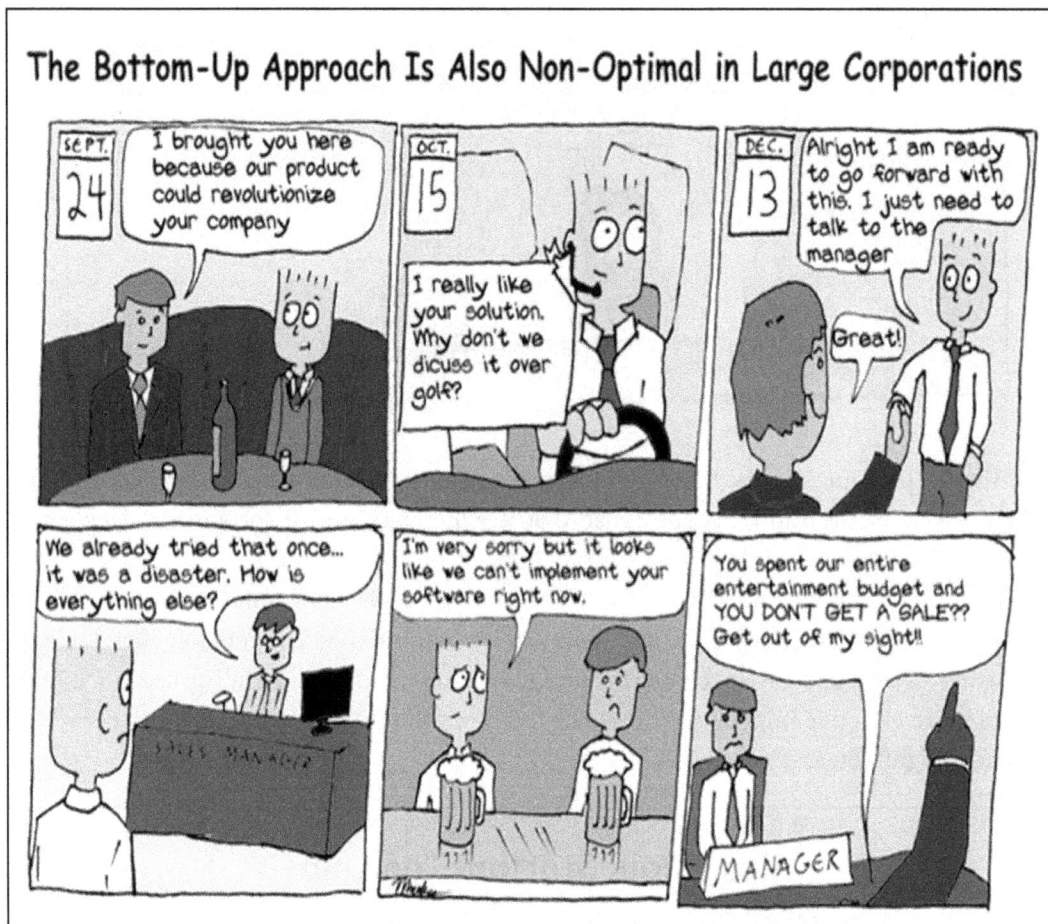

## Also Identify a Secondary Target Sponsor

*[Linda]:* "It's also important to have a **Secondary Target Sponsor**, just in case I don't connect with Roger for whatever reason. **My Secondary Target Sponsor with HD will be their Director**

*of Customer Service.* I don't know who that is yet, but you better believe that I will know quite a bit about the Director of Customer Service well before I start a discussion with HD."

[*Brian*]: "How do you find the names and positions of these folks at HD or any other company we might be targeting? I would think some companies don't make that specific information available to the general public."

[*Linda*]: "That's another good question, Grasshopper! You are right. Sometimes it is difficult to find out who is in a specific position at a target company. Many smaller companies and privately held companies, in particular, do not make that information public. Even many larger, publicly held companies keep that information to themselves because they do not want outsiders to have direct access to their key decision-makers."

[*Brian*]: "So, what do you if you are unable to find the name of a specific person to contact?"

[*Linda*]: "You didn't let me finish. In the past, that used to call for some creative 'detective work' – which consisted of using one's network to ask for the contact information and in more recent years, using various Internet search engines. Today, however, the social media tool **LinkedIn**[2] has given us a whole new vehicle for finding the key people we need to contact. Most of our sales team members, including me, use **LinkedIn** to find the names and contact information about the key decision-makers, including, specific Target Sponsors and Target Power Sponsors (which we will discuss in a moment), as well as other people in specific target customer companies who need specific visions. This is a really great tool to have, because, as I mentioned before, many companies restrict public information on specific decision-makers. LinkedIn benefits us because it looks at companies from the 'bottom up,' so we can often find out who the decision-makers are in various departments.

---

[2] LinkedIn offers the world's premier business network, with 722 million users (as of 2022). LinkedIn reports that 25% of all American adults use LinkedIn, with 22% of those use it every single day. It is no wonder, therefore, why LinkedIn has such great potential as a marketing aid for virtually any company. For example, refer to LinkedIn's own (2023) detailed review of multiple (10) ways to use LinkedIn to aid in performing critical marketing functions such as generating leads, building brand awareness, and establishing strategic partnerships. https://business.linkedin.com/marketing-solutions/how-to-market-on-linkedin, https://blog.hootsuite.com/linkedin-for-business/#3_important_LinkedIn_marketing_tips

"Another benefit of LinkedIn is that once we identify the right person, we can explore that person's network and interest groups. Having an idea of that person's specific professional and more personal interests can help provide you with a good platform for making the initial contact.

*[Brian]*: "Ok, let me take a shot at summing up what you just taught me. The way I understand it, your initial goal is to get your Target Sponsor - Roger, in this case - to enthusiastically endorse the SpeedyLane Self-checkout system. You will try to do this by convincing him that our system solution can make his day-to-day work more productive, more enjoyable, and less stressful. If you are successful in 'converting' Roger, then you and Roger will move forward *as a team* to try to convert the other key players at HD - players that you've listed up and down HD's corporate hierarchy. Is that right?"

### Relevant Issues & Related Visions of Important Internal Players
#### What Keeps Each Player Up at Night? – *Target Sponsor*

| Players | Operating Vision | Transition Vision | Financial Vision |
|---|---|---|---|
| CEO | Smooth Operations Throughout | Effective On Time Implementation Of All Plans | Higher Profits |
| CFO | efficient operations throughout the corporation | low cost vs benefits associated with all system changes | higher revenues, lower costs |
| Executive VP IT | Strong standardized systems and platforms | Effective IT Interface With All Depts. | keep IT costs down |
| Executive VP Operations | efficient operations throughout the corporation | effective, on-time implementation of all decisions | keep corporate costs down |
| VP of Marketing | Company Reputation of Customer Service Satisfaction | Smooth Transition for customers, employees | Higher Sales Revenue, lower costs |
| Director of IT | efficient and productive management of all IT matters | hassle free IT adaptation to all system changes | keep IT costs down |
| Corporate Director of In-Store Efficiency -*Target Sponsor* | efficient corporate-wide in-store operations | smooth transitions in any new in-store systems | keep in-store cost down |
| Director of Customer Service -*Secondary Target Sponsor* | Customer Service Satisfaction | Smooth Transition for customers, employees | Higher Sales Revenue, lower costs |

*[Linda]*: "Right on, dude! You *are* getting it! So, we'll do our research on Roger, spend quite a bit of time preparing for our meetings with him, and converse with him often in our efforts to convert him into our selling partner.

*[Brian]*: "Ok, got it. But before we move on, I have another question. I noticed that in the diagram showing Roger's position as your Target Sponsor, **you have also listed *'Don Johnson' as your 'Target Power Sponsor.'*** Who is this Don guy and what's a 'Target Power Sponsor'?"

*[Linda]*: "Looks like it's time for another break. You are doing great so far. Stick with me!"

CHAPTER 23

# Choose Target Power Sponsor

| | | Linda & SpeedyLane's Master Selling Plan |
|---|---|---|
| Ch | 20 | Meet Salesperson Linda Brown and Sales Trainee Brian Wilson |
| Ch | 21 | Linda's Master Selling Plan for House Depot (HD), Pt 1. Players & Visions Required |
| Ch | 22 | Linda's Master Selling Plan for House Depot (HD), Pt 2. Choose Target Sponsor |
| **Ch** | **23** | **Linda's Master Selling Plan for House Depot (HD), Pt 3. Choose Target Power Sponsor** |
| Ch | 24 | Linda's Master Selling Plan for House Depot (HD), Pt 4. Plan for Building Visions for All Important Players |

## Brian and Linda continue up their conversation...

*[Brian]*: "Wow, Linda, this Master Selling Plan of yours is really elaborate! I had no idea. Let's pick up with my question about Don Johnson, your designated Target Power Sponsor at HD. Who is this guy and how does he fit into the picture?"

## The "Money Line" & Target Power Sponsor, Don Johnson

*[Linda]*: "To understand where Don Johnson fits in, let's start by looking at the diagram of HD's corporate structure once more.

"Do you see that "Money Line" drawn across House Depot's (HD's) corporate structure? Well, HD folks above that line make the big money decisions. They have regular contact with one another in various top management committees, including a typical 'Top Management

Buying Committee.' If we hope to sell our 'game-changing' self-checkout system to HD, I'll have to get these folks on our side.

"This is where our friend Don Johnson comes into the picture. He has the 'Power' to get us and our HD selling partner Roger (assuming we get Roger on our side) access to all the powers above the Money Line – including the Top Management Buying Committee. That's why I refer to Don as my *'Target Power Sponsor.'* We'll need to get Don on our side if we hope to even get access to the various executives on the buying committee."

*[Brian]*: "So, we want to get Don on our selling team, just like Roger. Is that right?"

*[Linda]*: "That's a good way to put it – 'getting him on our selling team.' You catch on fast!"

*[Brian]*: "Gee, thanks! But, Linda, before you go on, I just thought of something. Why did you pick Don as your Target Power Sponsor instead of one of the other top executives above the money line?"

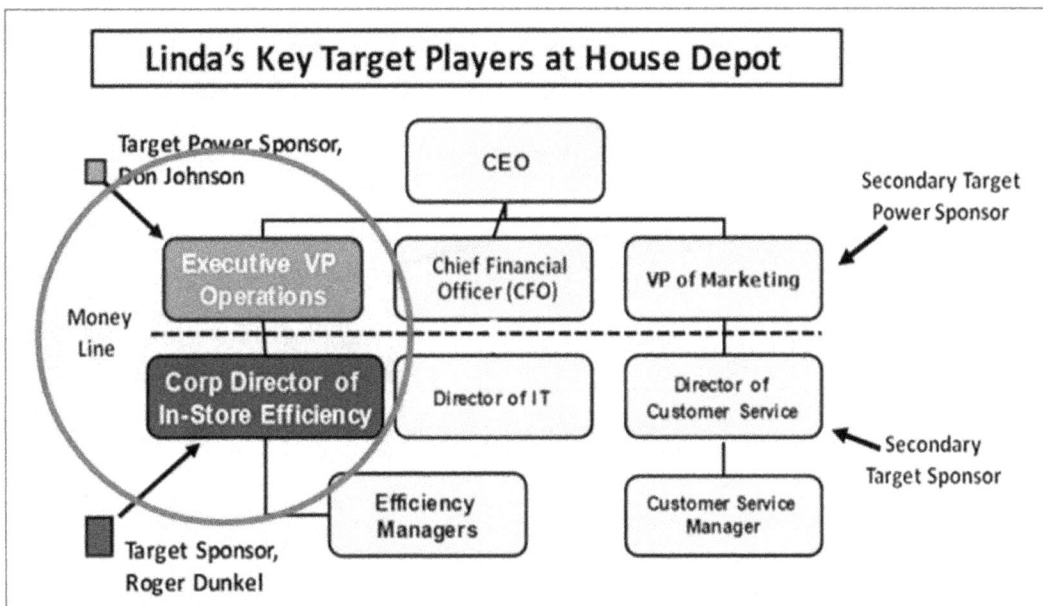

**Linda's Key Target Players at House Depot**

*[Linda]*: "Well, the primary reason I chose Don is because Roger reports directly to Don. As HD's Executive VP of Operations, Don is constantly looking for ways to improve the productivity and efficiency of all of HD operations. Our self-checkout system would be the perfect solution. If Roger and I can prove this to Don, he'll be anxious to connect us to the whole gamut of folks in need of 'self-checkout related visions' both above and below the money line. Recall that big list from a couple of chapters ago that includes all the players we want on our side!"

# Focus on Financial Issues & Benefits
# when Talking with the Target Power Sponsor

*[Brian]*: "I think I understand your logic, but is Don going to be converted using the same process that you plan to use on Roger?"

*[Linda]*: "Well, we will use the same vision building techniques, but the focus of our discussion with Don will be on the prospective *financial benefits* of our self-checkout system, because financial issues are Don's biggest concern. As you recall, our focus with Roger, on the other hand, was primarily with prospective operating benefits."

*[Brian]*: "Can you give me an example of this?

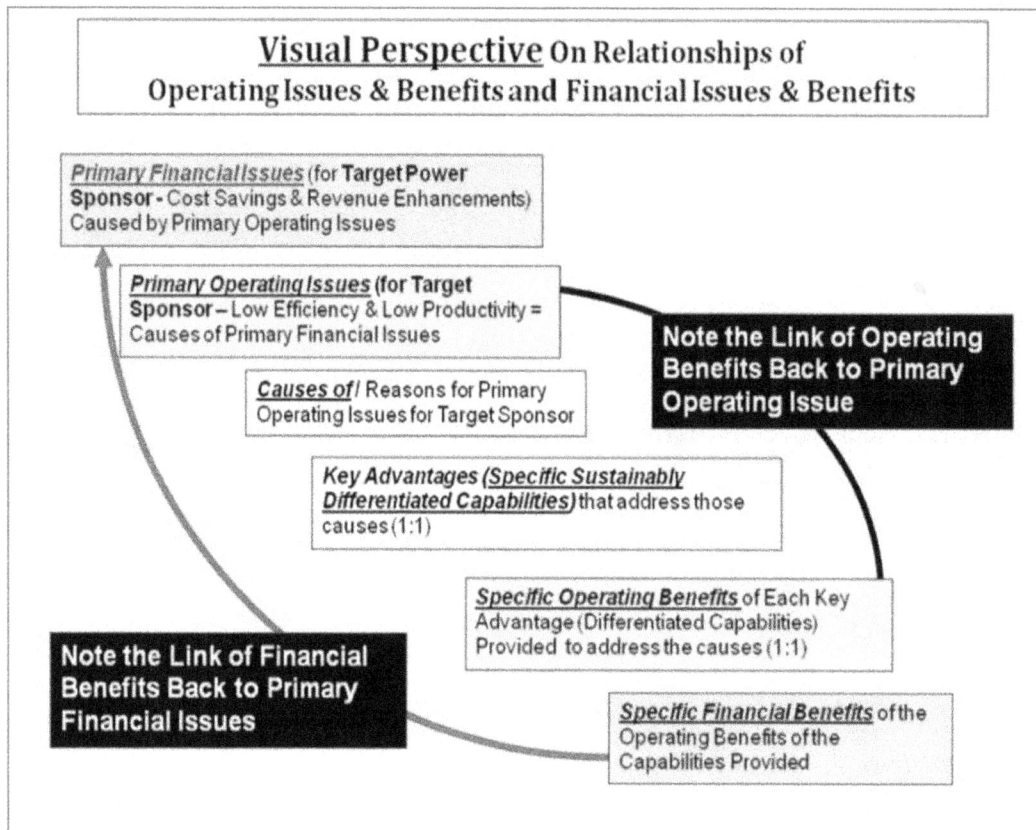

**Visual Perspective** On Relationships of Operating Issues & Benefits and Financial Issues & Benefits

*Primary Financial Issues* (for **Target Power Sponsor** - Cost Savings & Revenue Enhancements) Caused by Primary Operating Issues

*Primary Operating Issues* (for **Target Sponsor** – Low Efficiency & Low Productivity = Causes of Primary Financial Issues

*Causes of* / Reasons for Primary Operating Issues for Target Sponsor

*Key Advantages (Specific Sustainably Differentiated Capabilities)* that address those causes (1:1)

*Specific Operating Benefits* of Each Key Advantage (Differentiated Capabilities) Provided to address the causes (1:1)

*Specific Financial Benefits* of the Operating Benefits of the Capabilities Provided

**Note the Link of Operating Benefits Back to Primary Operating Issue**

**Note the Link of Financial Benefits Back to Primary Financial Issues**

*[Linda]*: "I'll do even better than that. – Take a look at my overall planning sheet for how to approach both Roger and Don. It's the same one you have in your SpeedyLane Selling Manual. The planning sheet shows how the concerns of both of these guys are closely linked. Check it out!"

*[Brian]:* "Umm.... That's a little over my head, Linda. Got anything more straight-forward?"

*[Linda]:* "Sure – how about this simpler diagram? It's also in your manual and points out the same relationships, but with less detail."

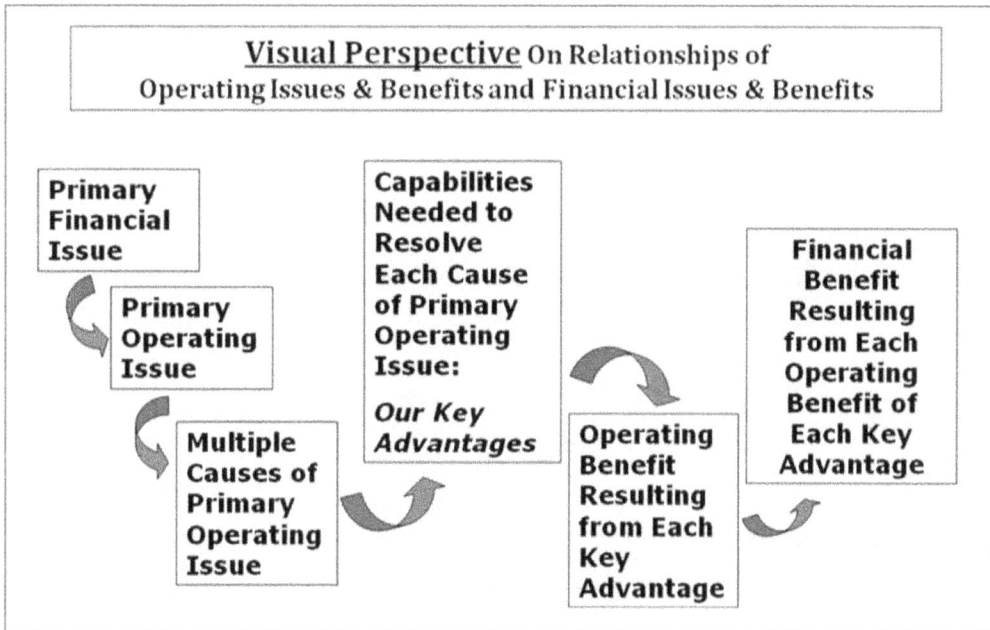

**Visual Perspective** On Relationships of
Operating Issues & Benefits and Financial Issues & Benefits

*[Brian]:* "That's much better. I think I get it now, but could you give me a more specific example using our SpeedyLane system?"

*[Linda]:* "No worries, you're not the first one to ask for that. In fact, let's look at the specific chart that I'll be using when I plan to approach Roger and Don. <u>*(NEXT PAGE)*</u> It's the same one I use when approaching any of my target customers for our self-checkout system."

(After looking it over carefully)

*[Brian]:* "Oh, that's much clearer - I like it! Especially because of your specific details about the operating causes and related capabilities, and the way you mapped out the very specific operating and financial benefits promised by our SpeedyLane system. I can see how this gives you some great talking points when you approach both Roger and Don. But just one thing, Linda -- what's with the "X" percentages that I see in the columns for specific Operating and Financial Benefits?"

*[Linda]:* "We call those '*critical success criteria.*' We get this data by carefully monitoring before-and-after measures for each client. Including specific data like this is key to getting and holding the attention of Roger, Don, and HD's entire buying committee. You'll see this in action later on when I take you through the actual process of building a financial vision in cooperation with Don and the HD buying committee (if we get that far in the selling process) and again when we talk about implementation and follow-up. Let's leave it at that for now. Just remember, as you already pointed out, that this data will be crucial for grabbing attention and for proving our solution to many key players at HD."

# Secondary Target Power Sponsor

*[Linda]:* "One last thing before we move on. Just like with our Target Sponsor, it's important to also have a secondary Target Power Sponsor, in case Roger and I don't connect with Don Johnson, for whatever reason. *My secondary Target Sponsor with HD will be their VP of Marketing.* You can see that in the summary within the "Internal Players" chart. Like Don, the VP of Marketing also has strong financial concerns regarding any prospective transition to self-checkout."

| Players | Operating Vision | Transition Vision | Financial Vision |
|---|---|---|---|
| CEO | Smooth Operations Throughout | Effective On Time Implementation Of All Plans | Higher Profits |
| CFO | efficient operations throughout the corporation | low cost vs benefits associated with all system changes | higher revenues, lower costs |
| Executive VP IT | Strong standardized systems and platforms | Effective IT Interface With All Depts. | keep IT costs down |
| Executive VP Operations - *Target Power Sponsor* | Efficient Operations throughout the corporation | Effective, on-time implementation of all new Operating Strategies | Keep Operating Costs down |
| VP of Marketing - *Secondary Target Power Sponsor* | Company Reputation of Customer Service Satisfaction | Smooth Transition for customers, employees | Higher Sales Revenue, lower costs |
| Director of IT | efficient and productive management of all IT matters | hassle free IT adaptation to all system changes | keep IT costs down |
| Corporate Director of In-Store Efficiency - *Target Sponsor* | efficient corporate-wide in-store operations | smooth transitions in any new in-store systems | keep in-store cost down |
| Director of Customer Service - *Secondary Target Sponsor* | Customer Service Satisfaction | Smooth Transition for customers, employees | Higher Sales Revenue, lower costs |

# Key Advantage Links Summary Sheet for SpeedyLane

| Primary Financial Issue for Target Power Sponsor | Primary Operating Issue for Target Sponsor | Multiple Causes of Primary Operating Issue | Capabilities Needed to Resolve Each Cause of Primary Operating issue (= Our 'Key Advantages) | % Operating Benefit (for Target Sponsor) Resulting from Each Key Advantage | % Financial Benefit (for Target Power Sponsor) Resulting from Each Key Advantage of Each Key Advantage |
|---|---|---|---|---|---|
| **High Costs & Lagging Revenue =Critical Financial Issues of the Target Power Sponsor Caused by: ==>** | **Inefficient Checkout & Dissatisfied Customers =Critical Operating Issues of the Target Sponsor and are Caused by:===>** | 1. Customer dissatisfaction with long lines leads reduces store loyalty. | 1. Self-checkout (feature) improves traffic flow and customer satisfaction by reducing time spent in line (advantage). | 1. More satisfied customers increases store traffic and customer loyalty (by X%). | 1. Satisfied customers lead to increased sales and store loyalty, resulting in increased revenue (by X%). |
| | | 2. A high number of cashiers is needed. | 2. Remote monitoring (feature) allows one cashier to operate ten lanes, so fewer cashiers are needed (advantage). | 2. Smaller workforce (by X%) is simpler to maintain. | 2. Fewer cashiers leads to less required labor and training, reducing overall costs (by X%). |
| | | 3. Customer dissatisfaction with long lines reduces store loyalty. | 3. Self-checkout (feature) allows customers the choice between a cashier or using self checkout, increasing customer satisfaction (advantage). | 3. More satisfied customers increases store traffic and reduces walkouts (by X%). | 3. Sastisfied customers lead to increased sales and store loyalty and reduce walkouts, resulting in increased revenue (by X%). |
| | | 4. Loss of prime floor space for impulse products. | 4. Compact configuration (feature) opens floor space, allowing more space for the sale of impulse products (advantage). | 4. Saved floor space and faster lines improve traffic flow and provides opportunity for placement of impulse products (by X%). | 4. Open floor space near front of store enables sale of more impulse products, increasing impulse sales revenue (by X%). |
| | | 5. Too much theft. | 5. Advanced weight system, security database, and remote monitoring (feature) result in higher security and less theft (advantage). | 5. Increased security reduces customer delinquency and saves retailer time and resources lost handling theft (by X%). | 5. Greater security reduces theft, leading to lower costs (by X%). |
| | | 6. Not enough employees on floor reduces customer satisfaction, which leads to fewer customers. | 6. Remote monitoring (feature) allows one cashier to operate ten lanes, so more employees available on floor (advantage). | 6. More employees on the floor means greater customer satisfaction and store loyalty (by X%). | 6. More employees on the floor leads to increased sales and store loyalty, resulting in higher revenue (by X%). |

## Converting Other Key Players

*[Brian]*: "Linda, I can sure see how much thought you've put into these upcoming efforts to 'convert' Roger and Don. But what about the other key players you've listed that all require seemingly different visions? How does the conversion of these players fit into your plan and how the heck are you going to approach that challenge?"

*[Linda]:* "I knew you'd ask that, Brian! Let's take another short break and then come back to that. Are you still with me?"

*[Brian]*: "You bet! This is fascinating!"

*[Linda]:* "By the way Brian, you haven't responded to the company e-mail we sent about the team luncheon. Are you coming or not?"

*[Brian]*: "Oh is that the one at the sushi restaurant? I don't think I can come. My mom said it's not a good idea to eat raw fish...it messes with my weak tummy. But I'll catch you guys at the next office luncheon for sure!"

CHAPTER 24

# Plan for Building Visions for All Key Players

| Linda & SpeedyLane's Master Selling Plan | | |
|------|------|------------------------------------------------------------------------------|
| Ch | 20 | Meet Salesperson Linda Brown and Sales Trainee Brian Wilson |
| Ch | 21 | Linda's Master Selling Plan for House Depot (HD), Pt 1. Players & Visions Required |
| Ch | 22 | Linda's Master Selling Plan for House Depot (HD), Pt 2. Choose Target Sponsor |
| Ch | 23 | Linda's Master Selling Plan for House Depot (HD), Pt 3. Choose Target Power Sponsor |
| **Ch** | **24** | **Linda's Master Selling Plan for House Depot (HD), Pt 4. Plan for Building Visions for All Important Players** |

*[Brian]*: "Linda, I know I mentioned earlier that I can see how much thought you've put into your upcoming efforts to 'convert' Roger and Don. But what about the other key players you listed that all require seemingly different visions? How does your conversion of these key players fit into your plan? And how are you going to approach that challenge?"

*[Linda]*: "We've thankfully got that covered too, Brian. If we don't take care of that, there will be no end to the problems we'll experience when installing, implementing, integrating and maintaining the system with HD, should I be lucky enough to even make the sale."

*[Brian]*: "What do you mean 'lucky'!? With your charm, good looks, and obvious selling savvy, this sale should be a no-brainer for you!"

*[Linda]*: "Aww, you're making me blush."

"But, moving right along.... let's review that list of key players we want to convert."

## Summary List of Relevant Players

----

# Internal Players

*[Linda]:* "Among others, this would include a number of different folks at **HD Corporate Headquarters** – for example:

- Those in charge of store operating efficiency;
- Those controlling the purse strings; and
- Other executives who would be responsible for implementing and integrating the new system into HD's current data and operating systems.

"Different **HD players at the store level** would also get involved with the go / no go decision to invest in the self-checkout system and would also be involved in the implementation of the system at the store level. These would include:

- Store managers & assistant managers,
- Cashiers,
- Customer service folks,
- IT folks, and
- In-store maintenance personnel.
- \

# External Players

"**Other players outside of HD** should also be taken into consideration. These would include external players such as:

- Stockholders.
- Customers,
- Independent suppliers
- Retail labor unions,
- External IT support,
- National and local business press,
- And others."

*[Linda]:* "That's quite a list, I know! As we discussed earlier and will expand upon later, different folks need the vision of how a "game-changing" self-checkout system might work to significantly improve efficiency, productivity, and profits at HD.

"Don Johnson (our designated '**Target Power Sponsor**') will really be a key player for us here. Once we convince Don of the attractive operating *and financial* benefits of the proposed self-checkout system, we will be counting on him to get us access to these players and to help us build the other critical visions.

[*Brian*]: "Well, why would Don want to spend his time doing that?"

[*Linda*]: "What? - You don't remember??? (*Linda showing her impatience, as sometimes happens*) I mean, as HD's Executive VP of Operations, Don is constantly looking for ways to improve the productivity and efficiency of all of HD's operations, and our self-checkout solution would do just that. If Roger and I can prove to Don that our system will solve his problems, he should be more than anxious to help us move the selling process forward. Such help would include getting us access to that whole group of folks listed above and assisting us in building the necessary visions wherever he can! Got it?"

[*Brian*]: "Oh, yeah.... My bad. I remember now. Like you were emphasizing at lunch, if you can convince Don to join your HD selling team, he should be

drooling over the financial benefits that self-checkout can bring to HD. It's a chance for him to be a hero!

"You mentioned that when you were doing background research on HD, Don seemed to be a 'chosen one' at HD who is making his way up the ladder. By saving HD big bucks and jacking revenues, Don could likely advance his career, for sure!"

[*Linda*]: "Exacta-Mundo! So, let's review the visions needed for our different key players and then identify the various steps we will use to try to convert all the other key players as well. I'm going to briefly list some logical steps for you now. Later, when you're shadowing me during the actual selling process, you can take note of the details of these steps. But for now, this overview should suffice."

# Steps in Linda's Account Marketing Plan

*[Linda]:* "Here's a simple list of the visions of the various players in our plan along with a list of the steps needed to build the visions & implement the Account Marketing Plan for House Depot. Brian, these summary charts are in the beginning of the 'Account Marketing Plan for HD.'" (Linda refers Brian to the Account Marketing Plan for House Depot Account document that she has now shared with her protégé.)

## Visions Needed in the Account Marketing Plan for House Depot

| Players | Operating Vision | Financial Vision | Transition Vision |
|---|---|---|---|
| Target Sponsor | X | | |
| Target Power Sponsor | X | X | |
| Buying Committee | X | X | X |
| Other Operating Players | X | | |
| Other Financial Players | | X | |
| Transition Players | | | X |

---

### Steps in SpeedyLane's
### Account Marketing Plan for House Depot

1. Convert Target Sponsor, Roger Dunkel, Corporate Director of In-Store Efficiency at HD.
2. Convert Target Power Sponsor, Don Johnson, Executive VP of Operations at HD.
3. Start converting the Buying Committee. Getting preliminary approval for doing a detailed audit of HD's current checkout situation and specific needs is critical.
4. Build remaining operating, financial, and transition visions for all important internal and external HD players (this is time-consuming and quite challenging, as you can likely imagine).
5. Negotiate the final price and breadth of the SpeedyLane self-checkout solution.
6. Implement the purchased solution in a timely and effective fashion, including follow-up to ensure a successful implementation.

---

*[Linda]:* "As you can see in the steps in the chart, after converting our Target Sponsor (Roger) and Target Power Sponsor (Don), the next challenge will be to get key members of the **Buying Committee** on board with us.

"At first, the Buying Committee will need an *Operating Vision* that proves that our system can actually deliver the operating benefits we detailed earlier. Next, they'll need a *Financial Vision*, which will provide absolute proof that the adoption and implementation of the proposed self-checkout system will yield a very attractive ROI (return on investment) and have a brief, low risk payback period. Finally, the members of the *Buying Committee* need a *Transition Vision* – i.e., to be convinced that key HD transition players such as IT staff, store managers, cashiers, and customers can all adapt to, implement, and run the system successfully in order to deliver the promised financial benefits."

"Sooner rather than later, we'll want to get the initial approval of the Buying Committee to start building the **financial vision**. That effort will require a detailed audit of HD's inventory of stores of various types and sizes so we can scale our proposed solution to fit HD's specific needs. You'll see me do a run-down of this audit with HD later, presuming we get that far with the selling process....Which we no doubt will, right, Brian!?"

[*Brian*]: "For sure!"

[*Linda*]: "Then, as we build enthusiasm among the various folks about their **operating and financial visions,** it'll be time to address the more important **transition challenges.** For example, it will take quite an effort from me, Roger and Don to convince HD's IT folks to commit to the pretty gargantuan task of integrating a whole new data gathering and analysis system into their existing system. If we can successfully convince all the key players at HD, we will then move on to the final negotiation, which can be another challenge, as you'll see. Finally, we hopefully procure the sale, implement the solution, and follow-up with HD.

"I know from personal experience that the whole Speedy-Lane selling process can seem overwhelming at first. The truth of the matter is that our selling process is quite involved and a bit complicated. That's why you'll be in training and will shadow me for two months before branching out on your own. I remember that when I started, my own mentor simplified the process by boiling it down to the six main steps, which made the process seem more doable to me."

---

# Summary of the Six Steps to Implementing the Account Marketing Plan

1. **Convert the Target Sponsor**
2. **Convert the Target Power Sponsor**
3. **Build Remaining Visions**
4. **Negotiation & Closing**
5. **Implementation & Follow-up**

## 6. Ensuring Continuous Sales Growth

"The whole Account Marketing Plan doesn't seem as complex if you think about it in these steps. You'll be using these same general steps on your own accounts in a couple of months, after you complete your shadowing and are out there selling on your own. What do you think, Brian?"

[Brian]: "I have to admit, I am a little overwhelmed right now. I'm sure it will seem much easier after I see you in action – starting on Thursday, when we first go to meet Roger Dunkel.

"But before that, I have a more personal question for you, Linda. What's been the secret to your success in becoming such a star salesperson for SpeedyLane?"

---

# Some Secrets to
# Linda's Selling Success

[Linda]: "Well, if you ask my boss Roberto, he is not likely to consider me as a 'star' right now, because I lost a couple of high potential sales opportunities last quarter and forfeited my 'Golden Sales Club' status in the process. That was a bummer, but I did learn from those lost sales that I should never count my chickens before they have hatched!

"But getting back to your question, Brian, in my view, there are a number of requirements for effective selling at SpeedyLane. First of all, you obviously have to know the self-checkout system inside and out. You also need to know as much as possible about the specific situation and checkout-related needs of the target segments to which you have been assigned. Then you have to gather as much information as you can about each individual target customer. Finally, as I've been emphasizing, having a super-organized selling process is key."

"Overlaying all of that, though, is the confidence that only successful selling efforts can bring. You'll see that soon enough when you complete your very first sale on your own. And the more successful you are, the more confident you will become. To get to that point, however, it will take considerable organization, patience, and perseverance. Bringing enthusiasm and fun energy to the selling process also helps a lot. Clients like working with enthusiastic, fun folks!"

[Brian]: "Well, it seems to me you have all those qualities in spades, Linda – especially being organized and fun to work with!"

[Linda]: "Thanks, that's kind of you to say. We'll see if I live up to your expectations when we get on the firing line later this week. I DO certainly have fun - I can guarantee you that! As for the patience part, let's just say I'm a bit... 'patience-challenged,' as you'll likely see. But I'm improving slowly on that too - especially as my three little boys are growing up. Talk about needing patience! Ha Ha!"

[Brian]: "I'm sure learning a lot today, Linda! Thanks for being so patient with me. I know I must be asking some pretty stupid questions."

[Linda]: "Not at all! How else are you going to learn? I really like working with young people like you – especially when I can help them succeed!"

[Brian]: "Glad to hear that, because I've still got some more questions for you."

[Linda]: "Fire away!"

---

# Next Up: the Inevitable Price Question

[Brian]: "I know from my introductory training class last week that the average sales contract for SpeedyLane is $3.2 million, plus a $500,000 annual service contract. That's a big chunk o' change for any target customer! How the heck do you even get in the door to talk with someone when they hear those numbers?"

[Linda]: "Are you a mind reader or something? That's a crucial question we like to expose our trainees to right off the bat. As you've already anticipated, it can be a real deal breaker from the get-go if you don't know how to properly address that price question right up front.

"Speaking of breaks, let's take a short one and talk about that price question as soon as we get back!"

=====

The nest chapter discusses and provides strategies for handling this 'inevitable price question.'

# Part 2, cont.

## *BUILDING THE ACCOUNT MARKETING PLAN, CONT.*

### *Preparing to Convert*
### *the Target Sponsor & Target Power Sponsor*

CHAPTER 25

# The Inevitable Price Question

Early in the selling process someone in the customer company is most likely going to ask the salesperson the inevitable question: "How much would this cost us?" This is only natural because the 'feared high cost' is most likely a reason why the relevant solution hasn't been considered seriously before. How should the salesperson respond to this question when it is asked at the beginning of the sales cycle? In this chapter, we address that concern.

## That Inevitable Price Question

*[Brian]*: "Like I was asking before our break, Linda (end of earlier chapter), how in the world do you even get in the door to talk with anyone when your target customer hears that our self-service checkout solution will cost millions of bucks?"

*[Linda, continuing]*: "Price can be a real deal breaker right from the get-go, if it's not handled properly. Let's consider this more carefully by looking at the SpeedyLane Selling Manual you received last week. I'm sure you've been studying it ever since... right? I mean, have you been studying it?"

*[Brian]*: "Of course! In fact, I only went out with my buddies a couple of times last weekend, because I really want to learn this stuff!"

*[Linda]:* "Let's go through that chapter in the Manual together. I want to make sure you understand how to respond to this critical question about price because undoubtedly, you'll have to deal with it once you're selling on your own.

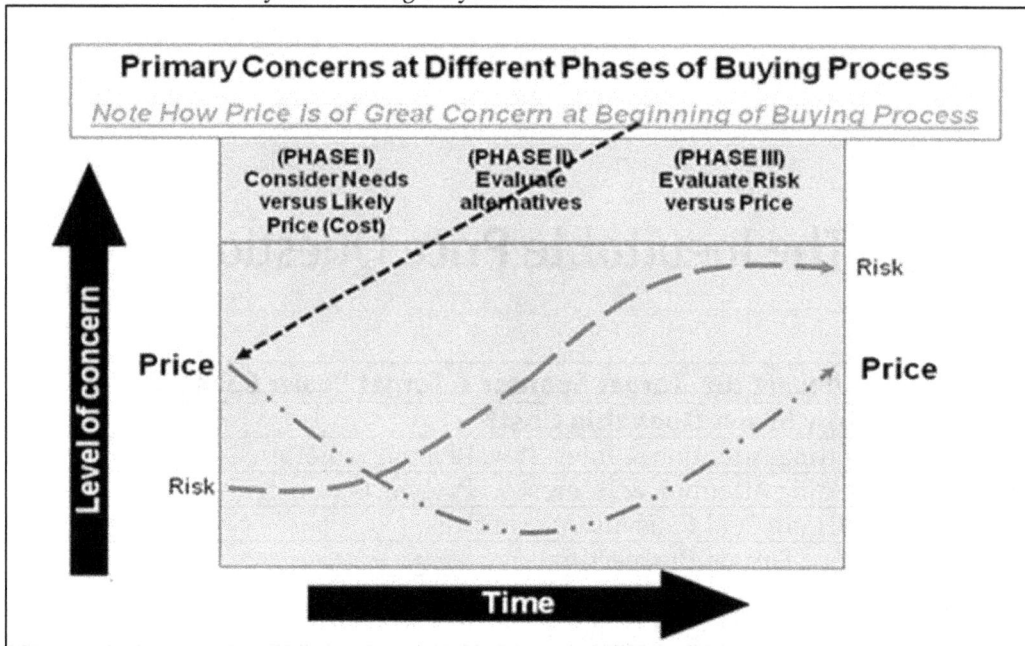

**Primary Concerns at Different Phases of Buying Process**

*Note How Price is of Great Concern at Beginning of Buying Process*

"First of all, you should know that price is a primary concern of any prospective buyer right out of the chute. Check out the chart (above) in the Manual that shows just that! Note also that this chart shows that if you can keep your buyer interested after the initial price inquiry, price should not be an issue again until much later in the selling process. This observation presumes that you answer the initial question effectively! Let's review that whole chapter in the Selling Manual."[16]

-----

*[Linda]:* "Before we do that, Bri, I have been meaning to ask you something. You're a smart kid and all, and I'd love to bring you along to my next meeting with Roger, but I have to be honest. If you wear a t-shirt like the one you're wearing now, I don't think he'll even let us in his office! Do you own ANYTHING professional that you could wear?"

*[Brian]:* "Oh sure I do! I have this great t-shirt with a picture of a tie on the front...I can fool anyone into thinking I'm dressed up with that one. It'll be perfect!"

*[Linda]:* "Another t-shirt!? That's not exactly what I had in mind. We have a long way to go here, Grasshopper..."

-----

## SpeedyLane Account Marketing Manual
## Answers the Inevitable Price Question

You can bet your bottom dollar that early in the discussions with your target customer, someone will ask you a question along the lines of, "What's your Price?" or "How much would this solution of yours cost us?"

We have seen earlier that the Target Sponsor is concerned primarily with resolving the day-to-day operational issues that our proposed solution promises to address. His immediate superior - who we have identified as our 'Target Power Sponsor'- is typically above the money line, meaning he is just as much concerned with financial ramifications as he is with the promised operational benefits of any new proposal.

Right off the bat, both the target sponsor and target power sponsor might ask "How much does this cost?" They won't be the last person who asks for our price. In fact, 'What's the price?' will likely be the first question asked by a number of people we meet as we try to move our sales process forward.

It would be a critical mistake to answer a question about price with a specific dollar amount early in the Account Marketing process before we can determine and prove the prospective value of our solution to the customer. Even mentioning a ballpark figure too early is a recipe for rejection and lost prospective sale.

---

# So, How Should We Answer
# a Premature Question about Price?

If planned, rehearsed, and backed by a solid, value-based pricing[17] framework (covered in a later chapter), there is an answer that should work every time to temporarily set aside our target customer's initial concerns about price. This answer should have the same essential components when used in response to every person in every prospective customer company. With that in mind, consider the points we want to make in answering the premature pricing question.

---

## Compact Response

Here's the short version of an effective response to the anticipated premature price inquiry. This short version is typically used with key players in the target company who may have some concern about the net financial benefits of the prospective new way solution but are primarily concerned with the operating benefits of our system. This well-practiced, short version should go like this:

*"Our price is different for every customer. We ourselves won't know the price for you until we have scaled the solution to exactly meet your particular needs. We can, however, guarantee you this – our price will, beyond a doubt, enable you to surpass your required Return on Investment (ROI) for this type of new venture. In fact, we only want your business if we feel confident that your company will be delighted with the financial outcome of this investment. Prior to making any price commitment to us, you will have ample opportunity to talk with our previous clients. We will encourage you to ask our previous customers whether they are happy with both the operational and net financial benefits of our solution. Is that an adequate answer for now?"*

## Lengthier Version

A lengthier answer to the premature question, 'How much does this cost?' would be more appropriate for justifiably persnickety executives above the money line. These executives have more direct financial responsibility for the outcome of such investments. That lengthier response should include the somewhat flexible components included in this sample response:

*"Our price is different for every customer. We ourselves won't know our price for you until we scale the solution to exactly meet your particular needs." (For example, for self-checkout systems, we would need to know the number of stores, the number of self-checkout units per store, etc. For online meetings, we would have to know the number, size, and types of meetings we would be hosting for each relevant pricing period.)*

Continuing ..., *"That said, we can guarantee you this: The price you pay for our solution will be designed to ensure, beyond a doubt, that you will surpass your required, risk-adjusted Return on Investment (ROI), and allow you to surpass your required payback period demands."*

*"We do not want your business unless you are certain that this will be a very attractive, successful investment for your company, returning far more in cost savings and new net revenues than any payment to us. We want this to be a successful adoption and implementation for you so that:*

- *You will be happy with us;*
- *You will do further business with us, should such opportunities be available; and*
- *You will gladly be willing to refer more business to us."*

*"We are in this for the long haul, and the best sale we can make is one that most delights you, our customer, at the end of the day."*

*"So, again, we can't tell you our exact price until we tailor our proposed market solution to your specific situation and needs."*

------

*"As a final note, prior to making any price commitment to us, you will have ample opportunity to talk with any number of our previous clients. You are certainly free to ask them what they paid -- remember that you will hear varying prices from different former clients, because we scale our solution to each client's specific needs. The one comment we are confident you will hear from each of our clients is that their investment in our solution greatly exceeded each one's required, risk-adjusted Return on Investment (ROI), and required payback period demands."*

*"Given that information, are you comfortable continuing our discussion?"*

# How Can We Possibly Guarantee a Profitable Price for a Client?

*[Brian]:* "But Linda, how can we possibly guarantee a profitable price for a client?"

*[Linda]:* "We can only guarantee a more than satisfactory price for a client if we meet two critical criteria:

"First, we must have a mature, inclusive, well-designed, transparent framework for **'Value-Based Pricing.'** A separate section of the Speedy-Lane Account Marketing Manual (covered later) shows how to develop and implement such a framework, but no need to detail that now.

"Secondly, our Value-Based Pricing process must actively involve those in the target customer company who are most familiar with and most concerned about overall financial ramifications of the proposed solution. There is much more on this later in the Value-Based Pricing section of the SpeedyLane Account Marketing Manual.

"So, Brian, what do you think?"

*[Brian]:* "I thought it was great. Not only did it give me a prepared response, but it also made total sense. How can we possibly price our solution until we scale it to each individual customer's needs? I have to be honest - before your response, I was dreading having to deal with the "price" question! But now I know to anticipate it and be ready to rock n' roll with a confident, solid, prepared response. There's that self-confidence factor again that you were emphasizing!"

*[Linda]:* "You got it! Your head must be spinning with all this new info you've been exposed to in such a short time."

*[Brian]:* "Actually it's not. Everything sounds so logical. I really like that. I was anticipating more of a "Rah! Rah! Let's go out and get 'em!" approach. I can be enthusiastic and my friends say I'm fun – ol' frat boy and all that – but I know that could only take me so far when selling such a game-changing, high-cost solution such as yours – or I should say, ours."

*[Linda]:* "Glad to hear that. You can achieve great success around here with that attitude. Are there any other questions on your mind right now?"

---

## Next up – Prepare Materials to Convert
## Our Target Sponsor (Roger) & Target Power Sponsor (Don)
## into Account Marketing Partners

*[Brian]:* "Well, I know you'll get around to it eventually, and that I'll get a better idea of it when I see you in action with Roger at House Depot on Thursday, but I have a couple of really basic questions.

"First of all, how did you initially get Roger interested enough to agree to meet with you Face-to-Face? Secondly, and I would think even more importantly, what specifically will you and Roger be talking about when you first walk in the door? I know you want to convert him into your 'Account Marketing partner' at HD, but I wouldn't even know where to start!"

[Linda]: "Funny you should ask, because that's the very next thing we are going to talk about -- that is, preparing materials for getting Roger's attention, building his interest, and vision building to convert both him and Don Johnson, our Target Power Sponsor, into full-fledged ' Account Marketing partners.'

"Again, our easiest way to do this is to look at the SpeedyLane Account Marketing Manual that you've been reviewing for the past week. Recall, the Manual has several chapters on this very point – '*Preparing Materials for Converting the Target Sponsor and Target Power Sponsor into Account Marketing Partners.*' Let's take a careful look at those chapters."

CHAPTER 26

# Getting Attention & Interest, with Reference Stories

| Preparing to Convert the Target Sponsor & Target Power Sponsor | | |
|---|---|---|
| Ch | 25 | How Much Does this Cost? |
| **Ch** | **26** | **Getting Attention & Interest w. Reference Stories** |
| Ch | 27 | Getting Attention & Interest w. Probing Questions |
| Ch | 28 | Turning Cold Calls into Warm Calls |
| Ch | 29 | More Tips on Prospecting |
| Ch | 30 | Prospecting with Social Media |
| Ch | 31 | Getting Attention & Interest w. Prepared Scripts |
| Ch | 32 | Big Growth Secret - Be Nice to Everyone! |

*Linda:* "Okay, here we are. Let's talk about preparing materials for getting attention, building interest, and building visions to convert Roger - our Target Sponsor- and Don - our Target Power Sponsor- into full-fledged 'selling partners.' Again, our easiest way to go about doing this is to look at the SpeedyLane Selling Manual. As you can see from the Manual Outline, the manual includes several chapters describing the various 'aids' designed to help us convert Roger and Don." (These are the same as the chapters in this book of the Sales Growth Secrets Book)

# Starting Point: Identify Operating Issues, Key Advantages, & Operating Benefits (Summary Sheet)

In an earlier chapter, we developed a summary sheet of relevant operating issues, key advantages, and operating benefits related to our proposed new way solution. We will now use this sheet as our starting point for developing reference stories, composing 'probing questions' on operating issues, and designing advertisements in order to capture initial attention. We will also use this summary sheet to help develop vehicles for generating leads and for developing flexible, planned scripts for both warm and cold calls.

Recall the **Operating Issues – Key Advantages – Operating Benefits** Summary Sheet, shown below.

| | Specific Relevant Operating Issues | New Capabilities (i.e., Generic Advantages) Needed to Resolve Each Relevant Operating Issue | Projected Operating Benefit from Each New Capability (i.e., from each new generic advantage) |
|---|---|---|---|
| **Target Sponsor = the one who is most concerned on a day to day basis with these primary operating issues & projected operating benefits** | Customer dissatisfaction with long lines leads reduces store loyalty | Self-checkout (feature) improves traffic flow and customer satisfaction by reducing time spent in line (advantage). | More satisfied customers increases store traffic and customer loyalty. |
| | A high number of cashiers is needed. | Remote monitoring (feature) allows one cashier to operate ten lanes, so fewer cashiers are needed (advantage). | Smaller workforce is simpler to maintain. |
| | Customer dissatisfaction with long lines reduces store loyalty. | Self-checkout (feature) allows customers the choice between a cashier or using self checkout, increasing customer satisfaction (advantage) | More satisfied customers increases store traffic and reduces walkouts. |
| | Too little prime floor space for impulse purchase items. | Compact configuration (feature) opens floor space, allowing more space for the sale of impulse items (advantage). | Saved floor space and faster lines improve traffic flow and provides opportunity for placement of impulse items. |
| | Too much theft. | Advanced weight system, security database, and remote monitoring (feature) result in higher security and less theft (advantage). | Increased security reduces customer delinquency and saves retailer time and resources lost handling theft. |
| | Not enough employees on the floor reduces customer satisfaction, which leads to fewer customers. | Remote monitoring (feature) allows one cashier to operate ten lanes, so more employees available on floor (advantage). | More employees on the floor means greater customer satisfaction and store loyalty. |

# Reference Stories

Without success stories of former clients, a seller faces a steep uphill battle when trying to capture the attention and interest of any prospective new customer. Thus, it is essential that our company partners with previous customers that have successfully adopted and implemented our solution. Here's an example of a multi-dimensional client case study that a Speedy-Lane salesperson can draw from in order to customize any reference story to emphasize the specific benefits perceived to be of the greatest importance to the target customer.

## Example of Broader, Documented Client Case Study

*[Linda]: "Pioneer Markets is a fast-growing superstore chain on the West Coast. Their Director of In-Store Efficiency* **told us** *that she was bothered by the company's inefficient checkout system and related customer dissatisfaction.*

*She* **told us** *that the primary* <u>Operating Issues</u> *were:*
- *Long checkout lines;*
- *The high number of cashiers needed to keep checkout times reasonable, leading to high wages, benefits, turnover, and training costs;*
- *Inability of customers to select faster checkout alternatives;*
- *Loss of prime floor space for impulse products due to so much prime, up front space being used for checkout stations;*
- *Profits lost because of cashier inaccuracies or outright theft; and*
- *Having too few employees on the sales floor to help customers.*

*"She* **told us** *that the* <u>Capabilities Needed</u> *to address each of these issues were:*
- *A faster checkout process to reduce the average customer time spent in the checkout process;*
- *A reduction in the number of cashiers needed without compromising customer satisfaction;*
- *A choice for customers between full service or self-service checkout;*
- *Allocating less prime, up front floor space to checkout stations and more for prominently displaying high margin impulse items;*
- *More advanced checkout technology to improve accuracy and reduce profits lost due to cashier inaccuracies or theft; and*
- *An ability to have more employees on the floor helping customers without increasing overall headcount or personnel expenses.*

*"Pioneer Markets adopted our SpeedyLane Self-checkout System, thereby acquiring each capability needed, and began reaping immediate <u>benefits</u>, including the following documented improvements:*

- *Average customer checkout time was reduced (by 20%);*
- *Average number of cashiers was reduced (by 25%) without reducing perceived customer service;*
- *Checkout alternatives were available (self-checkout or cashier checkout), which improved customer satisfaction and loyalty, and reduced the number of walkouts (by 15%);*
- *The more compact checkout area provided more space for displaying impulse items and increased impulse revenues (by 10%);*
- *Advanced checkout technology reduced profits previously lost to cashier inaccuracies or theft (by 12%); and*
- *More cashiers were free to help customers, increasing customer satisfaction and store loyalty (15%)."*

---

# Converting a Client Case Study into
# Shorter Reference Stories

The case study above includes a wide range of potentially relevant issues, advantages and benefits that might be of interest to any number of players in the target customer company. A reference story, on the other hand, is a much more compact version of this case study. A reference story focuses on only a few issues that are likely to be the most important to the target client beneficiary being addressed. Thus, the individual SpeedyLane salesperson extracts selected parts of the longer case study into a much briefer 'reference story' for the target player. The resulting reference story is intended as a teaser to raise the interest of the relevant player, such as the Target Sponsor.

For example, a short **reference story** from the case study above may sound like this:

*"A particular story that might interest you is that of Pioneer Markets. Their Director of In-Store Efficiency told us that she was bothered by the company's inefficient checkout system and related customer dissatisfaction.*

*"She said that she was particularly concerned about the long checkout lines and the high number of cashiers needed to keep checkout times reasonable in Pioneer Market stores.*

*"Pioneer ultimately adopted our solution and improved average customer checkout time by 20% while reducing its number of cashiers by 25% without reducing customer service.*

*"Would you like to hear more about how we were able to do this?"*

-----

Which specific issues to include in a reference story might vary from customer to customer, depending on the seller's knowledge or intuition regarding which specific issues are of the greatest concern to any particular Target Sponsor. Thus, SpeedyLane would have several different reference stories available and may even change stories during an initial meeting with the target customer if it becomes clear that the planned reference story is not the best match for the primary concerns of the Target Sponsor.

## Select a Reference Story about Someone
## with the Same Responsibilities as the Target Sponsor

Note that the reference story is about someone who was in the same position as the current Target Sponsor- Roger Dunkel - Director of In-Store Efficiency for House Depot. Titles may vary from company to company, so adjustments should be made to make the story about a manager who has the same responsibilities as the relevant Target Sponsor.

## Use a Subtle 'Self-Conclusion' Approach

People tend to believe what they conclude for themselves. We will emphasize this over and over again when describing the marketer's interface with the Target Sponsor.

In the case of the reference story, note the subtle language used to allow the Target Sponsor to make his or her own conclusions. We say:

- *"Their Director of In-Store Efficiency told us that she was bothered by the company's inefficient checkout system and related customer dissatisfaction. She told us that the primary operating issues were...."* T

This allows Roger, our Target Sponsor, to conclude that these were indeed the Director of In-Store Efficiency's issues, which should be similar to the issues that he too is facing at HD.

Contrast this with an alternative version that tries to draw conclusions for the listener. For example:

- *"Their Director of In-Store Efficiency's main overall issue was* the company's inefficient checkout system and related customer dissatisfaction. *The primary operating issues were..."*

In this second example, we are telling the Target Sponsor what the problems were, instead of guiding that person to make those same conclusions on his/her own. This goes directly contrary to the recommended 'self-conclusions' approach.

# Include Specific Documented Improvements
# in Describing Benefits

Note that the reference story above includes specific numbers -- general percentage (%) improvements -- to describe each operational benefit resulting from implementation of the proposed new solution. For example, it included documented improvements like:

- "Average customer checkout time was reduced by 20%." The specific % improvement grabs attention and makes the whole reference story more credible."

The source of these specific documented improvements must flow from previous successful adoptions of the proposed solution. (A later section of the book addresses the process of setting and carefully monitoring key before-and-after success measures).

# Avoid Using Reference Stories
# About Direct Competitors

This caveat falls under the category, *Common Sense*. If we are seen willingly sharing potential proprietary information of a direct competitor, then what assurance does our current target client company have that we will not also violate its own private information? The logical inference is to use reference stories of somewhat similar, but non-competing clients and only do so when you have permission from the reference client.

# Getting Former Customers
# to Agree to Serve as Reference Clients

Using a previous client's information without explicit permission not only violates assumed or specified confidentiality, but can also lead to costly, unhappy outcomes in a court of law (see the "Not Getting Permission" cartoon). With this in mind, why would any of our former clients who have successfully adopted and implemented our solution agree to serve as an enthusiastic reference client for us?

First, a former client might agree to share its specific success with our solution in a public forum as part of its broader effort to assure its stakeholders of its continuous efforts to enhance the company's efficiency and productivity. This might be accomplished through a cooperative win-win promotional campaign between us and the client. This helps us to promote the successful implementation of our solution and simultaneously helps the client broadcast its successful efforts to stay current.

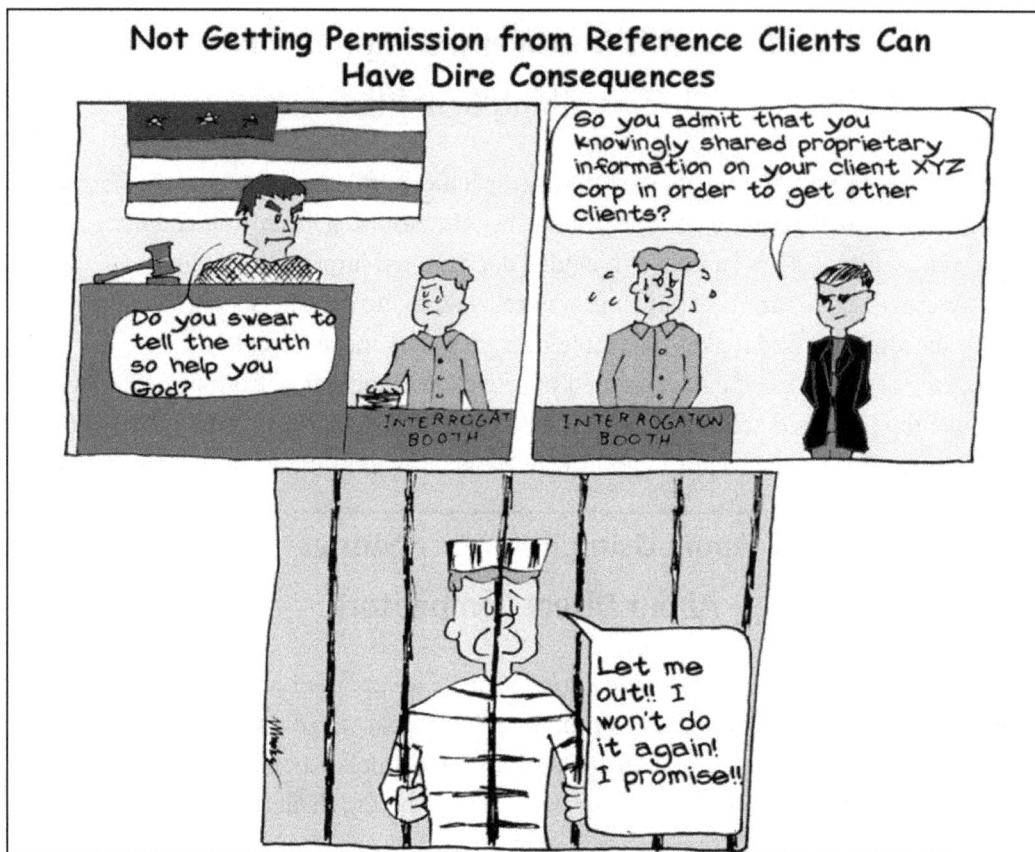

Not Getting Permission from Reference Clients Can Have Dire Consequences

Secondly, when closing a final deal with a target client, we might negotiate an agreement with that client to serve as a reference for us in return for something they deem as highly valuable. This might involve extra implementation support, free upgrades, an extended service agreement, or a variety of other offers. These offers are of high value to the customer and will help to enhance implementation of the system, yet typically involve little or no direct incremental cost for us. This is discussed in greater detail in the 'negotiation' section of the book.

## Reference Stories and Social Media

*[Brian]*: "Linda, you mentioned that we sometimes handpick the reference clients which we decide to show to our target customer. In this day and age, however, what prevents target customer companies from using social media to find their own reference clients?"

*[Linda]*: "Great point, Bri! We are well aware that our target customers are free in any stage of the evaluation or buying process to research other companies' experiences with us or with self-checkout systems in general. Social media has now empowered individuals to share their experiences with one another without the filters of corporate promotions and PR departments.

People are more honest when communicating one-on-one with their peers, which creates more credible and compelling references than canned success stories. As you know, these experiences appear in customer interest group discussions, industry blogs or wherever. Our target customers now regularly contact these more objective references on their own. It makes sense that self-selected references like these would be more credible for our customers than a specific reference contact that one of our sales folks has steered them toward.

"This has some critically important implications for us. *First of all*, this underlines the importance of indeed offering the best overall value for each of our target markets. But it *also* emphasizes how important it is for us to monitor and participate in these interest group discussions and industry blogs ourselves. Doing so keeps us up to date on the changing concerns of our various target segments. It also keeps us aware of what both former and prospective customers are saying about self-checkout systems in general and, even more importantly, about their specific experiences with and perceptions of our SpeedyLane brand.

"Today it's not just interest groups and blogs, though. Prospective buyers now ask questions directly to one another via social media sites like Twitter, Facebook and LinkedIn. Replies are almost instantaneous, and each response is tied back to an individual profile, which increases potential credibility. Not only can a prospective buyer now ask about others' experiences, but the buyer can also ask for experiential advice.

"We recognized several years ago that we have to be proactive about this, so we set up our own Social Media Department and related programs. For example, any time SpeedyLane or self-checkout systems in general are mentioned in customer interest groups, blogs, Twitter, or other social media, a call of action on our part may be necessary. If we come across *favorable mentions* -- whether they be of SpeedyLane or self-checkout systems in general -- we may reference them on our website and in one or more of our specialty blogs as well." (We *will talk about such specialty blogs in a later chapter*).

[*Brian*]: "What about negative mentions? I'd think those would be just as important."

[*Linda*]: "Right you are! Negative mention or critiques of SpeedyLane or self-checkout systems in general call for a different reaction. *If a relevant criticism is true and constructive*, we will relay it to product development, customer service and support, IT or other relevant departments for their consideration. If it affects our brand, we will generally take action to correct the problem and relay this corrective initiative on our website, in one or more of our specialty blogs, and as content for our participation in other customer interest groups or blogs.

"*If the criticism is negative but inaccurate* regarding SpeedyLane or self-checkout systems in general, we will get involved in the relevant blogs and discussion groups in the effort to try to set the record straight, while doing our best to not get defensive. In such informational, education initiatives, we would only refer to the SpeedyLane brand if the criticism is about us in particular. If it is about self-checkout systems in general, we would avoid mentioning our brand name. We can also cite objective studies and favorable experiences and case studies that counter the inaccuracies or bad experiences. Again, we do all of this as objectively as possible without getting defensive, so that our involvement in these discussions does not come off as a 'sales pitch.'"

*[Linda, continuing, but shifting gears a bit]*: "All that said, many of our Target Sponsors still depend on us to take them to see reference clients that we have used in our success stories. Most customers prefer the convenience of having us set up the opportunity for in-depth reference client visits, when they are encouraged to ask the reference clients drill-down questions about their experiences with self-checkout in general and with SpeedyLane in particular.

"Our target customers are no dummies. They realize they can complement such in-depth reference visits with their own reading of and participation in customer interest groups and industry blogs. In fact, more and more of our target customers today are consulting social media blogs and similar websites *before meeting with us and before their reference visits in order* to help them prepare detailed questions for both events. The whole process is much more transparent than it was before social media became so important.

"Because we have been so pro-active with our social media programs, we are finding that social media interest groups and blogs are beneficial for us at SpeedyLane. This is because we have a total commitment to providing the best solution value to our customers and communicating that value message as accurately as possible to them."

*[Brian]*: "Now I understand why you have me scheduled to attend that Social Media Workshop later this month and why we have a Social Media Department working with both our sales and marketing groups!"

*[Linda]*: "That's exactly right. A little later (*in a few chapters*), I'll give you an overview of the evolution, goals, and specific programs that our Social Media Department runs for both our Sales and Marketing Departments. You'll see that we even have our own SpeedyLane brand community, where we constantly seek customer feedback from our existing customers on product quality, support services, and the like. In addition to alerting us about specific customer concerns, the public nature of such online communities provides an active incentive to immediately address any relevant issues that may arise. At the same time, we use that same community to encourage our happiest customers to share their positive opinions."

CHAPTER 27

# Getting Attention & Interest, with

# Probing Questions

*Linda:* "Well Brian, next we're going to discuss how to develop 'Probing Questions,' and examine the role they can play in helping us to get attention, build interest, and create visions for converting Roger and Don into selling partners. Again, the easiest way for us to do this is to simply review the SpeedyLane Selling Manual. Let's look at the chapter on Probing Questions."

## What Are Probing Questions?

Probing questions are questions designed to stimulate the target sponsor to think about, admit to, and potentially discuss the various operating issues that are addressed by our solution.

Consider, for example, the operating issues introduced in the last chapter for our self-checkout systems. They were:

- Long checkout lines;
- The high number of cashiers needed to keep checkout times reasonable, which lead to high wages, benefits, turnover, and training costs;
- Inability of customers to select faster checkout alternatives;
- Loss of prime floor space for impulse products due to such valuable up front floor space being used for checkout stations;
- Lost profits due to either cashier inaccuracies or outright theft; and
- Having too few employees on the sales floor to help customers.

## Examples of Indirect / Subtle Probing Questions

What subtle, indirect questions might a seller ask in order to get each of the first three issues on the table? Try these:

- Long checkout lines;
  - o "How long does it take your average customer to check out?"
- The high number of cashiers needed to keep checkout times reasonable, leading to high wages, benefits, turnover, and training costs;
  - o "How many cashiers are needed to have what you consider to be a reasonable average checkout time?"
- Inability of customers to select faster checkout alternatives;
  - o "Do your customers have a choice regarding how they will check out?"

These are straightforward questions that simply ask for facts. They are non-accusatory and non-threatening. What are some similarly indirect, non-threatening questions for getting the other operating issues above on the table?

***Take a shot at filling in these examples:***

- Loss of prime floor space for impulse products due to a large amount of highly visible front floor space used for checkout stations;
  - o FILL IN

  _____

  _____

- Lost profits due to cashier inaccuracies or outright theft;
  - o FILL IN

  _____

  _____

- Having too few employees on the sales floor to help customers.

o   FILL IN

_____

_____

---

## Examples of Direct / In Your Face Probing Questions

What **more direct questions** might a seller ask in order to get the various issues on the table? Consider the following examples:

- Long checkout lines:
  - o   "Is your average checkout time too long?"
- A high number of cashiers needed to keep checkout times reasonable, leading to high wages, benefits, turnover, and training costs;
  - o   "Do you require too many cashiers on duty to provide a reasonable average checkout time?"
- Inability of customers to select faster checkout alternatives:
  - o   "How much do your customers complain about not having a faster checkout alternative?"

These are more direct, in-your-face questions that may be viewed by the Target Sponsor as accusatory or even threatening. These direct questions implicitly suggest that the client does indeed have each relevant issue. What might be other direct, potentially accusatory questions for each of the remaining operating issues introduced above? Take a shot at it.

Loss of prime floor space for impulse products due to a large amount of highly visible front floor space being used for checkout stations:

FILL IN _____

_____

Lost profits due to cashier inaccuracies or outright theft;

FILL IN _____

_____

Having too few employees on the sales floor to help customers.

FILL IN _____

_____

# Purpose of Probing Questions
# When and How Are They Used?

Each probing question addresses one of the specific operating issues that your proposed new way solution can resolve. These probing questions can be used in several different stages of the selling process.

## Using Probing Questions in Advertisements & Promotions

The first use for probing questions is to capture the target sponsor's initial attention and to generate potential leads. A lead, in turn, can transform a low probability cold call into a higher probability warm call. An individual ad can draw any perspective target sponsor's attention to a specific issue. For example, an ad for our self-checkout system might show a picture of a retail shop with a long line of obviously frustrated customers at the checkout counter -- or a picture of prime floor space up front in the store 'wasted' on an abundance of cashier checkout stations – as shown in this ad example.

## Using Probing Questions in
## Initial Conversation with Target Sponsors

Whether our initial contact with the target sponsor is at a convention, an informal get-together, a cold phone or office call, a warm/invited phone or office call, or any different form of initial contact, we will not be able to make progress on the sale unless we convince the prospect to admit to having one or more of the issues that our proposed solution can address.

After appropriate introductory remarks (covered later), we will likely start our initial discussion with our target sponsor with a compact reference story such as the one introduced in the last chapter and repeated below.

## Example of a Compact Reference Story

*"A particular story that might be of interest is that of Pioneers Market. Their Director of In-Store Efficiency told us that she was bothered by the company's inefficient checkout system and related customer dissatisfaction.*

*She said that she was particularly concerned about her stores' long checkout lines and the high number of cashiers needed to keep checkout times reasonable.*

*Her company, Pioneer Markets, ultimately adopted our solution and improved average customer checkout time by 20%, while reducing its number of cashiers by 25% without reducing customer service.*

*Would you like to hear more about how we were able to do this?"*

-----

If this brief story does not trigger the target sponsor's interest and fails to initiate some sort of discussion, ***then it's time for indirect, subtle, non-pushy*** **probing questions**. We want to guide the target sponsor to come to his/her own conclusions, and not push or project our views. To take this more subtle approach, we start with an indirect question, selecting one that we are quite certain should hit home with the target sponsor. For example, asking:

- "How long does it take your average customer to check out?"

This should lead the target sponsor to start talking about the issue at hand.

Next, try to get the target sponsor to admit that the average checkout time is too long. If he/she doesn't bite, then move on to a different issue with another indirect question. For example:

- "How many cashiers does it take if you wanted to achieve a reasonable average checkout time?"

Again, try to get the target sponsor to talk about it. Get him/her to admit that it's too expensive to have all the cashiers needed to have a reasonable checkout time.

If this indirect, subtle, non-pushy approach simply isn't working, then it's time to take the risk of switching to more direct questions, such as:

- *"Is your average checkout time too long?"* or
- *"Do you need too many cashiers on duty to have a reasonable average checkout time?"*

These questions pose a greater risk, because you may offend the target sponsor with this more accusatory, threatening questioning. At this point, however, since the indirect approach has not worked, you have little to lose. If the target sponsor isn't going to admit any of the operating issues or 'pains' that he or she is currently facing, you'll soon be 'dismissed' and will have to move on to your next target client anyway.

## Using Probing Questions in More Detailed Vision Building Conversation with Target Sponsor

Another time when your prepared indirect and direct questions will come in handy is after the target sponsor has admitted to one or more specific operating issues. At that point, it is important to schedule a face-to-face meeting with the target sponsor (we will elaborate on the importance of face-to-face contact in later chapters). The probing questions will certainly come in handy in vision building to expand the target sponsor's understanding of both the breadth of the relevant operating issues as well as the breadth of our proposed solution. We will do a drill down on this in the later chapters on 'Vision Building.'

*[Brian]:* "I didn't realize how 'touchy' our target customers are, and how subtle I'll have to be to avoid offending them."

*[Linda]:* "This is really important, Bri. I can't tell you how many potential customers have turned me away because I was much too direct when I first approached them."

"It's a lot like that T-shirt you have on today. Not really that subtle, Bri. No wonder you are having trouble getting any young ladies interested in you."

*[Brian:]* "It's actually one of my favorites – but I never let mom see it."

CHAPTER 28

# Getting Attention & Interest, cont.

# Turning Cold Calls into Warm Calls

*Linda:* "Here we are again, at the next chapter of the manual. This one deals with the importance of turning would-be cold calls into warm calls with our target client."

## Advantages of Turning Would-Be
## Cold Calls into Warm Calls

No one likes to make cold calls. Even more importantly, very few like to be on the receiving end of cold calls. Cold calls are uninvited and are often considered to be disrespectful to the person on the receiving end. Why would anyone want to talk with you out of the blue when they have better things to do with their time?

Why would anyone want to talk to you out of the blue?

"I don't know who you are.
I don't know your company.
I don't know your company's solutions.
I don't know what your company stands for.
I don't know your company's customers.
I don't know your company's record.
I don't know your company's reputation.
**Now, what was it you wanted to sell me?"**

A lead is any direct or indirect interest expressed by a potential customer. A lead turns a would-be cold call into a warm call. For example, a person walking into a shoe store is a lead, as he or she is obviously interested in browsing for and potentially purchasing a pair of shoes. The probability of engaging a potential customer in conversation and moving the sales process forward is much higher if the potential customer has initiated or expressed an interest in the seller and/or the solution. This emphasizes the importance of feeding the growth hopper with leads.

# Generating Leads:
## Social Media Channels Have Changed the Game[18]

*[Linda]*: "In the past for our SpeedyLane Self-Checkout System, like for most business markets, leads were traditionally generated by trade shows, trade advertising, direct mail campaigns, telemarketing and the like. Nowadays, that has changed dramatically with the advent and growth of social media channels. These new channels are much more effective and much less expensive than our traditional promotion channels.

"For example, our target segments no longer rely as heavily on traditional channels to find out about self-checkout systems. We used to spend $20,000 or more on a single trade print ad. Even when the ads were well-designed and well-targeted, they generated only a small number of leads. Part of the problem with such ads is that it is difficult to communicate the multiple benefits and overall value of our SpeedyLane solution in a single page advertisement, which leads to poor response rates. Even the leads that were generated were typically only at the very beginning stage of the buying cycle, which left us with a long and arduous selling process challenge ahead.

"Reflecting the transition to social media and digital formats, it is not surprising that overall dollars spent on trade publishing are plummeting, and most trade publications are now either going belly-up or migrating to digital formats only. Companies really do get more bang for the buck by using social media platforms."

*[Brian]*: "Linda, can you be more specific about how SpeedyLane generates leads today?

*[Linda]*: "Well, sure – that's just what I was getting at. Recall that the purpose of getting leads is to avoid cold calls, which involve prospective customers who aren't yet in the buying cycle. Cold calls are expensive, frustrating, and simply not very productive – at least for self-checkout systems. Our marketing and sales teams used to depend on a variety of promotional vehicles to try to stimulate prospective customers to express interest in self-checkout solutions. This included using promotional vehicles such as:

- Advertising (Print – trade and other magazines; Captive media – TV / radio),
- Industry trade shows,
- Direct mail campaigns,
- Informational seminars,
- Referrals from satisfied customers – either voluntary or requested,
- General networking,
- Public Relations releases about our new-way solution innovations and implementation successes,
- Casual contacts,
- Phone bank / Telemarketing, and
- Shotgun office cold calls.

"But now the game has changed significantly as the breadth of available media for contacting target customers has expanded so much in both coverage and complexity. Today, we have so many more alternatives for attracting customer interest. Fortunately for everyone, the new set of media available is both more efficient and more productive than the traditional media I listed above."

*[Brian]*: "How so? I would think it would be more expensive and more complicated if you were to utilize more media to try to generate target customer interest and leads."

*[Linda]*: "The new media environment is certainly more complicated. You are right about that. But the significant benefit of the new media – particularly the new social media channels – is that when a prospective customer contacts us today, that potential client is very often well into the buying / selling cycle. That is key because it not only speeds up and simplifies our selling challenge, but also yields higher closing rates."

*[Brian]*: "Why is that? I don't quite understand. For instance, why does a potential client who contacts you via social media channel tend to be further into the buying cycle?"

*[Linda]:* "To answer that fully, you would need a tutorial from our Social Media Department, which you will be getting later this month as part of your initial sales training. But I can at least give you an overview for now (more details appear in a subsequent chapter).

"As I mentioned earlier, historically our Marketing and National Sales Managers' Departments used to use scatter-shot techniques such as print advertising, direct mail, seminar events, trade shows, sales calls, public relations, and the like in order to generate leads. This was a real hit-or-miss proposition, with a huge percentage of our messages falling on deaf ears, since a vast majority of the contacts made were to those either not in the market or not ready to buy. Even when a lead is developed through such traditional media, the would-be customer tends to be at the very beginning of the buying cycle – which demands a long, arduous selling process for us to move the potential client toward an ultimate purchase.

## Using Search Engines and Educational Blogs to Generate Leads

*[Linda]:* "Now, consider a couple of examples of how a lead develops through social media. Let's take search engines, for instance. Search Engines cause self-selection, with leads flowing from prospective buyers taking the initiative, rather than from the seller making the move. After sifting through the wealth of information on the Internet, buyers then contact SpeedyLane when they are already well into the buying process. The Internet is always searchable. Now, that is an efficient lead generation system!"

"Another reason they are further along in the buying cycle is because of the nature of the information gathered through search engines. For example, we run a number of what we call Educational Blogs (or 'Knowledge Sharing' Blogs) that I mentioned previously when we were discussing reference clients. These blogs provide input from selected SpeedyLane in-house experts, but do so without mentioning the SpeedyLane brand name, except in the affiliation of the initial blog author.

"The marketing department started these blogs in partnership with the Social Media Department by developing a list of a couple dozen terms related to multiple dimensions of retail checkout systems that are of interest to prospective buyers – terms like 'retail pilferage', 'retail data integration', 'store walkouts', 'cashier costs' etc. Search engine hits on these blogs are often 'hot leads' to better qualified prospects because those consulting the blog are focused on specific issues and are often under pressure to solve a specific retail checkout related problem.

"For example, someone in charge of in-store efficiency whose cashier costs are getting out of hand is more likely to be comfortable interacting directly with professional peers involved with store efficiency (e.g., our in-house expert authoring the blog), rather than some unknown salesperson. These have become a veritable gold mine for us because these are ready prospects, who consult our blogs and are already contemplating the idea of self-checkout. In our national sales meeting last month, Marketing told the sales team that these blogs are now likely responsible for more than thirty percent of our sales! That was great encouragement for everyone to keep our specialty blogs fresh and exciting."

*[Brian]*: "OK, I definitely see why social channels can generate more ready buyers. So, who writes these specialty blogs? And how well have they worked to generate these so-called 'hot leads'?"

*[Linda]*: "Well, one question at a time. First, like I said, Marketing started these blogs in partnership with the Social Media Department. They then enlisted SpeedyLane experts (as 'volunteers') in marketing, product development, software development, IT, customer service, customer fulfillment, and even sales to write and maintain blogs on these specific topics. All these blogs are cross-listed and are prominently linked both within and to our SpeedyLane website. Additionally, we also link in our own expert-written white papers and podcast interviews and invite personal calls to our in-house experts for customized answers.

"In terms of how well they have worked, thanks to our twenty-plus specialty blogs that utilize search terms that retail professionals are likely to use, our blogs have quickly climbed the Google ladder, leading to a ton of hits. In fact, the Marketing and National Sales Departments told us in our January meeting that these blogs have been generating more than twenty percent of the leads for our sales force. And, like I said, these are hot leads from better qualified prospects because those consulting the blog are focused on specific issues and are often under pressure to solve a specific retail checkout related problem.

"For example, someone in charge of in-store efficiency whose cashier costs are getting out of hand is more likely to be comfortable interacting directly with professional peers involved with store efficiency (e.g., our in-house expert authoring the blog), rather than some salesperson. Social media really is a gold mine for us nowadays."

---

## Using LinkedIn, Facebook &
## Twitter Pages to Generate Leads[19]

*[Brian]*: "Wow, that's pretty amazing. Are we using any other social media vehicles to build leads? How about media like LinkedIn, Facebook, and Twitter – channels I'm more familiar with?

*[Linda]*: "We certainly do generate leads using LinkedIn, Facebook, Twitter and multiple other social media sites. In fact, these have become as critically important as regular sources of new leads and prospects for our SpeedyLane Self-checkout solution.[20]

"We view our presence on platforms like LinkedIn, Facebook, and Twitter as if they are our own radio or TV show. These platforms enable us to broadcast our dynamic, up-to-date messages to people who follow our postings. We use these popular channels to release news, educate potential customers, and get feedback. By utilizing these channels, we get leads, build relationships, and ultimately make sales.

"The coolest part is that this cuts down on the efforts we need to devote to searching out prospects – they come to us! Just look at some of the numbers for the folks now on LinkedIn, Facebook, and Twitter[21] -- and all these sites are continuing to grow at exponential rates each year. "

Linda shows the charts below.

"As of 2022, more than half (57.6 percent) of the global population used social media which is a 9.9 percent year-over-year since 2021.[22] The chart below shows social media user data estimates from a 2020 source[23]. The next pages show similar, a bit more up to date (2023) data.

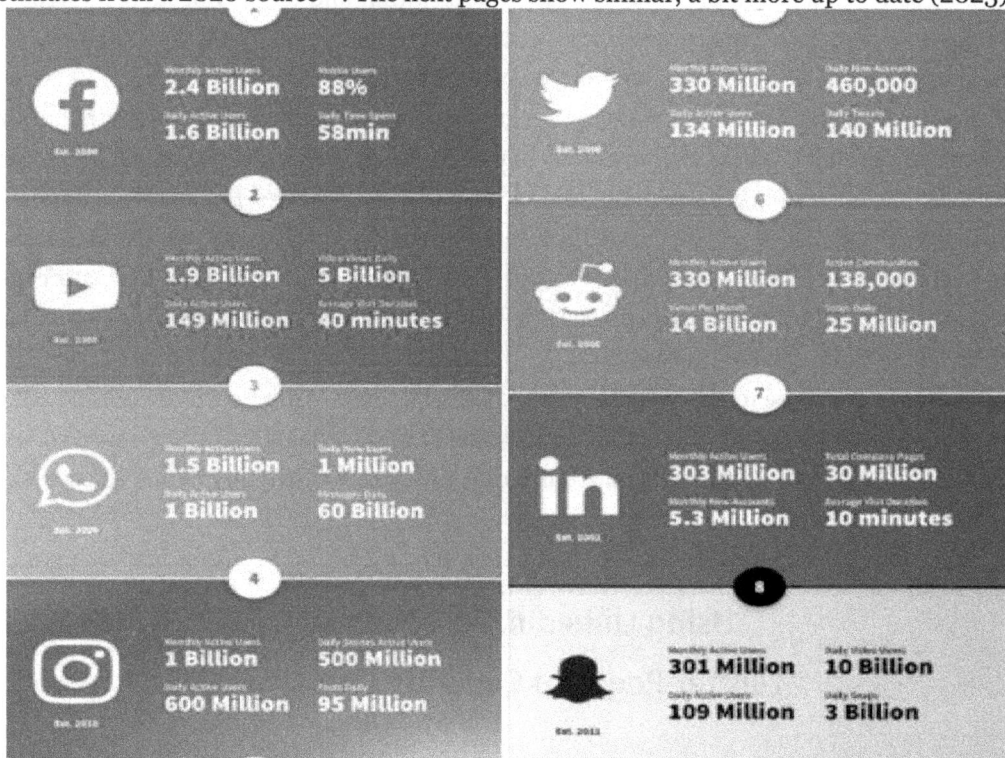

"The charts below  show more recent (2023) estimates of the number of users of the most popular social media as of 1/23[24] as well as estimates of the percentage marketers using different social media as of 2022-2023.

"With 2.9 billion active users in 2023, Facebook is the most popular social network worldwide. The market leader (Facebook) also remains the most important social media platform among marketers on the B2B and B2C spectrum. However, the social media landscape is quickly evolving and new players are fighting for attention from audiences and marketers alike, Facebook is facing increasing competition. With Instagram & YouTube gaining momentum, many advertisers are planning to reduce their Facebook activity in the future.[25]

**Most popular social media (by millions of monthly users) as of January 2023**

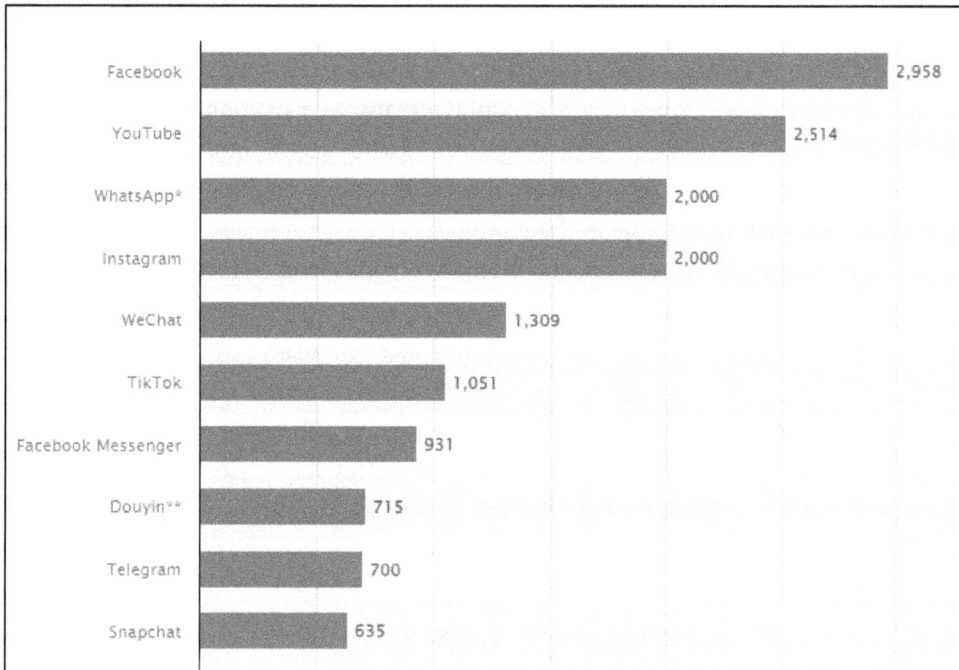

| Platform | Millions of monthly users |
|---|---|
| Facebook | 2,958 |
| YouTube | 2,514 |
| WhatsApp* | 2,000 |
| Instagram | 2,000 |
| WeChat | 1,309 |
| TikTok | 1,051 |
| Facebook Messenger | 931 |
| Douyin** | 715 |
| Telegram | 700 |
| Snapchat | 635 |

**Estimated % of marketers using different social media as of Jan. 202226**

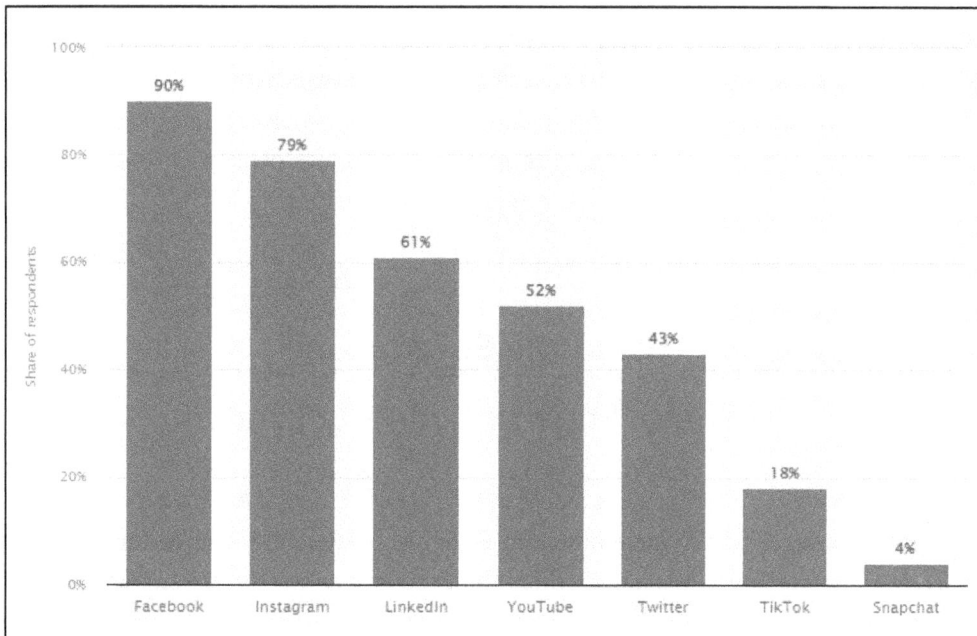

| Platform | Share of respondents |
|---|---|
| Facebook | 90% |
| Instagram | 79% |
| LinkedIn | 61% |
| YouTube | 52% |
| Twitter | 43% |
| TikTok | 18% |
| Snapchat | 4% |

"It doesn't really matter how many users any social network has. What really matters is how many people we are able to connect with in a relevant way. If 2.9 billion people are active on Facebook, but none of them have any interest in the stories we are telling (or if we you can't reach them efficiently), that social network is of little use to us. Our social media success isn't based on how many active users there are, but how many we can connect efficiently.

The point is this— we don't get caught up in the "who has the most active users" game. It's even more meaningless than our 'follower count.' Our social media presence is about serving your target audience, not everyone in the world."[27]

"We'll look in more detail at our Social Media Strategies later." (in a later Chapter)

*[Brian]*: "Where do you get the time to keep everything up to date and to regularly monitor our LinkedIn, Facebook, Twitter and other social media contacts?"

*[Linda]*: "That certainly is a challenge. Using LinkedIn, Facebook, Twitter and the other social media requires devoting considerable, consistent time and effort. We now need to monitor and update each site daily if we want to use them most effectively. Also, our updates need to be interesting and engaging for the potential customers following our postings. So now we need to have smart, engaging writers.

"It's no wonder so many businesses have started using LinkedIn, Facebook, Twitter and other social media -- beginning with initial burst of posts and enthusiasm, but then finding the time commitment so pressing that their activity soon dwindles and eventually stops altogether. In fact, that's the way we started a number of years ago, until we realized the importance of social media as a base for self-generated leads.

"At this realization, we decided to set up our own department to run it. Among many other responsibilities (more on this in a later chapter), our Social Media Department is charged with regularly (even daily) updating our LinkedIn, Facebook and Twitter pages and messages, consistently providing new postings, immediately following up on contacts, and answering any questions received. Their goal is to capture new SpeedyLane prospects and leads and to keep them engaged with follow-up contacts as our sales force attempts to advance the sale with each new prospect."

---

# Using the SpeedyLane
# LinkedIn Page to Generate Leads[28]

*[Brian]*: "Can you give me a specific example of how we use one of these media – say, LinkedIn?"

*[Linda]*: "Sure. Our SpeedyLane LinkedIn Page has been a great source for generating new leads. Here's how we use it. We have refined the Product and Services, Personal Contacts, and

Status Update sections of our SpeedyLane LinkedIn Page with the specific intent of generating solid new leads.[3]

## Showcase Pages & Updates

*[Linda]*: "Back 'in the day' LinkedIn used to offer subscribers a 'Products and Services' tab function. We used it to describe self-checkout system features as well as system operating and financial benefits. It also included a keyword-stuffed paragraph about the self-checkout solutions, designed to trigger hits from prospective customers exploring for information on self-checkout.

"With the products and services tab gone for a number of years now, we have been using LinkedIn 'Showcase Pages' and company updates to engage our audience and to reinforce our self-checkout physical product and supporting software and services array.

"Showcase Pages also let us personify SpeedyLane as a company by creating a specific page for members who want to follow different aspects of our business – like forthcoming product and software enhancements.

"Updates (more below) have always been important to us in developing and maintaining our relationships with our clients and followers and now even more so, since the product & services tab was dropped. Today, when our followers engage with our updates, it spreads our message to their networks and provides us with even greater exposure. Updates can be seen by our followers not just on our company page when someone looks at it, but also on the homepage of those that follow us, when we elect forwarding messages to them. [29]

"Our SpeedyLane product development, IT, and customer support teams have each developed specialty blogs, related white papers and YouTube videos to address frequently asked questions (FAQs) from prospective customers regarding self-checkout systems in general and our SpeedyLane brand in particular. The Product and Service section of our SpeedyLane LinkedIn page includes embedded links to all three of these information sources (blogs, white papers, and videos). Our compact videos on our LinkedIn page have proven to be especially popular with prospective customers and we have made it easy for them to indicate additional interest in SpeedyLane, each time providing a valuable new lead.

---

[3] LinkedIn offers the world's premier business network, with 722 million users (as of 2022). LinkedIn reports that 25% of all American adults use LinkedIn, with 22% of those use it every single day.[3] It is no wonder, therefore, why LinkedIn has such great potential as a marketing aid for virtually any company. For example, refer to LinkedIn's own (2023) detailed review of multiple (10) ways to use LinkedIn to aid in performing critical marketing functions such as generating leads, building brand awareness, and establishing strategic partnerships.[3][3]

"Our product and services tab also includes several Banner Ads. Each ad includes quick and easy access to specific contact information, which results in a regular flow of new leads. (Three Banner Ads are included free by LinkedIn).

## Personal Contact Information

*[Linda continues]:* "Our company's LinkedIn page also shows real SpeedyLane employees (with pictures and titles) whom prospective customers can contact for more information or to discuss the product. We typically include the names of some of our higher profile people with impressive titles, like Product Manager or Product Development Manager, to attract more interest. When someone clicks on one of those links, following an initial discussion with the SpeedyLane party contacted, this new contact often becomes a lead that is forwarded to our National Sales Management office and, eventually, to the appropriate regional sales manager.

## SpeedyLane Status Updates

"Our SpeedyLane LinkedIn page also includes a SpeedyLane 'Status Update' section that invites quick and easy access (links) to new Speedy-Lane blog posts, to new SpeedyLane white papers, to our regular Speedy- Lane webinar (that we offer to address especially perplexing issues holding prospects back from becoming active leads), and to important new third party articles and white papers. This Status Update section has become a gold mine for generating new SpeedyLane leads."

# More Traditional Prospecting with Probing Questions to Turn Would-be Cold Calls into Warm Calls

*[Linda concludes}:* "The 'Probing Questions' developed in the last chapter provide ideal content for converting would-be cold calls into invited warm calls using more traditional media – which is still an important part of most companies' lead generation strategy. These probing questions might be posed as in the ad -- see examples below -- which might appear in trade magazines, newspapers, or general magazines), or used in posters at trade shows, in headlines of direct mail or email campaigns, or in public relations releases about implementation successes. In each instance, the goal is to have target sponsors from our relevant segments initiate contact with us, which essentially opens the door for us to respond by contacting them."

====

## Examples: Using Probing Questions to Generate Leads for Self-Checkout Systems

**Long lines leaving your customers unsatisfied?**

*Speed up your checkout to keep even the most impatient customer happy.*

To check them out, check us out:

SpeedyLane

www.speedylane.com

WASTE OF SPACE

*SpeedyLane gives you more space for products without sacrificing the number of checkout lanes.*

To check them out, check us out:

SpeedyLane

www.speedylane.com

**Dealing with lots of mail?**

*Speed up your mail processing and avoid back-ups.*

To learn more, visit us at:

Xerox

www.xerox.com

**How do you process your mail?**

*Xerox Digital Mailroom offers you a fast and efficient way to process all your mail to save you time and money!*

To learn more, visit us at:

Xerox

www.xerox.com

**How have your employees adjusted to their new locations?**

*CORT's Turnkey Relocation Services will help make the transition smooth.*

www.cort.com/relocation
or call 1-888-360-2678

**How long does it take your relocated employees to find a new home?**

*CORT's Turnkey Relocation Services will help make the transition smooth.*

www.cort.com/relocation
or call 1-888-360-2678

CHAPTER 29

# Getting Attention & Interest, cont.
# More Tips on Prospecting

| Preparing to Convert the  Target Sponsor & Target Power Sponsor | | |
|---|---|---|
| Ch | 25 | How Much Does this Cost? |
| Ch | 26 | Getting Attention & Interest w. Reference Stories |
| Ch | 27 | Getting Attention & Interest w. Probing Questions |
| Ch | 28 | Turning Cold Calls into Warm Calls |
| **Ch** | **29** | **More Tips on Prospecting** |
| Ch | 30 | Prospecting with Social Media |
| Ch | 31 | Getting Attention & Interest w. Prepared Scripts |
| Ch | 32 | Big Growth Secret - Be Nice to Everyone! |

*L*inda: "This chapter gives us some additional tips on how to approach prospects, whether generated from cold calls or warm calls."

## Tips on Approaching Prospects - Whether Warm or Cold Calls[30]

### Importance of Having a Specific Value Proposition

*[Linda]:* "To interest prospects in our proposed solution, we must do whatever we can to avoid talking in generalities. We need to put some specific numbers (% or $s) on the promised benefits and improvements. We gather this data through carefully monitoring what we'll later call "key success factors", which capture and summarize the operating benefits of previous adoptions. Recall an example of specific benefits from an earlier example:"

## Important to include a specific $$ or % Projected Improvements

*[Linda]:* "Pioneer Markets adopted our SpeedyLane Self-Checkout System; thereby acquiring each capability needed, and began reaping immediate benefits including the following documented improvements:

- Average customer checkout time was reduced by 20%.
- Average number of cashiers reduced by 25% without reducing perceived customer service.
- Availability of checkout alternatives improved customer satisfaction and loyalty and reduced walkouts by 15%.
- Saved floor space and faster lines improved traffic flow and provided more space for impulse items and increased impulse revenues by 10%.
- Advanced checkout technology reduced profits lost due to cashier inaccuracies or theft by 12%.
- Less need for cashiers at registers enabled them to have 20% more employees on the floor to help customers, increasing customer satisfaction and store loyalty by 15%."

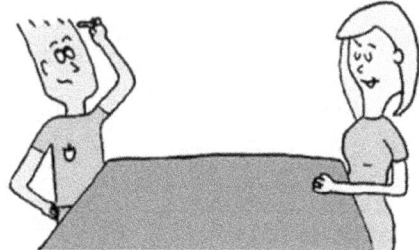

## Do Your Homework on the Target Customer Company

*[Linda]:* "Nothing will turn off a Target Sponsor more quickly than a salesperson's transparent ignorance of the sponsor's company. Our salesperson needs to carefully study the target customer before ever approaching anyone in that company. Despite having the information readily available on the Internet, many salespeople surprisingly ignore this advice. The successful salesperson will evidence in-depth familiarity with the target company by discussing current company news items, trends, promotions, and the like – all in addition to knowing about the target company's specific prospective benefits, should our solution ultimately be adopted."

## Specialize by Industry and by Target Sponsor

*[Linda]:* "Nothing will turn away more customers than a sales rep who is uninformed about a prospective customer's company and relevant challenges. Every industry is different. How companies in one industry might use and benefit from our proposed solution will often vary substantially from other industries. The variation among industries demands a specialization of our sales force by target segment (by industry in this case) and by the position of the relevant Target Sponsor. Very few Target Sponsors are willing to spend their valuable time talking with anyone not intimately familiar with their industry and well-aware of the specific operating

challenges related to the market solution in question. In the short term, this may dictate teaming with sales colleagues until the relevant salesperson is adequately familiar with the target industry and with the details of the specific operational challenges being faced by the Target Sponsor."

## Specialize by Industry and by Target Sponsor

*[Linda]:* "Nothing will turn away more customers than a sales rep who is uninformed about a prospective customer's company and relevant challenges. Every industry is different. How companies in one industry might use and benefit from our proposed solution will often vary substantially from other industries. The variation among industries demands a specialization of our sales force by target segment (by industry in this case) and by the position of the relevant Target Sponsor. Very few Target Sponsors are willing to spend their valuable time talking with sales representatives that are not intimately familiar with their industry or aware of specific operating challenges related to the market solution in question.

In the short term, this may dictate teaming with sales colleagues until the relevant salesperson is adequately familiar with the target industry and with the details of the specific operational challenges being faced by the Target Sponsor."

## Don't Waste Prospect's Time

*[Linda]:* "In selling to American companies, forget the small talk, unless it's initiated by the Target Sponsor. Managers are busy and often want to get right down to the business at hand. As you invade the Target Sponsor's typically tight schedule, respect the fact that time is incredibly precious to them. The Target Sponsor has a number of more important things to do than talking with a sales rep about an uncertain prospective new way solution. If a Target Sponsor wants to start the conversation with some small talk, leave it up to her or him. When selling to international companies, research the cultural values and manner guidelines. Each culture is different and respects unique types of interactions."

## Importance of Self-Discovery

*[Linda]:* "As mentioned earlier and emphasized numerous times throughout this SpeedyLane Selling Manual, people tend to believe what they conclude for themselves, especially when conversing with strangers. Therefore, the salesperson should spend more time asking than telling. To do this effectively, the salesperson must have in-depth knowledge of the target company in general and of the Target Sponsor's specific operating issues relating to the prospective solution. Beyond that, however, a skilled salesperson should have a list of carefully prepared questions (i.e., probing questions) and should be adept at posing such questions in an objective, non-accusatory, and non-threatening manner. This takes practice and is an important part of our SpeedyLane Sales Training Program."

## Have Thick Skin

*[Linda]:* "No one likes rejection, but our sales folks need to get used to it if they want to be successful over the long term. We must train our salespersons to be resilient. For even if we know that a particular company is in dire need of our solution and can significantly benefit from it, we may still be rejected for any of the reasons considered earlier (e.g., too much on the company's plate at the time, financial hard times, bad experience in the past, etc.). It's the sales manager's job to keep up the spirits of the sales force, especially when newer and younger salespersons may be experiencing outright rejection for the first time in their lives, let alone their business careers. A good mantra to ingrain in each salesperson is the "4 S's" – *Some Will, Some Won't, So What, Someone Else Is Waiting!*"

Don't Give Up! Someone Else Is Waiting!

---

## Don't Burn Bridges on the Way out the Door

"Cordial disengagement is always the best policy, even when you may be losing a long standing account. You never know when another opportunity with that same customer may arise. Furthermore, the maturity evidenced by cordial disengagement will be remembered and can lay the groundwork for easy future re-engagement with a lost client."

*Setting: Brian queries Linda about SpeedyLane's social marketing strategies.*

CHAPTER 30

# SpeedyLane's
# Social Marketing Strategies

| Preparing to Convert the Target Sponsor & Target Power Sponsor | | |
|---|---|---|
| Ch | 25 | How Much Does this Cost? |
| Ch | 26 | Getting Attention & Interest w. Reference Stories |
| Ch | 27 | Getting Attention & Interest w. Probing Questions |
| Ch | 28 | Turning Cold Calls into Warm Calls |
| Ch | 29 | More Tips on Prospecting |
| **Ch** | **30** | **Prospecting with Social Media** |
| Ch | 31 | Getting Attention & Interest w. Prepared Scripts |
| Ch | 32 | Big Growth Secret - Be Nice to Everyone! |

*Brian:* "Hey Linda, you mentioned social media earlier when we were talking about prospecting, lead generation, reference stories and contacts, help in surveying customers, and some other general topics. Could you please give me a little broader overview of our social media initiatives here at SpeedyLane?"

*[Linda]:* "Glad to, as that's really a hot topic in both our Marketing and Sales Departments. Let's look at the list of areas where we have started using social media to help our marketing and selling efforts. This list is from our Social Media Department. Then, if you'd like, I can give you a little history on how and why we've made such a commitment to using social media to build a whole social marketing program."

*[Brian]:* "Great! That would help me a lot."

**Estimated % of marketers using different social media as of Jan. 2022**[31]

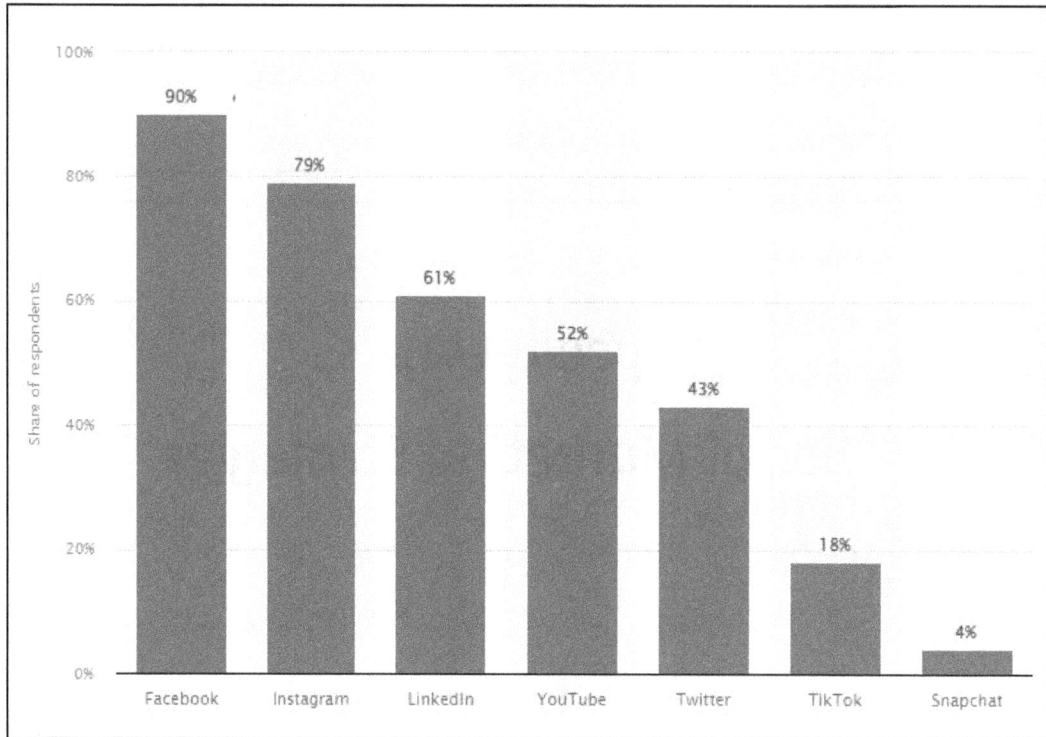

[Linda]: "Well, Bri, when our Social Media Department was established several years ago, they received a mandate from top management to build SpeedyLane's image as an industry leader in building, maintaining, and enhancing our market intelligence as well as our customer contacts and relations through social media. The goal was and still is to enhance the ways we listen to, engage with and build relationships with existing and potential customers.

"Here's a list the Social Media Department developed for our sales and marketing departments which summarizes the various ways we are now using social media to enhance our market intelligence and customer relationships."

## Some of the Many Ways SpeedyLane Uses Social Media to Enhance Market Intelligence and Customer Relationships

- Monitor Customers: We continually monitor the Internet to learn what specific concerns customer interest groups, blogs and white papers have about self-checkout systems in general and our brand in particular.

- Monitor Competitors: We also monitor and learn what self-checkout focused interest groups, blogs and white papers are saying about our primary brand competitors.
- Become Trusted Advisors: We at SpeedyLane established some interest groups of our own to position ourselves as a credible source of objective information, trying to position ourselves as trusted advisors regarding self-checkout systems and the specific functions of these systems.
- Getting Timely Suggestions for Further Improving Our Market Solution: We continually monitor the Internet in order to learn of specific new features or services our potential customers may want. This information is valuable to our product and technology developers and customer service department because they use the findings to guide product and service improvements.
- Online Surveys: We use low cost or even free online survey capabilities to monitor our customer community and to get quick and constructive answers to pressing questions. They also help us to engage our actual and potential customers in meaningful discussions to improve our SpeedyLane products and support services.
- Lead Generation: Social media helps us develop more and better leads through several vehicles, including:
  o Surveys, mentioned above, which can generate valuable, high quality leads for our sales team.
  o Aggressive use of our own knowledge-sharing blogs, which uncover hot leads because those consulting the blogs are focused on specific issues and are often already under pressure to solve a specific retail checkout related problem. Many of those consulting our blogs are ready prospects, who are already well into the self-checkout evaluation process.
- More Credible Reference Contacts and Stories: Our target customers are free at any time to read stories in our customer interest group discussions and industry blogs and contact these references themselves. This tends to be a more credible way for them to research results rather than having one of our sales folks steer them toward a specific reference contact (even though sales team-generated reference visits still remain a critical part of our selling process). We reference positive, objective remarks of our product on our website and in one or more of our specialty blogs as well.
- Responding to Critiques: Negative comments or critiques of SpeedyLane or self-checkout systems in general usually call for immediate action.
- Taking Corrective Actions. If a criticism of our SpeedyLane system is true and constructive, we will relay it immediately to product development, customer service, IT, or other relevant departments for their consideration. This may trigger corrective action, and these new initiatives may then receive prominent mention on our website and in one or more of our specialty blogs.

- Clarifying Misperceptions. If a criticism of SpeedyLane or self-checkout systems in general is negative, but inaccurate, then, we will become involved in the discussion in an attempt to set the record straight, while not getting defensive. Here we play the role of an educator in the discussion group, on our website, and perhaps in one or more of our specialty blogs.

===========

*[Brian]:* "That's a helpful summary of some of the uses you outlined earlier (in previous chapters). But as you anticipated, I could also use a little history on why and how we've made such a commitment to building our Social Marketing Program."

*[Linda]:* "I'm glad you are taking such an interest in our social marketing initiatives since it seems to be receiving more and more emphasis throughout the entire company.

"I should emphasize that I'm still learning about marketing with social media on the fly, as it were, but I'm more than willing to give you my perspective. While I'm no expert, I'm learning more each operating period, and you will have that same opportunity to learn. For example, we've been having at least one extended session on social media at each of our regional or national sales meetings for the last several years. In fact, you'll be attending a two-day training session on our social marketing program with our Social Marketing Managers, Kate Johnson and Chris Albertini, later this spring. They'll be bringing you, along with other new sales and marketing trainees, up to date on our rapidly evolving social marketing plans and strategies. It's really an exciting initiative for us and one that we are quite proud of."

*[Brian]:* "So when did this social marketing initiative start here at SpeedyLane? And who are these Social Marketing Managers, Kate Johnson and Chris Albertini?"

*[Linda]:* "We started emphasizing marketing with social media after a number of us attended a two-day Social Marketing Workshop back in 2007. At the time, our SpeedyLane website was about the extent of our social marketing strategy -- if you could even call it a 'strategy.' We ended up hiring two of the most effective presenters at the workshop – Kate Johnson and Chris Albertini, whom I mentioned earlier. Since that time, they have headed our Social Media Department and have worked tirelessly and effectively with both our marketing and sales groups to plan and implement our current broad-based social marketing efforts – some of which you saw in the table we just reviewed."

*[Brian]:* "What happened next? It sounds pretty innovative, proactive, and exciting."

## A Cooperative Effort between Sales and Marketing

*[Linda]:* "Well, as I said before, I'm no expert, but let me try to give you an overview of how social media developed here at SpeedyLane. First of all, it's been emphasized throughout SpeedyLane time and time again that this is a *cooperative effort of marketing and sales* – with each group supporting one another. Some companies think that creating initiatives in social marketing involves moving the selling effort up the channel to the marketing department, but we don't see it that way. We realize the importance of both groups working together in order to reach our mutual objective of consistent, profitable sales and revenue growth for SpeedyLane. For example, the Social Marketing Media group works with and reports to both our national VP of Sales & National Sales Manager - Catherine Russell- and to our VP and Director of Marketing - Todd Riley. They continually make known that a sound social marketing program, implemented aggressively and cooperatively by the two groups together, can really benefit our overall growth – and has certainly been doing so for us!"

## Why Participate in Social Media?

*[Brian]:* "I'm curious...Why did SpeedyLane first become interested in doing this?"

*[Linda]:* "That's an easy question. We found that our current customers and many of our prospective target customers talked more among themselves than with us. We wanted to get involved in the conversation to help inform the growing number of members of the various emerging social communities that focused on talking about the self-checkout process. In a nutshell, our desire to get involved in online discussions is what drew us toward the social media. The reason will be more evident as you become more familiar with some of the existing social communities and how SpeedyLane has become a part of them, including some communities we've started ourselves. It will likely take you some time to get familiar with this, but the Social Media Training Program will help you learn more."

## Importance of Establishing Ourselves as Trusted Experts in Self-Checkout Systems

*[Linda]:* "Before I get carried away describing more of our social marketing initiatives, I want to emphasize something that folks who are new to social marketing need to keep in mind, because it may initially sound counter intuitive. The point, however, is this: We do not try to sell using social media."

*[Brian]:* "Say what? Then why are spending all these valuable resources on our social marketing program?"

*[Linda]:* "We can't control what goes on in the discussions of the various social communities focused on self-checkout systems. These communities discuss a host of self-checkout related topics such as:

- Security of self-checkout systems;
- Accuracy of self-checkout readers;
- Integration of self-checkout data with a store's revenue, inventory, and warehouse databases;
- Self-checkout cashier training;
- Influence of self-checkout on store image;
- Customer challenges in learning how to use self-checkout;
- Using self-checkout for non-standard items (e.g., individual fruits & vegetables at a grocery store, or individual nuts and bolts at a hardware store);
- Down-time and related mechanical problems with self-checkout devices;
- And many other more related topics.

"We come in as 'unaffiliated' (i.e., no mention of SpeedyLane brand) experts to:

Provide immediate answers to specific, straight forward questions; and to refer (i.e., link) community members to studies, blogs, and white papers for more complex questions. Some of these studies, blogs and white papers may be our own, while others may be from more widely recognized industry sources."

*[Linda, continuing]:* "We always include the name of our (Speedy-Lane's) technical, marketing or other functional expert answering a question or authoring the study / blog / white paper and, as indirectly as possible, indicate their affiliation with SpeedyLane. However, we are extremely careful to stay away from 'pitching' our SpeedyLane brand."

*[Brian]:* "Why don't you pitch the brand? You're missing a golden opportunity to do so!"

*[Linda]:* "Community members are seeking objective information, not sales pitches. So, we try very hard to provide objective answers. In doing so, we attempt to position ourselves as a trusted source of information about self-checkout systems in general for our current and prospective customers. Believe me, if they think I am an expert and know that I'm associated with SpeedyLane, they will seek out me, and information on our SpeedyLane brand. When the prospective customer makes such an inquiry, it often results in starting a new buying cycle. That has proven much more effective than if we were to force feed or brag about our brand, while providing social media sourced 'supposedly objective' information.

"This leads to a couple of other points that our chief Social Marketing Managers, Kate and Chris, have emphasized time and time again with our sales and marketing departments and that I now want to emphasize to you."

## Social Media Helps SpeedyLane Build and Maintain the Best Overall Self-Checkout Solution Value in the Industry

*[Linda]:* "The first point is especially crucial. Our *'educational approach,' as opposed to a 'selling approach,'* will work for us *only if SpeedyLane does indeed offer the best overall solution value* for our target customers. Monitoring customer social communities can tell us what concerns they have with self-checkout in general and, perhaps, our brand in particular. This, in turn, can help us to ensure that we do indeed develop and maintain the best overall self-checkout solution."

## As Trusted Experts and Advisors, We Can Use Social Media to Influence What Self-Checkout Solution Dimensions Potential Customers Look For

*[Linda]*: "Before covering the second point, I need to stress again that we must truly believe that SpeedyLane does indeed offer the best overall solution value for our target customers. That said, we do not have to be superior to our primary direct competitors on every single dimension of self-checkout solution. With that warning in mind, I can *now move to the next point*. If we can become trusted advisors to target customers, we can influence what characteristics potential customers look for when evaluating alternative brands. Thus, we can essentially direct the evaluation process toward emphasizing self-checkout dimensions where we are clearly superior to our primary direct competitors."

-----------

*[Brian]:* "OK, I'm starting to understand why SpeedyLane is so actively involved with our social marketing program. But before you go on, I have a more fundamental question. So far you have only mentioned a few types of social media, like blogs and white papers. But what about Facebook, Twitter, Google, and all these other media sites that I am more familiar with? By chance, might you have a list of the different social media outlets SpeedyLane uses?"

*[Linda]:* "That's an expected question, Brian, and it's actually pretty funny, too."

*[Brian]:* "Why's that? Why is it a funny question?"

*[Linda]:* "Because when we all participated in that initial Social Marketing Workshop several years ago, it was about this time that Todd Riley, our VP of Marketing, asked the same question. Here's the answer that Kate and Chris flashed up on the screen."

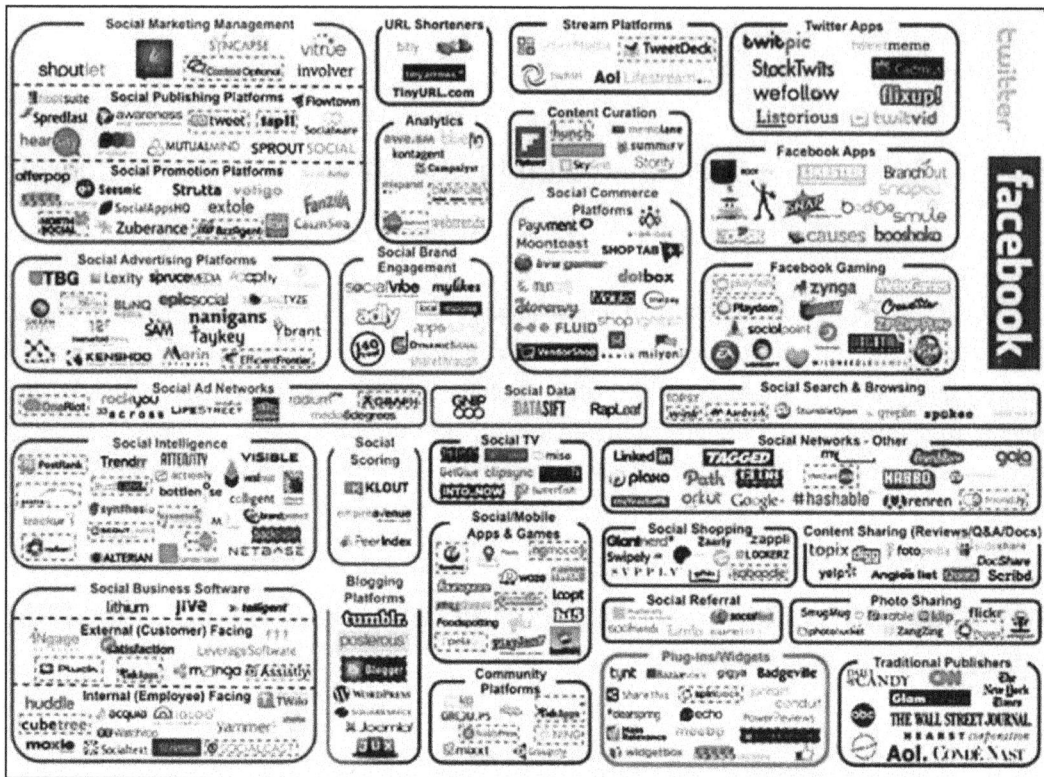

*[Brian]:* "Yikes!"

*[Linda]*: "Yikes, is right! And that was exactly the same reaction that most of us at the workshop had. The reason it's funny is because Todd told us that seeing this picture was the reason he decided to hire Kate and Chris to head our social marketing efforts. In a way, it's exactly what I was talking about earlier about remaining objective in the educational role. Kate and Chris weren't looking to get hired by SpeedyLane. However, by displaying this complex, informational, educational, factual diagram and then discussing some of the key pieces with us, we were immediately impressed by their expertise and credibility in this area.

"By the way, I'm not going to discuss it all with you for two reasons. First, I don't understand half of it myself; and secondly, we only actually depend on a relatively small subset of these social media tools for our own social marketing program."

*[Brian]:* "Before you continue, with so many social platforms and so many people talking about self-checkout and even SpeedyLane, how does our Social Media Department possibly keep track of it all?"

## Market Intelligence with a Social Media Dashboard

*[Linda]:* "Search engines such as Google offer our buyers access to entire communities of other buyers, such as customer interest groups, which make the buying process much more transparent. They also offer sellers, such as SpeedyLane, a vehicle for listening to and influencing what prospective buyers say about our brand at different stages of the buying process.

*[Brian]:* "But I don't think I see Twitter or Facebook links included when I use Google or other search engines. Don't we also want to monitor what's being said on these social networks?"

*[Linda]:* "That's very observant and important, Bri. You are right. Searching Google for our SpeedyLane brand name is just a start, but Google and other search engines index very little of what is being said on Twitter and other social networks. This is one of the reasons our Social Media folks have used Google Reader to set up our SpeedyLane Social Media Dashboard (similar dashboard services are available using My Yahoo, Pageflakes, and iGoogle). Each time we refresh our SpeedyLane dashboard, the latest search results are displayed. This enables us to catch almost any searches regarding self-checkout systems in general, our SpeedyLane brand, our competitors, target segments, current customers, and competitors as well. Google dropped Google Reader in mid-2013, but I am sure our Social Media Department came up with a suitable alternative.[32] I heard them talking about 'The Old Reader' and 'Flipboard,' for example, but I am not sure what they settled on. This is yet another example of how fast moving this whole area of social media is today.

"Our dashboard even goes beyond that, by allowing monitoring and indexing via indefinitely lasting RSS feeds. Our dashboard also allows us to monitor especially influential authors and journalists." (If you want to know more about these RSS Feeds, see this simple explanation on YouTube -- www.youtube.com/watch?v=0klgLsSxGsU.)

*[Brian]:* "You mean our dashboard also covers all of the information and discussions on blogs, Twitter, Facebook, and LinkedIn?"

*[Linda]:* "Hold on, I wasn't done. Yes, our dashboard does also monitor blogs, Twitter, Facebook, and LinkedIn and other niches, such as special interest social networks. But it doesn't stop there. It even covers Wikipedia, discussion forums, social book-marketing sites, and a variety of other sites as well.

"For example, the dashboard monitors Twitter content about the needs and frustrations of potential customers by looking for such terms as 'does anyone know ...?' pertaining to self-checkout in general or our SpeedyLane brand. Our SpeedyLane Social Marketing Manual also mentions aggregating potential opportunities through Twitter 'hashtags,' although I'm not exactly sure how that works. You can ask Kate or Chris about that when you attend their workshop.

"I also know that most of our sales team members, including me, use LinkedIn to find the names and contact information of the key decision-makers (including specific Target Sponsors and Target Power Sponsors) and others who are in need of visions in specific target customer companies. It's a really great tool, because many companies restrict public information on specific decision-makers. LinkedIn circumvents that by looking at companies from the 'bottom up,' so we can often find out who the decision-makers are in various departments. We also use LinkedIn company profiles to find people with connections to our own network, which often serves as a starting place for research to uncover new leads. Once we get a relevant contact – such as a target sponsor in a specific company, we can view that person's interest groups and lay the groundwork for more directed initial contacts.

-----------------

*[Linda]:* "Let's leave it at that for now, Brian, and wait until after you go through the social marketing training session with Kate and Chris to discuss more. In fact, I'll most likely be attending it myself, since I like to stay up to date on all the new opportunities available through social media."

---

## Appendix to Chapter

**The information in this Appendix is sourced directly from Dustin Stout website at:**
### https://dustinstout.com/social-media-statistics/

## Supplementary, More Detailed Information on Various Social Media Networks[33]

## Facebook Statistics

Facebook was founded by Mark Zuckerberg and launched in 2004. During creation, Facebook was only limited to Harvard students but was later available to everyone above 13 years old as long as you had a valid email address.

Now, after 15 years of existence, Facebook has become, by far, the largest social network in the world.

It has also become the most important social media site for marketers despite declining organic reach. Facebook marketing takes up a significant amount of digital ad spend in 2020.

And when it comes to social media statistics, Facebook tends to be the standard that all other networks are now compared to.

Here are some of the most current Facebook statistics (2020 source):

- As of June 2019, Facebook reports an estimated **2.4 billion Monthly Active Users**.
- Facebook also says it has **1.6 billion Daily Active Users**.
- 88% of Facebook's user activity is from a mobile device.
- The average amount of time a user spends on Facebook every day is 58 minutes.
- There are over 300 million photos uploaded to Facebook every day.
- On average, 5 Facebook accounts are created every second.
- Approximately 30% of Facebook users are aged between 25 and 34 years.
- Facebook video is still in high demand with approximately **8 billion video views per day**.

## YouTube Statistics

YouTube was created by Steve Chen, Chad Hurley and Jawed Karim (former PayPal employees) in 2005. Behind Google and Facebook, YouTube is considered the 3rd most popular website worldwide.

- Currently YouTube has more than **1.9 billion logged-in visits every month**.
- **149 million people** log in to YouTube daily.
- The average duration of a YouTube visit is **40 minutes**.
- Viewers are spending an average of 1 hour per day watching YouTube videos.
- On average, **300 hours of video are uploaded every minute** on YouTube.
- There are over **5 billion video views each day**.

## WhatsApp Statistics

WhatsApp is an instant messaging application for smartphones that comes with an end to end encryption. It was founded by Jan Koum and Brian Acton in 2009 and later bought by Facebook in 2014.

While some may mistakenly leave it out of the social media statistics studies, it's absolutely one of the social networking titans, IMO.

In the 10 years since its inception, it has achieved the following stats:

- WhatsApp is estimated to have approximately **1.5 billion monthly active users**.
- There are now over **1 billion daily active users on WhatsApp**.
- On average, 1 million people register on WhatsApp daily.
- Approximately 60 billion texts daily are sent.

## Instagram Statistics

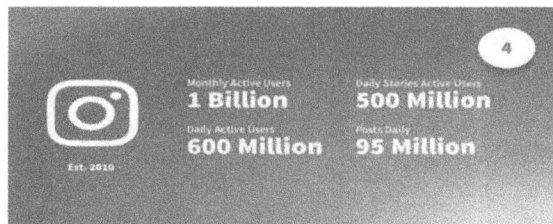

Instagram was created by Mike Krieger and Kevin Systrom in 2010. It was mainly meant to enable sharing of pictures and videos, both publicly and privately. It had been since acquired by Facebook in 2012.

After 9 years of its existence, take a look at some of these fascinating Instagram statistics:

- Instagram has over **1 billion monthly active users**.
- There are more than **600 million daily active users**.

- There are now **500 million daily Stories users.**
- Since its creation, more than **40 billion photos have been shared.**
- On average, **95 million photos are uploaded daily** on Instagram.
- There are approximately **4.2 billion likes per day.**
- Most Instagram users are between 18 to 29 years of age with **32% of Instagram users being college students.**

Some of these statistics were found on the Instagram Press page while others were found through third-party demographic research.

**Bonus:** Are you creating Instagram content? Make sure you grab my free Instagram Image Templates.

## Twitter Statistics

Twitter was founded by Jack Dorsey, Biz Stone and Evan Williams in March of 2006. It was an experiment that quickly became a messaging addiction for many.

It's one of my personal favorite social networks. And, if you know how to use Twitter right, it can be a big contributor to your social media success.

What started as a simple way to post status updates via text message has become one of the most popular go-to sources for what's happening in the world in real time. In Twitter's own words: *[Twitter is] what's happening in the world and what people are talking about right now.*

In its 13 years of existence, here are some of the noteworthy Twitter statistics:

- Nowadays Twitter has more than **330 million monthly active users.**
- There are **134 million daily active users** or at least that's how many "monetizable" daily active users (mDAU) according to Twitter.
- Of their monthly active users, **68 million MAU are form the United States.**
- The number of **mDAU from the US is 26 million.**
- Close to **460,000 new twitter accounts are registered every day.**
- Twitter users are posting **140 million tweets daily** which adds up to a billion tweets in a week.
- Each twitter user has on average 208 followers.
- 550 million accounts are reported to have at least sent a tweet.

I have dug through countless (and insanely boring) earnings reports to find these stats. Most recently the Twitter Q1 2019 Earnings Report was what informed most of the above data.

Now, even though Twitter is actually tied (so far as we know) with Reddit for Monthly Active Users, I've decided that Twitter should take the higher spot on the list because of mainstream adoption. I'd love to see some Daily Active User stats for Reddit though to see if they pull past Twitter.

## Reddit Statistics

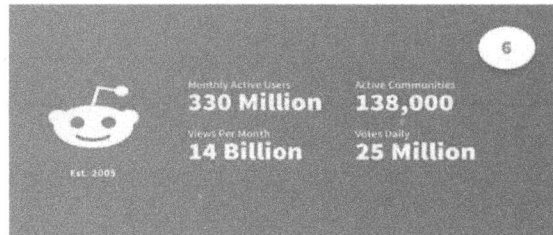

Reddit is a discussion and web content rating website. It was founded by Alexis Ohanian and Steve Huffman from the University of Virginia in 2005.

And while it isn't receiving anywhere near as much press buzz, it is a thriving and vibrant community of people. Many of them total trolls, but hey, trolls are people too.

It's also been known to completely tank websites by sending enormous, and unsustainable amounts of web traffic when things hit the front page. So, be sure to use it for your own blog posts with caution.

In the 14 years it's been around, it has accomplished the following:

- Reddit has approximately **330 million monthly active users**.
- It's estimated that Reddit gets over **14 billion views per month**.
- There have been more than 853,000 subreddits.
- It has more than **138,000 active communities**.
- On average, there are **25 million votes on Reddit daily**.
- The average time length of reddit visit is 13 minutes.

A lot of these statistics can be found if you search through their advertiser or press pages.

## LinkedIn[4] Statistics

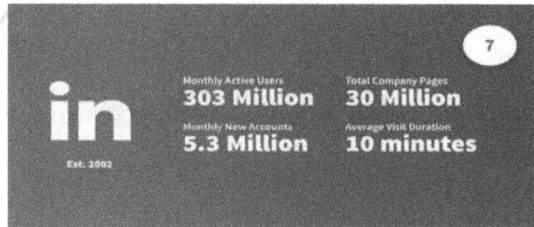

LinkedIn is a professional networking service that was founded in 2002 but later launched in 2003.

It is officially the oldest social network on this list.

And although it is the oldest, it's definitely struggled to grow its user base over the years. This is mostly due to the professional nature of the network.

It started as a place to simply keep your resume updated and didn't really turn into a full-on social network until Facebook was well into its prime.

Since launching 16 years ago, it can boast the following user stats:

- LinkedIn has over **560 million registered users**.
- It is estimated that LinkedIn has approximately **303 million monthly active users**.
- **5.3 million new accounts per month** are created on LinkedIn.
- There are over **30 million company pages**.
- The average visit duration is about **10 minutes**.
- Of all the users, 57% are male whereas 43% of the users are females.

LinkedIn has always been a bit cryptic in releasing usage statistics, but a few of the above points can be found on their About page.

---

4 LinkedIn offers the world's premier business network, with 722 million users (as of 2022). LinkedIn reports that 25% of all American adults use LinkedIn, with 22% of those use it every single day. It is no wonder, therefore, why LinkedIn has such great potential as a marketing aid for virtually any company. For example, refer to LinkedIn's own (2023) detailed review of multiple (10) ways to use LinkedIn to aid in performing critical marketing functions such as generating leads, building brand awareness, and establishing strategic partnerships. https://business.linkedin.com/marketing-solutions/how-to-market-on-linkedin, https://blog.hootsuite.com/linkedin-for-business/#3_important_LinkedIn_marketing_tips

## Snapchat Statistics

| Monthly Active Users | Daily Video Views |
|---|---|
| **301 Million** | **10 Billion** |
| Daily Active Users | Daily Snaps |
| **109 Million** | **3 Billion** |

Est. 2011

Snapchat is a multimedia mobile application which was created by Bobby Murphy, Evan Spiegel and Reggie Brown in 2011.

It started as a private messaging app that gave users the ability to create "snaps" or messages that would self-destruct (be automatically deleted) after being viewed. Unlike all the other social media apps and networks in which you had to manually delete posts you've shared.

For many, this was empowering because they didn't have to worry about sending something that they'd regret years down the road.

For others, it just seemed like a breeding ground for sexting and "unscrupulous" behavior that people wanted to hide.

When Snap, Inc. became a publicly traded company, it decided to evolve into calling itself a "camera company." Very few people understand that decision.

In that short 8 years, here's what the mobile messaging app has accomplished by way of user stats:

- Snapchat has approximately **301 million monthly active users**.
- Snapchat also reports **109 million daily active users** (a downward trend).
- Of those daily active users, **77 million** are from the United States.
- 60% of these snapchat users are aged between 18 and 34 years.
- Snapchat is competing closely with its rival, Facebook, by reporting more than **10 billion video views daily**.
- Approximately **3 billion snaps are created every day**.
- Snapchat users aged 25 years and above spend an average of 20 minutes on snapchat daily while those below 25 years spend on average 30 minutes.
- It's estimated that it would take you more than 950 years to watch all snaps made in a day.

Most of the data was found digging through Snap Inc. quarterly earnings reports. I wouldn't recommend it–unless you're literally reading everything else there is to be read on the internet first.

## Pinterest Statistics

Pinterest is a mobile application that enables you to find information on the World Wide Web. It was founded by Evan Sharp, Ben Silbermann and Paul Sciarra in 2010.

And Pinterest will be the first to tell you that it is not a social media platform. However, 99% of the people consider it one. Sorry, Pinterest.

It took some time for Pinterest to get on the social media marketing map, but it eventually showed itself to be a very powerful traffic driver.

And although it took Peg Fitzpatrick a couple years to get me on Pinterest, once I finally took her advice, I was a firm believer in the power of the platform. While it may not have the highest number of active users, the website traffic potential is through the roof.

While it developed a strong reputation for being mostly used by women, men have begun flocking to the network, probably thanks to Jeff Sieh at Manly Pinterest Tips.

In its 9 years, it has achieved the following milestones:

- Pinterest has **291 million monthly active users.**
- **70 million** of its active users are from the United States.
- The average Pinterest user visit lasts **14 minutes.**
- The total number of Pinterest pins is more than **175 billion.**
- The total number of Pinterest boards are approximately **1 billion.**
- In a day, Pinterest is visited by 2 million users who save shopping pins on their boards.

Some of these stats were found on the official Pinterest Blog while others had to be sourced through third-party data studies. And now since Pinterest is a publicly traded company, they also have quarterly earnings reports that anyone can view.

## Tumblr Statistics

This is a micro-blogging and social networking website which was launched in 2007 by David Carp.

You won't typically see Tumblr included in social media statistics because many people may think of it as a "blogging" platform. However, I believe it absolutely fits into the realm of social networks and should be counted among the top social media sites.

It's gone through a lot of evolutions, acquisitions, and changes, but it has stuck around for a long time. It's also developed a unique culture of users.

In its 12 years, it has accomplished the following user milestones:

- Tumblr has a total of over **452 million blogs.**
- There are approximately **371 million monthly visits.**
- Tumblr has more than **166 billion published posts.**
- There are approximately **7.2 million new blogs created each month.**
- Approximately 46% of Tumblr visitors are aged between 18 and 34 years.
- Of all the visitors, 52% are male and 48% female.

Of all the listed sites, Tumblr seems to be the most transparent as this data was pretty easy to get.

**Bonus Reading:** Check out list of the best Social Media Tools for professional social media marketers.

Other Social Networks

This section contains social networks that were previously a part of the primary list. I wanted to preserve these for historical purposes even though they no longer are included in the primary list.

## Google+ Statistics

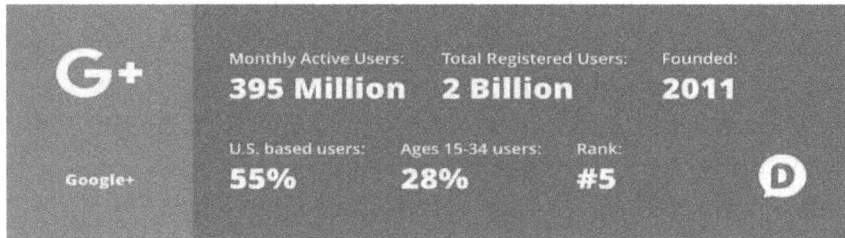

| | Monthly Active Users: | Total Registered Users: | Founded: |
|---|---|---|---|
| **G+** | **395 Million** | **2 Billion** | **2011** |
| | U.S. based users: | Ages 15-34 users: | Rank: |
| Google+ | **55%** | **28%** | **#5** |

Google plus is a social network owned by Google. It was launched in 2011 and was meant to be a social layer across all of Google's products. The purpose and objective of the social network has changed a lot over the years, and in early 2019 was officially sunset.

In its eight years of existence, it had accomplished some interesting milestones:

- At its high point, there were approximately **395 million monthly active users** on Google+.
- Google+ was estimated to have over **2 billion registered users** world-wide.
- 28% of Google plus users were aged between 15 and 34 years.
- United States alone made up 55% of all the users.
- 73.7% of the users were male while 26.3% were female.
- It is estimated that on average, a Google+ user will spend 3 minutes and 46 seconds per visit.

Some of this info was gained through reading the official Google Blog (before they got rid of the Google+ blog) as well as many other third-party research and data studies.

Unfortunately, it seems Google was in no way interested in the social media statistics game and has kept much of its data private.

## Periscope Statistics

| | Monthly Live-streams: | Daily Active Users: | Founded: |
|---|---|---|---|
| | **9.3 Million** | **1.9 Million** | **2015** |
| | Total Registered Users: | Daily streamed video: | Rank: |
| Periscope | **10 Million** | **350k hrs.** | **#12** |

Periscope is a live video streaming app that was created by Joe Bernstein and Kayvon Beykpour and before even launching was bought by Twitter in 2015.

It quickly dwarfed its predecessor, Meerkat, and became very popular among live-streaming apps. I even tried it for a while and came up with a handful of Periscope pro tips that you might want to check out.

In its short 3 years after launch Periscope has accomplished the following milestones:

- There are over **9.3 million live streams monthly** on Periscope.
- Periscope has over **10 million registered users.**
- Daily active users are approximately **1.9 million.**
- The number of active users on Periscope using android is 1.2 million.
- There have been 200 million broadcasts on periscope to date.
- On average, **350,000 hours of videos are streamed every day.**

Twitter doesn't reveal many of Periscope's usage stats, but you can dig through their quarterly reports and get some interesting info.

CHAPTER 31

# Getting Attention & Interest
# with Prepared Scripts

| Preparing to Convert the Target Sponsor & Target Power Sponsor | | |
|---|---|---|
| Ch | 25 | How Much Does this Cost? |
| Ch | 26 | Getting Attention & Interest w. Reference Stories |
| Ch | 27 | Getting Attention & Interest w. Probing Questions |
| Ch | 28 | Turning Cold Calls into Warm Calls |
| Ch | 29 | More Tips on Prospecting |
| Ch | 30 | Prospecting with Social Media |
| **Ch** | **31** | **Getting Attention & Interest w. Prepared Scripts** |
| Ch | 32 | Big Growth Secret - Be Nice to Everyone! |

*[L inda]:* "This chapter in the Account Marketing Manual discusses the development and role of *Prepared Scripts*[34] for both cold & warm calls. Let's review it together."

## Are Face-to-Face Communications Still Important?

*[Linda]:* "New communication methods such as texting, email and video conferencing are rapidly replacing face-to-face business communication. College students today much prefer these new communication vehicles over face-to-face gatherings. It comes as no surprise, therefore, that most students send more than 50 text messages per day. As these young adults move into the workplace, they'll be more comfortable with new technology than previous generations.

## Scripts for Warm Calls and Cold Calls Constitute the Final Pieces of the Growth Plan Puzzle

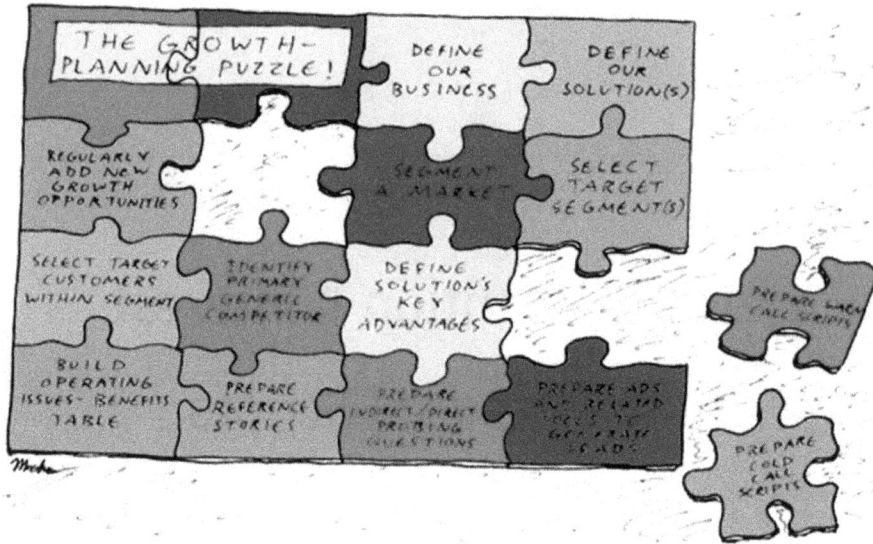

## Keep the Goal in Mind – To Arrange a Face to Face Meeting with the Target Sponsor

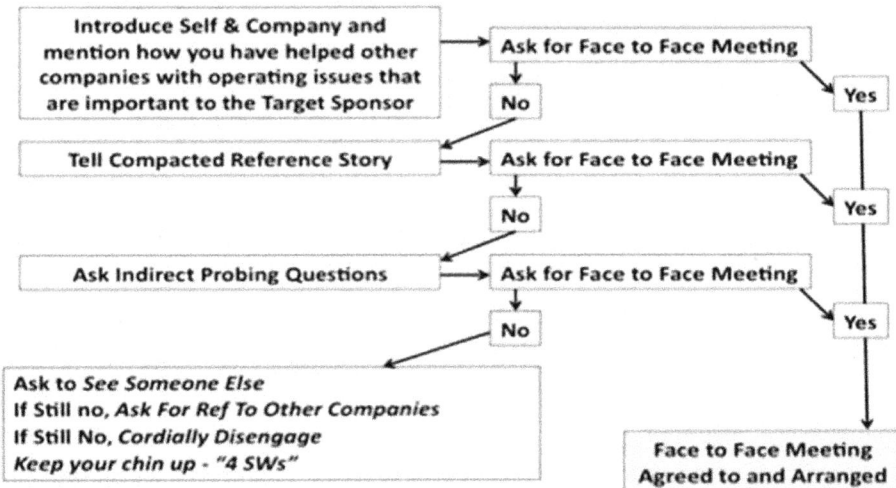

"In this rapidly changing communications environment, are face-to-face communications still important? You bet. In fact, eight out of ten executives today feel that face-to-face communication is still essential for business and actually prefer face-to-face meetings over technology-enabled meetings such as videoconferencing.[35] They believe that face-to-face meetings are critical for building stronger and more meaningful business relationships and allow for better social opportunities to bond with target clients. It is also easier to read body language and facial expressions and to interpret nonverbal communication signals when interacting in person. The consensus is that face-to-face communication is better for persuasion, engagement, inspiration, accountability, candor, focus and reaching decisions. That's quite a list and it suggests that face-to-face get togethers will continue to play a crucial role in many different selling scenarios.

"All that said, for straight forward repeat purchases, face-to-face gatherings may or may not be important. The importance of these face-to-face meetings depends on the cost of the solution, the history and strength of the seller-buyer personal relationship involved, and the intensity of competition for the relevant prospective sale. For example, face-to-face meetings are seldom necessary when selling incidental, low cost solutions that are of relatively small importance to the target customer. In fact, given the ease of buying electronically nowadays and the busy schedules of our prospects, it may be counter-productive for our sales team to always strive for face-to-face meetings.

"On the other hand, for more expensive solutions and/or solutions that could be 'game-changing' for our target customer, important new visions need to be built with key players in the target customer's organization. In such instances, the best way to build such visions is through face-to-face interactions, for all the reasons mentioned above.

---

## The Goal of Our Warm or Cold Call to the Target Sponsor is to Set up a Face-to-Face Meeting

*[Linda]:* "We are not trying to 'sell' when we first contact the Target Sponsor. Getting a target customer to commit to a significant change will take a great deal more time and effort than a simple initial sales call.

"So, what is our immediate goal in making the initial warm or cold call to the Target Sponsor in a more complex selling scenario? Simple -- our goal is to get the Target Sponsor interested enough to be willing to meet in person for a continued discussion. It is only through a face-to-face-meeting that we can hope to convince the Target Sponsor of the breadth of benefits our solution provides and its ability to alleviate the Target Sponsor's daily worries and pains.

"[In the event that the initial warm or cold call is an office visit, where we have already achieved our goal of meeting Face-to-Face, then the goal will be to get the Target Sponsor to admit "pain" – that is, that he or she is facing one or more operating problems that our market solution is equipped to resolve. Later on, we'll talk more about 'getting pain admitted.']"

---

## The What & Why of Prepared Scripts

*[Linda]:* "A script is a prepared statement for introducing ourselves, our company, and our solution to a Target Sponsor. The purpose of using a prepared, rehearsed script is to provide our sales folks with a template for starting a fruitful conversation with the Target Sponsor. A well-designed script, delivered in a confident, 'natural' manner, improves the salesperson's chances of capturing the attention and building the interest of the Target Sponsor.

"Prepared scripts are particularly useful for sales training, and for newer, less-seasoned sales professionals. However, a veteran salesperson may find a reminder useful, for example, when checking a planned script just prior to making sales calls in order to quickly review important talking points.

"Having a script in hand can enable both new and veteran sales professionals alike to focus on informal, personal and effective delivery, while still not missing anything important in an initial contact with a Target Sponsor.

"The confidence instilled by having a well-designed and well-practiced script in hand can help a salesperson - particularly the newer, younger salesperson to persevere after each failed call. Following each sales call, a well-prepared script and practiced, informal, natural delivery should leave a salesperson with the feeling that, "Hey, I took my best shot," regardless of whether or not the sales call was successful.

---

## Think of This Warm / Cold Call Process as a Flow Chart

*[Linda]:* "To better understand, plan, and keep track of this overall initial contact with the Target Sponsor, think of it in the context of a flow chart, as in the exhibit.

## Keep the Goal in Mind – To Arrange a Face to Face Meeting with the Target Sponsor

**Use Flow Chart of Alternatives to Try to Arrange for 1st Face to Face Meeting with Target Sponsor**

Introduce Self & Company and mention how you have helped other companies with operating issues that are important to the Target Sponsor → Ask for Face to Face Meeting → No / Yes

Tell Compacted Reference Story → Ask for Face to Face Meeting → No / Yes

Ask Indirect Probing Questions → Ask for Face to Face Meeting → No / Yes

Ask to *See Someone Else*
If Still no, *Ask For Ref To Other Companies*
If Still No, *Cordially Disengage*
*Keep your chin up - "4 SWs"*

**Face to Face Meeting Agreed to and Arranged**

---

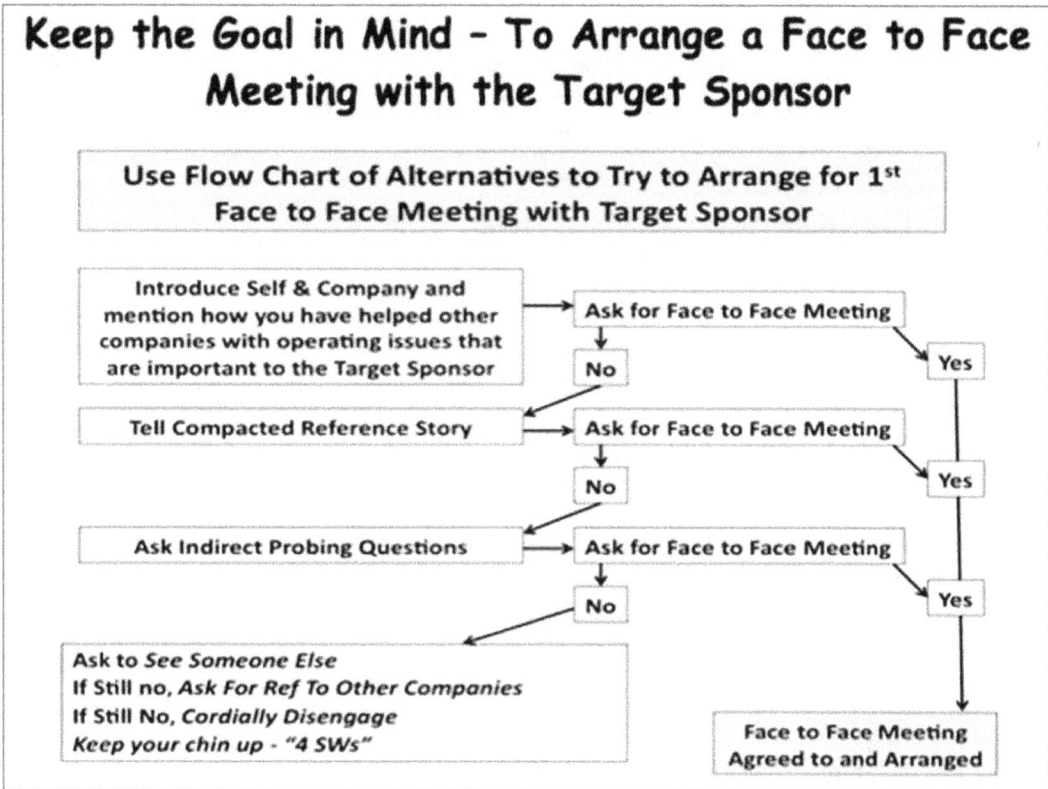

## Warm & Cold Call Scripts: Example

*[Linda]:* "Let's look at an example of a set of warm and cold call scripts and their various components.

---

## Warm Call Intro

Here, we start with a specific lead. We will assume this is a follow-up phone call to a contact made earlier with the Target Sponsor.

- *"Hi, my name is Linda Brown, from SpeedyLane Self-checkout.*
- *We met at the XYZ Trade Show last week in Boston.*
- *Or we received a postcard / e-mail / etc. from you seeking more information about our services.*
- *Have I reached you at a bad time?*
- *(Wait for an answer. If yes, find a more convenient time to call back. If no, continue.)*

- *We have been working with checkout solutions for the past 10 years. Other Efficiency Managers we have talked to are mainly concerned with a lack of efficiency and retail customer satisfaction during the customer checkout process. With our solution, we have been able to help our customers address this issue. Would you like to know how?"*

(Wait for confirmation. If enthused immediately, <u>Set up First Face-to-Face Meeting</u>. If not, continue on to the compacted reference story below.)

*(Tell compacted reference story)* – EXHIBIT BELOW

---

## Cold Call Intro

In this case, we start without any specific lead.

- *"Hi, my name is Linda Brown, and I'm from SpeedyLane Self-checkout. You and I haven't spoken before, but, here at SpeedyLane, we have been working with checkout solutions for more than 10 years.*
- *The main concern we are hearing from other Efficiency Managers is a lack of efficiency and retail customer satisfaction during the customer checkout process. With our solution, we have been able to help our customers address this issue. Would you like to know how?*

(Wait for confirmation. If enthused immediately, <u>Set up First Face-to-Face Meeting</u>. If not, continue on to the compacted reference story below.)

(Tell compacted reference story) – EXAMPLE BELOW

---

## Share Our Planned Compact Reference Story

Here is an ***example of a compact reference story*** – assuming we have not yet succeeded in scheduling a face-to-face meeting.

### Example of Compact Reference Story

*"A particular story that might interest you is that of Pioneer Markets. Their Director of In-Store Efficiency told us that she was bothered by <u>the company's inefficient checkout system and related customer dissatisfaction</u>.*

*She said that she was particularly concerned about her stores' long checkout lines and the high number of cashiers needed to keep checkout times reasonable.*

*Her company, Pioneer Markets, ultimately adopted our solution and improved average customer checkout time by 20% and reduced its number of cashiers by 25% without negatively impacting customer service.*

*Would you like to hear more about how we were able to do this?"*

<u>**Next**</u> – Push the ball over to the Target Sponsor's Court

*"Would you like to hear more about this?"* or *"Are you curious to know how we helped them accomplish that turnaround?"*

If yes, <u>set up First Face-to-Face Meeting. RECALL, THIS IS OUR GOAL IN WARM/COLD CALLS.</u>

*"Well, what I'd like to do is stop by:*

- *To introduce myself and my company;*
- *To talk with you about your specific situation; and*
- *To see if we might be able to help you address any checkout efficiency issues you may be facing."*

*"Is there a day and time that would be convenient for you?"*

Or *"I'll be in town tomorrow afternoon. Would there be a convenient time for you to meet with me?"*

**If No**, consider asking one or more of our *Indirect Probing Questions,* until you've triggered enough interest to convince the Target Sponsor to meet Face-to-Face with you.

**If interest is triggered**, suggest that we have helped other firms with other specific issues by relaying another custom reference story. Then, loop back to ask, "Would you like to hear more about how we have helped XYZ Company?"

**If Yes**, set *up a Face-to-Face Meeting* (as outlined above).

---

## What if the Warm or Cold Call Fails?

What if the Target Sponsor does not agree to meet Face-to-Face?

**If No,** ask to *See Someone Else*: "Is there anyone else in the company with whom I might speak? Possibly someone for whom these issues might be more relevant?" Remember, you should have previously identified a potential 'secondary' target sponsor.

**If Still No**, *Ask for a Reference to Other Companies / Contacts:* "Are you aware of any other companies who might be facing the issues we talked about?" You will lose nothing by asking this question.

**If Yes**, ask for contact information and permission to use this person as a reference name to help 'get a foot in the door.'

---

After that, whether or not the Target Sponsor provides a reference to another company, *Cordially Disengage*. Remember, don't burn bridges!

"Well, thank you for your time. It has been very nice talking with you. Here's my card (and/or, I'll send you my e-mail address). Please keep us in mind, should these issues become more important to you. Thanks again for speaking with me."

---

## Keep your chin up – remember the "4 SWs"

### "Some will, some won't, so what, someone else is waiting!

*[Brian]:* "I can see how that step-by-step approach could really help me out, preventing me from giving up when my first strategy isn't successful."

*[Linda]:* "That's right, young grasshopper! You know, there are a lot of times in life when a step-by-step approach can be a good idea. For instance, most men replace their mom with a girlfriend at some point in their life. Maybe you should give it a try."

*[Brian]:* "I don't know, Linda, I would have to ask my Mom first."

CHAPTER 32

---

# Big Growth Secret -
# Be Nice to Everyone!

| Preparing to Convert the Target Sponsor & Target Power Sponsor | | |
|---|---|---|
| Ch | 25 | How Much Does this Cost? |
| Ch | 26 | Getting Attention & Interest w. Reference Stories |
| Ch | 27 | Getting Attention & Interest w. Probing Questions |
| Ch | 28 | Turning Cold Calls into Warm Calls |
| Ch | 29 | More Tips on Prospecting |
| Ch | 30 | Prospecting with Social Media |
| Ch | 31 | Getting Attention & Interest w. Prepared Scripts |
| **Ch** | **32** | **Big Growth Secret - Be Nice to Everyone!** |

*Linda:* "My seven little nieces and nephews, ages 3-10, love to go turtle hunting in the channel near Grandma and Grandpa's home. They are pretty clever kids who, with a bit of luck, nearly always manage to catch a couple of the little critters whenever they set off on one of their great turtle expeditions. They bring a couple of the captured turtles home, name each of them (of course), play with them for a couple hours, and then release them back into the wild down at the creek. It's quite a riot for everyone, including the friendly neighbors who always crowd around to take part in the children's excitement and to see the 'big catch' of the day.

"Given this regular fun activity, last year, the kids started their own club, which they appropriately dubbed the "Turtle Club." My precocious nine-year-old niece wrote the charter for the club, and together all seven came up with the only three rules for membership, displayed prominently in both the charter and on the membership card below."

Turtle Club Executives at Grandma and Grandpa's House at the Lake

"It's easy to have fun. If you have a good imagination, it's easy to think about turtles from time to time as well. But what about the third rule – '***Being nice to everyone***?' Not so easy. Yet even these inexperienced loveable youngsters know how important it is to follow that rule.

"It's no different for salespersons. People prefer working with people they like. That's common sense... Or is it? It is hard to like someone who is not nice. Target customers have a choice of suppliers for virtually everything they buy, so why not favor the supplier with a nice salesperson? Being nice has real value and is an important part of the 'equation' used when selecting one supplier over another, especially when different suppliers are perceived as offering more or less the same alternative.

" So, how can one be nice? Here's a simple rule. As they say, the good Lord gave us two ears and only one mouth for a reason - listen more than you talk. Take a genuine interest in people with whom you are dealing in the target customer company. When small talk is acceptable (which is the customer's call, not yours), ask more than you yap, and remember what that individual person says. Jot down a few notes after you leave this informal discussion. Does the person have a family? How many kids does he or she have? How old are the kids? What are the person's interests and hobbies? What school did he or she attend? Next time you see this person, ask specifically about one or more of those little details."

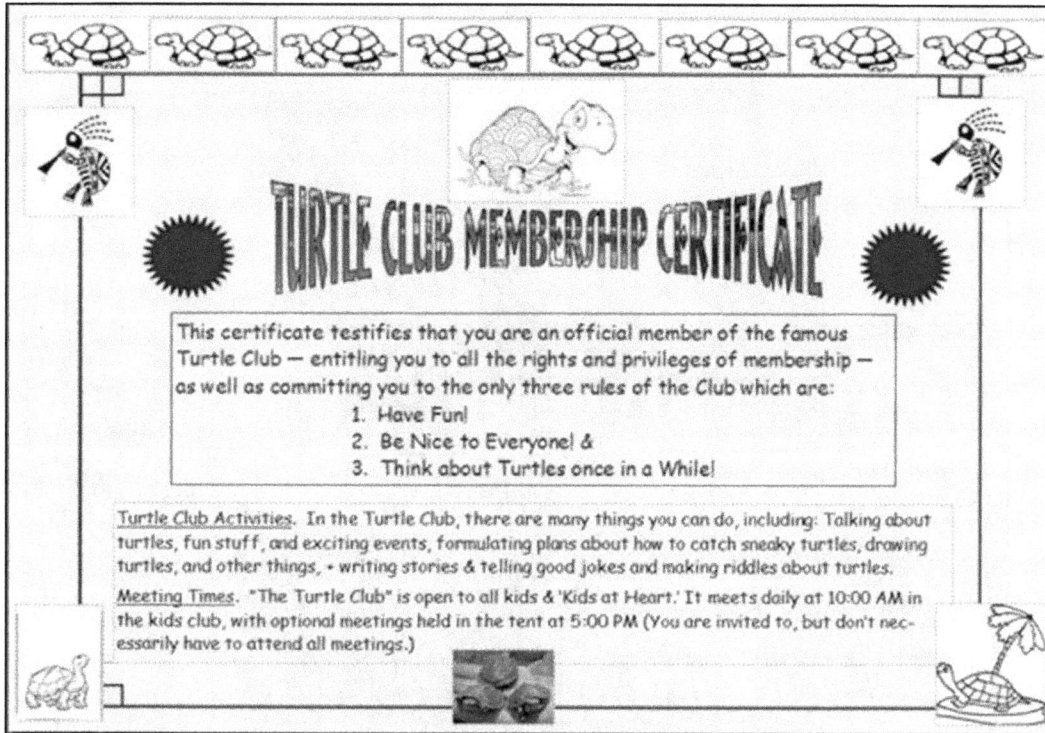

**TURTLE CLUB MEMBERSHIP CERTIFICATE**

This certificate testifies that you are an official member of the famous Turtle Club — entitling you to all the rights and privileges of membership — as well as committing you to the only three rules of the Club which are:

1. Have Fun!
2. Be Nice to Everyone! &
3. Think about Turtles once in a While!

Turtle Club Activities. In the Turtle Club, there are many things you can do, including: Talking about turtles, fun stuff, and exciting events, formulating plans about how to catch sneaky turtles, drawing turtles, and other things, • writing stories & telling good jokes and making riddles about turtles.

Meeting Times. "The Turtle Club" is open to all kids & 'Kids at Heart.' It meets daily at 10:00 AM in the kids club, with optional meetings held in the tent at 5:00 PM (You are invited to, but don't necessarily have to attend all meetings.)

*[Brian]:* "Isn't that being kind of artificial if you pretend to be interested in someone?"

*[Linda]:* "Not if you have a genuine interest in the other person, which is a key part to being nice. So, the next time you are waiting in the entryway to meet with a Target Sponsor or another key player in a customer company, strike up a conversation with the all-important 'gatekeeper' or administrative assistant

"Get into a personal conversation; listen more than you talk and remember (jot down later, if your memory is as bad as mine) exactly what you heard (family, kids, interests, hobbies, schools, vacation, etc.). Next time you see this person, initiate a conversation with a specific question relating to the last time you talked. Again, you might ask if that is an artificial thing to do. But it's not if you're truly showing genuine interest, – which is essential to being considered nice.

"Try to show others that you really care, if you don't do it already. Have your salespersons practice on one another, and then have them share stories about how their personal relationships with key client players - originally cultivated by being nice - have blossomed into more profitable business deals.

"It's obvious that being nice does pay big dividends – in life in general and in business dealings. Kids are pretty smart!"

# Sales Growth Secrets

## Part 3: Implementing Your Account Marketing Plan: Making the Individual Sale (4 Steps)

---

1. Converting the Target Sponsor
2. Converting the Target Power Sponsor
3. Using an 'Evaluation Plan' to Convert All Remaining Key Players
4. Negotiation, Closing, and Implementation

# Implementing Your Account Marketing Plan: Making the Individual Sale

----

# Step 1 (of 4 Steps) Converting the Target Sponsor

---

## *Step 1: Converting the Target Sponsor*

33. Meet Linda's Target Sponsor and Target Power Sponsor at House Depot
34. Linda's Warm Call to Arrange a Face-to-Face Visit with Roger, the Target Sponsor
35. Linda Builds Rapport with Roger's Gatekeeper
36. Linda Introduces Herself & SpeedyLane to Roger
37. First Face-to-Face Meeting: Linda Gets Roger's Admitted 'Pain' Back on the Table
38. Overview of the Vision Building Process
39. Linda Diagnoses Roger's Issues with House Depot's (HD) Current Checkout System
40. Linda Builds Roger's Anxiety over HD's Checkout Problems
41. Linda Helps Roger Envision an Ideal Solution
42. Linda Closes Her Vision Building with Roger
43. Linda Follows Up with Roger
44. Linda Converts Roger into Her Selling Partner Using a Reference Client

CHAPTER 33

# Meet Linda's Target Sponsor & Target Power Sponsor at House Depot

| Step 1 – Linda Converts Roger, Her Target Sponsor | | |
|---|---|---|
| Ch | **33** | **Meet Linda's Target Sponsor & Target Power Sponsor at House Depot** |
| Ch | 34 | Linda's Warm Call to Arrange a Face-to-Face Meeting with Roger |
| Ch | 35 | Linda Builds Rapport with Roger's Gatekeeper |
| Ch | 36 | Linda Introduces Herself & SpeedyLane to Roger |
| Ch | 37 | Linda Gets Roger's Pain (Back) on the Table |
| Ch | 38 | Overview of the Vision Building Process |
| Ch | 39 | Linda Diagnoses Roger's Issues with HD's Checkout System |
| Ch | 40 | Linda Builds Roger's Anxiety Over HD's Checkout Prob;ems |
| Ch | 41 | Linda Helps Roger Envision an Ideal Solution |
| Ch | 42 | Linda Closes Her Vision Building with Roger |
| Ch | **43** | Linda Follows up with Roger |
| Ch | 44 | Linda Converts Roger into a Selling Partner with Reference Client Visit |

Following on from the previous chapter, let's begin the selling process. As outlined earlier, Linda's first challenge is to arrange a face-to-face meeting with her Target Sponsor at House Depot (HD).

---

## Target Sponsor
## Roger Dunkel, Corporate Director of In-Store Efficiency, House Depot

Meet Linda's Target Sponsor, Roger Dunkel, Corporate Director of In-Store Efficiency, House Depot (HD)

**Full Name**: Roger Dunkel

## Family Background & Romantic Interests:

- Grew up in London, UK as an only child. His father owns and continues to run the Chandos Pub in Central London, just off Trafalgar square. Roger bartended there for two years after secondary school, before entering Oxford University.
- Followed Christine Abernathy (Oxford classmate) to Atlanta, GA, USA, in 1997 -- with hopes of marriage in mind.
- Shunned by Christine immediately after following her to the USA, Roger has tirelessly sought to find a mate. Still unsuccessful many years later, despite continual efforts of his many friends and House Depot colleagues to fix him up. He is now desperate!

## Education:

- Bachelor's degree from Oxford University, Class of 1993.

## Career:

- Sold for Random House Publishing in UK – 1993-1997, following graduation from Oxford.
- Joined House Depot in 1998, starting in Customer Service at House Depot's Atlanta, GA headquarters.
- Rose to current position as Corporate Director of In-Store Efficiency in 2006. No likely prospects for promotion on the horizon, which is fine with Roger because he is effective at and content with his current position.

## Current Position & Company:

- Corporate Director of In-Store Efficiency, House Depot

## Hobbies:

- Horror movies. Loves to watch any and all horror movies and is addicted to things that just give you the creeps. His favorite movie is "Chainsaw Massacre."
- Prolific reader. Favors crime thrillers – Patterson, et al, -- as he aspires to be a hero in all facets of his life. He talks to himself in the mirror every morning when shaving to remind himself of his hero status.
- Cricket. Claims Cricket as a hobby, although he hasn't played in over twenty years. The 1992 season saw Roger play for the Oxford side, and his final aggregate of 46 wickets was the highest he managed in any year, as was his total of several five-wicket innings. His

best inning return that season was the 6-11 he claimed against Free Foresters in late May. Not a stellar achievement by any Cricket standard, but a plaque hangs in his office at House Depot commemorating this supposed outstanding achievement. Uninformed SpeedyLane colleagues are convinced by this plaque and Roger's bravado that he was a candidate for the all England team that year. NOT!!!

- Weight-Lifting. Roger also claims weight-lifting as a hobby because he lifted weights three times a week for a whole month back in the 1995. Has not lifted since.
- Eating. Roger is a little overweight. He enjoys snacking on whatever he can get his hands on while watching his horror movies. His favorite late-night snack is nachos.
- Dieting. Dieting is not really a hobby by choice, but rather a futile effort as he tries to keep up his physical appearance as part of his continuing quest to find a mate.

## Physical:
- Less than average height – about 5'7"
- Portly
- Balding
- Mustache -- he has a mustache that kind of resembles a paint brush, not like an artist's paintbrush, but a paintbrush you use to paint the walls in your room...straight, thick and bristly
- Stodgy wardrobe – still wearing polyester slacks for special occasions.

## Nickname:
- Paintbrush, for his unrefined mustache

## Automobile
- Blue 2009 Volvo V60 Family Sedan

---

## *Target Power Sponsor*
## *Don Johnson*, Executive VP of Operations, House Depot

Meet Linda's Target Power Sponsor, *Don Johnson*, Executive VP of Operations, House Depot (HD)

# Dr. John A. Weber

**Full Name**: Don Johnson

**Education**:
- University of Illinois, BBA, 2005; Stanford MBA, 2010

**Career**:
- Booze, Allen Hamilton Consulting 2004-2008; joined House Depot in 2008, quickly rising up the corporate ladder. Destined for continued leadership role at House Depot.

**Current Position & Company**:
- Executive VP of Operations, House Depot

**Romantic Interest**
- Women named Michelle who works at the office. She has no idea he's in love with her, because he only admires her from afar. One day he might have the courage to actually talk to her.

**Hobbies**:
- Collecting fine wines to place in his extensive wine cellar
- Fine dining
- Getaways to his weekend home on Lake Allatoona, just north of Atlanta
- Reading classics – he's quite cultured (except for his musical tastes)
- Listening to punk rock music – a carryover from when he played bass guitar with a rock band in his high school days.

**Physical**:
- Tall ever since childhood. Always lost at Hide and Seek because he could never find a good spot to hide that was big enough for his long legs. Has peaked at 6'3".
- Thin
- Sharp dresser – wears dark, expensive suits daily to work -- specially made to fit his long legs
- Youthful look
- Dark hair parted straight down the middle.
- Other:
  - Shy and soft-spoken
  - Very articulate on all business matters

- When he gets angry, his nostrils flare out and he will actually raise his voice -- rather a scary sight to see due to his height.

## Automobile:

- White 2012 Porsche Boxter

-----

So, now we know a little more about Linda's Target Sponsor, Roger Dunkel, and Target Power Sponsor, Don Johnson, at House Depot. Let's see how Linda tries to convert them each into selling partners. She knows that she must succeed at converting them if she wants a chance to convince House Depot to adopt the SpeedyLane self-checkout system.

*Mon., January 23, 10 am*

CHAPTER 34

---

# Linda's Warm Call to Arrange a Face-to-Face Visit with Roger, the Target Sponsor

The big day has arrived. It's finally time for Linda to take her protégé Brian into the fires! After spending three days last week at the SpeedyLane booth at the Home Improvement National Trade Show in Las Vegas, Linda is about to call one of the 'hot leads' that she discovered at the show. Brian is a little over-excited as he looks over Linda's shoulder.

*[Linda]:* "Brian, ya might wanna cool your jets a bit. This may or may not work out right away. Remember, we talked about that along with the need to have a backup plan ready to go. Plus, since we are targeting customers who are not currently looking for a new system, this will

be challenging. Keep in mind that if this call doesn't go the way we want it to, there's a lot of fish in the sea."

*[Brian]:* "I got it, boss! I know, 'some will, some won't, so what, someone else is waiting.' I think I was saying that in my sleep last night, because you've been pounding that into my head so many times lately!"

*[Linda]:* "I'm not your boss. I'm just here to help you get started. I thought we went through that!"

*[Brian]:* "Got it, boss!" Brian says with a chuckle or two. "I know, just kidding." *Brian is a fun guy and these two are getting along just fine.*

*[Linda]:* "OK, I'm ready to make that phone call. I don't have to remind you of what's going down here because we've been over the 'Sales Manual' together and you've had plenty of time to carefully study it on your own. Plus, you have all the notes you took during our talks earlier in the week."

Here goes that warm phone call to her lead, Roger Dunkel, the Corporate Director of In-Store Efficiency at House Depot (HD). Linda plans to start the phone call by using a compact reference story to generate Roger's interest, hoping that he will agree to meet her face-to-face. If she can't get a face-to-face meeting, her chances of heightening Roger's interest, building a shared vision, and ultimately converting him into a selling partner are slim to none.

## Linda's Warm Call.

In her 'Warm Call', Linda's goal is simply to set up an initial face-to-face meeting with roger, her target sponsor

*[Linda, SpeedyLane Salesperson]:* "Hi again, Roger, this is Linda Brown, from SpeedyLane Self-checkout. As you might recall, we met and spoke for a few minutes at the Trade Show in Las Vegas last week. You gave me your card and asked me to give you a buzz. Have I reached you at a bad time?

*[Roger Dunkel, House Depot (HD), Target Sponsor]:* "No problem, I have a few minutes. In fact, I was actually hoping that you would follow up. What'ya got for me?"

*[Linda]:* "Well, as I started telling you at the trade show, we've been working with self-checkout solutions for the past 10 years. The main concern we are hearing from other Retail Efficiency Managers is a lack of efficiency and customer satisfaction during the checkout process. We've been able to help dozens of customers address this issue with our solution. Would you like to know a little more about how we do this?"

*[Roger Dunkel]:* "Fire away! I'm all ears."

*[Linda]:* "Well, a particular story that might interest you is that of Pioneer Markets. Like you at HD, they have a couple hundred retail outlets. You might know someone who works there, because they are also headquartered in Atlanta. At any rate, their Corporate In-Store Efficiency Manager told us that she was bothered by <u>her company's inefficient checkout system and related customer dissatisfaction</u>. She said she was particularly concerned about her stores' long checkout lines and the high number of cashiers needed to keep checkout times reasonable. Pioneer ultimately added our self-checkout system and reduced average customer checkout time by 20% and its number of cashiers by 25% without reducing customer service."

## Linda then passes the ball over to Roger's court.

*[Linda]:* "Are you curious to hear how we helped them make that turnaround?"

*[Roger]:* "I sure am! As I mentioned to you at the trade show, the inefficiency of our checkout system in general is at the top of my 'fix it' list!"

## Linda then sets up her initial face-to-face meeting with Roger.

*[Linda]:* "Well, if it's OK with you, what I'd like to do is stop by to introduce myself and our SpeedyLane Self-checkout system, to talk with you about your specific situation, and to see if we might be able to help you address some of the checkout efficiency issues you may be facing. I'm located right here in Atlanta and could meet with you any time tomorrow, if that would be convenient for you."

*[Roger]:* "Great! How about 2 o'clock at my office? Here's my address and office number..."

*[Linda]:* "Perfect! See ya then!"

*[Brian]:* "Okay!! Ya done it. It worked out just liked you hoped it would. High five!"

*[Linda]:* "Good Lord, young Grasshopper. That's no biggie, it's just the start. At this rate, you are going to wear us both out!" *She says with a sly smile on her face. Inwardly, she is very pleased to be working with such an enthusiastic, ready-to-learn young upstart.*

*[Brian]:* "Do you think you'll get this contract?"

*[Linda]:* "Heck no! It's way too early to predict that. In fact, I'll now enter the completion of this second step on my iPhone into our 'cloud-based' sales force automation system. You'll learn more about that as we move along."

*[Brian]:* "What exactly do you enter? And why do you do that before you actually have the sale locked down?"

*[Linda]:* "Well, just to give you a quick overview, our Southeast Regional Sales Manager, Roberto Garcia, whom you met yesterday, is responsible for eight sales folks in this region, including you and me. This SpeedyLane sales automation system enables Roberto to keep track of the progress of the sales effort on every lead for each sales person in the region. That way he can realign his energies and resources to improve his chances of making his overall growth and profit numbers for the quarter and the year.

"For example, I met with Roberto yesterday and we pegged this HD opportunity to be worth about $3.2 million up-front, based on our previous experience with a similar sized customer. This price is in addition to a continuing service agreement --but let's forget about service contracts for the moment.

"Now, because I was just successful in moving our friend Roger from warm call status to securing a face-to-face meeting with him, I will remotely input that information. Our 'system' projects that I now have a 10% chance[36] of ultimately landing that $3.2 million contract. This shows up immediately as a $320,000 sales projection on Roberto's computer screen."

*[Brian]:* "What's the point in doing that?"

*[Linda]:* "The point is that if Roberto wants to keep his job and keep moving up in the company ranks – perhaps to National Sales Manager or ultimately even Chief Marketing Officer, then he has to continue to regularly make his numbers. So, he uses the sales automation system to keep track of all of the opportunities that I'm currently working on. You should remember, these are the opportunities that I showed you yesterday. Roberto also keeps careful track of all the opportunities that the other four regional sales reps are working on as well. Like I said, this system helps to keep Roberto and our four other regional sales managers on track to hit their numbers.

"Our National Sales Manager, Catherine Russell, whom you met at the beginning of the sales trainee induction session last week, carefully monitors how each of our five regional sales managers are doing on a day-to-day basis. She meets with the individual regional sales managers regularly in order to re-align energies and resources. She does this in order to improve chances of making SpeedyLane's overall growth and profit numbers for the quarter and the year. Ultimately, this may be achieved by being more aggressive in generating new leads, trying to speed along individual sales efforts of specific sales reps, or by using a number of other pro-active strategies you'll learn about later." (This is covered in considerable detail in the last book of the Sales Growth Secrets Book.)

*[Brian]:* "My head is starting to ache. Can we go to lunch?"

*[Linda]:* "Sure, I'm up for lunch. You buy, because you are the rookie. Just kidding! But hey, try not to worry about the whole sales automation system thing at this point. We'll have plenty of opportunities to go over it as this sales effort with HD progresses – or, I should say, as it *hopefully* progresses! You and the other sales rookies are already scheduled for a separate training session on the sales automation system in two weeks with Catherine's national sales management team.

"This training session will give you plenty of opportunities to get up to speed on how to use that system yourself. It will also allow you to see how Catherine and her crew use the system to significantly improve chances of hitting our corporate-wide sales and profit numbers for the quarter and the year. If the sales automation system enables us to achieve our goals, then all the sales folks who have hit their numbers can celebrate at the annual week-long Corporate Blowout in Hawaii at the end of the year! Hopefully that will include us!"

*[Brian]:* "Sounds good! Lunch it is!"

CHAPTER 35

# Linda Builds Rapport with Roger's Gatekeeper

| **Step 1 – Linda Converts Roger, Her Target Sponsor** | | |
|---|---|---|
| Ch | 33 | Meet Linda's Target Sponsor & Target Power Sponsor at House Depot |
| Ch | 34 | Linda's Warm Call to Arrange a Face-to-Face Meeting with Roger |
| Ch | 35 | Linda Builds Rapport with Roger's Gatekeeper |
| Ch | 36 | Linda Introduces Herself & SpeedyLane to Roger |
| Ch | 37 | Linda Gets Roger's Pain (Back) on the Table |
| Ch | 38 | Overview of the Vision Building Process |
| Ch | 39 | Linda Diagnoses Roger's Issues with HD's Checkout System |
| Ch | 40 | Linda Builds Roger's Anxiety Over HD's Checkout Problems |
| Ch | 41 | Linda Helps Roger Envision an Ideal Solution |
| Ch | 42 | Linda Closes Her Vision Building with Roger |
| Ch | 43 | Linda Follows up with Roger |
| Ch | 44 | Linda Converts Roger into Her Selling Partner with a Reference Client |

## Linda Starts Building Rapport with the Gatekeeper

Linda and Brian enter House Depot (HD) headquarters in Atlanta and are sent up to Roger's office on the 6th floor. But, before they go in to see Roger, Linda introduces herself and Brian to Roger's Administrative Assistant, Lois Pancratz.

Linda strikes up a little conversation with Lois while they are waiting. Linda's goal is to start developing a cordial relationship with this 'gatekeeper.' This is an important relationship for Linda to nurture, because Linda would like to receive 'priority welcoming' whenever she may contact Roger over the next several months should this deal start to pan out. Recall the discussion and related cartoon in the "Be Nice to Everyone" chapter. Relationships with gatekeepers can be deal makers or deal breakers!

Much to her delight, Linda soon discovers that her six-year-old son, Robby, goes to the same school as two of Lois's children. They talk briefly about their children and their mutual experiences at the school. Score one for Linda! She has successfully jumpstarted the process of building a relationship with the important gatekeeper, Lois. Linda will make some notes as a reminder that Lois' children attend the same school as her own -

- along with anything else that came up in her informal conversation with Lois. She will review these notes just prior to her next call or visit to Roger's office in order to continue building rapport and a relationship with Lois.

## Why the Small Talk with Lois?

While they are waiting, Brian looks somewhat concerned and pulls Linda aside.

*[Brian]:* "Hey, what's the deal with spending time chatting up Lois? I thought we were here to sell to Roger! Why are you wasting our time with her?"

*[Linda]:* "My, oh my, Grasshopper, you certainly have lots to learn... I was personable and nice to Lois in order to try to build rapport with her. If I can successfully do that, then she will be more likely to cut me some slack and help me get access to Roger in the future – even if he is super busy."

*[Brian]:* "So, that was kind of a phony-baloney conversation with Lois, eh? You were just *pretending* to be really interested in becoming friends with Lois. That seems a little sketchy to me... I'm not sure that I'd personally be comfortable doing that myself. It just doesn't seem that sincere."

*[Linda]:* "Yikes, you don't get it! I thought you read the chapter on 'Being Nice to Everyone.' I'm not being artificial if I have a genuine interest in her, which is essential to being nice. What

is wrong with being civil and cordial to everyone you meet? It's not artificial, it's just common decency. Sure, in this case, you may think I have an ulterior motive and, to a degree, that is true. But I genuinely enjoy being nice to people and was truly interested in getting to know Lois!

Let me toss the ball back into your court. I am sure that you 'chat up' the young ladies when you go out with the guys. Is your behavior there any different than what I just did? It's probably not different at all. When you are out talking with the ladies, you are trying to be nice in order to potentially build relationships. Tell me this – how many times in the last month alone did you do just that – i.e., chat with a girl whom you did not know, introducing yourself, etc.?

I'm sure you've done it lots!"

[Brian]: "Umm... Well... I actually don't really approach girls that I don't already know... I just don't feel comfortable doing that."

[Linda]: "What!? You're kidding, right? A decent looking guy like you, with a job and everything, is scared to talk to the ladies? You certainly have talked to new young ladies when you are out on the town, don't you? You've already told me about your regular visits to the Buckhead bar scene!"

[Brian]: "Umm... Well... Umm... It's pretty much negatory on that whole chatting with the ladies stuff.... It's just not my strong suit."

[Linda]: "Say what? What are you talking about? Tell me this. When was the last time you had a date with a young lady?"

[Brian]: "Oh, well, don't get me wrong. I've had a date and everything."

[Linda]: "What do you mean _a_ date? When did you last have _a_ date? And what do you mean by _everything_?"

[Brian]: "Can we talk about something else!? I'm sorry I brought up the thing about you being so friendly with Lois. I think I get it now."

237

*[Linda]:* "We'll let it lie now, but next time we are out with the sales team bar-hopping, I think we should do a drill down on this and explore the potential 'socialization of the Grasshopper.' You are going to need some strong social skills if you are to be successful in this new sales position."

*[Brian]:* "Whatever... Can we just let it go for now? Hey, looks like Lois is waving us in to see Roger." *Brian says with an obvious look of chagrin on his face.*

----------

That's the end of this uncomfortable conversation between Linda and Brian ... for now. Brian obviously needs to enhance his social skills if he wants to be successful in selling for SpeedyLane. And who knows? Maybe Linda can help bring about what Brian's mother and four sisters have been trying to do unsuccessfully for years – the 'socialization' of the Grasshopper! I guess we'll have to wait and see. Hmm...it could be interesting, and maybe even amusing.

CHAPTER 36

# Linda Introduces Herself & SpeedyLane to Roger, the Target Sponsor

| Step 1 – Linda Converts Roger, Her Target Sponsor | | |
|---|---|---|
| Ch | 33 | Meet Linda's Target Sponsor & Target Power Sponsor at House Depot |
| Ch | 34 | Linda's Warm Call to Arrange a Face-to-Face Meeting with Roger |
| Ch | 35 | Linda Builds Rapport with Roger's Gatekeeper |
| Ch | 36 | Linda Introduces Herself & SpeedyLane to Roger |
| Ch | 37 | Linda Gets Roger's Pain (Back) on the Table |
| Ch | 38 | Overview of the Vision Building Process |
| Ch | 39 | Linda Diagnoses Roger's Issues with HD's Checkout System |
| Ch | 40 | Linda Builds Roger's Anxiety Over HD's Checkout Problems |
| Ch | 41 | Linda Helps Roger Envision an Ideal Solution |
| Ch | 42 | Linda Closes Her Vision Building with Roger |
| Ch | 43 | Linda Follows up with Roger |
| Ch | 44 | Linda Converts Roger into a Selling Partner with Reference Client Visit |

## Linda's First Face-to-Face Meeting with Roger, the Target Sponsor[37]

Linda is now ready for her first face-to-face meeting with Roger, her Target Sponsor at House Depot (HD). The broad objective of this meeting is to get Roger excited about how Linda's proposed self-checkout solution could make his day-to-day life easier and more productive. Linda would like to get Roger so enthused, in fact, that he would become her selling partner and help her take the self-checkout proposal to other important players and decision-makers at HD.

Linda is armed and ready to try to accomplish this objective by using:

239

- Solid knowledge of her target customer, HD;
- Intimate familiarity with the operating issues that most likely keep Roger up at night;
- A mix of reference stories, giving Linda the flexibility to best match Roger's most important operating concerns;
- Both indirect and direct probing questions to help her expand the breadth of relevant operating issues and introduce a broader array of SpeedyLane's unique capabilities;
- A plan and a related script to help her start this first face-to-face meeting with Roger; and
- A conversational, vision-building 'tool' to try to convert Roger's initial interest into full-fledged enthusiasm regarding the SpeedyLane Self-checkout solution and its ability to make his workday easier and more productive.

## Linda Lets Roger Take the Lead in Potential 'Small Talk'

Linda knows from experience that she will be interrupting Roger's busy day. If he is into small talk, he'll signal it by taking the lead. Even then, Linda shouldn't dawdle on the small talk without Roger's lead. He's got a lot of things to do. Linda is there for a specific purpose, and it does not include wasting Roger's time. This same principle applies to Linda for the future, when hopefully she will get the opportunity to introduce herself, her company (SpeedyLane), and her self-checkout solution to others both above and below Roger in HD's corporate hierarchy.[38]

### Linda Introduces Herself, SpeedyLane and Its Self-checkout System – Establishing Rapport and Credibility

Linda sidesteps the small talk and gets right into why she's here and what she has to offer Roger. Her goal in this introductory conversation with Roger is to motivate him to engage her (and SpeedyLane) in serious discussion.

She starts with a short personal introduction to begin developing rapport and credibility as a knowledgeable business professional. Once that's completed, she quickly provides relevant information on SpeedyLane and its self-checkout – evidencing that she's been around this block successfully more than a few times.

Let's watch along with protégé, Brian, as Linda takes on this challenge.

### Linda Gets Right Down to Business by Stating the Exact Objective of Her Sales Call

*[Linda, SpeedyLane]:* "Nice to see you again Roger. Thanks for agreeing to meet with me. I've been on the SpeedyLane sales and marketing team for the past eight years and I'm really excited about the self-checkout solutions we have to offer.

"What I would like to do today is to introduce you to SpeedyLane and our self-checkout capabilities and tell you a story or two about other retail chain stores we've been able to help out. I would then like to learn more about your situation at HD. After that, we should be able to decide whether or not we should proceed any further."

*[Roger, HD Target Sponsor]:* "Sounds good to me. What d'ya got?"

### Linda Positions Herself

Here, Linda provides a straight-forward, unembellished overview of her selling background with SpeedyLane and its self-checkout solution – letting Roger know indirectly that she's a master in the self-checkout business.

*[Linda]:* "I've been a SpeedyLane sales rep for eight years and have successfully placed self-checkout systems with thirty-five different retailers, several having more than three hundred retail outlets."

**Desired self-conclusion** (Roger's): Linda is well-experienced and knows retail checkout challenges and understands how a self-checkout solution can help address such challenges.

### Linda Positions SpeedyLane

Here, Linda provides a simple, general overview of her company, making it clear to Roger that this is not a fly-by-night operation.

*[Linda]:* "SpeedyLane is a part of NAC, the National Automation Corporation, a 5 billion dollar company that has been creating a variety of checkout solutions for over a hundred years."

**Desired self-conclusion**: SpeedyLane is a legitimate, well-established company with many years of experience and is backed by a multi-billion dollar corporation.

### Additional Facts About SpeedLane

Then, Linda provides additional facts about speedylane and its Self-Checkout System – Again Letting Roger Draw His Own Self-Conclusions

Here, Linda's goal is to build credibility in the SpeedyLane self-checkout system. Note again that she does this by presenting only the straight-forward facts and then letting Roger draw his own self-conclusions. Remember, people tend to believe what they conclude for themselves.

*[Linda]:* "We are the largest provider of self-checkout systems in the world."

**Desired self-conclusion**: SpeedyLane has significant experience in self-checkout solutions.

*[Linda, continuing, without pause]:* "We have over 500,000 self-checkout machines working worldwide."

__Desired self-conclusion__: SpeedyLane is a company with experience and worldwide reach.

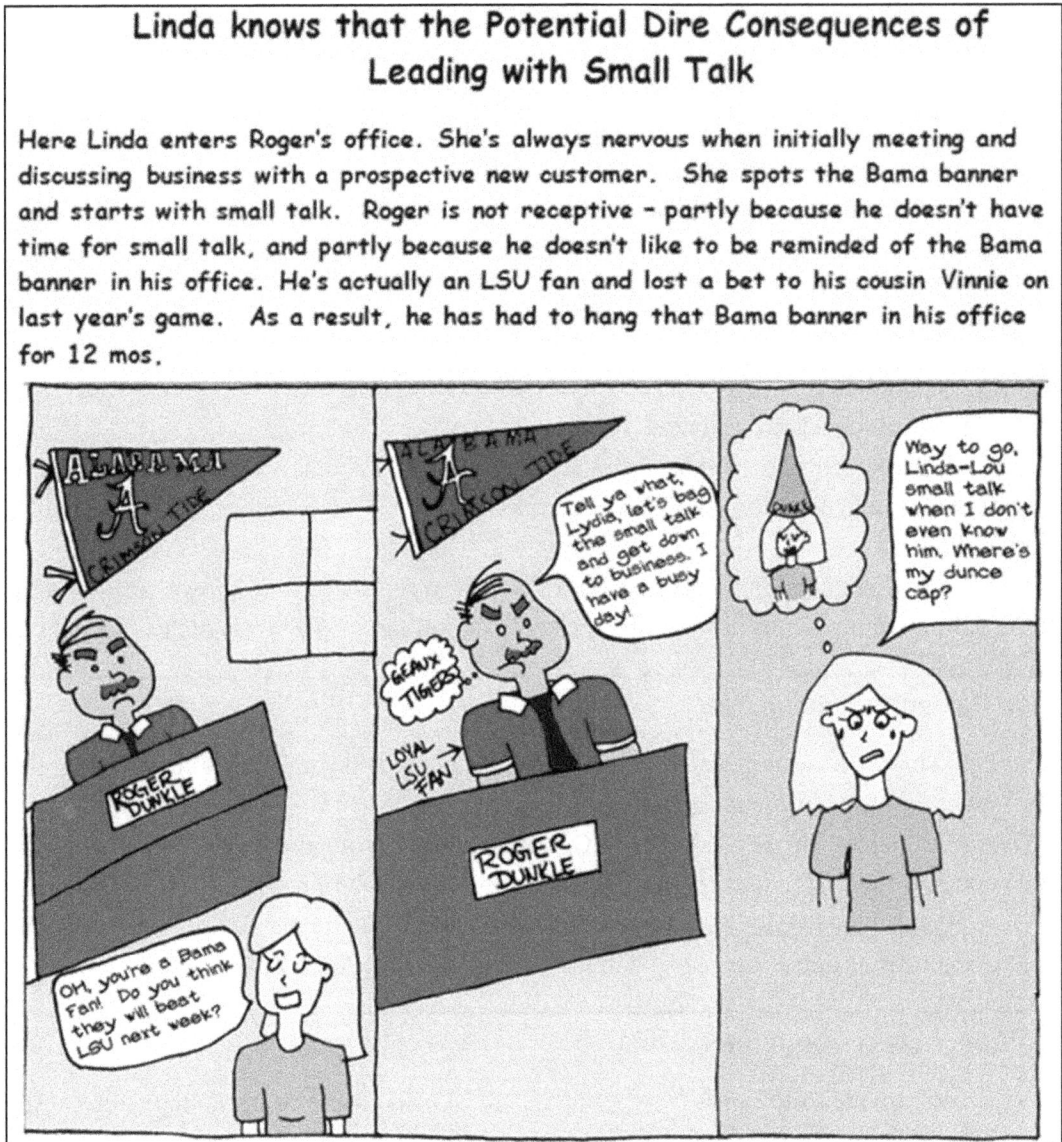

----------

Later on, during a break in the discussion with Roger, Brian asks Linda about why she doesn't just tell Roger what to think about SpeedyLane and its super self-checkout solution.

*[Brian]*: "So, Linda, what's the deal with you being so indirect in 'bragging about' our great company and self-checkout system?"

*[Linda]*: "Well, this is a good lesson for you. More than once when I was starting out, just like you are now, I was so excited about our company and our self-checkout system that I would blurt out what I thought, instead of being subtle and letting my Target Sponsors draw their own conclusions. That's why now I just provide facts, such as, *"We have over 500,000 self-checkout machines working worldwide"* and let my Target Sponsors draw their own conclusions.

I was embarrassed more than once when I was a rookie – sometimes getting the boot out the door by my Target Sponsor before I even got rolling. I finally realized that outright boasting can be perceived as braggadocio and can be a real turn-off for many Target Sponsors. The lesson is this: just stick with the facts and let your Target Sponsors draw their own conclusions about 'how great' your company and solution truly are.

*Tues., January 24, 2:15 pm*

C H A P T E R  37

---

# First Face-to-Face Meeting: Linda Gets Roger's Admitted 'Pain' Back on the Table

| Step 1 – Linda Converts Roger, Her Target Sponsor | | |
|---|---|---|
| Ch | 33 | Meet Linda's Target Sponsor & Target Power Sponsor at House Depot |
| Ch | 34 | Linda's Warm Call to Arrange a Face-to-Face Meeting with Roger |
| Ch | 35 | Linda Builds Rapport with Roger's Gatekeeper |
| Ch | 36 | Linda Introduces Herself & SpeedyLane to Roger |
| Ch | 37 | Linda Gets Roger's Pain (Back) on the Table |
| Ch | 38 | Overview of the Vision Building Process |
| Ch | 39 | Linda Diagnoses Roger's Issues with HD's Checkout System |
| Ch | 40 | Linda Builds Roger's Anxiety Over HD's Checkout Problems |
| Ch | 41 | Linda Helps Roger Envision an Ideal Solution |
| Ch | 42 | Linda Closes Her Vision Building with Roger |
| Ch | 43 | Linda Follows up with Roger |
| Ch | 44 | Linda Converts Roger into a Selling Partner with Reference Client Visit |

In her original 'warm call,' Linda Brown, the SpeedyLane salesperson, got Roger Dunkel, her Target Sponsor at House Depot (HD), to admit that he does face some significant everyday operating challenges with HD's current checkout system. Indeed, the only reason Roger agreed to meet with Linda face-to-face today is because he hopes her solution might be the cure for his checkout system headaches, which would mean he could stop with the double dose of tranquilizers he's been taking every day!

## Linda Gets Roger's 'Pain' Back on the Table

After introducing herself, her company and solution (as she did in the last chapter), Linda's next step is to get the "pain" that Roger originally acknowledged back on the table[39].

Once she gets Roger to admit that pain again, Linda can then:

- Explore a range of operating problems that Roger may have with HD's current checkout system. She will look especially for specific issues that the SpeedyLane Self-checkout system can address (i.e., that cater to SpeedyLane's unique advantages & capabilities);

- Intensify Roger's anxiety over his day-to-day operating problems, making him extremely anxious to seek a solution for his daily challenges; and

- Help Roger to articulate the desired dimensions of a potential solution for the whole set of checkout-related operating issues that will have been brought to the forefront.

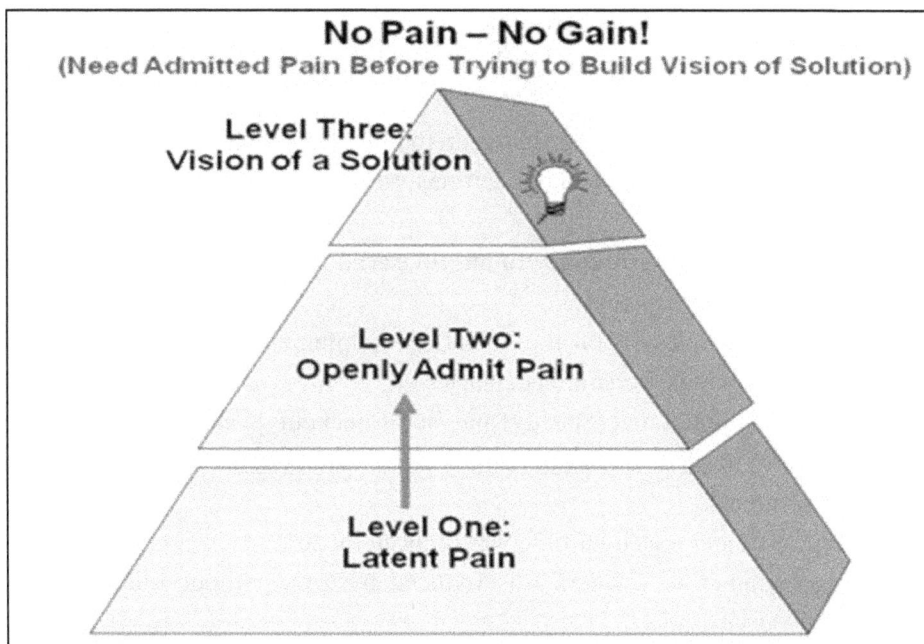

**No Pain – No Gain!**
(Need Admitted Pain Before Trying to Build Vision of Solution)

**Level Three: Vision of a Solution**

**Level Two: Openly Admit Pain**

**Level One: Latent Pain**

## Linda Starts with an In-Depth Reference Story

To get the original pain that Roger expressed back on the table, Linda follows the same process she did before – beginning with the same reference story that she used for the warm call. This time, however, instead of the compact story, she will use an extended version. This longer version introduces additional dimensions of the overall operating issues that were not mentioned in the compact version. Linda's extended reference story goes like this:

*[Linda]:* "I'd like to return to a story I already started about Pioneer Markets, a fast-growing super-store chain on the West Coast. Their Director of In-Store Efficiency told us she was bothered by the company's inefficient checkout system and related customer dissatisfaction.

She told us the primary operating issues were:

- Long checkout lines;
- A large number of cashiers needed to keep checkout times reasonable, and related high wage, benefits, turnover, and training costs;
- Inability of customers to select faster checkout alternatives;
- Loss of prime floor space for high margin impulse products, due to large amounts of prime space used for checkout stations;
- Lost profits due to cashier inaccuracies or outright theft; and
- Too few employees on the sales floor to help customers.

She said that the Capabilities She Needed to address each of these issues were:

- Faster checkout process for customers;
- Reduction in the number of cashiers needed, without compromising customer satisfaction;
- Ability of customers to choose between full-service or self-service checkout;
- Less space allocated to checkout stations, to increase high margin impulse selling space;
- Advanced checkout technology to improve accuracy and reduce profits lost due to cashier inaccuracies or theft;
- Having more employees on the sales floor helping customers, without increasing overall headcount or personnel expenses.

Pioneer ultimately adopted our SpeedyLane Self-Checkout System. By doing so, they acquired each capability needed and began reaping immediate Benefits including the following documented improvements:

- Average customer checkout time was reduced by 20%;
- Average number of cashiers was reduced by 25% without reducing perceived customer service;
- Providing checkout alternatives improved customer satisfaction and loyalty and reduced walkouts by 15%;
- Saved floor space and improved traffic flow provided more space for impulse items and increased impulse revenues by 10%;
- Advanced checkout technology reduced profits lost due to cashier inaccuracies or theft by 12%;
- Reduced the number of cashiers needed at registers, enabling them to be on the sales floor helping customers, which increased customer satisfaction and store loyalty by 15%."

## Linda Closes her Reference Story by Tossing the Ball to Roger's Court

After completing the extended reference story, including citing specific quantitative improvement numbers, Linda immediately passes the ball over to Roger.

*[Linda]:* "But enough about us, what about your situation, Roger?"

At this point, Linda is hoping that Roger will key in on at least one of the operating issues highlighted in the reference story. Or, he might acknowledge that he faces many of these same issues.

*[Roger]:* "Oh man, that sounds a lot like the situation I am faced with every day."

Whether acknowledging a single issue, multiple issues, or the overall set of operating issues, the important point is that ***Roger's pain is now back on the table***.

This opens the door for Linda's next step, which is to launch into a more in-depth conversation with Roger in order to explore the wide array of checkout system-related operating headaches that he faces on a daily basis. We will start with that in the next chapter.

### What if Linda's Extended Reference Story Does Not Trigger Explicit Acknowledgement of Any of Roger's Operating 'Pains?'

What happens if the extended reference story does not cause Roger to clearly admit to one or more of the operating 'pains' that he previously expressed? Well, Linda should then go back to the flow chart that was previously introduced during the warm call. Here's the logical flow of alternative strategies that Linda can then use in order to get Roger's operating pain back on the table.

## The Importance of Citing Quantified Improvements to Heighten the Target Sponsor's Interest

Later on, during a break in their discussion with Roger, Brian asks Linda about where the 'quantitative improvement' numbers come from.

*[Brian]:* "Linda, What's up with the numbers? For example, where do you get off claiming to Roger that you can reduce average customer wait time by 20%? Are you just 'BSing' and hoping he's naïve enough to believe you?"

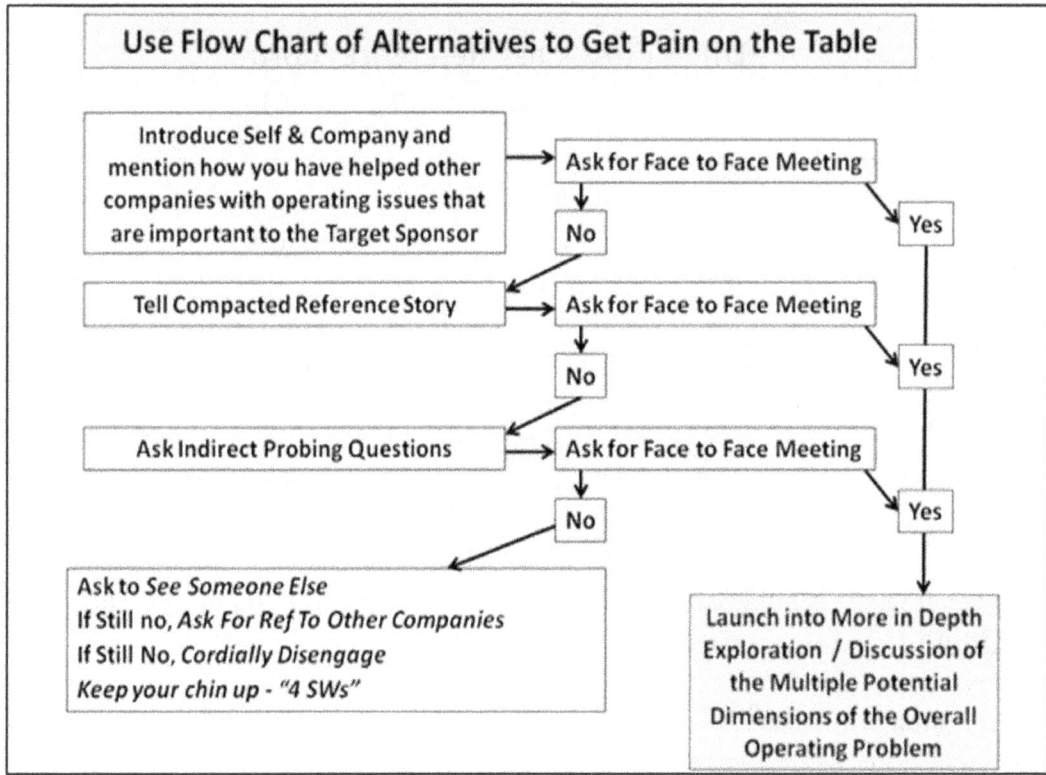

**Use Flow Chart of Alternatives to Get Pain on the Table**

Introduce Self & Company and mention how you have helped other companies with operating issues that are important to the Target Sponsor → Ask for Face to Face Meeting → No / Yes

Tell Compacted Reference Story → Ask for Face to Face Meeting → No / Yes

Ask Indirect Probing Questions → Ask for Face to Face Meeting → No / Yes

Ask to *See Someone Else*
If Still no, *Ask For Ref To Other Companies*
If Still No, *Cordially Disengage*
*Keep your chin up - "4 SWs"*

Launch into More in Depth Exploration / Discussion of the Multiple Potential Dimensions of the Overall Operating Problem

*[Linda]*: "Far from it, Grasshopper. In fact, as you will see, we call these specific numbers our 'critical success factor' numbers ('CSF') at SpeedyLane Sales Headquarters. Yes, we do use these numbers to build initial interest. But just as importantly, we also plan to use these specific improvement numbers as critical input for making credible projections for Return on Investment (ROI) and Payback Period calculations in cooperation with the HD Buying Committee (should this sales effort get that far.)

"As to where we get the numbers from, we certainly do not 'just make up' these improvement results. Rather, in cooperation with each new client, we carefully monitor concrete before-and-after measures of each of these critical success factors. The bottom line is that, when the time comes for it, we can 'prove' to HD that these are realistic projections. As suggested earlier, we will use these proofs as critical inputs to cooperatively build HD's 'financial vision' for our proposed solution."

*[Brian]*: "Wow, that's pretty impressive if you can pull it off. I'm anxious to see how you'll that. But why can't you just talk in generalities about reducing wait time or reducing the number of required cashiers? That seems a lot less risky and a whole lot easier than making inferred promises about specific improvements."

*[Linda]:* "Well, that's another lesson I learned the hard way. If I would have talked in generalities to Roger, I might have been quickly headed for the exit, because my conversation may have sounded like this:"

*[Linda]: ".....Pioneer Markets adopted our SpeedyLane Self-Checkout System, acquiring each capability needed and immediately began reaping <u>Benefits</u> by: Reducing Average checkout time; reducing the number of cashiers; providing more space for impulse items; and reducing cashier inaccuracies and theft; and putting more customer service reps on the floor helping customers."*

"To which Roger might have responded like some of my other Target Sponsors did in the not-so-distant past, saying:

*[Roger]:* "Well, so you claim, Linda. But we can't move forward with just general promises of improvements! You'd be surprised at how many sales pitches I hear each week claiming general improvements – similar to those you are mentioning. But without documented evidence, I've got better ways to spend my time. So, thanks, but no thanks. It's been nice ....."

*[Linda]:* "In fact, that's exactly what used to happen to many of us SpeedyLane sales reps all around the country. Finally, several of us in the 'Golden Sales Club' got together with our National Sales Manager, Catherine Russell, at our annual boondoggle to Hawaii. There, we all had a serious heart-to-heart discussion about the problems we were facing, and ultimately it resulted in Catherine getting Corporate Marketing to hand over to us our 'Critical Success Factor numbers (or 'CSF's'). Because our sales success ratio across the country spiked almost immediately, I got some kudos and an additional bonus that year for being a part of that initiative!"

*[Brian]:* "Wow! Cool. It's nice to know that corporate will listen to us 'lowly' sales folk once in a while!"

*[Linda]:* "You said it! I think SpeedyLane is miles ahead of our competitors on that."

-------------

Over the next several chapters, we will introduce a conversational 'vision building' tool that Linda will use to convert Roger's initial interest into full-fledged enthusiasm about SpeedyLane's proposed solution. This will provide Roger with a vision of a solution that can make his daily life easier, less stressful, and much more productive.

# Overview of the Vision Building Process

| Step 1 – Linda Converts Roger, Her Target Sponsor | | |
|---|---|---|
| Ch | 33 | Meet Linda's Target Sponsor & Target Power Sponsor at House Depot |
| Ch | 34 | Linda's Warm Call to Arrange a Face-to-Face Meeting with Roger |
| Ch | 35 | Linda Builds Rapport with Roger's Gatekeeper |
| Ch | 36 | Linda Introduces Herself & SpeedyLane to Roger |
| Ch | 37 | Linda Gets Roger's Pain (Back) on the Table |
| Ch | 38 | Overview of the Vision Building Process |
| Ch | 39 | Linda Diagnoses Roger's Issues with HD's Checkout System |
| Ch | 40 | Linda Builds Roger's Anxiety Over HD's Checkout Problems |
| Ch | 41 | Linda Helps Roger Envision an Ideal Solution |
| Ch | 42 | Linda Closes Her Vision Building with Roger |
| Ch | 43 | Linda Follows up with Roger |
| Ch | 44 | Linda Converts Roger into a Selling Partner with Reference Client Visit |

In this chapter, we will introduce a conversational 'tool' that Linda will use to try to convert Roger's initial interest into full-fledged enthusiasm. Enthusiasm about what, you may ask? Enthusiasm about how the SpeedyLane Self-checkout system might be able to put an end to Roger's sleepless nights and make his days less stressful and more productive.

This process starts by making sure that Roger's pain is back on the table – i.e., Linda must have Roger openly admit that he is very concerned about House Depot's (HD's) inefficient checkout system. Well, if you recall, Roger just admitted pain at the end of the last chapter, so Linda is now ready to start her vision building effort with him.

## Brian Questions Linda about the Need for the Seemingly 'Over-Complicated' Vision Building Process

*[Brian]*: "Say Linda, I want to ask you something before you get all involved in describing this so-called 'Vision Building Process.' It seems like you're making it waaay too complicated if you ask me. Roger has a problem and we have a solution. To me, it's as simple as that. Now that Roger has admitted his problem, why don't we simply tell him that we at SpeedyLane have a super solution for him? Why make it so complicated?"

*[Linda]*: "Bri, that's a natural inclination for new sales folks – thinking it'd be best to just tell Target Sponsors that we have a solution for their admitted checkout problems. But WRONG!!! Guess what will happen nine times out of ten if you take that direct approach?"

*[Brian]*: "You're the mentor. How about you tell me the secret?"

*[Linda]*: "It's not a secret at all. Review the cartoon in your selling manual (next page), which pretty much says it all."

*[Linda]*: continuing ... "It's common sense if you keep in mind what we have emphasized over and over again – folks are much, much more likely to believe and act upon things they conclude for themselves. In this case, that means we will be using a very subtle approach to get Roger to self-conclude that we at SpeedyLane do indeed have the ideal solution for House Depot (HD)."

*[Brian]*: "That seems kind of devious to me. What? Are we trying to 'trick' Roger into thinking we have a great solution for him?"

*[Linda]*: "Trick, schmick! What are you talking about?" *Linda is obviously losing some of her patience with her young protégé, Brian.* "Recall what we have emphasized over and over again, from the time we hired you through all of your training and up until now. We need to truly believe that we do indeed have the best overall solution value available for our target customers! If we don't believe that, then what do we do? .... This is a TEST!!"

*[Brian]*: "OK, I remember. If we don't offer the best solution value for a specific target segment and customer, then we have no business selling to them. In such a case, we need to either enhance our solution value for the target segment and customer or choose a different target segment for which we do indeed have the best solution value."

*[Linda]*: "Very good, Grasshopper, you make me proud with that 'right on' answer! You *are* learning – glory beeeeeeee!"

## Purpose of the 9 Block Vision Processing Model®⁴⁰

The 9 Block Vision Processing Model® is intended to help Linda guide Roger to self-conclude that SpeedyLane might indeed have the ideal solution for his checkout challenges. Linda's goal with the '9 Block Vision Building Process' is to help Roger create his own vision of an ideal solution for HD's checkout problems. Only after Roger has constructed his vision can Linda suggest that SpeedyLane has a solution that matches this vision more or less perfectly.

Immediately after Roger has admitted that he has significant problems with HD's checkout system, Linda begins the vision building process.

## Overview of 9 Block Vision Building

Here's how the '9 Block Vision Processing Model®' works. Once Roger's general pain is clearly admitted, Linda will launch into an in-depth, three-phase conversation with Roger. Subsequent chapters will go into more detail on each part of this process as we watch Linda in action, but for now, here's an overview.

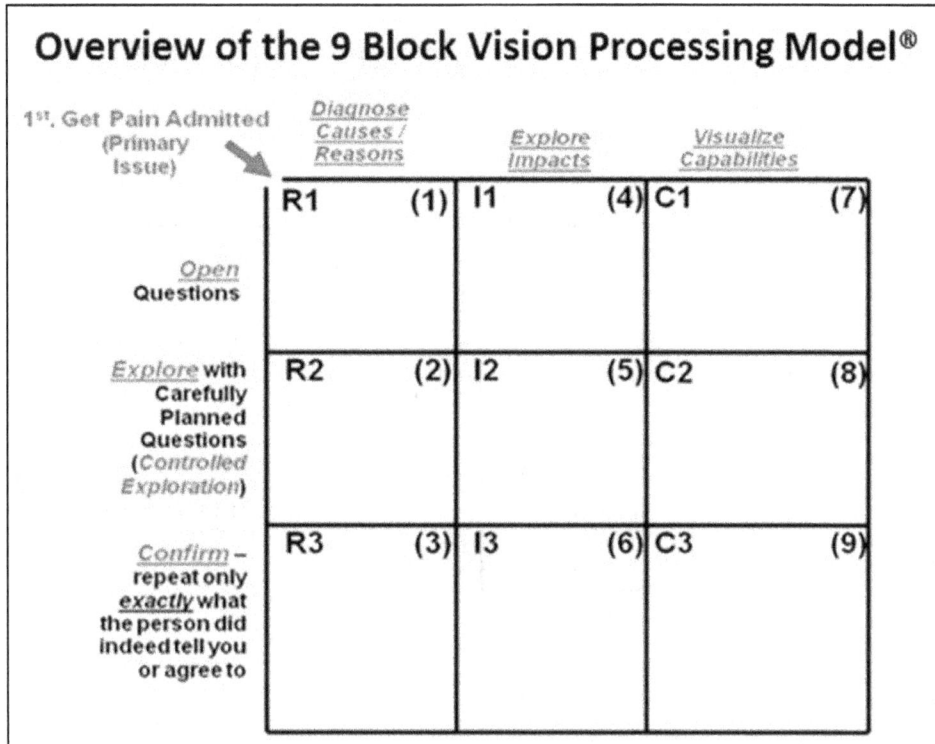

## Overview of the 9 Block Vision Processing Model®

| | Diagnose Causes / Reasons | Explore Impacts | Visualize Capabilities |
|---|---|---|---|
| 1st. Get Pain Admitted (Primary Issue) → | | | |
| *Open* Questions | R1 (1) | I1 (4) | C1 (7) |
| *Explore* with Carefully Planned Questions (*Controlled Exploration*) | R2 (2) | I2 (5) | C2 (8) |
| *Confirm* – repeat only *exactly* what the person did indeed tell you or agree to | R3 (3) | I3 (6) | C3 (9) |

## Three Columns

**Column 1:** Linda's goal in Column 1 is to explore and mutually conclude with Roger the specific Reasons for his general pain with HD's current checkout system. In the process of this drill down, Linda will try to make sure that the list of specific reasons acknowledged by Roger includes problems for which SpeedyLane has a uniquely attractive solution (note: Linda's solution alternatives themselves will not arise until Column 3).

**Column 2:** In Column 2, Linda helps Roger to identify and acknowledge the wide ranging Negative Impacts of the inadequacies of HD's current checkout system. Linda's goal in Column 2 is to heighten Roger's anxiety about his checkout problem to the point where he is *begging* for a solution.

**Column 3**: Linda's goal in Column 3 is to help Roger visualize a set of potential Capabilities that would resolve his heightened pains over HD's current checkout system. Roger will own this vision.

---

## Summary of the Appropriate Contents for Linda to Use in Each Block in the 9 Block Vision Building Process

### 9 Block Vision Processing Model® – Block Contents

| 1ˢᵗ. Get Pain Admitted (Primary Issue) | Diagnose Causes / Reasons | Explore Impacts | Visualize Capabilities |
|---|---|---|---|
| **Open Questions** | **R1 (1)** Can you tell me more about that? What's causing .. Repeat the issue / pain | **I1 (4)** Besides you, who else is impacted by this (briefly repeat issue / pain) and how are they affected? | **C1 (7)** What's it going to take for YOU to address this problem? What can you do about it? |
| **Explore with Carefully Planned Questions (Controlled Exploration)** | **R2 (2)** Indirect Qs to get each Cause /Reason on the Table (Cause 1, 2, 3, etc.) | **I2 (5)** Is your 'x' (name a position) also affected? How about 'y' position,' is that also affected? Etc. | **C2 (8)** Could I try some ideas on you? What if when C1, you could ... Capability 1 ? Wait for response. What if when C2, you could ... Capability 2 ? Etc. |
| **Confirm – repeat only *exactly* what the person did indeed tell you or agree to** | **R3 (3)** So, if I am hearing your right, you .. Repeat Issue / Pain .. because 1, 2, 3, etc. Is that correct? | **I3 (6)** From what I've just heard, it sounds like this is a challenge for # of others as well as for you. Now repeat all of those mentioned along with the specific challenge for each | **C3 (9)** So, I hear you saying that if you had this, this & this, then the issue / pain (repeat it) would be addressed as well as the challenges faced by, & all those others affected (mention them each). Is that an accurate summary? |

---

## Three Rows

**Row 1**: Linda begins each Column of the 9 block conversation with an <u>Open Question</u> for Roger, which allows her to search for input from him before she enters into and guides the conversation. For example, to start off Column 1, Linda asks: "What do you think is causing your checkout problems?"

**Row 2**: In the second row of each column, Linda introduces <u>Extend and Control Questions</u>. This is the most important row in the 9 block process, as it gives Linda the opportunity to influence Roger's search for Reasons (Column 1), Impacts (Column 2), and Capabilities (Column 3). We'll see more details on this in the next chapter.

**Row 3**: In the third and final row of each column in the 9 block process, Linda concludes with a <u>Summary</u>. Linda simply repeats what Roger has said or agreed with in the first two rows and does so without distorting or exaggerating his words. This confirms Roger's own stated vision.

---

# Appendix to this chapter
## <u>9 Block Vision Building Planning Worksheet</u>

### Identify Key Player
### Identify Issues & Related Reasons
- Identify Primary Overall Issue
- Get the Primary Overall Issue on the Table (i.e., Get Pain Admitted)
- Get Reasons Acknowledged
- Open Question regarding Specific Reasons for this main overall issue
- Indirect & Direct Probing Questions to try to get each reason on the table
- Summarize & Verify acknowledgement of all Specific Reasons

### Identify Impacts
- Get Additional Impacts Acknowledged
- Open Question regarding potential negative impacts on other players
- Probing Questions to get impacts on additional players admitted, which builds anxiety
- Summarize & verify acknowledgement of all the folks negatively impacted by the primary overall issue

### Identify Capabilities Needed (i.e., overall solution)
- Get 'Ideal' Solution Acknowledged (i.e., Needed Capabilities)
- Open Question regarding what Capabilities are needed to address all reasons for the Overall Issue
- Suggestions imbedded in questions to get player to acknowledge the key capabilities needed
- Summarize & Verify acknowledged key capabilities needed to address each reason for the overall issue, the overall issue itself, and the negative ramifications of the overall issue on many different players

### Plan Closing Statement

---

In the next several chapters we will run through the three phases of the 9 block process with Roger -- Diagnosing Reasons, Exploring Impacts, & Visualizing Capabilities Needed.

*Tues., January 24, 2:30 pm*

# CHAPTER 39

# Linda Diagnoses Roger's Issues with House Depot's (HD) Current Checkout System[41]

| | | Step 1 – Linda Converts Roger, Her Target Sponsor |
|---|---|---|
| Ch | 33 | Meet Linda's Target Sponsor & Target Power Sponsor at House Depot |
| Ch | 34 | Linda's Warm Call to Arrange a Face-to-Face Meeting with Roger |
| Ch | 35 | Linda Builds Rapport with Roger's Gatekeeper |
| Ch | 36 | Linda Introduces Herself & SpeedyLane to Roger |
| Ch | 37 | Linda Gets Roger's Pain (Back) on the Table |
| Ch | 38 | Overview of the Vision Building Process |
| Ch | 39 | Linda Diagnoses Roger's Issues with HD's Checkout System |
| Ch | 40 | Linda Builds Roger's Anxiety Over HD's Checkout Problems |
| Ch | 41 | Linda Helps Roger Envision an Ideal Solution |
| Ch | 42 | Linda Closes Her Vision Building with Roger |
| Ch | 43 | Linda Follows up with Roger |
| Ch | 44 | Linda Converts Roger into a Selling Partner with Reference Client Visit |

After Linda told Roger her detailed reference story about Pioneer Markets (several chapters ago), she tossed the ball over to Roger, who admitted pain by acknowledging HD's checkout problems, which are similar to those previously faced by Pioneer.

[*Linda, SpeedyLane*]: "Enough from me – tell me about your situation."

[*Roger, HD*]: "Well, we certainly have some of those same problems that Pioneer saw– our checkout system is nowhere near as efficient as we'd like it to be. It's a big money drain on our bottom line, which is why I'm always getting pressure from my boss, Don Johnson."

Now that Roger has admitted his pain – i.e., his dissatisfaction with House Depot's (HD's) current, inefficient checkout system – Linda's real work can begin. Her next goal is to help

Roger self-conclude the specific causes for why he is unhappy with HD's present checkout system. Importantly, Linda also wants to make sure that Roger provides reasons that include at least some specific problems for which SpeedyLane has unique, sustainable, differential capabilities.

## Linda Diagnoses the Causes of HD's Inefficient Checkout System

|  | Diagnose Causes / Reasons | Explore Impacts | Visualize Capabilities |
|---|---|---|---|
| **1st, Get Pain Admitted** (Primary Issue)<br><br>*Open* Questions | **R1** (1)<br>Can you tell me more about that? What's causing .. Repeat the issue / pain | **I1** (4)<br>Besides you, who else is impacted by this (briefly repeat issue / pain) and how are they affected? | **C1** (7)<br>What's it going to take for YOU to address this problem? What can you do about it? |
| *Explore* with Carefully Planned Questions (*Controlled Exploration*) | **R2** (2)<br>Indirect Qs to get each Cause /Reason on the Table (Cause 1, 2, 3, etc.) | **I2** (5)<br>Is your 'x' (name a position) also affected? How about 'y position,' is that also affected? Etc. | **C2** (8)<br>Could I try some ideas on you?<br>What if when C1, you could ... Capability 1 ? Wait for response. What if when C2, you could ... Capability 2 ? Etc. |
| *Confirm* – repeat only *exactly* what the person did indeed tell you or agree to | **R3** (3)<br>So, if I am hearing your right, you .. Repeat Issue / Pain .. because 1, 2, 3, etc. Is that correct? | **I3** (6)<br>From what I've just heard, it sounds like this is a challenge for # of others as well as for you. Now repeat all of those mentioned along with the specific challenge for each | **C3** (9)<br>So, I hear you saying that if you had this, this this & this, then the issue / pain (repeat it) would be addressed as well as the challenges faced by, & all those others affected (mention them each). Is that an accurate summary? |

The tricky part for Linda is to avoid force-feeding Roger answers. The checkout system is Roger's problem and both the analysis of his dilemma and any envisioned ideal solution have to be his as well. Let's see how she handles this challenge. Brian is also watching and listening closely!

## Open Question: Linda Gets Roger Talking More about His Problem – "Can You Tell Me More about That?"

As soon as Roger admits that HD's checkout system is keeping him up at night, Linda asks an *open-ended question*:

[Linda]: "Tell me more about that!"

Linda encourages Roger to talk, purposefully relinquishing control of the conversation. When Roger mentions any specific problematic dimension of his checkout system, Linda asks him to elaborate. During this general conversation, Linda is hoping that Roger will acknowledge a number of specific causes for HD's inefficient checkout system, which hopefully her SpeedyLane solution can effectively address.

### The causes that Linda hopes to get on the table include:

- Long checkout lines;
- A high number of cashiers needed to keep checkout times reasonable, and related high costs for wages, benefits, turnover, and training;
- Inability of customers to select faster checkout alternatives;
- Loss of prime floor space for high-margin impulse products, because checkout stations currently use so much prime selling space;
- Lost profits due to cashier inaccuracies or outright theft; and
- Having too few employees on the sales floor helping customers.
- Let's see what Roger has to say.

--------------

[Roger]: "Well to begin with, our customers have no choice but to use the cashier checkout, because it's the only system we have in place. Because of the lack of alternatives, if we want to keep a reasonable number of checkout lanes open at any given time, we need a lot of cashiers. Also, we seem to need more and more cashiers as we are continually expanding our store hours. As if that isn't bad enough, more customers are getting fed up with waiting in long lines at each register. You can see the frustration in their body language. Some even walk out. Who knows if they'll ever come back. So, as you can see, we have lots issues with our current system."

### Linda Explores Further – Using Indirect Questions to Get Additional Specific Causes for Roger's Problem on the Table

Linda listens carefully and *takes notes*! Once she senses that Roger is done talking or is at least running out of steam, she asks herself which specific causes Roger has admitted and which he has not yet acknowledged. In this instance, Roger mentioned 3 of the 6 operating issues Linda was looking for. Three other specific potential operating issues remain, which Linda then hints at with indirect questions.

---

### The first additional cause Linda wants to get on the table is the large amount of prime, high-margin, impulse selling space currently occupied by HD's checkout lanes.

*[Linda]:* "How much space do your current checkout stations take up near the front of the store?" Note the indirect nature of her question. She doesn't want to risk turning off Roger like a pushy know-it-all (e.g., she avoids phrasing such as "Do you feel you have a problem with your many checkout stations taking up too much impulse selling space?")

*[Roger]:* "That's a good question. We are always trying to squeeze in more impulse racks near the front of the store. You'd be surprised at how much extra, high-margin revenue those racks can generate. It would be great if we could free up more of that prime space, but right now, most of that area is required for our checkout stations." *(Linda should ask Roger to elaborate, if she'd like more detail.)*

---

### With impulse item space now added to Roger's list, Linda moves on to the next issues not yet on the table – cashier errors and outright theft.

*[Linda]:* "Do you worry about cashier errors or outright cashier theft?"

*[Roger]:* "Oh, for sure. We don't have a good way to carefully monitor all of the products that goes through our cashier lanes. Between cashier errors and outright customer and employee theft, I hate to imagine how much money we actually lose each quarter." *(Linda should ask Roger to elaborate, if she'd like more detail. She wants to keep Roger talking.)*

Now Linda has one last issue for Roger to address – the number of customer service reps on the sales floor at any given time.

*[Linda]:* "How many employees do you typically have on the floor to help out HD customers?"

*[Roger]:* "Well, not nearly enough! That's for sure. So many of our employees are wrapped up in the checkout process that a number of our customers don't get the assistance they need. I guess it's no wonder that our customer satisfaction is far below where we'd like it to be." *(Again, Linda should ask Roger to elaborate, if she'd like more detail.)*

---

After Linda has tried to get all of the desired causes acknowledged and discussed, it's time for Linda to review her notes and summarize and confirm the causes that are on the table. Here, it is critical for Linda not to exaggerate or embellish what Roger has told her. As accurately as possible, Linda must repeat *exactly what she has just heard <u>and nothing more.</u>*

All six causes are now on the table. It's time for Linda to summarize and confirm what she and Roger just discussed.

Let's See What Happens if Linda Exaggerates What Roger Has Told Her

**So, it sounds like you're telling me your checkout system's a mess, and everything about it is just plain going wrong! Is that about right?**

**Well, it has its problems, but it's certainly not as bad as you say! Why doncha leave your materials up front and I'll get back to you. Bye now!**

**Hey, you can just trash anything that Lydia sends us. What a pushy gal!**

**OK!**

ADMIN ASSISTAN

## Let's hear Linda's summary ('world's longest sentence')

*[Linda]*: "So, it sounds like you're telling me that your checkout system is inefficient and that your customers are dissatisfied because they have no choice but to use the one system you have in place – the cashier checkout.

- You feel you need too many cashiers to keep a reasonable number of your checkout lanes open. Furthermore, as your store hours expand, additional cashiers are needed.
- You feel that many customers get fed up with waiting in long lines – you've even witnessed some customers walk out – and you are concerned that some may not return.
- You believe that too much of your floor space is being taken up by checkout lanes, thereby causing a loss in a lot of prime, high-margin retail space at the front of the store.
- You also said that you are losing a lot of money each quarter due to cashier errors and outright theft by customers and employees because you don't have a good way to carefully monitor all of the products that go through your cashier lanes.

- And, finally, you feel that because too many of your employees are wrapped up in the cashier checkout process, a number of your customers don't get the assistance they need, which causes significant customer dissatisfaction."

*[Linda]:* "Is that an accurate summary?"

*[Roger]:* "Wow! That was a mouthful! How'd you remember all that? You've got it *exactly!* You've really hit the nail on the head!"

Roger now thinks Linda is "brilliant!" Well, of course she is, because she listened attentively, took careful notes and repeated more or less exactly what Roger just told her! Brilliant indeed! Linda is now ready to move on to the next phase of vision building with Roger – building his anxiety about all the HD checkout problems he has just admitted. The next chapter will address this.

*But first Brian has a question, which he asks Linda during a short break.*

*[Brian]:* "Linda, it seems that you are biasing Roger's perception of his problems specifically toward those causes for which we at SpeedyLane have the best solution. Do you feel right about that? Is that really in Roger's and HD's best interest?"

*[Linda]:* "Yes, I feel very right about biasing Roger's perception of his problems toward those causes for which SpeedyLane has the best solution. That's because we sincerely believe that SpeedyLane offers a better overall value for HD than any of our competitors."

*[Brian]:* "That makes sense now. I just have to keep in mind that we have HD's and Roger's best interests in mind when purposefully steering Roger toward our SpeedyLane system. Good enough! I also can't forget that we do offer a better overall value than anyone else in the market."

*[Linda]:* "Well said! You are growing out of Grasshopper status a lot faster than I thought you would!"

*Tues., January 24, 2:50 pm*

CHAPTER 40

---

# Linda Builds Roger's Anxiety over HD's Checkout Problems[42]

| Step 1 – Linda Converts Roger, Her Target Sponsor | | |
|---|---|---|
| Ch | 33 | Meet Linda's Target Sponsor & Target Power Sponsor at House Depot |
| Ch | 34 | Linda's Warm Call to Arrange a Face-to-Face Meeting with Roger |
| Ch | 35 | Linda Builds Rapport with Roger's Gatekeeper |
| Ch | 36 | Linda Introduces Herself & SpeedyLane to Roger |
| Ch | 37 | Linda Gets Roger's Pain (Back) on the Table |
| Ch | 38 | Overview of the Vision Building Process |
| Ch | 39 | Linda Diagnoses Roger's Issues with HD's Checkout System |
| Ch | 40 | Linda Builds Roger's Anxiety Over HD's Checkout Problems |
| Ch | 41 | Linda Helps Roger Envision an Ideal Solution |
| Ch | 42 | Linda Closes Her Vision Building with Roger |
| Ch | 43 | Linda Follows up with Roger |
| Ch | 44 | Linda Converts Roger into a Selling Partner with Reference Client Visit |

In this chapter, Linda continues her effort to convert Roger's initial interest into full-fledged enthusiasm for her SpeedyLane Self-checkout system. Last chapter, Linda helped Roger to self-conclude the specific causes for his unhappiness with House Depot's (HD's) current checkout system. By astutely using indirect questions, Linda also made sure that Roger's set of causes included those for which SpeedyLane has unique capabilities. Now, Linda can move on to the next phase of vision building with Roger, which involves building his anxiety about his acknowledged problems.

# Don't Jump the Gun

After accurately summarizing what Roger has told her are the primary causes behind the inefficiencies in HD's checkout system, Linda might be tempted to immediately propose a solution for Roger. But, not so fast! *Roger is not yet ready for a solution.* In fact, he may be in active denial of his day-to-day operating prob-lems because he sees no way to effectively address these issues.

But Linda's been making progress. So far Roger has overcome two important hurdles, which include:

- Admitting that HD has a problem with its current checkout system; and
- Detailing and acknowledging the specific causes for HD's checkout inefficiencies.

## Now that she's laid this groundwork, Linda is ready for her next strategy.

Note that Roger still feels that he's stuck with his checkout problems. Who likes to dwell on their problems when no solution is in sight? No one! Nevertheless, if Linda is to move her sales effort forward, she must keep Roger talking about HD's checkout problems. Her goal now is *to build Roger's anxiety about HD checkout problems to the point where he decides he must take action!* Yikes, this could be touchy – but our smart, experienced friend Linda is aware of that. She's been through this process many times before, and she, therefore, understands that Roger won't beg for a solution until he recognizes the broad-ranging negative impacts that may arise if he does nothing about HD's checkout problems! Linda charges forward with additional, subtle, indirect questions.

| PAIN (Primary Issue) | Diagnose Causes / Reasons | Explore Impacts | Visualize Capabilities |
|---|---|---|---|
| *Open* **Questions** | **R1** (1)<br><br>Can you tell me more about that? What's causing .. Repeat the issue / pain | **I1** (4)<br><br>Besides you, who else is impacted by this (briefly repeat issue / pain) and how are they affected? | **C1** (7)<br><br>What's it going to take for YOU to address this problem? What can you do about it? |
| *Explore* with **Carefully Planned Questions** (*Controlled Exploration*) | **R2** (2)<br><br>Indirect Qs to get each Cause /Reason on the Table (Cause 1, 2, 3, etc.) | **I2** (5)<br><br>Is your 'x' (name a position) also affected? How about 'y position,' is that also affected? Etc. | **C1** (8)<br><br>Could I try some ideas on you? What if when C1, you could ... Capability 1 ? Wait for response. What if when C2, you could ... Capability 2 ? Etc. |
| *Confirm* – **repeat only** *exactly* **what the person did indeed tell you or agree to** | **R3** (3)<br><br>So, if I am hearing your right, you .. Repeat Issue / Pain .. because 1, 2, 3, etc. Is that correct? | **I3** (6)<br><br>From what I've just heard, it sounds like this is a challenge for a # of others as well as for you. Now repeat all of those mentioned along with the specific challenge for each | **C1** (9)<br><br>So, I hear you saying that if you had this, this & this, then the issue / pain (repeat it) would be addressed as well as the challenges faced by, & all those others affected (mention them each). Is that an accurate summary? |

## Linda Builds Roger's Anxeity

So, how might Linda build Roger's anxiety about his host of interrelated day-to-day operating problems without turning him off and having him send her away? How can Linda make Roger beg for a solution? In preparation for this purposeful tension-producing discussion with Roger, Linda uses her previous experience to identify all of the players both inside and outside of HD, who, in addition to Roger, are also likely being negatively affected by HD's current inefficient checkout system.

Let's watch as Linda now uses indirect questions to get Roger to explore and acknowledge the wide-ranging negative impacts of HD's inefficient checkout system. Let's see how she subtly works to heighten his anxiety to the point where he realizes he absolutely must do something about his problem!

## Open Question. Linda Gets Roger Thinking and Talking About Other Important Players Who Are Negatively Impacted by HD's Inefficient Checkout system

Linda starts the conversation immediately after she successfully sumarizes and confirms the reasons for Roger's problem (at the end of the last chapter). The anxiety building now begins with Linda's open-ended question:

*[Linda]:* "Well, besides you, is anyone else negatively affected by this checkout inefficiency?"

With this question, Roger has to think and talk about any other players inside or outside his company who might also be negatively affected by the same operating issues that haunt him. Discussing these other folks who are also negatively affected should start building Roger's anxiety. As Linda listens, she carefully notes down all players mentioned and how they are each negatively impacted.

## Roger Lists Some Players and Describes How Each is Negatively Impacted by HD's Inefficient Checkout System

*[Roger]:* "Yes, I know plenty of people are affected by this issue. Our Executive VP of Operations, Don Johnson, comes immediately to mind, as he constantly complains about the costs of inefficiency. He is also in charge of monitoring how customers flow through the store, including their time spent at the checkout." (*With some parties that Roger mentions, Linda should ask him to elaborate in order to get him to think further about the negative impacts on these folks.*)

*[Linda]:* "Care to elaborate on that?"

Linda then asks for more input from Roger.

*[Linda]:* "Anyone else come to mind?"

*[Roger]:* "Well, our CEO is definitely affected because of his concern with the bottom line. He can't be happy about the costs of inefficiency, such as customer walkouts and the high labor cost of having too many cashiers."

*[Linda]:* "Care to elaborate?"

Linda will now encourage Roger to bring as many negative impacts as possible out into the open.

*[Linda]:* "Anyone else?"..... Anyone Else? ... Linda has a whole list of players who she believes are negatively impacted by HD's current system. But before using her list, she would prefer that Roger himself identify them.

## Linda Expands Roger's Acknowledged List of Players Who Are Negatively Affected – Hopefully Enhancing Roger's Anxiety & Readiness to Address His Problem

Some of the many players Linda is hoping Roger will mention include:

- Customers;

- Current in-store cashiers, managers, assistant managers, departmental heads, etc.;
- Corporate Floor Planners & Merchandisers;
- Corporate Director and individual managers of Retail Operations;
- Chief Executive and Chief Financial Officers;
- Board of Directors & Shareholders;
- Suppliers; and
- Roger's own career prospects.

The more of these players she can get Roger to acknowledge and discuss, the more anxious he should become to find a solution.

So, once Roger has run out of steam, Linda refers to her prepared list and asks Roger about other affected players that he has not yet mentioned. For example, she asks, "What about the CFO?" Again, note that she uses indirect questioning because it is less accusatory and less likely to trigger a defensive response from Roger. When Roger acknowledges that any new player is negatively affected, Linda should consider asking him to elaborate, hopefully building further anxiety.

[Linda]: "How about the cashiers and other in-store personnel?" Linda awaits Roger's response and asks him to elaborate ... "How about corporate and in-store merchandisers?" etc.

## When does Linda stop her indirect questioning?

Well, she has to sense that on her own. She won't quit until either her whole list of negatively affected players has been acknowledged, or until it becomes obvious that Roger's increased agitation has made him ready for a solution. An effective last player to mention is Roger himself, by asking a question such as, *"What about you? Are any of these operating inefficiencies affecting the assessment of your performance?"* These personal questions regarding Roger's specific performance can be an effective way to ensure that anxiety is indeed etched in Roger's mind.

[Linda]: "Finally, how about your own career? Are these problems affecting your advancement opportunities?"

[Roger]: "I can't say that these aren't huge issues for me. I can't really perform my job well when we have such an inefficient checkout system. That's part of the reason why I approached you at the trade show. Now that we are discussing all of these negative effects, I'm getting even more worried. This whole situation is horrible!"

## Linda Summarizes and Confirms All of the Broader Negative Impacts that Roger Has Openly Acknowledged

Even after all of that, Linda is still not done building Roger's anxiety. Recall that her goal is to make Roger effectively beg for a solution. So, Linda must rub in Roger's anxieties even further. To do this, she now repeats all of the folks who Roger has described as negatively affected and summarizes how each player is impacted by the relevant inefficiencies. This summary should not exaggerate what Roger himself has recognized as a vast list of negative ramifications that came about due to HD's current inefficient system.

Now, Roger should be more than ready to consider virtually any potential solution for this horrible situation.

## Linda's Summary & Confirmation

*[Linda]:* "So let me see if I can accurately summarize what you have told me. What I believe you said is that the overall inefficiency of HD's current checkout system is not only frustrating YOU but is also negatively impacting:

- Your EXECUTIVE VP OF OPERATIONS, DON JOHNSON, because he is concerned about the costs of inefficiency and the poor flow of customers through the store;
- Your CEO, because of his concern with the high costs of customer walkouts and the high labor costs associated with too many cashiers;
- Your CASHIERS, who feel the brunt of customer dissatisfaction and experience pressure to move quickly due to the long lines;
- Your FLOOR PLANNERS AND MERCHANDISING MANAGERS, who constantly struggle with the floor layout because the lanes consume so much floor space and take away this valuable space from impulse products;

- Your LOCAL STORE MANAGERS, who feel the brunt of customer dissatisfaction and are not in a position to change the system;
- Your CUSTOMERS, who are pressed for time and frustrated by the long lines; and
- Even your own CAREER, which may be at a stand-still because the design of HD's current checkout system is preventing you from reaching your assigned In-Store efficiency goals.

*[Linda closes]:* "Is that an accurate summary?"

*[Roger]:* "I have to say, that's right on! Yikes! No wonder I am so frustrated and unhappy! I've gotta do something about this!!!"

---

## Mission Accomplished for Linda! Roger is READY FOR ACTION

---

### Another Question from Brian

Before moving on, however, the ever-inquisitive Brian has yet another question which he asks Linda during a short break.

*[Brian]:* "Linda, it seems that you are purposefully causing Roger to get really upset. Don't you feel bad about that?"

*[Linda]:* "Certainly not. Roger has a problem and he needs a solution. And we have the best solution available. At the end of the day, if I can get Roger and HD to adopt our solution, then Roger and all of HD will be better off, and they'll love us for it. Think of it as kind of a 'Tough Love' scenario. I have to dig deep in order to get him to act, because up until an hour ago, he was in major denial that he and HD even had major checkout problems."

*[Brian]:* "It just seemed kind of harsh. Hasn't anyone ever got upset with you for twisting the knife like that again and again?"

*[Linda]:* "That can happen and actually did happen to me on a selling effort just last year. I made a Target Sponsor so upset that she refused to talk about it anymore and rather unceremoniously told me to leave!

"End of that selling effort, so I thought. But she called me back the very next week and we were able to turn the selling effort into a successful sale and implementation. She's now actually a pretty good friend of mine because of the help our solution has provided her. I've even used her as a reference client several times.

"So, yes, you have to determine when 'enough is enough' – which I obviously didn't do in that case. I lucked out in the end, but that doesn't always happen. You just have to learn to feel people out as you become more experienced in building the 'right amount' of anxiety."

*[Brian]:* "So now you're all set to tell him we have the best solution, right?"

*[Linda]:* "Hardly, oh foolish one! I thought you said you studied the Manual! Listen and learn as I move to the next step."

## Moving Right Along

*[Linda]:* "By the way, Bri, where did you get that tweed sport coat with the leather elbow pads? You look like some kind of long in the tooth, worn out professor or something."

*[Brian]:* "I'll have you know that my grandpa gave it to me. He was a professor at Bucknell for 43 years! It's actually the only sport coat I own."

*[Linda]:* "You are kidding, right? Actually, knowing you, you're probably not. Remind me to take you shopping before we visit another client. You are a tad bit embarrassing to even be seen with, if you don't mind my saying so. Not exactly a chick-magnet, are you?"

*[Brian]:* "Cheese 'n crackers, Linda, you really say what's on your mind, don't you? My clothes have nothing to do with my struggle with the ladies. In fact, my mom says this coat looks great on me. And it almost even fits, except for the sleeves which may be a little short!"

*[Linda]:* Thought bubble -- "***Help!!***"

269

CHAPTER 41

# Linda Helps Roger to Envision an Ideal Solution

| Step 1 – Linda Converts Roger, Her Target Sponsor | | |
|---|---|---|
| Ch | 33 | Meet Linda's Target Sponsor & Target Power Sponsor at House Depot |
| Ch | 34 | Linda's Warm Call to Arrange a Face-to-Face Meeting with Roger |
| Ch | 35 | Linda Builds Rapport with Roger's Gatekeeper |
| Ch | 36 | Linda Introduces Herself & SpeedyLane to Roger |
| Ch | 37 | Linda Gets Roger's Pain (Back) on the Table |
| Ch | 38 | Overview of the Vision Building Process |
| Ch | 39 | Linda Diagnoses Roger's Issues with HD's Checkout System |
| Ch | 40 | Linda Builds Roger's Anxiety Over HD's Checkout Problems |
| Ch | 41 | Linda Helps Roger Envision an Ideal Solution |
| Ch | 42 | Linda Closes Her Vision Building with Roger |
| Ch | 43 | Linda Follows up with Roger |
| Ch | 44 | Linda Converts Roger into a Selling Partner with Reference Client Visit |

Last chapter, Linda got Roger all hyped up about the negative impacts that House Depot's (HD's) inefficient checkout system is having on a wide range of important players. With his anxiety sky high, Roger is begging for a solution! [43]

**Danger.** Given Roger's obvious eagerness for a solution, it is important for Linda to *avoid the temptation to immediately 'jump to the rescue' with SpeedyLane's 'perfect solution.'* Recall the cartoon from a couple chapters ago about not jumping the gun. Rather, Linda should continue on with the well-thought-out natural progression and conclusion of the Vision Building Process – following the specific guidelines outlined below for the last phase of the process.

As she begins the final phase of vision building with Roger, Linda must remember that *this is Roger's problem and the vision of an 'ideal solution' must be his as well.* Linda can't try to force-feed Roger her own magic SpeedyLane solution.

Linda reminds herself again that people tend to believe what they conclude for themselves. From her experience, she knows she can only guide Roger toward his own vision of an ideal solution. This does not mean, however, that she can't help *shape* Roger's vision. Indeed, recall when she used indirect questions a couple chapters back in order to help Roger identify the key causes for HD's checkout inefficiencies. Then, Linda complemented the causes Roger mentioned by suggesting (and later confirming with Roger) additional causes which the SpeedyLane brand is uniquely qualified to address.

Now, in concluding her vision building with Roger, one of Linda's critical goals is to see that Roger's vision of an ideal solution includes SpeedyLane's unique advantages over its direct competitors. Perhaps it helps to think of it like setting up the bowling pins (specific causes in Column 1 of Vision Building) and then knocking each of them over (with specific capabilities) in the last column.

## Let's See How Linda Does With This Last Phase of the Vision Building

After heightening Roger's anxiety with her summary of the negative impacts (last Chapter - in Cell 6 or I3), Linda then immediately begins the effort to help Roger envision a solution – starting with an open-ended question (from the top cell in 'Column 3 – cell 7 or 'C1').'

# Linda Helps Roger to Envision an Ideal Solution

## 9 Block Vision Building – Cell Content Summary

| 1st, Get Pain Admitted (Primary Issue) | *Diagnose Causes / Reasons* | *Explore Impacts* | *Visualize Capabilities* |
|---|---|---|---|
| *Open* Questions | **R1** (1)<br><br>Can you tell me more about that? What's causing .. Repeat the issue / pain | **I1** (4)<br><br>Besides you, who else is impacted by this (briefly repeat issue / pain) and how are they affected? | **C1** (7)<br><br>What's it going to take for YOU to address this problem? What can you do about it? |
| *Explore* with Carefully Planned Questions (*Controlled Exploration*) | **R2** (2)<br><br>Indirect Qs to get each Cause /Reason on the Table (Cause 1, 2, 3, etc.) | **I2** (5)<br><br>Is your 'x' (name a position) also affected? How about 'y position,' is that also affected? Etc. | **C2** (8)<br><br>Could I try some ideas on you?<br>What if when C1, you could ... Capability 1 ? Wait for response. What if when C2, you could ... Capability 2 ? Etc. |
| *Confirm* – repeat only *exactly* what the person did indeed tell you or agree to | **R3** (3)<br><br>So, if I am hearing your right, you .. Repeat Issue / Pain .. because 1, 2, 3, etc. Is that correct? | **I3** (6)<br><br>From what I've just heard, it sounds like this is a challenge for # of others as well as for you. Now repeat all of those mentioned along with the specific challenge for each | **C3** (9)<br><br>So, I hear you saying that if you had this, this this & this, then the issue / pain (repeat it) would be addressed as well as the challenges faced by, & all those others affected (mention them each). Is that an accurate summary? |

*[Linda]:* "Roger, what's it going to take for you to solve this problem?"

---

## Roger Has Some General Ideas, but Vents His Frustration

*[Roger]:* "I know there must be a better way, but I don't know what else to do. We have to check-out our customers somehow! But it's just not efficient the way we are doing it right now. We require too many cashiers and our customers have to wait too long. It's just frustrating."

---

Note that Roger may mention some desired capabilities that have not yet come up in the conversation. Included may be one or more capabilities in which SpeedyLane does not have a competitive advantage. Linda should carefully note these and include such desired capabilities in her summary later on (see below).

Time for Linda to Pose Some Prospective Capabilities

# Linda's Vision of an Ideal Solution for Roger

Linda senses Roger's frustration and wants to help. In fact, she has a solid list of capabilities that she feels would make an ideal solution for Roger. The capabilities she has in mind exactly parallel the causes for the problem that Roger confirmed earlier and match SpeedyLane's unique advantages over its direct competitors. More specifically, Linda's vision of an ideal solution for Roger includes the following capabilities:

- Reducing the time customers spend waiting in line;
- Reducing the number of cashiers needed, as well as HD's related requirements for recruiting and training cashiers;
- Enabling customers to choose their preferred method of checkout;
- Opening up more prime high-margin impulse selling space near the front of the store;
- Reducing cashier errors and outright theft at the checkout stations; and
- Having more employees on the floor to help customers, without increasing overall employee headcount.

## What's Linda to Say?

How can Linda make Roger feel as if these are his own ideas? How can she get Roger to agree that this set of capabilities make up an ideal solution for addressing HD's checkout inefficiencies? It is a challenge for any salesperson, but Linda is an experienced pro. She knows that if she just throws the 'perfect' SpeedyLane solution in Roger's face, he will be turned off to her suggestions. The solution has to be Roger's idea.

Hmm... how is Linda going to pull this off? Let's watch as Linda tries to get Roger to articulate his own vision of an ideal solution, one that includes SpeedyLane's unique advantages.

## Linda Asks for Permission -- Before Throwing Out Possible Ideas for an Ideal Solution

Nobody likes the 'know-it-all' who assumes that he or she has all the answers. If Linda acts like that, she could immediately blow her whole vision building effort. But she's too smart and too experienced for that. So before she can offer any ideas for Roger to consider, she asks for his permission to do so.

**Ask Permission Before Offering Suggestions**

[Linda]: "Can I try a few things on you?" [44]

[Roger]: "Of course! I need all the help I can get!"

Linda Poses Her Solution Ideas as Questions, Trying to Make them Roger's Ideas -- "What if ........?"

Even though Linda now has permission to make suggestions, she is careful not to assume too much. She avoids the temptation to simply rattle off her ideas for an ideal solution. Instead, she addresses one capability at a time while posing each as a question to Roger. This soft-sell approach helps Roger buy in, because he is more likely to feel that these are *his ideas*. Let's see how Linda tries this approach. Note that Linda awaits Roger's confirmation after each idea before moving on to the next, and that she avoids any overt suggestion that SpeedyLane has these capabilities.

[Linda]: "What if when customers were ready to check out, they could choose to go to a cashier's line or go to one of the quicker self-checkout aisles, thereby spending an average of 5 minutes less time waiting in line?"

**Linda awaits a response.**

[Roger]: "That would be great!"

Hopefully Roger responds in an affirmative way like this after each proposed capability. Linda is careful not to include more than a single prospective capability at a time, allowing Roger a chance to acknowledge the attractiveness of each specific capability.

Linda continues with the rest of her 'What if...' questions, awaiting Roger's response before moving on to the next capability.

*[Linda]*: "What if you could reduce the average checkout time while also reducing both the number of cashiers needed and your related requirements for recruiting and training cashiers?" <u>She awaits a response</u>.

*[Linda]*: "What if customers could choose their preferred method of checkout?" <u>She awaits a response</u>.

*[Linda]*: "What if your checkout lanes were configured so that you could open up more prime high-margin impulse selling space near the front of the store?" <u>She awaits a response</u>.

*[Linda]*: "What if you had a system that would enable you to reduce cashier errors and theft at the cashier stations?" <u>She awaits a response</u>.

*[Linda]*: "What if you could have more employees on the floor helping customers, without increasing overall employee headcount?" <u>She awaits a response</u>.

**Reminder.** Linda does *not mention her specific brand, SpeedyLane, or its specific competitive advantages a single time* during vision building. This is because Linda is trying to *build a 'generic vision' of an ideal solution*. The *ideal vision created will indeed include specific important capabilities where SpeedyLane has clear and sustainable advantages over its direct competitors.*

Linda Summarizes and Confirms <u>*Roger's Vision*</u> of an 'Ideal Solution'

Through her careful planning and wording, Linda has just helped Roger develop a vision of his own 'ideal solution' for HD's inefficient checkout system – and a way to get rid of his own day-to-day headaches at work.

---

## Linda not only summarizes this solution, but confirms it.

*[Linda]*: "Let me see if I understand you correctly. From what you've just told me, it sounds like you feel you could dramatically improve the efficiency of your checkout system and your customers' satisfaction if you had a way to:

- Reduce the time customers spent waiting in line;
- Reduce the number of cashiers needed as well as your related requirements for recruiting and training cashiers;
- Enable customers to choose their preferred method of checkout;
- Open up more prime high-margin impulse selling space near the front of the store;
- Reduce cashier errors and outright theft at the checkout stations; and
- Have more employees on the floor to help customers, without increasing overall employee headcount."

[Note: Linda should also include mention *any additional capabilities* that Roger may have mentioned – whether or not SpeedyLane has a unique advantage with these capabilities.]

*[Linda, closing her long summary]:* "These benefits, in turn, would not only greatly improve your own day-to-day efficiency, but would also help:

- Your EXECUTIVE VP OF OPERATIONS, Don Johnson;
- Your CEO;
- Your CASHIERS;
- Your FLOOR PLANNERS AND MERCHANDISING MANAGERS;
- Your LOCAL STORE MANAGERS;
- Your CUSTOMERS; and
- Even your own CAREER!"

"Does that sound about right?"

*[Roger]:* "Brilliant! That says it all! That would be super – BUT... how could we possibly accomplish all that?"

------------

Indeed, how could HD accomplish all that? Let's jump to the next chapter to see what Linda suggests!

*Tues., January 24, 3.45 pm*

# CHAPTER 42

# Linda Closes Her Vision Building with Roger

| Step 1 – Linda Converts Roger, Her Target Sponsor | | |
|---|---|---|
| Ch | 33 | Meet Linda's Target Sponsor & Target Power Sponsor at House Depot |
| Ch | 34 | Linda's Warm Call to Arrange a Face-to-Face Meeting with Roger |
| Ch | 35 | Linda Builds Rapport with Roger's Gatekeeper |
| Ch | 36 | Linda Introduces Herself & SpeedyLane to Roger |
| Ch | 37 | Linda Gets Roger's Pain (Back) on the Table |
| Ch | 38 | Overview of the Vision Building Process |
| Ch | 39 | Linda Diagnoses Roger's Issues with HD's Checkout System |
| Ch | 40 | Linda Builds Roger's Anxiety Over HD's Checkout Problems |
| Ch | 41 | Linda Helps Roger Envision an Ideal Solution |
| Ch | 42 | Linda Closes Her Vision Building with Roger |
| Ch | 43 | Linda Follows up with Roger |
| Ch | 44 | Linda Converts Roger into a Selling Partner with Reference Client Visit |

*L*inda *thinks:* "OK, that vision building effort with Roger went super! This is exciting! Even though I know we have the 'perfect solution,' I just can't jump right in and tell Roger 'Boy, do we have the perfect solution for you.' I'd love to do that, but, I've fallen into that trap before and that's not gonna happen again! I know Roger must self-conclude that we have the right solution for him. And I can only get him to do that if I can first PROVE beyond a doubt that SpeedyLane can indeed deliver the 'ideal solution' we worked out together and that he now visualizes."

Roger would obviously be turned off if Linda takes an aggressive approach, rather than letting him self-conclude.

## What Should Linda Say Next?

OK, we know that Linda can't just jump in and tell Roger that SpeedyLane has the exact solution he has just described as his 'ideal solution.' So what should she say?

Here Linda teaches us and Brian what she has learned the hard way over her years of selling experience. Her closing statement to Roger will include a number of critical parts – each with a specific intended purpose.

## Linda's Closing Statement to Roger

Linda's closing statement begins immediately after Roger confirms that the 'ideal solution' just summarized by Linda will indeed enable him to overcome HD's checkout challenges.

*[Linda]:* "Does that sound about right?"

*[Roger]:* "Brilliant! That says it all! That would be fantastic! But how could we possibly accomplish all that?"

Linda Suggests that SpeedyLane Can Deliver the Ideal Solution Roger Now Envisions.

*[Linda]:* "Well, I'm quite confident that SpeedyLane can deliver the capabilities that you just said you needed."

## Linda Checks to see if Roger is still 'with her.'

Linda then tests for Roger's continuing interest. She wants to confirm that she and Roger are on the same wavelength and that he wants to continue their discussion -- if she can prove that SpeedyLane can deliver the desired capabilities.

*[Linda]:* "If we could prove these capabilities to you, would you be willing to take a serious look at our SpeedyLane Solution?"

*[Roger]:* "Sure would, if you could prove it. But I don't know how you're going to do that!"

Linda Tests for Power to find out who handles the purse-strings for this potential purchase commitment by House Depot. OK, here's a danger point. Linda doesn't know for sure who at HD would likely have the power to make the purchase decision to buy the SpeedyLane self-checkout system – but it's probably not Roger, since he's an operating guy and below the so-called 'money line'. Therefore, Linda will <u>not ask</u> Roger how he would like her to try to prove that SpeedyLane can deliver the promised capabilities. Roger could easily respond with a laundry list of things he would like Linda to do to prove her solution's capabilities. For example, he might ask Linda to:

- take him on several reference visits to previous SpeedyLane clients;
- take others in his company on reference visits;
- run trials at several HD stores;
- do a detailed audit of HD's current checkout system in order to come up with a specific price, etc.

All these proofs would require time and would involve considerable expenses for SpeedyLane, in addition to killing the momentum of the sale. And, more importantly, even if all these 'requirements' were completed successfully, Linda would be no further along in her sales effort than she is now, since Roger is unlikely to have the power to buy.

Even After Building a Vision of an Ideal Solution, It's Still Not Appropriate for Linda to Brag About SpeedyLane's Self-Checkout Solution!

**So what should Linda say or do at this point?**

The answer is: *Test for Power.* Linda needs to find out who has the power to make this prospective purchase decision at HD. Linda would be more than willing to jump through some hoops for those decision makers, given the game-changing nature of potentially moving to a self-checkout system. Linda wants to move on with the sales process right now as she has piqued Roger's enthusiasm. She questions Roger to see who would ultimately have the power to commit to and buy the SpeedyLane Self-checkout system.

## Here's Linda's Test for Power

*[Linda]:* "Well, assuming for the moment that we could prove to your satisfaction that we can deliver those capabilities, and that you would want to move forward, what would be the next step?"

*[Roger]:* "Well, then our Executive VP of Operations, Don Johnson, would be the first one we'd have to talk with about potentially changing the way we handle our customer checkout.

Others would also eventually have to get involved, including our Directors of IT and Customer Services, our CEO and others as well. But Don is the first one we'd have to see."

Ah ha! Linda just found out who has the power, and it's not Roger. We will designate Mr. Johnson as our *Target Power Sponsor*! (We will talk much more about the Target Power Sponsor in upcoming chapters.) We already saw Don's personal profile a few chapters back.

---

## Linda Asks for Immediate Access to Don Johnson, her Target Power Sponsor.

If Roger is already 'sold' on us and our solution (i.e., is already a *'Converted Sponsor'*[45]), he might be willing to risk taking us to see his boss, Don Johnson, right now. This would reflect Roger's confidence that we can indeed deliver the capabilities promised. He would have to be quite certain that he would not be wasting Mr. Johnson's valuable time, thus losing his own credibility with his boss. After all, he has only been talking with us for a couple hours and has no definite proof that we can indeed deliver the ideal solution envisioned.

At any rate, Linda has nothing to lose and can potentially shortcut the selling process by asking Roger if he is willing to take her to see Don right now – in a sense, striking while the iron is hot!

*[Linda]*: "Can we go and see him now?"

*[Roger]*: "Hmmm ... that would be a negatory. I just don't know enough about SpeedyLane and your proposed solution to take you to Don right now. First, I'd need to know a lot more about the specifics of your system. I wouldn't feel comfortable taking you to him until I'm confident that you can deliver the capabilities we've been talking about."

**Bargaining for Access to Don**

So, Roger wants more proof that Linda and SpeedyLane can deliver the capabilities promised before he's willing to take Linda to see his boss, Don Johnson. First, Linda will make sure that Roger is indeed willing to take her to see Don if she can prove the SpeedyLane solution to him.

*[Linda]*: "If I can prove that we can deliver the set of capabilities you have indicated you need and that we just talked about, then will you take me to see Don?"

*[Roger]*: "Of course -- why not? If I have confidence that you can deliver all those capabilities effectively, I'd be more than anxious to introduce you to Don. The sooner we get this ball rolling, the sooner my daily headaches could be over! I'm really excited about the possibilities here – I just need more proof that you can deliver."

That's just the response Linda was hoping for. Time to move forward![46]

## Closing the Initial
## Face-to-Face Conversation with Roger

Linda starts her wrap-up by indicating that she will immediately send an e-mail (+ hard copy for HD files). Linda confirms that her e-mail (and letter) will summarize today's conversation with Roger and will also suggest a specific next step to prove that SpeedyLane can deliver the desired capabilities.

*[Linda]:* "That sounds great. Here's what I'm going to do. I'll go back to my office and first thing in the morning I'll send you an e-mail, along with a hard copy for your files. In that e-mail, I will summarize my understanding of everything you've told me today. I will also suggest a way I might be able to prove to your satisfaction that SpeedyLane does indeed have a solution that can provide you with the capabilities you said you needed. How does that sound?"

*[Roger]:* "Perfect! I look forward to getting your e-mail. I'm really anxious to continue working with you if you can prove your solution."

### Linda Indicates and Confirms Her Next Steps and Cordially Closes

*[Linda]:* "Thanks very much for your time, Roger. I will e-mail you first thing in the morning, summarizing our conversation and proposing a way for me to try to prove our capabilities to your satisfaction. I'll then call you later tomorrow to plan our next step."

*[Roger]:* "Great! I look forward to getting your note. I like everything I've heard so far and would love to move this forward, if it all works out."

## THAT IS THE END OF INITIAL FACE-TO-FACE MEETING WITH ROGER

-------------------

Brian & Linda in the Parking Lot, Just Leaving HD Headquarters

*[Brian]:* "Wow, that was really something! You da Man! I mean, da Woman! You can just about mark down this sale! I am sure Roberto will be excited too!"

*[Linda]:* "What are you talking about? Roger isn't even our Converted Sponsor yet. We still have to prove to him that our solution can deliver all those promised operating benefits!"

*[Brian]:* "Well, do you at least think you'll get this contract?"

*[Linda]:* "It's looking better, but it's still way, way too early for projecting that. In fact, I'll now indicate our third step forward in this particular selling effort on my iPhone – where it'll somehow go into our 'cloud-based' salesforce automation system."

*[Brian]:* "What are you entering this time?"

*[Linda]:* "I'm indicating on my sales planning sheet that I've successfully helped Roger build a vision of a solution that matches what we at SpeedyLane have to offer – nothing more. Once I enter that info, Roberto's sales management automation system will project that I now have a 20% chance[47] of ultimately landing this $3.2 million contract. This shows up immediately as a $640,000 sales projection on Roberto's computer screen – up from the $320,000 'credit' I had going for this account prior to our successful meeting with Roger today."

*[Brian]:* "If you can prove our SpeedyLane solution to Roger, and get him to partner with us as our Converted Sponsor, then what will this so-called sales automation system of yours project as the likelihood of getting this contract?"

*[Linda]:* "The answer is 30%, but, hold the show for now! First of all it's not 'my' system, it's *our system* and you'll also be using it, once you get out there selling on your own. But, wait for now -- you're getting way ahead of the game. All that in due time."

"Hey, I have a great idea, to 'celebrate' this little victory, why don't we go downtown and look at some new clothes for you? At least a new sport coat?"

*[Brian]:* "Well, I'd have to call my mom about that first. Besides, I have a badminton match I've got to get to. I'd have time for an ice cream cone though!"

*Tues., January 24, 7:00 pm*

# CHAPTER 43

# Linda Follows Up with Roger

| Step 1 – Linda Converts Roger, Her Target Sponsor | | |
|---|---|---|
| Ch | 33 | Meet Linda's Target Sponsor & Target Power Sponsor at House Depot |
| Ch | 34 | Linda's Warm Call to Arrange a Face-to-Face Meeting with Roger |
| Ch | 35 | Linda Builds Rapport with Roger's Gatekeeper |
| Ch | 36 | Linda Introduces Herself & SpeedyLane to Roger |
| Ch | 37 | Linda Gets Roger's Pain (Back) on the Table |
| Ch | 38 | Overview of the Vision Building Process |
| Ch | 39 | Linda Diagnoses Roger's Issues with HD's Checkout System |
| Ch | 40 | Linda Builds Roger's Anxiety Over HD's Checkout Problems |
| Ch | 41 | Linda Helps Roger Envision an Ideal Solution |
| Ch | 42 | Linda Closes Her Vision Building with Roger |
| Ch | 43 | Linda Follows up with Roger |
| Ch | 44 | Linda Converts Roger into a Selling Partner with Reference Client Visit |

Linda's next challenge is to convince Roger that SpeedyLane can indeed deliver the capabilities promised. If she can do this, she will likely be successful in converting Roger into a full-fledged, enthusiastic selling partner.[48]

## Some Background on
## Linda's Reference Client, Pioneer Markets

Pioneer Markets is a national general merchandise retailer with over 2000 outlets in the USA and Canada. Like HD, Pioneer is headquartered in Atlanta. Three years ago, Linda was successful in selling Pioneer on SpeedyLane's Self-checkout system. Prior to their SpeedyLane adoption,

Pioneer faced most of the same checkout challenges faced today by HD. Since the SpeedyLane adoption, Pioneer's checkout system, related costs, and general customer satisfaction have improved significantly. The prime players at Pioneer are delighted with SpeedyLane's system, including SpeedyLane's efficient, on time implementation, continuing customer service and updating, and, most of all, the fact that SpeedyLane met or surpassed all of the success criteria they established with Pioneer as part of the original purchase agreement.

Linda's original Target Sponsor at Pioneer was *Danielle Starke*. After converting Danielle into a selling partner at Pioneer, Linda and Danielle worked together at Pioneer for nearly six months to convert other important Pioneer players. Together with Danielle's boss, *Sally Cartwright* (Pioneer's Executive VP of Operations), they were successful in creating all of the operational, transitional and financial visions necessary to ensure a successful SpeedyLane sale and implementation.

In the process, Linda developed a close personal relationship with Danielle. In fact, they now have a weekly racquetball game and regularly socialize.

### *Tues., January 24, 7.00 pm*

Linda's planned strategy for proving the SpeedyLane solution to Roger is to take him to see Danielle Starke, the Director of In-Store Efficiency at Pioneer Markets (see insert). Danielle has more or less the same responsibilities at Pioneer as Roger has at House Depot (HD).

Linda Makes Arrangements with Danielle of Pioneer Markets (Linda's Reference Client) to Meet with Roger

Linda calls her friend Danielle and asks her if Pioneer would be willing to serve as a reference client for her new target customer, House Depot. Based on their long-standing personal and professional relationship, Danielle says she is certainly game. She texts Sally Cartwright, her boss and Executive VP of Operations at Pioneer, and immediately gains approval. Sally is one of the most enthusiastic folks at Pioneer in terms of what SpeedyLane has done for them. She is delighted with both the original installations and the continuing technical support that SpeedyLane has provided to make their recently adopted self-checkout system such a resounding success. Danielle gives Linda several alternative days and times for the first meeting with Roger.

### *Nest up – Linda's Follow Up Letter*

---

## Linda Sends a Follow-up Letter to Roger, Her Target Sponsor

Having made preliminary arrangements with Danielle of Pioneer Markets, Linda drafts and sends a follow-up e-mail to Roger the next morning. The e-mail is quite detailed and includes:

- Summary highlights of the meeting with Roger; and
- A proposal for a reference visit to Pioneer Markets as a way to prove that SpeedyLane can indeed deliver the promised capabilities for HD.

**Here is the follow-up letter from Linda to Roger.**

*"Dear Roger,*

*It was a pleasure talking with you yesterday afternoon. Thank you for your interest in SpeedyLane. This letter summarizes my understanding of our meeting and proposes a next step.*

*Reviewing our conversation, you told me you feel that HD's current checkout system is inefficient because of:*

- *Needing a high number of cashiers to keep checkout times reasonable;*
- *Not having enough space up front for selling more high-margin impulse items; and*
- *Having too many cashier errors and too much outright theft at checkout stations.*

*In addition, you said that you feel that HD customers are dissatisfied with your current checkout system because of:*

- *Long average checkout time;*
- *Lack of a faster checkout alternative available for smaller purchases; and*
- *Having too few employees out on the floor to help customers.*

*You told me that you feel HD could significantly improve checkout efficiency if your checkout system provided ways to:*

- *Reduce the number of cashiers needed;*
- *Open up more prime impulse selling space near the front of the store; and*
- *Reduce cashier errors and outright theft at the checkout stations.*

*You also said that you feel you could significantly improve HD customer satisfaction if your checkout system could:*

- *Reduce your average checkout time;*
- *Provide a faster checkout alternative available for smaller purchases; and*
- *Enable more employees to be out on the floor helping customers.*

*You said that if you had these capabilities, you could improve House Depot's overall checkout efficiency as well as your customer satisfaction and loyalty.*

*You also agreed to seriously consider SpeedyLane's solution, if we could prove to your satisfaction that we can effectively deliver those capabilities.*

*In an effort to prove to your satisfaction that we can indeed deliver those desired capabilities, I propose that we meet with Danielle Stark, the Director of In-Store Efficiency at Pioneer Markets, one of the companies I told you about during our discussion. We helped Pioneer to address some of the same checkout issues you currently face at House Depot. You will have a chance to meet Danielle and ask her about anything you'd like. I think you will like what you hear.*

*Following that meeting, I am confident you will want to keep this ball rolling, like we talked about, and that you'll be willing to introduce me to your boss, Executive VP of Operations, Don Johnson.*

*I will call you later today to answer any questions you might have and to arrange for our visit to see Danielle at Pioneer Markets.*

*Sincerely,*

*Linda Brown, SpeedyLane"*

**Wed., January 25, 3.00 pm**

---

## Linda Calls Roger Later That Day

Later that same day, Linda calls Roger confirming that her e-mail accurately summarized their conversation about HD's checkout challenges.

*[Linda]:* "Well, Rog, what do you think? Does my letter accurately summarize our conversation?"

*[Roger]:* "Right on! This is getting exciting! I just hope you can prove these capabilities to me so we can get this ball moving into upper management here at HD."

To provide the proof Roger is looking for, Linda proposes a visit to Danielle at Pioneer Markets.

*[Linda]:* "Well, I've talked with my friend Danielle, the Director of In-Store Efficiency over at Pioneer Markets – one of the companies I mentioned during our conversation. She said she would be more than happy to meet with us to talk about how our SpeedyLane self-checkout solution has helped Pioneer overcome some of the same checkout issues you said you have at HD."

*[Roger]:* "That would be great. I am anxious to meet her. How soon can we do it?"

Linda selects the earliest available date from the alternatives Danielle has given her, and puts that date on Roger's schedule, while immediately confirming that meeting time with Danielle as well.

----------------

[Brian]: "Linda, why would Danielle be willing to spend time acting as a reference client for you? I don't get that."

[Linda]: "Danielle and I worked together for almost six months trying to convert everyone at Pioneer, and we became good friends. She also agreed to serve as a reference client if the implementation was successful. We, in turn, agreed to provide Pioneers with extra IT support to integrate our two data systems."

[Brian]: "Oh! Ok that makes sense."

----------------------

[Linda]: "Hey, by the way Brian, my niece Lucy is coming into town next week. I thought I might introduce her to you."

[Brian]: "Uggg....mmmmm....gulp....errrrrrr."

CHAPTER 44

---

# Linda Converts Roger into Her Selling Partner with a Reference Client Visit[49]

| Step 1 – Linda Converts Roger, Her Target Sponsor |||
|---|---|---|
| Ch | 33 | Meet Linda's Target Sponsor & Target Power Sponsor at House Depot |
| Ch | 34 | Linda's Warm Call to Arrange a Face-to-Face Meeting with Roger |
| Ch | 35 | Linda Builds Rapport with Roger's Gatekeeper |
| Ch | 36 | Linda Introduces Herself & SpeedyLane to Roger |
| Ch | 37 | Linda Gets Roger's Pain (Back) on the Table |
| Ch | 38 | Overview of the Vision Building Process |
| Ch | 39 | Linda Diagnoses Roger's Issues with HD's Checkout System |
| Ch | 40 | Linda Builds Roger's Anxiety Over HD's Checkout Problems |
| Ch | 41 | Linda Helps Roger Envision an Ideal Solution |
| Ch | 42 | Linda Closes Her Vision Building with Roger |
| Ch | 43 | Linda Follows up with Roger |
| Ch | 44 | Linda Converts Roger into a Selling Partner with Reference Client Visit |

Linda is quite excited. The face-to-face meeting with Roger -- her Target Sponsor at House Depot (HD) -- seems to have gone very well. She is now ready to try to prove her solution to Roger so that he may become even more enthusiastic about adopting SpeedyLane's self-checkout system. Linda's goal is to gain Roger as her selling partner in moving forward at HD. The next step, assuming a proved solution, would be for Roger to take Linda for a joint visit to Don Johnson, Linda's Target Power Sponsor at HD.

## Linda Should Re-Confirm
## Her Access to Power, Just Prior to Reference Visit

If Linda had not confirmed access to her power sponsor Don prior to proving the SpeedyLane solution to Roger, she may have been left out in the cold. Consider this scenario.

# Meet Linda's Reference Client, Danielle Stark, Director of In-Store Efficiency at Pioneer Markets

**Full name:** Danielle Stark

**Education:**

- Florida State University, Class of 2010. Cheerleader, all four years.

**Career:**

- Started right out of Florida State as a Merchandising Assistant for Pioneer Markets. Has moved up steadily to her current management position at Pioneer.

## Company & Current Position:

- Pioneer Markets, Director of In-Store Efficiency.

## Romantic Interest/Family:

- Unmarried, but total babe-o-rama! Tons of suitors, but linked most closely with Gustavo Bianchi. He and his family own a line of Italian restaurants in the Southeastern USA. Danielle met him when she was a waitress at the Bianchi restaurant in Tallahassee during her college years at Florida State.

## Hobbies:

- Visiting Gustavo in Tampa and enjoying his delicious Italian cooking (she is not much of a cook herself and survives mainly on instant pancakes and canned soup).
- Road Rallies – most weekends, Danielle can be spotted in her red BMW convertible with any one of her many local Atlanta boyfriends
- Clubbing
- Reading romantic novels
- Making puzzles

## Physical:

- Tall, slender, looong legs
- Very well-proportioned for her height
  Long, flowing brunette hair

Sweet smile
Laughs easily

**Nickname:**
Movie Star

**Vehicle:**
- Red BMW Convertible

---

## Why Would Danielle of Pioneer Markets Be Willing to Meet with any of Linda's Target Customers?

Danielle of Pioneer Markets is happy to help Linda by serving as a reference client for several reasons:

During the final negotiations with SpeedyLane several years ago, Pioneer agreed to serve as a SpeedyLane reference client in return for SpeedyLane agreeing to provide extra IT support to integrate the two data systems;

Danielle is quite proud of and likes to boast about the efficiency improvements she has spearheaded at Pioneer through her lead role in getting Pioneer to adopt and implement the SpeedyLane self-checkout system; and finally,

Linda and Danielle spent a lot of time together as partners in cooperatively building the visions with key players at Pioneer. Through all this time spent together, they have developed a close personal relationship, so Danielle has no problem helping when Linda asks for favor.

---

## Reference Client Visit
## Linda & Roger Go to See Danielle

Roger asks many questions and receives many satisfying answers from Danielle. He comes away with a very positive overall impression. In fact, he is nearly overwhelmed by all the positive reactions he hears about SpeedyLane's interface with Pioneer Markets from Danielle including:

*Fri., Jan 27, 9 am*

- The effectiveness of the overall SpeedyLane self-checkout system;
- The helpfulness of a wide variety of SpeedyLane people with whom she and others at Pioneer worked during assessment, adoption, and implementation of the SpeedyLane system;

- How well SpeedyLane IT professionals helped Pioneer IT and database folks to seamlessly integrate the new SpeedyLane system with Pioneer's existing IT and database systems;
- SpeedyLane's effective training initiatives and programs for store managers, cashiers, and customers;
- The thoroughness of the audit used to determine Pioneer's specific needs;
- The subsequent scaling of the SpeedyLane system to exactly match Pioneer's specific situation;
- And much more – including an inquiry from Roger on price – to which Danielle and Linda gave the 'standard answer.' [I.e., That Speedylane would only ask for a price with which House Depot is completely comfortable. (This is covered in depth in a later chapter.)

Danielle also shared with Roger some detailed metrics she had on hand, documenting specific improvements Pioneer made in its checkout efficiency and customer satisfaction after changing to the SpeedyLane system. Roger was impressed not only by the level of the improvements, but also by the metrics themselves – confirming that SpeedyLane welcomed accountability for delivering on promised improvements.

## Linda Confirms Her Newly Gained Access to Don Johnson -- Her Target Power Sponsor at House Depot

After meeting with Danielle, Linda asked Roger for his general reaction to visiting with Danielle and Pioneer Markets. No surprise here, Roger loved what he had just heard – envisioning solving his own day-to-day headaches in the same way!

[Linda]: "Well, Rog, what do you think?"

[Roger]: "Wow, I can hardly believe Danielle's enthusiasm over your SpeedyLane solution. Did you bribe her or something? Just kidding! That was really impressive!"

This strongly suggests that Roger is now a *Converted Sponsor* – someone now willing to partner with Linda in trying to jointly move this sales effort to the next level. Linda confirms this:

[Linda]: "So, can we move forward now and talk with your boss, Don, to see if we can get him excited about this?"

[Roger]: "You bet. I'll get ahold of him right away when I get back to the office and set up a meeting. I'm really looking forward to helping you convince our uppity-ups to go for your self-checkout system."

Linda now has a Converted Sponsor and a selling partner, Roger, who is just as anxious as her to move this sales effort forward.

Next up. It's now time for Linda and Roger to go see the Target Power Sponsor, Don Johnson, who is both Roger's boss and HD's Executive VP of Operations. Linda wants to try to add him to her sales team!

--------

Before that, however, Linda wants to set up a racquetball match with her good friend Danielle.

[*Linda*]: "Hey Danielle, wanna play racquetball next Tuesday?"

[*Danielle*]: "Sure! Although, I can't seem to find my pocket calendar with all these guys' phone numbers in the way!!!"

# Sales Growth Secrets

---

## Implementing Your Account Marketing Plan: Making the Individual Sale

----

## Step 2 (of 4 Steps)
## Converting the Target Power Sponsor

---

### *Step 2: Converting the Target Power Sponsor*

45.  Plan for Converting the Target Power Sponsor

46.  Vision Building with the Target Power Sponsor

47.  Closing Statement with the Target Power Sponsor

48.  Follow-up Letter & Proposed Evaluation Plan

CHAPTER 45

# Plan for Converting Don Johnson, the Target Power Sponsor

| Step 2 – Linda Converts Her Target Power Sponsor, Don Johnson | | |
|---|---|---|
| Ch | 45 | **Plan for Converting Don - the Target Power Sponsor** |
| Ch | 46 | Vision Building with Don - the Target Power Sponsor |
| Ch | 47 | Closing Statement with Don - the Target Power Sponsor |
| Ch | 48 | Follow-up Letter & Proposed Evaluation Plan |

Presuming a successful reference visit like we saw last chapter, Linda, our salesperson, now has Roger, as a 'Converted Sponsor' and a partner to help her proceed with the selling effort. At this point, Roger is anxious to introduce Linda to his boss, Don Johnson. Don is House Depot's (HD's) Executive VP of Operations. Linda and Roger regard him as their primary "Target Power Sponsor."

If they can add Don to their selling team, then they can have both Roger and Don help to 'convert' other important HD players to join the 'self-service checkout' bandwagon. Without buy-in from these other players, the sale and successful implementation of the proposed self-checkout system will simply not occur.

The range of such players to be addressed may be wide indeed (see 'Bandwagon' Exhibit below) – especially for proposed game-changing solutions, as shown in this case.

# Who Else Will Linda & Roger Need to Get on the Bandwagon?

**The Salesperson and Sponsor Need to get Lots of Folks on the Bandwagon Before a Game Changing Sale is Likely to Occur**

Corporate Managers · C-Level Executives · Customers · Store Managers · Outside Players

## Converting Don Johnson, the Target Power Sponsor

What focus should Linda and Roger have when trying to convince Don to embrace the proposed self-checkout system for HD? Well, as Executive VP of Operations, Don is constantly on the lookout for any new strategies that provide financial benefits to help HD's bottom line. Fortunately, the operating benefits promised by the proposed SpeedyLane solution will yield direct financial benefits for HD.

Thus, Linda and Roger's challenge will be to convince Don of the prospective operating *and financial benefits* of the proposed SpeedyLane self-checkout system. In order to do this, it would be helpful to draw up a planning sheet showing the direct links between each promised operating benefit and its corresponding financial benefit. So far, we have been focusing on the efficiency problems HD is having with its current system, specific reasons for these problems, how to resolve individual inefficiencies, and the specific operating benefits projected from resolving each issue. Now, we will also consider the specific financial benefits of each promised operating benefit. Conceptually, those relationships look like this:

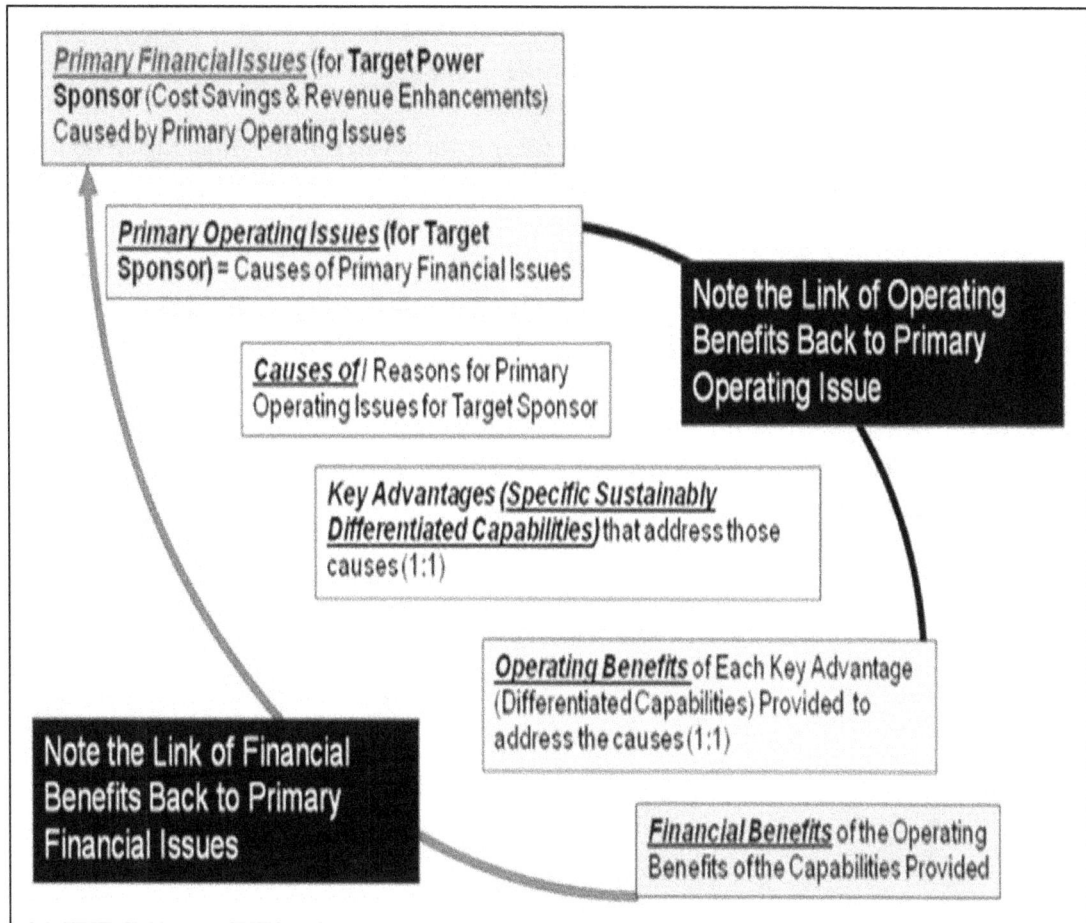

## Vision Building with the Target Power Sponsor

We will use the same Vision Building Process with the Target Power Sponsor as we did earlier with the Target Sponsor. This time, however, both Linda and Roger will participate, and the focus will be not only on the operating issues and benefits, but on the financial issues and benefits as well. Again, the components of the Vision Building Process will be as follows.

- **Capture the initial attention** of the Target Power Sponsor;
- **Establish and build the Target Power Sponsor's interest** in specifically how the promised new operating capabilities can help the Target Power Sponsor and his

company to resolve relevant, critical financial issues, by reducing specific costs and/or increasing specific revenues profitably;

- **Get the Target Power Sponsor to admit a specific relevant financial pain;**
- **Frame the in-depth exploration** (with the Target Power Sponsor, and later with the 'buying committee,' if relevant) of the relevant operational issues and their direct relationship with critical financial issues;
- **Explore** with the Target Power Sponsor (& potentially later with the 'buying committee, if relevant) the significance and breadth of **the long term financial impacts** of living with the current operating inefficiencies – hopefully stimulating the Target Power Sponsor to move the prospective resolution of those issues to the front burner;
- **Help the Target Power Sponsor to visualize how the set of proposed new operating capabilities might help his company resolve its overall financial issues.**

The next chapter presents an example of the detailed conversation that might take place as the salesperson and her Converted Sponsor together try to build a vision of the proposed solution with the Target Power Sponsor.

The Expanded Working Chart for Vision Building with the Target Power Sponsor Might Look Like This:

## Planning Sheet for Addressing the Target Power Sponsor

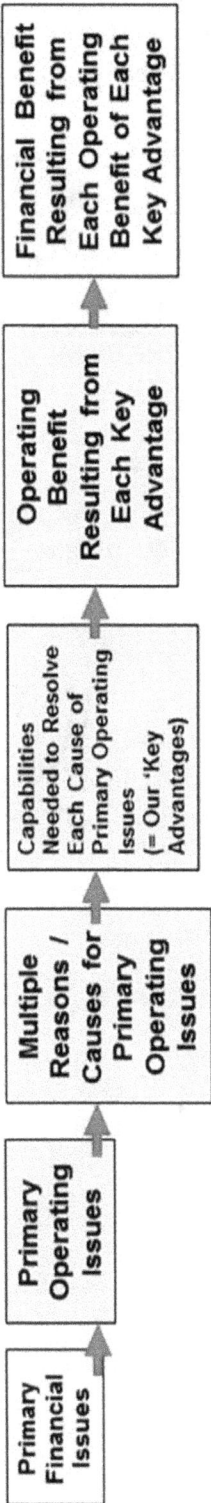

| Primary Financial Issues | Primary Operating Issues | Multiple Reasons / Causes for Primary Operating Issues | Capabilities Needed to Resolve Each Cause of Primary Operating Issues (= Our 'Key Advantages) | Operating Benefit Resulting from Each Key Advantage | Financial Benefit Resulting from Each Operating Benefit of Each Key Advantage |
|---|---|---|---|---|---|
| High Costs & Lagging Revenue = Critical Financial Issues for *Target Power Sponsor* and are Caused by: ==> | Inefficient Checkout System & Dissatisfied Customers =Critical Operating Issues for *Target Sponsor* and are caused by: ==> | 1. Customer dissatisfaction with long lines leads reduces store loyalty. | 1. Self-checkout (feature) improves traffic flow and customer satisfaction by reducing time spent in line (advantage). | 1. More satisfied customers increases store traffic and customer loyalty (by 15%). | 1. Satisfied customers lead to increased sales and store loyalty, resulting in increased revenue (by 5%). |
| | | 2. A high number of cashiers is needed . | 2. Remote monitoring (feature) allows one cashier to operate ten lanes, so fewer cashiers are needed (advantage). | 2. Smaller workforce (by 15%) is simpler to maintain. | 2. Fewer cashiers leads to less required labor and training, reducing overall costs (by 15%). |
| | | 3. Customer have no option for reducing long line wait - compromises satisfaction & loyalty. | 3. Self-checkout (feature) allows customers the choice between a cashier or using self checkout, increasing customer satisfaction (advantage) | 3. More satisfied customers increases store traffic and reduces walkouts (by 15%). | 3. Satisfied customers lead to increased sales and store loyalty and reduce walkouts, resulting in increased revenue (by 15%). |
| | | 4. Loss of prime floor space for impulse products. | 4. Compact configuration (feature) opens floor space, allowing more space for the sale of impulse products (advantage). | 4. Saved floor space and faster lines improve traffic flow and provides opportunity for placement of impulse products (by 15%). | 4. Open floor space near front of store enables sale of more impulse products, increasing impulse sales revenue (by 20%). |
| | | 5. Too much theft. | 5. Advanced weight system, security database, and remote monitoring (feature) result in higher security and less theft (advantage). | 5. Increased security reduces customer delinquency and saves retailer time and resources lost handling theft (by 15%). | 5. Greater security reduces theft, leading to lower costs (by 20%). |
| | | 6. Not enough employees on floor reduces customer satisfaction, which leads to fewer customers. | 6. Remote monitoring (feature) allows one cashier to operate ten lanes, so more employees available on floor (advantage). | 6. More employees on the floor means greater customer satisfaction and store loyalty (by 15%). | 6. More employees on the floor leads to increased sales and store loyalty, resulting in higher revenue (by 15%). |

----------------------

**_Meanwhile,_** on Linda's day off, she scurries over to her friend Danielle's place, proud of the new car she just bought. She has finally upgraded from her old, beat-up 2005 VW Polo.

*[Linda]*: "Hey, Danielle! How do you like my new BMW? It's just like yours!"

*[Danielle]:* "Very nice, Linny. That is actually my old clunker BMW which I just traded in. How do you like my new Ferrari?"

It's my brand new Ferrari 458 Italia! Do you like it?

*Mon., Jan 30, 9 am – 10 am*

CHAPTER 46

# Vision Building with the Target Power Sponsor

| Step 2 – Linda & Roger Team to Convert Target Power Sponsor, Don | | |
|---|---|---|
| Ch | 45 | Plan for Converting Don - the Target Power Sponsor |
| Ch | 46 | Vision Building with Don - the Target Power Sponsor |
| Ch | 47 | Closing Statement with Don - the Target Power Sponsor |
| Ch | 48 | Follow-up Letter & Proposed Evaluation Plan |

## Overview of the Vision Building Effort with Don, Linda's Target Power Sponsor

In this chapter, Linda and Roger will jointly attempt to add Don Johnson (the Target Power Sponsor) to their selling team. Don is a critical player for SpeedyLane because he has access to multiple important players both above and below him on House Depot's (HD's) corporate ladder. In talking with Don, Linda and Roger will focus on the financial issues and benefits that flow from the operating issues already discussed with Roger.

The components of the Vision Building Process with Don will be as follows[50]:

- *Capture Don's initial attention*;
- *Establish and build Don's interest* in discussing how SpeedyLane's Self-checkout operating capabilities might help resolve Don's relevant financial issues, by reducing checkout costs and/or increasing HD's revenues and profits;
- *Get Don to openly admit that he suffers financial pain* related to one or more operating issues that can be addressed by the SpeedyLane Self-checkout system;

- *Explore the relevant financial issues* with Don;
- *Explore the breadth of negative financial impacts* that flow from not addressing relevant operating inefficiencies, hopefully encouraging him to move the resolution of those issues to the front burner;
- *Help Don to visualize the set of new checkout capabilities* that can help him resolve his financial issues related to HD's current inefficient checkout system; and
- *Provide appropriate closing comments* and proposed follow-up with Don.

---

## Here's A Quick Review of the '9 Block' Vision Building Process Itself (Full Scale Exhibit Later in Chapter Provides Details)

## Linda and Roger Get Don's Pain on the Table

*[Roger]:* "Hi Don. I'd like you to meet Linda Brown, from SpeedyLane – the company I told you about that offers solutions for streamlining checkout systems."

[*Don Johnson*]: "Nice to meet you, Linda. I've heard exciting things about your company from Rog. After visiting Pioneer Markets with you, he is really enthusiastic about the possibility of having you work with us to help improve our own checkout system. Tell me more. Exactly what is it that you do?"

[*Linda*]: "Well, let me try to answer your question by summarizing my understanding of House Depot's current checkout system based on what Roger has told me so far. Please jump in whenever you want to correct, clarify, or ask any questions."

"Roger told me that he feels HD's current checkout system is inefficient because it:

- Requires a high number of cashiers to keep checkout times reasonable;
- Lacks space up front for selling more high-margin impulse items; and
- Has too many cashier errors and too much outright theft at checkout stations.

In addition, he told me he feels that your customer satisfaction and loyalty are being hurt by your current checkout system due to:

- Long average checkout time;
- Lack of a faster checkout alternative available for smaller purchases; and
- Having too few employees out on the floor to help customers.

[*Linda*]: "Is that an accurate summary, Roger?"

[*Roger*]: "That's pretty much exactly what we concluded."

[*Linda*]: "I believe Roger also told me that he feels House Depot could significantly improve checkout efficiency if your checkout system provided ways to:

- Reduce the number of cashiers needed;
- Open up more prime high-margin impulse selling space near the front of the store; and
- Reduce cashier errors and outright theft at the checkout stations.

In addition, he told me he feels you could significantly improve customer satisfaction and loyalty if your checkout system could:

- Reduce your average checkout time;
- Provide a faster checkout alternative available for smaller purchases; and
- Enable more employees to be out on the floor helping customers.[51]

[*Linda*]: "Again, Roger, is that an accurate summary?"

[*Roger*]: "That's what we talked about all right – again, pretty much exactly what I told you!"

"Don, I got particularly excited when we visited Pioneer Markets, and their Director of In-Store Efficiency, Danielle Stark, confirmed that SpeedyLane did indeed provide that whole range of capabilities Linda just summarized – and did so very effectively! That's when I decided to call you, to see if we could at least discuss this possibility."

*[Don]:* "Well, I have to admit, that really sounds interesting, since I have some of the same concerns as Roger. As you probably know, I am in charge of the bottom line implications of all those efficiency challenges that Roger faces. And nearly all of the points raised by Roger hurt my bottom line financials."

## Pain Has Now Been Admitted

'Pain' is now clearly admitted. Linda and Roger's next challenge is to take Don on a deep dive in order to flesh out the Causes / Impacts / Capabilities needed (i.e., do the 9 Block Vision Building). This time, however, the conversation will focus on the negative financial impacts of all the operational challenges that Roger has admitted. Linda can be more direct in her questioning of Don than she was with Roger since Don has already heard and presumably (from his reactions we observed) agreed with Linda's list of 'Issues /Pains' and the 'needed capabilities' which Roger just confirmed.

## Next Comes Linda's Vision Building Effort with Don, Using the Same '9 Block Process' Used Earlier to Get Roger on her Selling Team

Without providing all the details of the questioning and discussion in each cell of the 9 Block Vision Building with Don, here we move on to show Linda's wrap up in Cell 9 ('C3'). If you need a review of what questioning and discussion takes place in each cell, we suggest you refer back to the previous chapters where we applied this same process in Vision Building with Roger, the Target Sponsor.

## Planning Sheet for 9 Block Vision Building with Don Johnson, Linda's Target Power Sponsor

| 1st Get Pain Admitted | *Diagnose Reasons* (Causes) (Block R1, R2, R3) | *Explore Impacts* (Block I1, I2, I3) | *Visualize Capabilities* (Block C1, C2, C3) |
|---|---|---|---|
| **Open Questions** | R1. What do you feel is causing the operating & related financial problem(s) you just mentioned? | I1. Who else are these operating & related financial problems affecting besides yourself? | C1. What is it going to take for you to solve these problems that are affecting not only you but so many others as well? |
| **Control Questions** | R2. Ask pretty direct questions to get all potential issues on the table. Are your current checkout station costs too high? Why? Do you: • Need too many cashiers active to keep waiting times reasonable? • Have enough prime floor space up front for impulse racks? • Have high too many cashier errors and too much outright theft at your cashier stations? Are your customer satisfaction and related customer loyalty lagging? Why? Do you: • Have an average checkout time that is too long? • Have customer dissatisfaction for not having a choice on how fast they can checkout? • Have too few employees on the floor assisting customers? | I2. Is this affecting: ■ Your store layout planners? ■ Your store managers? ■ Your cashiers? ■ Your customers? ■ Your CEO? ■ Your Board of Directors? ■ Your Shareholders? ■ Your career? | Would you mind if I threw out some ideas? Sure! C2. *What if you could improve operations and reduce your operating costs by:* -Having fewer cashier stations open, without increasing your average checkout time? -Having more space up front for impulse racks & related high margin sales? -Having fewer cashier errors and less theft at your checkout stations.?? **Furthermore,** What if you could improve customer satisfaction and sales by: -Reducing your average checkout time? -Having a faster checkout alternative available for smaller purchases; and -Having more few employees helping customers on the floor? |
| **Confirmation** | R3. So, from what I believe you've told me, it seems like you are having operating problems and related high costs because of: having too many cashier stations open, with related high direct costs and high costs of recruitment and training; having too little space up front for impulse racks & related high margin sales; having too many cashier errors and outright theft at your checkout stations. Furthermore, you have a high customer walkouts and dissatisfaction and lagging customer loyalty because of: your long average checkout time; not having a faster checkout alternative available for smaller purchases; and having too few employees helping customers on the floor. Is that an accurate summary? | I3. So, if I'm hearing your right, you are saying that this is hurting your CEO, your store layout planners who must compromise prime floor space due to the huge number of check lanes needed, your managers and cashiers who feel the brunt of customer dissatisfaction and, of course, your unhappy customers. On top of all of that, you must deal with the high costs and lagging revenues resulting from all of these problems. Is that an accurate summary? | C3. So let me get this straight... *SEE 'C3' in the text* |

# Wrapping Up the Vision Building with Don
## (Block 9 = 'C3')

Linda concludes her vision building effort with Don by succinctly summarizing what Don has acknowledged would help him to address his day-to-day operating and financial headaches caused by HD's current checkout process.

*[Linda]:* "So, Don, if I'm hearing you correctly, you said that you feel you could improve your checkout efficiency and, in the process, significantly lower your costs by:

- Having fewer cashier stations open, without increasing your average checkout time;
- Having more space up front for impulse racks & related high margin sales; and
- Having fewer cashier errors and less theft at your checkout stations.

I believe you also said that you could improve customer satisfaction and sales by:

- Reducing your average checkout time;
- Having a faster checkout alternative available for smaller quantity purchases; and
- Having more employees on the sales floor helping customers.

Furthermore, you said that these capabilities would benefit not only your customers, but also your store managers and cashiers who bear the brunt of customer dissatisfaction. You also said that Roger, your efficiency manager, would be able to improve his performance, and that your CFO, CEO, and stockholders would all benefit from improvements in your bottom line. You also said that these operating and related financial improvements might even enhance your own personal career opportunities."

*[Linda]:* "Is that an accurate summary?"

*[Don]:* **"Well, Linda, that's a good summary of what I said -- but I can't imagine how we could possibly bring about all those changes!"**

## Just Listening Carefully Can Make a Salesperson Look Pretty Smart!

So, Don, if I'm hearing you correctly, you say that you could improve your check-out efficiency and in doing so fix a host of other aspects of your system?

WOW, this Linda gal's sure got her act together-- she's brilliant!!

------------

In the nest chapter, Linda's details her and critically *important* closing comments to Don, her Target Power Sponsor.

CHAPTER 47

# Closing Statement with the Target Power Sponsor

| Step 2 – Linda Converts Her Target Power Sponsor, Don Johnson | | |
|---|---|---|
| Ch | 45 | Plan for Converting Don - the Target Power Sponsor |
| **Ch** | **46** | **Vision Building with Don - the Target Power Sponsor** |
| **Ch** | **47** | **Closing Statement with Don - the Target Power Sponsor** |
| Ch | 48 | Follow-up Letter & Proposed Evaluation Plan |

In this chapter, we see how our salesperson, Linda Brown, closes her first face-to-face conversation with House Depot's (HD's) Target Power Sponsor, Don Johnson. This closing statement includes some major differences from her earlier closing statement to her Target Sponsor, Roger Dunkel.

## Linda's Closing Statement with Don Johnson, Her Target Power Sponsor[52]

Linda's closing statement begins immediately after Don confirms Linda's succinct summary of the capabilities Don said he needs in order to address his checkout-related financial challenges. (Refer back to Linda's summary in 'Cell C3' in the previous chapter.)

*[Linda]:* "Is that a good summary?"
*[Don]:* "Right on, but I can't imagine how we could possibly bring about all those changes!"

# Linda's Closing Statement

## 1. Linda Confirms that SpeedyLane Can Deliver the Capabilities Promised.

*[Linda]:* "Well, I'm quite confident that SpeedyLane can deliver the capabilities that you said you needed."

## 2. Linda Tests for & Confirms Don's Real interest

*Next,* Linda confirms that Don would indeed be interested in continuing the discussion if she can prove to his satisfaction that SpeedyLane can indeed deliver the desired capabilities

*[Linda]:* "If we could prove these capabilities to you, would you be willing to take a serious look at the SpeedyLane system?"

*[Don]:* "Yes-sir-ree, Linda! Our whole executive team would be extremely interested in a serious look at SpeedyLane -- if you can prove to our satisfaction that you can indeed deliver all the capabilities we just talked about."

## 3. Linda Gets a Better Read on Don's Level of Power

*[Linda]:* "Well, assuming for the moment that I could prove to your satisfaction that SpeedyLane can deliver those capabilities, and that you would want to move forward, what would be the next step?"

*[Don]:* "Since this would be such a big step for us – indeed, a game-changer – our whole executive team would have to get involved in any potential decision to move forward on this.

"What we typically do with big decisions like this is to set up a specific 'Top Management Buying Committee' to evaluate and ultimately make the Yes-No decision."

## 4. Linda Re-Confirms that Don is Serious About Moving Forward

Linda re-confirms Don's Vision by double-checking for access to the next level of authority (Top Management Buying Committee, in this case) if she can prove her solution to Don

*[Linda]:* "So, if I can prove to your personal satisfaction that we can deliver the set of capabilities we just talked about, then could we together take this to your buying committee?"

*[Don]:* "No doubt! In fact, I'd lead the charge – but you've got a lot to prove to me before we get to that stage. I'm sure you understand that I can't put my reputation on the line with our top management team with some half-baked 'might possibly work' idea."

*[Linda]:* "I can certainly understand that."

## 5. Linda asks Don what proofs he will need

**Linda asks Don what proofs he will need.** Linda will NOT ask Don to take her to the buying committee at this point. This is because she fully realizes that Don will want more 'proof.'

*[Linda]:* "How would you like us to try to prove that we can deliver the set of capabilities we've been discussing?"

Linda listens carefully, writing down all of Don's apparent proof 'demands' (see "Wanted Proofs" cartoon). Linda *does not, however, agree verbally or even nod her head in agreement after any of the requests*, as that would infer her commitment to indeed honor any or all of Don's proof requests.

## 6. Linda Purposefully Does NOT Commit to Providing Any of the 'Proofs' Requested by Don

***Why doesn't Linda agree to provide the proofs requested?*** For the same reasons that Linda did not ask Roger, her Target Sponsor, for his desired proofs. Fulfilling all the proofs requested would require momentum-killing time as well as considerable expense. *More importantly, Linda has a tried & true method for proving her solution beyond a doubt. Her approach is much faster, better, and less expensive than running Don's gauntlet of required proofs. She knows from experience that Don will like her method – even though it will omit some - perhaps many - of Don's specific proof requests.*

On a short break, Brian queries Linda.

*[Brian]:* "So, Linda, if you don't intend to honor all of Don's 'proof demands,' then *how can you possibly continue to move this selling effort forward?*"

*[Linda]:* *"Just watch and see."*

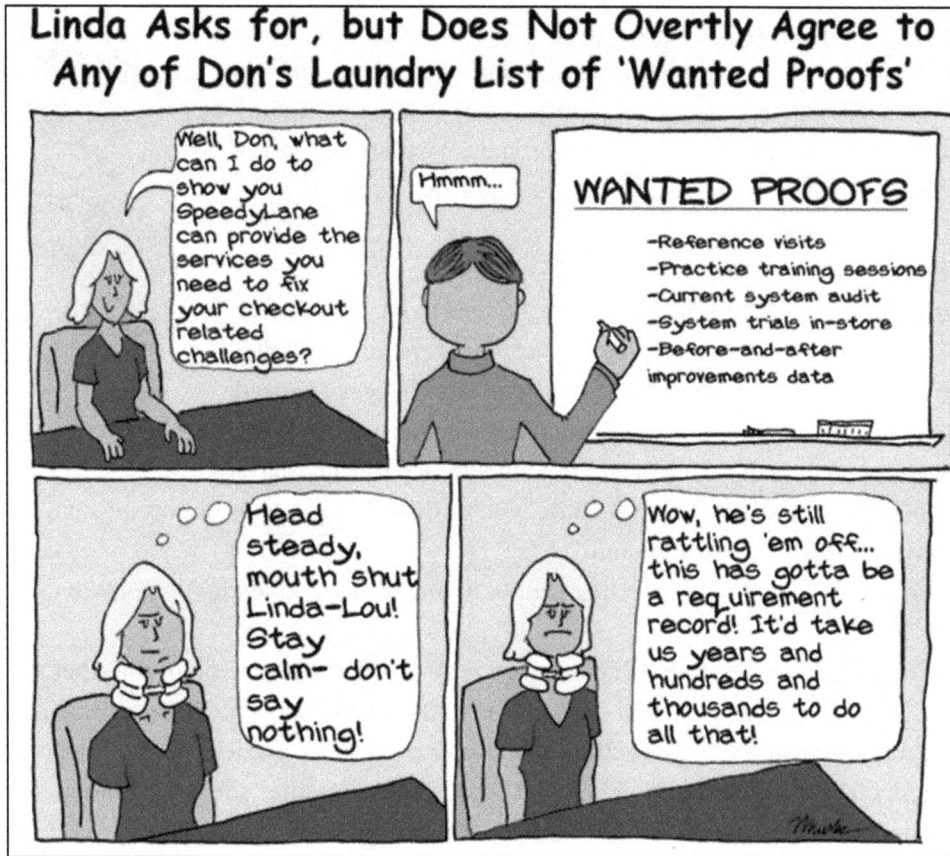

Linda Asks for, but Does Not Overtly Agree to Any of Don's Laundry List of 'Wanted Proofs'

## 7. Linda expands on Don's list of requested proofs.

**Next Linda expands on Don's list of requested proofs. By** doing so, Don will gain confidence in Linda as he sees her in-depth knowledge of the Home Store Industry (of course, it's her target segment). He is also impressed that Linda adds some insightful additional steps to prove beyond a doubt that SpeedyLane can indeed deliver the promised capabilities.

To do this, Linda starts by expanding Don's list of 'required proofs' – including many proofs that hadn't crossed Don's mind yet, but would be expected by others at HD.

*[Linda]:* "How about your IT folks? Will there be a technical review?"

*[Don]:* "No doubt! In fact, one of the critical elements will be to see how easily and how well SpeedyLane can interface their retail data gathering and analysis systems with our current HD systems. I know for a fact that our IT folks would be very concerned about the prospect of having to integrate whole new data systems with their current ones. Yes, we would definitely need you to get our IT group on board."

*[Linda]:* "How about your HR department – would they need to check off on this?"

*[Don]:* "Ya, that's another good point I should have thought of. Our HR group is in charge of recruitment, training, and managing our overall retail headcount at each of our stores. They would have to buy in to any HR related changes that would be required with the adoption of the SpeedyLane system. Good idea! Let's add that to the list, for sure."

*[Linda]:* "Will there be a legal review?"

*[Don]:* "When isn't there? They seemingly need to stick their nose into every change we try to make here at headquarters. In this case, I am sure they would have something to say about any changes required for those HD workers who are unionized. Furthermore, if the SpeedyLane system may require layoffs, I am sure legal would have some important input there as well. Linda, you're thinking of lots of important matters that I should have included in my list of 'must do's.'"

*[Linda]:* "Will you require a formal proposal and an ROI projection, when we get to that point?"

*[Don]:* "Well, I assumed that. When Laura Taylor, our CFO, gets wind of this, that's the first thing she'll ask about. Yes, we will certainly need to generate detailed financial projections, including a risk-adjusted ROI projection as well as a projected Payback Period. Roger said that the reference client he visited at Pioneer Markets told him that she was impressed by the detailed model SpeedyLane uses to project ROI. Our folks in the financial group are likely to want to get their hands on that – they are seldom willing to let vendors do such analysis on their own. Another good point to add to the list of proof requirements."

As Linda presents these additional potential proofs – ___importantly ones that she DOES intend to deliver___ – Don should be thinking, "Wow, this Linda gal really knows her stuff – she's got a better list of proofs than I have. If she commits to getting all these important folks on board, it will really smooth the potential approval process with the buying committee, and in addition help to make the potential implementation go as smoothly as possible."

## 8. Linda assures Don of no end-game surprises – i.e., no last minute changes from SpeedyLane.

*[Linda]:* "Well, I want to assure you that, when we do prepare a proposal for you, it will contain no new information. It will simply document and confirm all the specific business arrangements we will have already discussed – no more and no less. Does that make sense?"

*[Don]:* "We would assume that."

## 9. Linda suggests a 'Pre-Proposal Review.'

**Next, Linda will suggest a "Pre-Proposal Review."** A Pre-Proposal Review is a meeting that Linda will schedule in her detailed 'Evaluation Plan' (see below). She schedules this meeting for right after she, Roger, and Don have completed all important operating, transition & financial proofs. This will be roughly a week before the planned final negotiation and closing in her evaluation plan.

*Importantly, Linda's behind-the-scene / real purpose of this Pre-Proposal Meeting* is to confirm that all proofs have met SpeedyLane's expectations and to subsequently try to close the deal right then and there at the 'pre-proposal meeting.' Doing so would help to avoid all the consternation, bickering, last-minute pressures, tensions, and hard feelings that typically do arise during a formal negotiating session.

*[Linda]:* "Also, I would like to suggest if we get that far, that we come out with a rough draft a week in advance of the delivery of our final proposal. We call this a pre-proposal review. This will provide an opportunity for a last-minute check on all important items for both SpeedyLane and for all of your important players at HD. It will also help to ensure that you and your management will have no surprises in the final proposal. How does that sound?"

*[Don]:* "Why not? That makes sense. Sure."

## 10. Linda reviews with Don her next step

**Linda then reviews with Don her next step: to send a summary letter and draft of a proposed Evaluation Plan**

*[Linda]:* "Well, what I will do now is take my notes back to my office and summarize my understanding of the entire conversation we've had today. I will e-mail you if I have any important questions or need any clarifications while I am preparing that summary. Then I will send you an e-mail with that summary along with a hard copy letter for your files. I will also include a preliminary draft of a proposed step-by-step plan to help you and your top management team to thoroughly evaluate all dimensions of our proposed solution. You will receive my e-mail and the draft of that 'Evaluation Plan' by early tomorrow afternoon. I'll then call you on Thursday to discuss it with you, answer any questions, or provide any clarifications you may like. We'll then plan our next steps. How does that sound?"

===

Don is delighted. He's thinking that he may be on his way to finally addressing some major operating and related financial headaches he experiences every day.

315

*[Don]:* "Perfect. You really have your act together. I'm anxious to get your summary and 'evaluation plan' tomorrow. Thanks so much for coming in today. It's been a real pleasure. Thanks, Roger, for bringing in Linda. I think we may really have something here!"

*[Roger, HD]:* "No problem. I figured you'd be impressed -- especially after I got all those good vibes from my visit with Danielle at Pioneer Markets."

---

### 11. Review of 'Next Steps' – Summary Letter & Evaluation Plan – Cordial Close

Linda concludes the discussion.

*[Linda]:* "It's been a pleasure talking with you both today. I'm very hopeful that we'll be able to move forward together on this. Thanks much for your time. You will be hearing from me tomorrow."

**Follow up Letter to Don, accompanied with a** *"Proposed Evaluation Plan"* (covered in the next chapter)

---

## End of Face-to-Face Meeting with Don

CHAPTER 48

# Follow-up Letter & Proposed Evaluation Plan

| Step 2 – Linda Converts Her Target Power Sponsor, Don Johnson | | |
|---|---|---|
| Ch | 45 | Plan for Converting Don - the Target Power Sponsor |
| Ch | 46 | Vision Building with Don - the Target Power Sponsor |
| Ch | 47 | Closing Statement with Don - the Target Power Sponsor |
| **Ch** | **48** | **Follow-up Letter & Proposed Evaluation Plan** |

## Linda's Follow up E-Mail to Don, Accompanied by a Proposed 'Evaluation Plan'[53]

*"Dear Don:*

*Thank you and Roger for meeting with me yesterday. I believe that the time was well spent for both SpeedyLane and House Depot (HD). In our meeting, you said that you feel you are facing both cost and revenue pressures related to your inefficient checkout system. Here is my summary of our discussion and conclusions during that meeting.*

*You identified the following checkout-related reasons for your checkout inefficiency:*

- *Too many open cashier stations, with related high direct costs as well as high costs of recruitment and training;*
- *Too many cashier errors and too much outright theft at your checkout stations; and*
- *Too little space up front for impulse racks & related high margin sales.*

You then indicated the following checkout-related reasons for your customer dissatisfaction, walkouts, and lagging customer loyalty and sales:

- Long average checkout time;
- Lack of a faster checkout alternative available for smaller purchases; and
- Having too few employees on the sales floor helping customers.

You said that you feel you could improve your overall checkout efficiency by:

- Having fewer cashier stations open, without increasing your average checkout time;
- Reducing cashier errors and eliminating theft at your checkout stations; and
- Creating space up front for impulse racks and related high margin sales.

Furthermore, you said you thought you'd improve customer satisfaction by:

- Reducing your average checkout time;
- Providing a faster checkout alternative available for smaller quantity purchases; and
- Moving some employees from cashier stations to the sales floor in order to help customers.

In addition, you also said that you would take a serious look at SpeedyLane's potential for providing these capabilities. I have attached a preliminary draft of an **Evaluation Plan** designed to help you and your management team thoroughly explore SpeedyLane's capabilities. I will contact you tomorrow to discuss that plan with you, to answer questions you may have, and to plan our next steps.

Sincerely,
Linda Brown, SpeedyLane

Attachment: Rough Draft of Proposed 'Evaluation Plan'"

## Linda's Proposed 'Evaluation Plan'

**DRAFT** **DRAFT**

## Rough Draft of Proposed Evaluation Plan

| | GO / NO GO | BILL-ABLE | Proposed Evaluation Plan | Week |
|---|---|---|---|---|
| | | | The 'Evaluation Plan' is your Proposed Vehicle for Building and Proving all Visions Necessary to Thoroughly Convince all Important Internal & External Players of Operating, Transition & Financial Efficacy of the Proposed Solution | |
| Following Up on the Initial Meeting with Target Power Sponsor | X | | Reference visit with target power spons (Tgt power sponsor may | fill in |
| | X | | Summary of findings on Visit (s) to Top Managem | |
| Operating Visions | | | Continue to Extend Operati | |
| | X | | Gain Operating Vision Confirm Management & the Buying Con | |
| Transition Visions | | | Build transition vision with all int | X |
| | | | · HR | X |
| | X | | · Legal | X |
| | | | · Store Personnel (Managers an ...oyees) | X |
| | | | · Other Important Transition Players | X |
| | X | | Gain Transition Vision Confirmation & Transition Plan Approval from all Transition Players as well as from Top Management & the Buying Committee | X |
| Financial Visions | | X | Audit of existing systems (Scale solution, filing in Customer Usage Profile, 'Placeholder' Value-add parameters, etc.) | x |
| | | | Agree on Financial Criteria for Monitoring Results ('Key Success Factors') | x |
| | X | | Gain Top Management & Buying Committee Check Off and Agreement re Financial Vision, related ROI & Break Even Projections & Key Success Criteria | x |

*As you notice, we will mutually decide to go forward with this project six times during this process (at each go/no go step). Remember this is my first shot, so please feel free to make revisions as you deem necessary. I'll call you to discuss.*

## What is the Evaluation Plan?

The Evaluation Plan is a roadmap for 'converting' all of the other key internal and external players – getting all on board to enthusiastically support and subsequently implement this game changing solution.

Linda purposefully refers to her proposed Evaluation Plan as a 'Rough Draft' and prominently labels it accordingly. She wants Don to buy into this plan so that he will enthusiastically launch it and move the selling effort forward more efficiently. Don's enthused buy-in of the Evaluation Plan is more likely to occur if he regards the plan as *his,* not Linda's. It will become ***Don's plan*** as soon as he makes some changes and returns it to Linda as the '***Final Evaluation Plan.***' Fortunately for Linda and SpeedyLane, the changes Don makes are likely to be pretty minor. Linda has been around this block many times before and has offered up a very thorough 'rough draft' of the proposed Evaluation Plan.

### Tues., Jan 31, 3 pm

Don carefully reviews the proposed Evaluation Plan and generally likes what he sees. He makes a few changes, which include:

- Changing the dates of a few events based upon HD's own schedule and projected availability;
- Adding a few items: for example, adding a trial program for training in-store managers and cashiers;
- Asking for more detail regarding how HD's financial team will be involved in making the financial projections;
- And perhaps a few other, mostly minor, details.

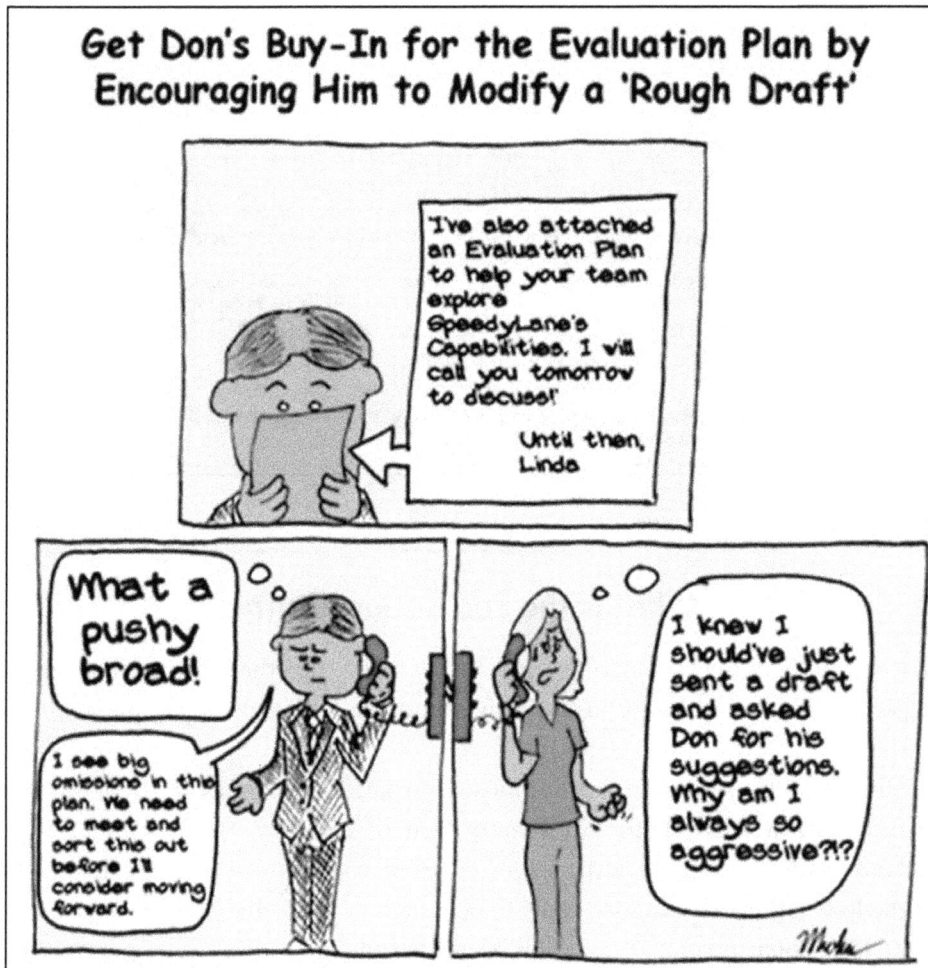

### Tues., Jan 31, 4 pm

Don sends the **Revised Evaluation Plan** back to Linda. ***The plan is now Don's!*** This is important since he is responsible for bringing the plan to the Buying Committee to try to move the plan forward. If a number of significant changes are suggested by Don, then it is important to meet to agree on these specific changes.

---

## Don's Revised Evaluation Plan

| | GO / NO GO | BILL-ABLE | Proposed Evaluation Plan | Week |
|---|---|---|---|---|
| | | | The 'Evaluation Plan' is your Proposed Vehicle for Building and Proving all Visions Necessary to Thoroughly Convince all Important Internal & External Players of the Operating, Transition & Financial Efficacy of the Proposed Solution | Week |
| Following Up on the Initial Meeting with Target Power Sponsor | X | | Reference visit with target power sponsor & other key members of the Buying Committee (Tgt power sponsor may or may not want others to accompany at this point) | fill in |
| | X | | Summary of findings on Initial 'Operating, Transition, & Financial Visions' from Reference Visit (s) to Top Management & the Buying Committee | X |
| Operating Visions | | | Continue to Extend Operating Vision up & down the Chain of influence | x |
| | X | | Gain Operating Vision Confirmation from all Important Operating Players as well as from Top Management & the Buying Committee | X |
| Transition Visions | | | Build transition vision with all internal & external transition players (e.g.) | x |
| | | | - HR | x |
| | X | | - Legal | X |
| | | | - IT = Revision | x |
| | | | - Store Personnel (Managers and Employees) | x |
| | | | - Other Important Transition Players | x |
| | X | | Gain Transition Vision Confirmation & Transition Plan Approval from all Transition Players as well as from Top Management & the Buying Committee | X |
| Financial Visions | | X | Audit of existing systems (Scale solution, filling in Customer Usage Profile, 'Placeholder' Value-add parameters, etc.) | x |
| | X = revision | | Cooperatively Determine ROI and Break Even Payback Period = Revision | x |
| | | | Agree on Financial Criteria for Monitoring Results ('Key Success Factors') | x |
| | X | | Gain Top Management & Buying Committee Check Off and Agreement re Financial Vision, related ROI & Break Even Projections & Key Success Criteria | X |

Revised Draft of Evaluation Plan (now belongs to Don)

*[Brian]:* "What if he rejects the whole Evaluation Plan because it doesn't include some of the things he asked for? Like doing a test market?"

*[Linda]:* "In my experience, that hasn't happened, because the Evaluation Plan which we've suggested is so inclusive. But if it DOES happen, and Don won't move forward without a test market, then I would talk to my sales manager about whether or not we can do that."

---

### Linda adds an aside to Brian

*[Linda]:* "By the way, Brian, tonight's the night I'm going to introduce you to Lucy!"

# Sales Growth Secrets

---

## Implementing Your Account Marketing Plan: Making the Individual Sale

----

## Step 3 (of 4 Steps)
## Using an 'Evaluation Plan' to Convert All Remaining Key Players

*Step 3, cont., Using an 'Evaluation Plan' to Convert All Remaining Key Players*

### Converting All Remaining Key Players Identified in the Evaluation Plan

49.  Principles to Incorporate in the Evaluation Plan
50.  Start Implementing the Evaluation Plan
51.  Build & Confirm Additional Operating Visions
52.  Build & Confirm Transition Visions
53.  Build & Confirm Financial Visions

CHAPTER 49

# Purposes and Components of the Evaluation Plan[54]

| Step 3 – Linda, Roger & Don Team to Convert the Remaining Key Players | | |
|---|---|---|
| Ch | 49 | **Purpose & Components of the 'Evaluation Plan'** |
| Ch | 50 | Principles to Incorporate in the Evaluation Plan |
| Ch | 51 | Start Implementing the Evaluation Plan |
| Ch | 52 | Build & Confirm Additional Operating Visions |
| Ch | 53 | Build & Confirm Transition Visions |
| Ch | **54** | Build & Confirm Financial Visions |

## Purposes of the Evaluation Plan

Detailed Definition of the Evaluation Plan: The 'Evaluation Plan' is SpeedyLane's proposed vehicle for building and proving all visions necessary to thoroughly convince all-important internal & external House Depot (HD) players of the operating, transition, and financial feasibility of the SpeedyLane Self-checkout System. This is summarized in the Exhibit below.

## Purposes of the Evaluation Plan

**1. To Build All Required Operating Visions.**
Meet and thoroughly convince all parties needing 'Operating Vision' that your solution can deliver the specific vision needed.

→ Operating Vision Proves 'It Works' as Promised

**2. To Build All Required Transition Visions.**
Meet and thoroughly convince all parties needing 'Transition Vision' that your solution can deliver the specific vision needed.

→ Transition Vision Proves 'It Can Be successfully Implemented' as Promised

**3. To Build All Required Financial Visions.**
Meet and thoroughly convince all parties needing 'Financial Vision' that your solution can deliver the specific vision needed.

→ Financial Vision Proves 'It Makes Financial Sense' as Promised

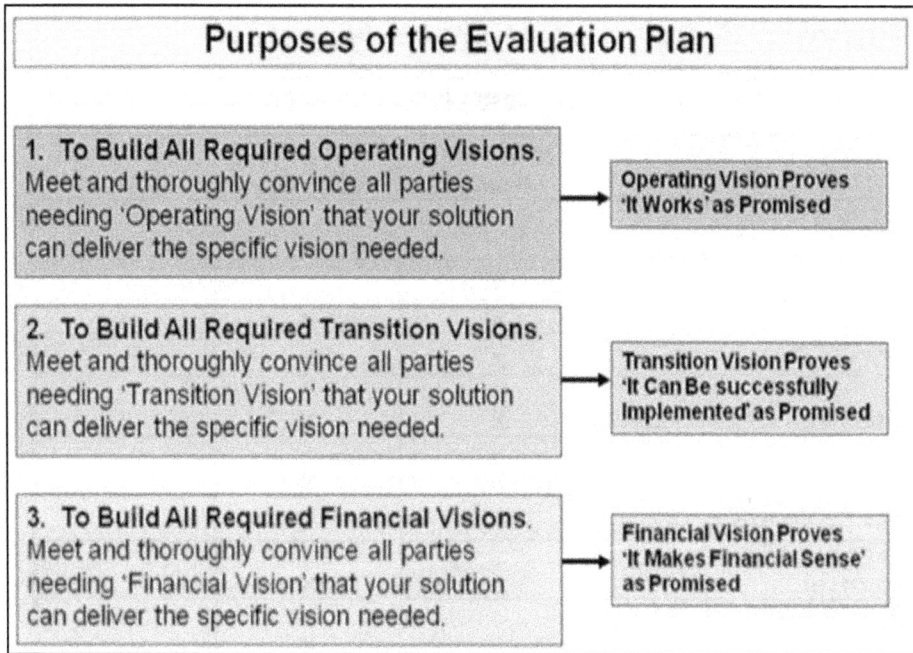

Note in the **next Exhibit -- "Players and Related Visions"** -- how many HD players will need one or more visions built if this is to be a successful sale and implementation. As shown, some players require only a single vision, while others demand multiple visions before they will buy into the proposed SpeedyLane solution. In practice, one should think of this as a 'master table of visions to be built', intended to build awareness of the wide array of *potential concerns* that may exist within a target customer company when a game-changing solution - like self-checkout - is proposed.

The "Players" table below, therefore, is a master list of *potential* visions of concern. In actual practice, the   salesperson will likely be building only a subset of this whole array of visions. Some of these folks may be bypassed altogether. And most of the other individual players will, in practice, typically require but a single vision built (for example, a single operating vision, transition vision, or financial vision).

Then, *why is it such an extensive list?* We want our sales folks to be aware of the breadth of *potential* concerns within the target customer company. That way, when hearing an objection or question about a vision requirement from a particular player, the salesperson is not caught off guard.

## Players & Related Visions Needed

| Market solution: | Self-Service checkout | | |
|---|---|---|---|
| **Players** | Operating Vision | Transition Vision | Financial Vision |
| **Internal Players** | | | |
| CEO | X | X | X |
| CFO | X | X | X |
| COO | X | X | X |
| EXEC VP - OPERATIONS | X | X | X |
| Director of In-Store Efficiency | X | X | |
| Corporate HR Manager | | X | |
| Corporate Legal Counsel | | X | |
| Director of Corporate IT | | X | |
| IT Managers | | X | |
| Corporate Merchandising | X | X | |
| Corporate Customer Svc Manager | X | X | |
| Store Managers | X | X | X |
| Stoe Assistant Managers | X | X | X |
| Cashiers | X | X | |
| In-store customer service reps | X | X | |
| **External Players** | | | |
| **Players** | Operating Vision | Transition Vision | Financial Vision |
| Customers | X | X | |
| Independent suppliers | X | X | |
| Retail Labor Union(s) | | X | |
| Nat'l Business press | | X | |
| Local press | | X | |

## Components of the Evaluation Plan

The following steps in the Evaluation Plan are intended to get all important HD players on board with the proposed addition of the SpeedyLane Self-checkout System.

## 1. Don Makes a Reference Visit to Pioneer Markets

Linda and Roger take Don, the Target Power Sponsor, on a reference visit to Pioneer Markets. Don may elect to bring along additional members of the HD Buying Committee.

## 2. Report to the Top Management Buying Committee

Don and Roger summarize the findings from their Reference Visit(s) to the Top Management Buying Committee regarding the projected 'Operating, Transition, and Financial Visions.' Linda is also there to help answer any questions.

## 3. Initial Go-Ahead from Top Management Buying Committee

The Top Management Buying Committee gives the go-ahead for Linda, Roger and Don to move forward with the proposed Evaluation Plan. They will try to build positive operating, transition, and financial visions for all HD players who will be affected by the prospective addition of the proposed SpeedyLane Self-checkout System.

## 4. Get Buying Committee's OK for Auditing HD's Current Checkout System

The Top Management Buying Committee approves an audit of HD's current checkout system and the related charge from SpeedyLane to conduct this audit (e.g., $50-$100K). Upon Linda's insistence, this audit approval will be required as an integral part of the Buying Committee's initial approval for moving forward with the Evaluation Plan.

This up-front financial commitment is intended to ensure that the HD Buying Committee has a serious interest in evaluating the potential of using SpeedyLane as a solution. If Linda senses a lack of enthusiasm from the Buying Committee, she may want to lighten the potential shock of the up-front charge. She can do this by adding: *"However, if we go through with the sale and implementation, we will rebate that audit charge."*

The information from the audit is required in order to scale the solution for determining the prospective financial benefits, ROI, Payback Period, etc. as well as for setting the price that SpeedyLane will charge HD for the system.

But we always have to be careful not to test the Buying Committee's sincerity before they have been convinced of an initial, concrete vision of how the proposed solution might make sense regarding both operating and financial benefits. Refer to the "Buying Committee" cartoon.

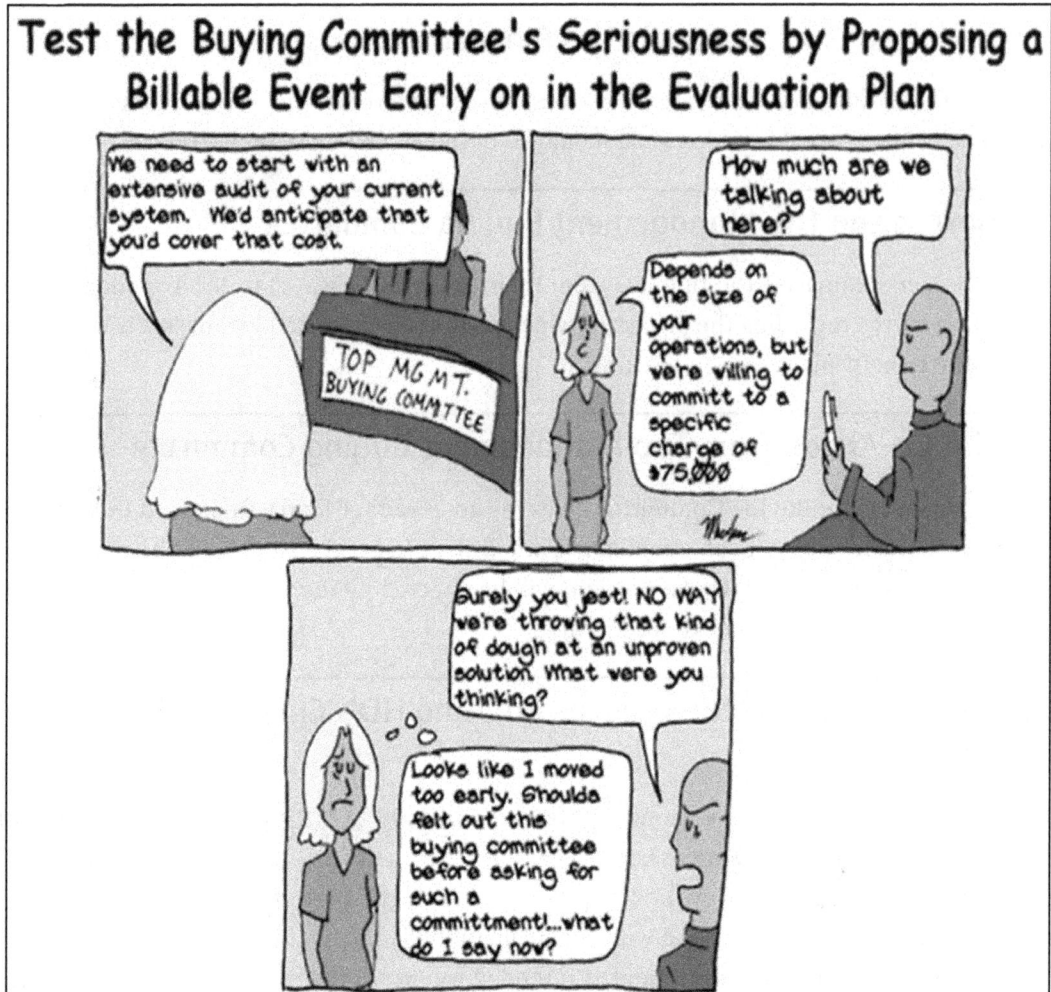

Test the Buying Committee's Seriousness by Proposing a Billable Event Early on in the Evaluation Plan

## 5. Build All Visions with Key Players

Now it is time for Linda, Roger, and Don to build each vision with key players at HD. These visions will all be explained in separate chapters, but the list includes:

a.  Build & Confirm the Full Range of Required *Operating Visions* up and down the corporate ladder.

b.  Build & Confirm the Full Range of Required *Transition Visions* up and down the corporate ladder.

c.  Build & Confirm the Full Range of Required *Financial Visions* with results from the detailed audit scaling to HD's specific needs.

## 6. Finish & Confirm All Visions

With help from Roger, Don, and selected reference clients, Linda provides any final individual operating, transition, and financial proofs still needed by key internal and external HD players. She does this in order to ensure that everyone is on board for an expedient closing and smooth implementation of the SpeedyLane Self-checkout system.

## 7. Pre-Proposal Review

Linda has planned a "Pre-proposal Review" for one week prior to the official planned closing. This review appears prominently in the Evaluation Plan. It is promoted as an opportunity for Linda, Roger, Don and key HD players to confirm that all operating, transition, and financial visions have indeed been built to the satisfaction of the Top Management Buying Committee. We will consider this Pre-Proposal Review in greater depth in the next chapter.

## 8. Final Negotiation, Implementation, and Monitoring Results

This final component of the Evaluation Plan is covered in a later, after reviewing how to build all the necessary visions.

# CHAPTER 50

# Principles to Incorporate in the Evaluation Plan

| Step 3 – Linda, Roger & Don Team to Convert the Remaining Key Players | | |
|---|---|---|
| Ch | 49 | Purpose & Components of the 'Evaluation Plan' |
| **Ch** | **50** | **Principles to Incorporate in the Evaluation Plan** |
| Ch | 51 | Start Implementing the Evaluation Plan |
| Ch | 52 | Build & Confirm Additional Operating Visions |
| Ch | 53 | Build & Confirm Transition Visions |
| Ch | 54 | Build & Confirm Financial Visions |

This chapter reviews a number of important principles to follow when Linda develops and communicates her Evaluation Plan to Don and the House Depot (HD) Top Management Buying Committee.[55]

## Suggest a Specific Schedule for All Planned Activities

Linda shows Don (and eventually the entire Top Management Buying Committee) that she has a very thorough, well-thought-out proof plan. She makes sure to include specific proposed timing for all important stages of the plan.

Have an Organized Proof Plan that Includes Specific Dates for All Planned Activities

# Detailed Schedule for All Planned Activities in Evaluation Plan

## Send the Plan in 'Draft' Form

Clearly label the proposed Evaluation Plan sent to Don as a 'Draft' or 'Rough Draft.' This will encourage Don to make changes in the plan. By doing this, it will then become 'his' plan, which improves the chances of his buy-in.

Not having a well-organized 'proof plan,' (including specific dates, who will do what, etc.) can leave the prospective buyer with little confidence that you can actually complete the evaluation plan both efficiently and effectively. See the "Organized Proof Plan" cartoon for what can happen if a  salesperson offers an incomplete or haphazard evaluation plan.

**DRAFT**   **DRAFT**

## Rough Draft of Proposed Evaluation Plan

| | GO/ NO-GO | BILL-ABLE | Proposed Evaluation Plan | Week |
|---|---|---|---|---|
| | | | The 'Evaluation Plan' is your Proposed Vehicle for Building and Proving all Visions Necessary to Thoroughly Convince all Important Internal & External Players of Operating, Transition & Financial Efficacy of the Proposed Solution | |
| Following Up on the Initial Meeting with Target Power Sponsor | X | | Reference visit with target power sponsor (Tgt power sponsor may or...) | fill in |
| | X | | Summary of findings on Visit (s) to Top Management | |
| Operating Visions | | | Continue to Extend Operati... | |
| | X | | Gain Operating Vision Confirm... Management & the Buying Con... | |
| Transition Visions | | | Build transition vision with all int... | X |
| | | | - HR | X |
| | X | | - Legal | X |
| | | | - Store Personnel (Managers an ...oyees) | X |
| | | | - Other Important Transition Players | X |
| | X | | Gain Transition Vision Confirmation & Transition Plan Approval from all Transition Players as well as from Top Management & the Buying Committee | X |
| Financial Visions | | X | Audit of existing systems (Scale solution, filling in Customer Usage Profile, 'Placeholder' Value-add parameters, etc.) | X |
| | | | Agree on Financial Criteria for Monitoring Results ('Key Success Factors') | x |
| | X | | Gain Top Management & Buying Committee Check Off and Agreement re Financial Vision, related ROI & Break Even Projections & Key Success Criteria | X |

*As you notice, we will mutually decide to go forward with this project six times during this process (at each go/no go step). Remember this is my first shot, so please feel free to make revisions as you deem necessary. I'll call you to discuss.*

## Include Numerous "Go-No Go" Points
## in the Proposed Evaluation Process

Observe that the draft Evaluation Plan Linda sent to Don includes seven Go-No Go Points that are spread throughout the entire evaluation process.

By including these points, Linda enhances the likelihood that Don and the HD Top Management Buying Committee will accept the Evaluation Plan because it reduces perceived risk. They know that they can end the buying process idea at almost any time prior to committing to the purchase.

## Include a Billable Event Early-on in the Plan

Include a billable event near the beginning of the Evaluation Plan. As we saw in the last chapter, this is a good way to test whether or not the Buying Committee does indeed have a serious interest in the SpeedyLane solution.

In this example, Linda used a billable audit to tailor the solution to HD's specific needs. If the Buying Committee is really serious about continuing with the Evaluation Plan, they'll be willing to pay the $50,000-$100,000 to pay SpeedyLane for the audit. If they balk, then Linda obviously has more vision building to do with the Buying Committee.

*We will talk more about this up-front 'audit charge' in the next chapter.*

## Delay Indicating the Price until the Value of the Solution Is Proven (Note – Price must be determined in order to do the ROI and Payback Period Projections)

Linda already knows that one of the first questions asked by the Buying Committee will be, 'What would this cost us?' Linda avoids the trap of stating even an approximate price, as that often causes more harm than good when selling any substantive market solution. Rather, Linda's automatic response (reviewed in earlier chapters) is the following: *"We can't price it until we scale it to your specific situation and needs. But I will tell you this -- your cost will be far less than the proven value provided!"*

Linda can't determine or justify the SpeedyLane price until she has proven its value to HD's satisfaction. She will do this while working cooperatively with HD financial folks to project ROI and Payback Period.

## Schedule a Pre-Proposal Review for a Week Prior to the Planned Formal Closing

Linda has planned a "Pre-Proposal Review" for one week prior to the official planned closing. Outwardly, this is promoted as an opportunity for Linda, Roger, Don and key HD players to confirm that all operating, transition, and financial visions have indeed been built to the satisfaction of the Top Management Buying Committee's requirements.

But Linda has an important additional reason to try to close the deal right then and there at the pre-proposal meeting. She wants to try to strike while the iron is hot, because she is fully aware that the negotiation process itself can be stressful and may frequently force last minute 'gives' on price, add-ons, updates, guarantees, etc.

So, once the visions for all the important players have already been built and an attractive price (for HD, the buyer) has been agreed upon, why not move ahead right now? That's the point that Linda will make at the pre-proposal meeting. To encourage this desired early signing, Linda can emphasize that every week of delay is costing HD big bucks (e.g., $25 K or whatever the number turns out to be when cooperatively developing and proving the final financial vision).

------------

***Meanwhile,*** *i*t's finally time for Brian's 'big date' with Lucy

*[Linda]*: "Tonight's the night! It's your big date with Lucy. She's staying with me for the weekend, so why don't you come by my house at 8pm to pick her up?"

*[Brian]*: *Gulp* "Ok, Linda... but do you think she'll like me?"

*[Linda]*: "As long as you wear something presentable and act maturely, I don't see why not!"

Later that evening ...

*Thurs, Feb. 2, 10 am – 12 pm; and Mon, Feb 6, 9am – 11 am*

CHAPTER 51

# Start Implementing the Evaluation Plan[56]

| Step 3 – Linda, Roger & Don Team to Convert the Remaining Key Players | | |
|---|---|---|
| Ch | 49 | Purpose & Components of the 'Evaluation Plan' |
| Ch | 50 | Principles to Incorporate in the Evaluation Plan |
| **Ch** | **51** | **Start Implementing the Evaluation Plan** |
| Ch | 52 | Build & Confirm Additional Operating Visions |
| Ch | 53 | Build & Confirm Transition Visions |
| Ch | **54** | Build & Confirm Financial Visions |

## Meet Linda's Reference Client (for Target Power Sponsor, Don Johnson),

## Sally Cartwright,
### Exec. VP of Operations for Pioneer Markets

**Full name**: Sally Cartwright

**Education**: University of Wisconsin, Class of 1995.

**Career**:

- Started right out of college as a Merchandising Assistant for Pioneer Markets. She has moved up steadily to her current executive position at Pioneer.

**Company & Current Position**: Pioneer Markets:

- Executive VP of Operations

**Family/Romantic Interest**

- Sally is a hopeless romantic who will fall in love with essentially any member of the male gender. She still hasn't found "the one" yet but is on the prowl every day. She's getting a little worried, though, because she's not getting any younger and wants to have a family.

**Hobbies:**

- *Off-Roading* in her Jeep Wrangler, showing off her wild, adventurous side
- *Crocheting* scarves and blankets for her friends
- *Daydreaming* about her wedding and future husband
- *Scrapbooking*
- *Listening to soundtracks* from musicals
- *Visiting her folks* on their dairy farm in Wisconsin

**Physical:**

- A little on the short side (5'1")
- Slightly plump
- Rosy cheeks
- Light brown curly hair

**Other:**

- Drinks several cups of tea every day
- Loves malt liquor – a carryover from her sorority days at UW

**Nickname:**

- Curly (from her dad, for her ultra-curly hair as a child)

**Vehicle:**

- Two year old Yellow Jeep Wrangler

---

*Thurs, Feb. 2, 10 am*

## Linda and Roger Take Don to Visit Sally

Prior to meeting with Don, Linda and Sally are waiting for Roger and Don in the lobby at Pioneer HQs

[*Linda*]: "Is everything okay, Sally? You seem stressed. There's nothing to worry about, just explain to Don how SpeedyLane has helped Pioneer to increase revenue and cut costs."

338

*[Sally]:* "I'm not nervous about our meeting. I just met this really cute guy last night at my crocheting class and he's all I can think about."

## Don & Roger in the parking lot

*[Don]:* "Is everything okay, Roger? You seem stressed."

*[Roger]:* "I'm not nervous about our meeting. I just met this really cute girl last night at my crocheting class and she's all I can think about."

## Don & Roger enter lobby

*[Linda to Sally]:* "I'd like you to meet Don and Roger."

*[Sally to Roger]:* "Oh my gosh! It's you! I thought I'd never see you again!"

*[Roger]:* Thinking to himself – *I can't believe it! At long last, I may have found my soulmate!*

# Start Implementing the Evaluation Plan

The first step in the Evaluation Plan will be for Linda and Roger to take Don to talk with the folks at Pioneer Markets, the same company that Roger visited earlier. The three will talk with both Danielle Stark - Roger's counterpart at Pioneer - and with Sally Cartwright, who is Pioneer's Executive VP of Operations and has more or less the same responsibilities and challenges that Don has at House Depot (HD).

Given Linda's successful vision building effort with Don, he is already excited about all the potential benefits the SpeedyLane solution *might* bring, but he still needs confidence that SpeedyLane can indeed deliver the promised capabilities. If he's convinced by these discussions at Pioneer Markets, then he will have a strong self-interest in moving the selling process forward. The next step for Don would be to introduce Linda and the SpeedyLane proposal to HD's Top Management Buying Committee.[57]

## Don Asks a Slew of Questions

Don is likely to ask Sally – as well as Danielle and potentially others at Pioneer – a wide array of questions during his visit. His own questions will parallel the questions he himself anticipates being asked by his Buying Committee, if and when he decides to move this proposal forward. His list will include questions such as:
- "Did the SpeedyLane solution generally live up to the hype built by Linda during the selling process?" "What were the results?"
- "Has your average checkout time improved? How much?"

- "What were the results?"
- "Has Pioneer reaped significant cost savings from:
  - Having fewer cashier stations open & using fewer cashiers?
  - Having fewer cashier errors?
  - Having less theft at your checkout stations?
- "What before-after metrics did SpeedyLane use to monitor these improvements?"
- "Have you captured more space for impulse racks - &, if so, by how much have impulse sales improved?"
- "Did Pioneer determine the projected ROI and Payback Period? & did you at Pioneer meet these goals?"
- "What key success variables did you monitor to determine financial improvements?"
- "How have your customers reacted to having a faster checkout available for smaller purchases; and to having more employees out on the sales floor helping customers?"
- "What primary challenges did Pioneer run into when transitioning to SpeedyLane's self-checkout system?"
- "How long did the transition take after Pioneer gave the final go-ahead? Were there any big delays or deviations from the planned implementation schedule? Please elaborate."
- "Did the SpeedyLane database system interface seamlessly with Pioneer's existing database system?"
- Etc.

Don asks any or all of these and other probing questions of Sally and others at Pioneer in order to help decide whether or not to move this selling effort forward at HD. *Don needs these answers because he knows that his Buying Committee is likely to ask him similar questions* prior to authorizing continuation of the evaluation process.

---

## Linda Confirms Don's Continuing Interest

### *Thurs, Feb. 2, 12 pm*

Out in the parking lot, at the close of Don's visit, Linda confirms that Don is satisfied with the answers he has received from Sally and others at Pioneer. She will also confirm that Don will now enthusiastically take the proposed Evaluation Plan to the Top Management Buying Committee for review and, hopefully, for approval.

---

# Don Confirms He is now a
# Converted Power Sponsor& Selling Partner

*[Linda, SpeedyLane]: "Well, what do you think Don?"*

[Don, HD]: "Wow! That was impressive. I can't wait to take this to my superiors to see if we can push it forward. If we have an experience similar to Pioneer's, this will significantly improve the efficiency of our checkout processes – helping to both reduce cost and increase revenues."

Don's enthusiastic reaction has now made him a *Converted Power Sponsor,* and he will now join Linda and Roger on the 'selling team.' He may or may not want to talk with additional reference clients for two reasons First, he may need more convincing himself, or second, he may be anxious to move the selling effort forward and feels that, with additional success stories, he could make a more convincing proposal to the Buying Committee.

## Have Additional Reference Stories and Contacts Ready at Hand

While Don was very impressed with what Pioneer had to say, he may ask for some additional references that he might call in order to confirm that other businesses have had favorable reactions and similar results to Pioneer. Linda has to be ready to provide such references for both Roger and Don to potentially check out and volunteer to take them to witness firsthand SpeedyLane's other success stories.

### Brian wants to know what Linda feels the chances are now of ultimately making this sale

*[Brian]*: "Hey, what are the chances now? This looks to be going great!"

*[Linda]*: "We still have a long way to go because we still have to implement all those proofs. I would say we're only 40% of the way to making the sale. "

*[Brian]*: "Is that all? Seems like we're much closer than that!"

*[Linda]*: "You would be surprised how many sales go bust because we're not able to actually implement every proof step we've listed. For example, it might only take one transition player like the head of IT to ruin the whole deal."

*Mon, Feb 6, 9am – 11 am*

## Don Meets with the Top Management Buying Committee

Next, Don meets with the Top Management Buying Committee to present his proposal to move forward with the Evaluation Plan. Linda and Roger accompany him to lend support and to help answer questions the Buying Committee may have. Don's goals are to present his Pioneer reference visit findings to the HD Buying Committee, to answer their questions, and to seek their authorization to take the next steps.

Some Buying Committee members may hesitate to approve the more in-depth exploration of the feasibility of SpeedyLane's self-checkout alternative. This may occur despite hearing the glowing reports from Don and Roger's SpeedyLane reference client visit(s). In this case, Linda will invite those more cautious Buying Committee members to take one or more reference visits themselves -- until they are comfortable with at least moving to the next step of the Evaluation

Plan. To help soften up these dubious folks, Linda will also present the overall Evaluation Plan and will emphasize that the plan includes multiple 'no-go opportunities' that allow HD's Buying Committee to back out prior to making any final commitment to purchase the SpeedyLane solution.

*Mon, Feb 6, 11 am*

## Linda Gets Some 'Skin in the Game' From HD with an Early Required Audit of HD's Current Checkout System

Before starting the intense, time consuming Evaluation Plan effort to cooperatively build operating, transition, and financial visions with key players at HD, Linda wants HD to put some 'skin in the game' in order to ensure that the Buying Committee has true interest in moving forward from the get go. Linda can provide this opportunity through the next step of the Evaluation Plan: an audit of HD's current checkout system.

SpeedyLane will do the audit and will charge for this service – say anywhere from $50,000 to $100,000. Approval for the audit and the related charge will be included as an integral part of the Buying Committee's initial approval for moving forward with the Evaluation Plan. If the final deal goes through, SpeedyLane may plan to rebate the audit charge. Linda may or may not want to mention this to help both Don and Roger to get the Buying Committee's approval. By not mentioning the rebate at this moment, Linda could potentially use it later as a 'give-back' in the final negotiation of the deal if necessary.

The next step will be to start a company audit. This involves scaling the solution specifically for HD, filling in a 'Customer Usage Profile,' identifying 'Placeholder' Value-added parameters, etc.[58]. Simultaneously, the selling team of Linda, Roger, and Don will begin approaching all key HD players who may affect or be affected by this game-changing addition of self-checkout. The goal is to build all the positive operating, transition, and financial visions necessary to get all key players on board and enthusiastic about the prospective adoption of the SpeedyLane Self-checkout system.

*Expanding Operating Visions to all Key Operating Players in HD Will Occur over Several weeks during February and perhaps running into March.*

CHAPTER 52

# Build & Confirm
# Additional Operating Visions

| Step 3 – Linda, Roger & Don Team to Convert the Remaining Key Players | | |
|---|---|---|
| Ch | 49 | Purpose & Components of the 'Evaluation Plan' |
| Ch | 50 | Principles to Incorporate in the Evaluation Plan |
| Ch | 51 | Start Implementing the Evaluation Plan |
| **Ch** | **52** | **Build & Confirm Additional Operating Visions** |
| Ch | 53 | Build & Confirm Transition Visions |
| Ch | **54** | Build & Confirm Financial Visions |

## The Most Important Operating Players to Get on Board

Many players at House Depot (HD) will have their day-to-day operating responsibilities affected in fundamental ways if the game changing SpeedyLane Self-checkout system is adopted. For example, see the list of affected operating players in the exhibit below. Most are *internal HD players* at the *corporate level* or at the *store level*. There are also some important *external players* who need to be convinced that the SpeedyLane solution actually works as promised.

# Vision Building with Additional Important Operating Players

While the list of potential Key Operating Players in the Exhibit below is very extensive, Linda knows from her previous discussions with Don Johnson (her now converted Power Sponsor), which Operating Players will be most important to get 'on board.'

Next, Linda, together with Roger (Sponsor) and Don (Power Sponsor) will operate as a team to approach and vision build with and convert as many of these Key Operating Players as possible in order to keep the sales effort moving forward. The goal is to convince each targeted Key Operating Player that SpeedyLane can indeed deliver the promised new capabilities. These are specific new capabilities that will help all of the affected Key Operating Players to better address their day-to-day operating challenges.

## Converted Operating Players Are Critical for Smooth and Effective Solution Implementation

Getting the most important operating players behind the SpeedyLane solution will certainly help to push the selling effort forward. Very importantly, converting this set of players now will both facilitate and accelerate the effective implementation of the SpeedyLane Self-checkout System at HD if adopted.

## Confirm the Conversion of Important Operating Players with the Buying Committee

As the SpeedyLane selling team gains the backing of the important operating players, they inform the Buying Committee about these 'conversions.' Committee members are well aware of the importance of these conversions because they will both contribute to HD's overall operating performance and be critical for effective implementation of the SpeedyLane system.

# Players & Related Visions Needed

## Market Solution: Self-Service checkout system

| Players | Operating Vision | Transition Vision | Financial Vision |
|---|---|---|---|
| **Internal Players** | | | |
| Board of Directors | efficient operations throughout the corporation | effective, on-time implementation of all decisions | Meet profit expectations |
| Chairman of the Board of Directors | efficient operations throughout the corporation | effective, on-time implementation of all decisions | Meet profit expectations |
| Top Management Buying Committee | efficient operations throughout the corporation | effective, on-time implementation of all decisions | Meet profit expectations |
| CEO | efficient operations throughout the corporation | effective, on-time implementation of all decisions | Meet profit expectations |
| CFO | efficient operations throughout the corporation | low cost vs benefits associated with all system changes | higher revenues, lower costs |
| EXEC VP - OPERATIONS (or COO) | efficient operations throughout the corporation | effective, on-time implementation of all decisions | keep corporate costs down |
| VP of Marketing | Productive & efficient Revenue Enhancement & Marketing Plans | Smooth implementation of all Rev. Ehancement & Mkting Plans | Keep Revenue growing steadily |
| Corporate Director of In-Store Efficiency | efficient corporate-wide in-store operations | smooth transitions in any new in-store systems | keep in-store cost down |
| Corporate Customer Svc Director | develop & monitor customer satisfaction initiatives - keep customers happy! | ensure smooth implementation of any new corporate-wide programs customer satisfaction initiatives | keep customer service manpower costs under control |
| Corporate Director of Merchandising | continuous creative development of in store revenue generating merchandising initiatives | effective implementation of all new merchandising initiatives | continuous creative development of in store revenue generating merchandising initiatives |
| Corporate Director of Human Resources | effective recruitment and handling of all HR decisions | ensure proper training with all new systems | control headcount |
| Corporate Legal Counsel | | avoid potential legal entanglements | avoid costly legal judgments |

# Players & Related Visions Needed, cont.

## Market Solution: Self-Service checkout system

### Internal Players

| Players | Operating Vision | Transition Vision | Financial Vision |
|---|---|---|---|
| Corporate Director of Information Technology | efficient and productive management of all IT matters | hassle free IT adaptation to all system changes | keep IT costs down |
| IT Managers | manage all IT systems efficiently | ensure seamless integration of all data systems | implement IT efficiency initiatives |
| Store Managers | smooth in-store operations | ensure smooth implementation of corporate in-store initiatives | store level profit responsibility |
| Store Assistant Managers | run smooth operations | implement new systems | efficiently run the store |
| Cashiers | efficiently & courteously checkout customers | learn and effectively implement any new checkout systems | minimize cashier errors |
| In-store customer service reps | handle all in store customer complaints & requests | implement new corporate customer satisfaction initiatives | |

### External Players

| Players | Operating Vision | Transition Vision | Financial Vision |
|---|---|---|---|
| Stockholders | | | Meet profit expectations |
| Customers | know how to use potential new self-checkout system | get in and out of store quickly | pay reasonable price |
| Independent suppliers | efficient interface with retail outlets | seamless adaptation to new systems of stores | high, profitable sales of our products |
| Retail Labor Union(s) | keep retail union members happy & help keep their jobs | help members to adapt to new system requirements | help ensure jobs & favorable wages and benefits for members |
| Nat'l & Local Business press | | announce and publicly evaluate new retail self-checkout system initiatives | |

Here's A Quick Review of the '9 Block' Vision Building Process Itself (Details provided earlier)

## 9 Block Vision Building Summary

| PAIN (Primary Issue) | Diagnose Causes / Reasons | Explore Impacts | Visualize Capabilities |
|---|---|---|---|
| Open Questions | **R1** (1) Can you tell me more about that? What's causing .. Repeat the issue / pain | **I1** (4) Besides you, who else is impacted by this (briefly repeat issue / pain) and how are they affected? | **C1** (7) What's it going to take for YOU to address this problem? What can you do about it? |
| Explore with Carefully Planned Questions (Controlled Exploration) | **R2** (2) Indirect Qs to get each Cause /Reason on the Table (Cause 1, 2, 3, etc.) | **I2** (5) Is your 'x' (name a position) also affected? How about 'y position,' is that also affected? Etc. | **C2** (8) Could I try some ideas on you? What if when C1, you could ... Capability 1 ? Wait for response. What if when C2, you could ... Capability 2 ? Etc. |
| Confirm – repeat only exactly what the person did indeed tell you or agree to | **R3** (3) So, if I am hearing your right, you .. Repeat Issue / Pain .. because 1, 2, 3, etc. Is that correct? | **I3** (6) From what I've just heard, it sounds like this is a challenge for # of others as well as for you. Now repeat all of those mentioned along with the specific challenge for each | **C3** (9) So, I hear you saying that if you had this, this & this, then the issue / pain (repeat it) would be addressed as well as the challenges faced by, & all those others affected (mention them each). Is that an accurate summary? |

## Example of Linda, Roger & Don Teaming in the Effort to Convert Additional Key Operating Players[59]

**Key Operating Player Example:**

Theresa Chambers, Corporate Customer Service Director, HD

## Theresa's Primary Overall Operating Issue:

There's a decline in customer satisfaction and loyalty due to HD's current checkout system. Linda knows that any "Customer Service Director" would be concerned about that issue.

## Linda Gets the Primary Overall Issue on the Table (i.e., Gets Theresa to Admit 'Pain':

Linda starts with *"So Theresa, can you tell me about HD's current checkout system."*

If this doesn't get Theresa's relevant pain out in the open, Linda goes to indirect questions below, focusing on specific reasons for the overall issue.

## Linda Gets Theresa to Acknowledge Reasons for the Overall Inefficiency of HD's current Checkout System (Column 1 of the '9 Block' Framework)

Linda has a good idea of which specific checkout inefficiencies are likely to be of greatest concern to Theresa, as Customer Service Director – essentially any checkout inefficiencies that might negatively impact customer satisfaction or loyalty. Examples of such problems might include:

- Checkout times that are too long;
- lack of a faster checkout alternative available for smaller quantity purchases; and
- having too few employees out on the floor to help customers.

Linda's goal (in Col 1 of the 9 block) is to get Theresa to talk more about how specific HD checkout inefficiencies can negatively impact HD customer satisfaction and loyalty. Linda tries to trigger this by asking ***Indirect (or Direct, if needed) Probing Questions*** such as:

- *"What's your average checkout time?"* Await answer. Then maybe ask: *"Are you satisfied with that?"*
- *"Do customers have a faster alternative checkout available for smaller quantity purchases?"* Await answer. Then maybe ask: *"Are any customers frustrated with not having fast checkout available for smaller purchases?"*

Linda might then ask additional indirect questions, such as

- *"Do you monitor and record walkouts?"*
- *"Are some walkouts caused by customers being frustrated with not having fast checkout available for smaller purchases?"*
- *"Tell me about the customer service folks you have roaming the floor helping customers."*

Linda then summarizes exactly what Theresa has acknowledged as specific problems. This closes 'Column 1' (Reasons) and moves on to 'Column 2' (Impacts) of her "9 block" vision building effort with Theresa

## Linda Gets Theresa to Acknowledge Negative Impacts (Column 2 of the 9 Block)

Linda runs up and down the list of the internal & external player in the matrix introduced above to search for players with Operating Checkout System Issues. The goal is to heighten Theresa's awareness about how the same checkout efficiencies that impact her job, also negatively affect many others in House Depot.

To get these impacts acknowledged, Linda starts with: "Besides yourself, is anyone else negatively affected by these issues?" Linda awaits Theresa's answer and then asks her to elaborate on specifically how each person is negatively impacted by HD's inefficient checkout system. Through this discussion, Linda is trying to heighten Theresa's anxiety in order to make her (Theresa) more anxious to seek out a solution.

Linda continues her effort to heighten Theresa's anxiety by getting more and more negatively impacted HD internal and external players on the table. Linda does by asking, over and over again: "Anyone Else?"

Each time, Linda awaits a response, and then asks Theresa to elaborate on how that particular person is negatively impacted by HD's checkout inefficiencies. Using a prepared list of internal and external players such as the one above, Linda asks: "How about ...?" ... "How about ...?" Thus, Linda builds Theresa's anxiety about more and more affected parties.

Just prior to moving on to 'Column 3' (Capabilities Needed), Linda summarizes the entire list of negatively impacted operational players that Theresa has mentioned or acknowledged. This is intended to peak Theresa's anxiety about HDs inefficient checkout system, just prior to 'coming to the rescue' with some idea for a solution (next up, in 'Column 3' of the 9 Block). At this point, Theresa should be more than ready for a solution.

## Get 'Ideal' Solution Acknowledged (i.e., Capabilities Needed -- Column 3 of 9 Block

Linda & her selling team are confident that the overall inefficiency of HD's current checkout system could be remedied if HD had a way to:
- Reduce the average checkout time;
- Provide a faster checkout alternative for smaller quantity purchases; and
- Enable more employees to be out on the floor helping customers.

Immediately after summarizing (in Cell 6 of the 9 block) the entire list of negatively impacted operational players that Theresa has mentioned or acknowledged, Linda moves to Column 3 of the 9 Block and starts with:

*"What can you do about this problem?"* Linda awaits Theresa's answer and then asks her to elaborate to see if Theresa mentions any of the specific 'capabilities needed,' – as inferred by the specific checkout issues Theresa acknowledged in Column 1

Depending on Theresa's ideas for a solution and assuming it does not include remedies for each of the issues acknowledged by Theresa in Column 1, Linda then asks:

*"Mind if I offer some other suggestions?"*

Given her heightened anxiety, Theresa should quickly grant that permission, after which Linda launches into describing a full gamut of capabilities related to the specific issues acknowledged in column 1. For example, Linda asks:

- *"What if you had a way to reduce your average checkout time?"* Linda awaits Theresa's confirmation, prior to moving to the next item.
- *"What if you could provide a faster checkout alternative for smaller quantity purchases?"* Linda awaits Theresa's confirmation, prior to moving to the next item.
- *"What if you could have more employees on the floor helping customers, without increasing your employee headcount?"* Linda awaits Theresa's confirmation, prior to moving to the next item.

Linda then summarizes the Acknowledged Needed Capabilities (Col. 3, Cell 'C9).

*[Linda, SpeedyLane]* summarizes to Theresa:

> *"So, if I'm hearing you right, you said that if your checkout system had these capabilities (mention the 3 above), you feel you could improve customer satisfaction and loyalty, alleviate the primary checkout-related issues that concern the CEO, CFO ( continue the list ) and in the process make your own day-to-day job more productive and enjoyable. Is that an accurate summary?"*

Linda would hope for and wait for a positive response from Theresa – for example, "Yes, that would be great."

## Closing Statement – Linda Confirms Theresa as Yet Another Converted Operating Player

Assuming Theresa's positive response confirming her summary, Linda would make a closing statement such as this:

"Well, I think our SpeedyLane solution can deliver these capabilities you said you needed in order to address the main operational issues with HD's current checkout system."

"I believe your colleagues here (pointing to her converted Sponsor and Power Sponsor, Roger and Don, respectively) can verify this claim – as they have each visited with some of our previous clients, personally witnessing their successful implementation of our SpeedyLane checkout system."

## 'Proof' and Verification

Linda would then simply ask Roger and Don to verify SpeedyLane's ability to deliver the promised capabilities and to answer any specific questions Theresa may still have.

That verification should be enough to convert Theresa, with no need for a more elaborate proof step. If Theresa asks for more proof, then Linda should offer to take her to visit a former client company (reference client) to talk with someone in a parallel position (Customer Service Director or similar) in order to discuss and resolve any doubts Theresa may have about the promised capabilities of the game changing new system.

[Note: This same principle of offering reference client visits applies when building transition and financial visions for any important players.]

## Do We Have to Try to Convert
## Every Operating and Transition Player?

*[Linda to Brian]:* "Bri, now our next step is to get access to the other key operating and transition players shown in the 'Key Players Chart' (above) and to move on to convert them one by one – trying to get them all on board, supporting the adoption and implementation of our checkout system."

Be Ready to Take Any Important Operating Player to See a Reference Client if Necessary

[Brian]: "You mean, we have to vision build with that entire list of people? That seems like it would take a lot of time and effort. Since Roger and Don are already on board and enthusiastic about adopting our system, I don't see why we need to or how we can justify trying to convert all the key players on that list."

[Linda]: "That's a good and fair point, Brian. In reality, it is likely that we may indeed end up skipping vision building with some operating or transition players. For example, it might be impossible or quite difficult to get timely access to certain operating or transition players. In such cases, we do not want our vision building efforts to drag on and on.

"Also, after we build the financial vision with the key C-Level (CEO, CFO, CMO, President, etc.) and other key members of the Buying Committee, that Committee may be anxious to adopt the solution ASAP. In this latter case, we may simply not have the time to convert all of the key operating or transition players. When our buyer agrees to buy, we always jump on it.

## Focusing our Vision Building Efforts, with Help from Our Converted Sponsor and Target Sponsor

*[Linda continues with Brian]*: "Finally, and very importantly, we can ask Roger and Don, now our selling partners as our "Converted" Sponsor and Power Sponsor, respectively, to identify which specific internal and external players THEY feel are the KEY internal and external players for HD related to this prospective purchase and implementation of this game changing new checkout system. That is, who do Roger and Don feel might be most likely to negatively affect and/or simply delay HD's Buying Committee's progress toward committing to and ultimately purchasing and adopting our SpeedyLane checkout system.

"Given that insight from Roger and Don, we can prioritize and focus our Key Player targets and respective vision building efforts. "

## Be Aware of the Significant Risks in Overlooking Vision Building for Any Potentially Influential Internal or External Key Player

*[Linda]*: "BUT, and I emphasize this BUT, there can be significant risk and potential cost to us if we overlook our vision building efforts for any specific key operating or transition players during the implementation of our Account Marketing Plan."

*[Brian]*: "Risks? Like what? I don't get it."

*[Linda]*: "As we move closer to the 'Closing' for this sale, I'll talk with you more about those risks and potential cost to us of not trying to get all the key internal and external players on board prior to closing. But, for now, let me just say this. You would be surprised how many sales go bust because we've overlooked an important player prior to trying to close a deal. For example, it might only take one transition player, like the head of IT, to ruin the whole deal."

"Elaborating a bit now, and more later, consider two potential bad things that can happen at or near closing, if we overlook vision building with some key operating or transition players, thus failing to get them on board prior to the Closing.

"First, let's say:

- we overlook the **legal department** and we find out at closing time that we have a locked-in contract with our current checkout system provider; or

- we overlook a **cashiers union** and the would-be new solution violates a part of their contract with HD; or,

- we overlook the **HD IT department**. Then, at or near closing, they obviously find out and scream about the difficulties the new system will create – and demand significant new resources if they are to go along with the adoption. Not clearing it with IT (through prior vision building) might also add unanticipated extreme delays in successful implementation. Any of those cases would, at a minimum, delay the purchase decision at the last minute and possibly cancel it – and we certainly do not want that!

"Secondly, every key player – internal or external – that we fail to convert prior to closing introduces a risk factor for the Buying Committee. Risk factors include unanticipated extra time, trouble, and/or cost in addition to decreasing the probability of an overall successful implementation of our game changing solution. Any of these risks provide leverage for the Buying Committee – through their well-experienced, astute negotiator (covered in detail in the later chapters) to insist on a lower price and/or other more favorable buying terms than we have in our proposed contract.

"So, in sum, yes, we can overlook vision building with any internal or external key player we choose. But each potentially important player we fail to get 'on our side' prior to closing, the greater the leverage House Depot will have for pressuring us at closing time."

*[Brian]*: "OK, I get it now! Though it still seems like a lot of effort to go through for one potential sale."

*[Linda]*: "Ummm.... don't forget we are talking about one sale that will reap SpeedyLane several million dollars up front and ongoing annual service revenues of $500,000 or more.

*[Brian]*: "Ah, I kind of forgot about that. Now it all makes sense."

---

## The Team of Linda, Roger and Don Then Move on to Vision Build and Convert the Other Key Operating Players

*Next Up (Next Chapter) – Get the Transition Players on board.*

*Vision Building Transpires over a 4-6 week period, starting in February, running into March.*

CHAPTER 53

# Build & Confirm Transition Visions

| Step 3 – Linda, Roger & Don Team to Convert the Remaining Key Players | | |
|---|---|---|
| Ch | 49 | Purpose & Components of the 'Evaluation Plan' |
| Ch | 50 | Principles to Incorporate in the Evaluation Plan |
| Ch | 51 | Start Implementing the Evaluation Plan |
| Ch | 52 | Build & Confirm Additional Operating Visions |
| **Ch** | **53** | **Build & Confirm Transition Visions** |
| Ch | **54** | Build & Confirm Financial Visions |

## What Is a Transition Vision?

The SpeedyLane Self-checkout System promises many important potential operating and financial benefits for House Depot (HD). However, these benefits and the related positive visions they create can only be realized if the solution is effectively implemented. Now enter Transition Players and their necessary Transition Visions. [60]

For some players, the prospect of adopting the SpeedyLane System may cause nightmares. More importantly, some of these very same players may be in a position to delay or even impair the successful implementation of the new system, if and when purchased. Linda and her sales team have to make sure that such players have full knowledge of and are at least 'OK' with the prospective adoption of the new system. That is, Linda has to do some positive vision building with these folks as a critical part of the Evaluation Plan! A positive Transition Vision is one that verifies that the proposed solution can be implemented in a way that will enable the client to reap the full operating and financial benefits promised.

The Transition Players exhibit presents a list of important transition players who could most easily kibosh the whole idea of adopting the SpeedyLane Self-checkout System. Note in the exhibit that both internal and external players are important when dealing with the transition vision.

---

# 'Can Do,' 'Can't Do,' and 'Wanna Do It' Transition Players

---

## Can Do Transition Players

"Can Do" Transition Players are folks who, despite envisioned disadvantages for them in the short term, will reap long-term net benefits from the proposed new self-checkout system. Store Managers serve as a good example of *"Can Do Players."* Store Managers will certainly have initial perceived pains, summarized in unanswered questions/reasons such as:

"Will the new self-checkout system work properly?"

"How will it prevent more theft from occurring?"

"Will customers try it? Will customers continue to use it?"

"How long will it take to re-train cashiers to use the new system?"

"What will be the overall effect on my costs and profits?"

"Over the longer term, Store Managers will benefit from higher profits through increased revenues and reduced overall costs. We refer to the Store Managers as "Can Do players," because if we can convert them, they will add fuel to the fire for adoption of the new system."

---

## "Can't Do" Transition Players

"Can't Do" Transition Players are folks who would have to expend effort to help successfully implement the proposed new solution, but who typically would not reap long-term net benefits from the new solution. IT folks serve as a good example of *"Can't Do Players"* -- from the IT Director down to 'rubber meets the road' IT technicians. The thought of adopting the SpeedyLane Self-checkout System could easily be perceived by HD's IT folks as a prospective disaster waiting to happen. In fact, just thinking about it could cause untold pain! IT has some especially important reasons for that pain - related to unanswered questions/reasons such as these.

## Most Important Transition Players

**Market Solution:  Self-Checkout Service**

| Players | Operating Vision | Transition Vision | Financial Vision |
|---|---|---|---|
| **Internal Players** | | | |
| Corporate Director of Human Resources | effective recruitment and handling of all HR decisions | ensure proper training with all new systems | control headcount |
| Corporate Legal Counsel | | avoid potential legal entanglements | avoid costly legal judgments |
| Corporate Director of Information Technology | efficient and productive management of all IT matters | hassle free IT adaptation to all system changes | keep IT costs down |
| IT Managers | manage all IT systems efficiently | ensure seamless integration of all data systems | implement IT efficiency initiatives |
| Store Managers | smooth in-store operations | ensure smooth implementation of corporate in-store initiatives | store level profit responsibility |
| Store Assistant | run smooth operations | implement new systems | efficiently run the store |
| Cashiers | efficiently & courteously checkout customers | learn and effectively implement any new checkout systems | minimize cashier errors |
| **External Players** | | | |
| **Players** | **Operating Vision** | **Transition Vision** | **Financial Vision** |
| Stockholders | | | Meet profit expectations |
| Customers | must be convinced the new self-checkout system works | learn how to use potential new self-checkout system | pay reasonable price |
| Retail Labor Union(s) | keep retail union members happy & help keep their jobs | help members to adapt to new system requirements | help ensure jobs & favorable wages and benefits for members |

- "How can we interface the SpeedyLane data system infrastructure and data collection methodology with our current HD data systems?"
- "Where are we going to get the time and manpower to work on learning about the SpeedyLane data system and integrating that system with ours?"
- "What if HD adopts the SpeedyLane System, but we (IT) are not successful in integrating the SpeedyLane data system with the current HD system? In that case, we would certainly have mud on our face! No?"

- "What about prospective new day-to-day challenges such as 'How is the data collected at the self-checkout station?', 'Is that data accurate?', and 'Is that data secure?'

Bottom line for IT: this is a non-starter! Forget it! Bad Idea! No way! We have too much on our plate already!

A realistic goal in vision building with 'Can't Do' transition players is to convince them at least to not oppose the selling process – thus not retard the final implementation of the proposed new solution. This means the IT team must at least give its OK to implementing the new system. We'll consider how to convince them in a moment.

## Converting 'Can't Do' Transition Players into Supporters

With some imagination and creativity, the SpeedyLane selling team may be able to convert HD's 'Can't Do' IT folks into pro-active supporters of adopting the new self-checkout system. See that example -- where Linda and Don try to do just that.in the exhibit below.

## Building Positive Transition Visions

The questions raised by Store Managers and IT folks represent *'Reasons'* why these important players experience *'Pain'* regarding the risks that come with the addition of the SpeedyLane Self-checkout System.

Well, from our learning last chapter in building Operating Visions, we know how to deal with *Pain* and the *Reasons for the Pain*. The key is to be prepared with a set of prospective capabilities that will address each reason, thereby dampening or even eliminating the overall pain envisioned by the Store Managers or IT folks. That is, yes, *we can '9 block' vision build with these folks too*!

For the Store Managers, our goal is to make them enthusiastic supporters.

For the IT folks, we may not be able to get them to back the proposed SpeedyLane System adoption with enthusiasm. However, with a proper set of creatively planned capabilities, we can significantly alleviate their specific concerns to the point where they would be 'OK' with the proposed new solution. If we can accomplish that, we can continue to move the sale forward with less concern that IT will hinder eventual implementation, upon adoption of the system.

## Two Important Differences Between Building Transition Visions and Building Operating Visions.

There are two important differences in building Transition Visions versus building Operating Visions. Let's contrast the two approaches

**When Building Operating Visions,** Linda focused on pains that would be alleviated by the proposed new solution itself. She focused on HD's overall 'Pain' with its current checkout system. First (column 1 of the 9 block), Linda broke out the specific reasons for that overall pain. Then (in column 2), she tried to increase the anxiety about the overall pain and its components. She did this in order to motivate key HD operating players to more aggressively seek out capabilities that would address the pains felt with the current checkout system.

Finally (in column 3), Linda proposed specific new capabilities to address all the reasons for the pain.

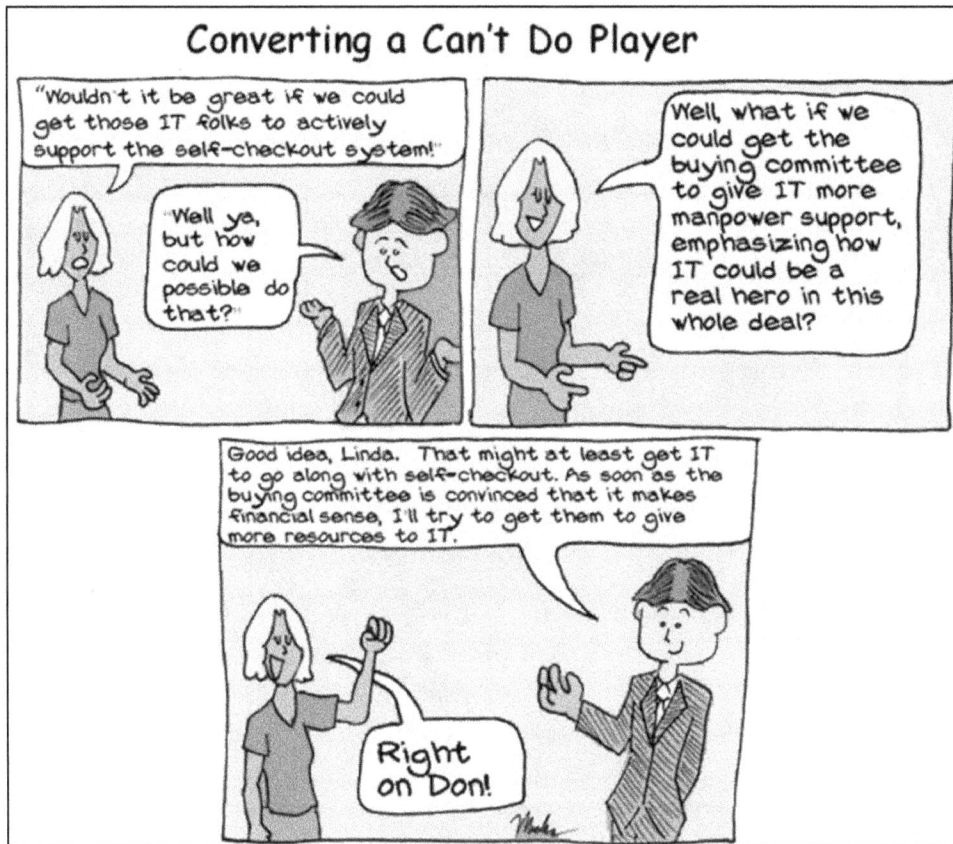

**_Building Transition Visions varies from building Operating visions_** Consider the IT example to understand the differences.

The IT transition folks regard the proposed SpeedyLane Self-checkout System *itself* as a prospective pain, rather than as a solution for a specific pain (as envisioned by operating players).

The goal of vision building with the IT transition players is, therefore, to downplay and *decrease* the prospective pain related to the possible adoption of the new self-checkout system.

This is a big contrast to building visions with an operating player, where Linda would want to *increase* the pain (in column 2) in order to get operating players more anxious to adopt her SpeedyLane System (in column 3).

In order to downplay and reduce the prospective pain that IT folks would face if the new system were adopted, *Linda will totally eliminate 'anxiety building' (Column 2) in vision building with HD's IT folks.* Instead, she will move directly from exploring the reasons for the prospective new pain (Column 1) to itemizing how each of IT's major concerns (reasons) might be addressed (column 3). See the visual below.

Linda's goal is to get the IT folks to give their 'official OK' to the prospective adoption of the new self-checkout system. That OK, once communicated to the Buying Committee, will enhance the Buying Committee's own positive Transition Vision of smooth implementation of the new checkout system.

Thus, the vision building process for transition players looks like this.

| Start with Admitted Pain | Diagnose Reasons | Explore Impact | Visualize Capabilities |
|---|---|---|---|
| Open Questions | R1 | I1 | C1 |
| Control Questions | R2 | I2 | C2 |
| Confirmation | R3 | I3 | C3 |

---

## Sample Dialog of Building a Positive Transition Vision
### (Turning a "Can't Do It Player" into a "Wanna Do It Player!")

**Key Player: Greg Stewart – Store Manager** – *Currently a 'Can't Do It' player*

**Overall Concern and Projected Pain**: Several important transition challenges if asked to add the new self-checkout system to his store's current checkout system

**Reasons for the Greg's Concern / Pain**
- Will the new self-checkout system work properly?
- How will it prevent more theft from occurring?
- Will customers try it? Will customers continue to use it?
- How and how long will it take to re-train cashiers to use the new system?
- What will be the overall effect on the store's costs and profits?

**Capabilities Included with the System to Address these Specific Challenges**
- System is time tested, with proven dependability over many years.
- Built-in Anti-theft system is an award-winning, state of the art system.
- Experience and refined research data show that 60% of customers will try it and 50% will continue to use it as their favored checkout alternative.
- SpeedyLane provides DVD training videos and on-site training for up to two years, as part of the contract. The refined training module trains cashiers in less than six hours.
- SpeedyLane will reduce costs, increase revenues, and increase profits.

**Pain is already on the table** – Most Store Managers immediately express concerns about the challenges they envision in the prospective addition of self-checkout capabilities.

---

# Dialog (using the 9 Block Framework to Convert Greg into a Wanna Do It Player)

---

## Column 1: Diagnose the Reasons

**R1.** *[Linda]*: "Tell me about your concerns."

*[Greg, HD Store Manager]*: "Well, I foresee all sorts of potential problems – for example, does the system even work? And how will it affect my costs and profits?"

**R2.** Get more challenges on the table. [Linda's thought]: "I might as well get all the real issues on the table now, lest they show up later and then Greg rethinks his support – assuming I can get his enthusiastic support."

Linda knows that two concerns are already on the table. Now she tries to get Greg to acknowledge other likely concerns.

*[Linda] to Greg:*

- "Are you concerned about how the system will prevent more theft from occurring?" Linda awaits response.

"Are you concerned whether customers will use it? And whether they will continue to use it?" Linda awaits response.

"Are you concerned about re-training cashiers to use the new system properly?" Linda awaits response.

"Anything else?" Linda awaits response.

**R3.** *[Linda summarizes]:* "So, if I'm hearing you right, your primary concerns are ... " (she simply repeats all of Greg's concerns).

Then *[Linda]*: "Is that an accurate summary?" Greg agrees.

## Column 2: Explore the impacts (<u>PURPOSEFULLY OMITTED</u>)

***Linda now omits column 2,*** trying to downplay Greg's anxiety, rather than build it like she did for operating players. She moves directly to Column 3 and the potential capabilities that Greg needs to address his primary concerns.

## Column 3: Visualize Capabilities

**C1:** *[Linda]:* "Can you think of any ways the new system might address these prospective challenges?" Greg tosses out a few ideas.

**C2 & C3**: *[Linda]: "Well, can I offer some more ideas that might help?"*

*[Greg, Store Manager]:* "Fire away!"

*[Linda]:*

- "What if the system is time tested, with proven dependability over many years?" Linda awaits a response. [Greg, Store Manager]: "That would be great!"
- "What if it had a fail-safe, integrated anti-theft system?" Linda awaits a response.
- "What if you could be assured that 60% of your customers would try it and that 50% would continue to use it as their favored checkout alternative?" Linda awaits a response.
- "What if you had both DVD training videos and on-site cashier re-training?" Linda awaits response.

**Now Linda adds the kicker – in the effort to convert Greg from a 'Can't Do Guy' to a 'Wanna Do It Guy!'**

*[Linda]:* "Beyond all that, what if you could be assured that:

- Your average checkout time would go down by over 25%;
- Your overall cashier costs would go down by 30%;
- Your total store revenues would increase by over 15% within one 1 year; and that
- Your net store profits would increase by over 20% within one year?"

*[Greg, Store Manager]:* "Wow, that would be fantastic – but can all that really happen?"

*[Linda]:* "You bet, and I've got the data to prove it from stores remarkably similar to yours that have added our self-checkout capability. Here's a packet with specific data supporting all the claims I've just made. Check it out and I'll get back to you tomorrow so you can ask about any additional concerns you may have."

=========

**That ought to do it! After a review of the 'proofs' Linda has provided, Greg becomes a 'Wanna Do It Guy.' Whooo hooo!!**

-----

*Meanwhile*....

***So, how did Brian's date with Lucy go?***

*[Linda]:* "So, Brian, how'd that date go? What did you do?"

*[Brian]:* "Well I took her to Windy's."

*[Linda]:* "Well, how did it go?"

*[Brian]:* "I mean I had fun, but we didn't really talk so I don't know if she did or not. The food was good at least."

*[Linda]:* "I see. Are you going to go out with her again?"

*[Brian]:* "I don't know. Maybe. I don't understand this whole dating thing. Did she say anything to you?"

*[Linda]:* "She told me she had a ***great*** time!"

*[Brian]:* "Really? Oh wow! Maybe I will ask her out again! Is that the next step? I think I need a step-by-step plan of attack. I guess I could ask my sisters for some advice. Hmmmm...."

*Building the Financial Vision at House Depot will start with an Audit (charged to House Depot) that will take a couple weeks in February, followed by detailed discussions and analysis running through February and well into March.*

CHAPTER 54

---

# Build & Confirm Financial Visions

| Step 3 – Linda, Roger & Don Team to Convert the Remaining Key Players | | |
|---|---|---|
| Ch | 49 | Purpose & Components of the 'Evaluation Plan' |
| Ch | 50 | Principles to Incorporate in the Evaluation Plan |
| Ch | 51 | Start implementing the Evaluation Plan |
| Ch | 52 | Build & Confirm Additional Operating Visions |
| Ch | 53 | Build & Confirm Transition Visions |
| **Ch** | **54** | **Build & Confirm Financial Visions** |

[*B*]*rian]:* "I think I'm getting a good understanding of how we build those operating and transition visions for all those different folks at House Depot. But it seems to me that **unless we can prove that this whole proposal makes financial sense to the uppity ups on the House Depot buying committee, we won't get this sale.**"

*[Linda]:* "No question, Bri. You are exactly right about that. This brings us to our next challenge in this selling cycle -- '**Proving the Financial Vision.**'[61] In fact, you'll be going to a three-day seminar on this later in the spring with the rest of our new sales folks."

*[Brian]:* "That's what they told me at orientation, and now I can't wait to hear about how we try to build the financial vision. Do you suppose you can give me a quick overview of what I'll hear at that Financial Vision Building Seminar?"

*[Linda]:* "Well, I can take a shot at it. But you'll get more details in the seminar when you can ask and get solid answers to as many questions as you like. I can't say I'll do a particularly good job of answering all the questions you may have, but I'll try.

"Some of our sales folks are really good at cooperatively building financial visions with their clients. I'm a bit more 'challenged' than most in doing this with my clients. So, I frequently bring in one or more of our financial vision building experts from our home office staff to help me work with my prospects on this – especially my multi-million dollar prospects. Neither I nor the home office wants me to lose any sales because I'm not very skilled at building financial visions. Fortunately, they are always ready to help if I need it. You'll be able to call on them as well. In fact, you will be encouraged to do so by our Regional Manager and the home office as you get your feet wet during your first year or so in the field."

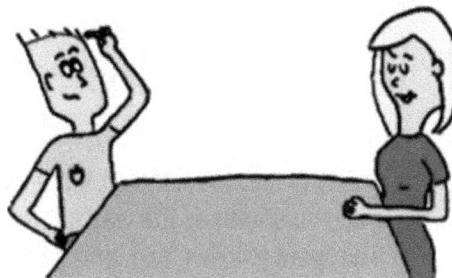

[Brian]: "Glad to hear that, because I'd also hate to blow a sale after taking all that time and effort to work with everyone needing operating and transition visions."

## When to Start Building the Financial Vision?

[Linda]: "Actually, you'll start building the financial vision while simultaneously building the other visions, but your point is well taken. At any rate, here's my overview of how we build financial visions with our target customers."

## Building a Financial Vision is a Cooperative Process

[Linda]: "First off, we don't build the financial vision by ourselves and then just lay it on the prospective customer. It can be a real turn-off if we just tell the client our price and 'claim' the price will produce a certain return on investment and payback period. Rather, we keep the process as transparent as possible, while guiding the prospect through the process."

"To do this, we have a formal, menu-driven framework in Excel that we use to ask the client specific questions.[62] The model helps us tailor the solution to the customer's specific needs and price our solution so that it will provide an attractive Return on Investment and Projected Payback Period for our client. Here's the cover page for the model."

## SpeedyLane Self-Checkout Systems

The SpeedyLane self-check out system is an automated retail self-checkout system that revolutionizes the way customers make store purchases. This system enables shoppers to scan, bag, and pay for their purchases with limited (or no) assistance from store personnel. In addition, the SpeedyLane Sel-checkout System helps generate sales revenue through increase prime retail selling space, improved customer assistance and more efficient flow of customers.

Go to Table of Contents

| Customer Usage Profile | Value In Use Analysis | Justifications | Investment Costs | ROI | Pricing & Financial Projections | Keys to Success |

Let's Get Started!!

"And here is a description of each component of the model.

| Table of Contents | | |
|---|---|---|
| **Page of Framework** | | |
| 1. Home | Home | Includes overview of what the model is, SpeedyLane value proposition and starting place for framework. |
| 2. Customer Usage Profile | Customer Usage Profile | Includes all Customer usage profile variables: variable from CIU and BIU formulas and placeholder values. |
| 3. Value In Use Analysis | Value In Use Analysis | Includes value in use analysis and totals, looks at financial numbers such as Pricing, ROI and BEPP. |
| 4. Justifications | Justifications | Includes formulas used to calculate value in use analysis, explanation and justification of these formulas. |
| 5. Investment Costs | Investment Costs | Includes formulas used to investment costs in use analysis, |
| 6. ROI | ROI | Includes CIU and BIU calculation, discounted cash flow and ROI/IRR calculation. |
| 7. Pricing & Financial Projections | Pricing & financial Projections | Includes pricing strategy explanation, value pillar analysis, ROI and the Breakeven point graph. |
| 8. Keys to Success | Keys to Success | Includes BIU and CIU that largely influence success. Demonstration of how these keys to success will benefit the company. |

## Need to Do a Customer Audit Up-Front

"We can't price our solution or estimate a Return on Investment (and/or Projected Payback period) until we adapt our proposed solution to the specific needs of the individual client. We call this scaling process our 'Customer Audit,' for which we charge our customer typically $50,000 to $75,000."

*[Brian]:* "How do we get away with charging that much money, especially since at that point we haven't proven we can provide an attractive Return on Investment?"

*[Linda]:* "Well, if you look back at our 'Account Marketing Plan' structure, you'll see that we don't propose the audit – including the charge - until we already have the full support of our Target Sponsor and Target Power Sponsor, which we get by proving our Operating and Financial Visions to them. They, in turn, will have made recommendations to the Top Management Buying Committee.

"After some consideration, the buying committee will have given their approval for further exploration. This approval includes consent for conducting and paying for the audit in order to tailor the solution to the customer's specific situation. The buying committee knows the audit

*Dr. John A. Weber*

is needed before we can price our solution or prove that we can provide an attractive Return on Investment for our client.

"Furthermore, the $50,000-$75,000 audit charge not only pays for our time and trouble in conducting the audit, but *also tests the seriousness of the buying committee in its commitment to explore the promise of our proposed solution*."

[Brian]: "What if they balk at the proposed audit charge? What do you do then?"

[Linda]: "If they balk, it means we haven't done as ideal job of converting our Target Sponsor and our Target Power Sponsor. So, if they balked at the audit charge (in the Evaluation Plan), consider it a point of negotiation and indicate that "We will refund that charge if we eventually do business together." Assuming the Target Sponsor and Target Power Sponsor are on your side, this compromise will enable you to move forward in nearly all instances.

## Scaling the Solution for House Depot

[Linda]: "So, assuming the audit has been approved, the next step in the model is to ask the key players specific questions that help us scale the solution to the customer's specific situation and needs. We call this 'filling in the Customer Usage Profile.' You can see that option on the model cover page within the above "Table of Contents". When we click on that option with the prospect, up comes this worksheet page."

"Once our prospect fills out that profile, the model does the rest. The model automatically:

- Calculates a value-based price;
- Leaves enough Customer Incentive to Purchase; so that it surpasses the customer's required minimum Return on Investment and Required maximum Payback Period.

"The model does this by assessing the data from the Customer Usage Profile in a series of 'Value in Use' formulas that reflect value-added criteria. The individual criteria are justified through SpeedyLane's careful monitoring of the results (in the form of *'Success Criteria'*) of previous adoptions of our \ system by customers in the same segment as the current prospect.

NEXT

## Customer Usage Profile

### Customer: House Depot

### Retail Outlet Information

|  |  |
|---|---|
| Total Number of Stores | 0 |
| Avg Annual Sales / Store presently | 0 |
| Avg direct cost of goods sold overall (%) | 0 |
| Avg Annual # of Customers / Store entering presently | 0 |
| Avg Annual # of Customers / Store purchasing presently | 0 |
| Avg # of Checkout Stations / Store Presently | 0 |
| Avg Sq FT taken up by each Checkout Station | 0 |
| Avg Sq Ft total selling space / Store Presently (w/o checkout) | 0 |
| Avg % of sales $ in unplanned purchases (impulse items) | 0 |
| Avg cost of goods sold for unplanned purchases only (%) | 0 |

### Employee Information

|  |  |
|---|---|
| Avg # of Employees / store presently | 0 |
| Avg Annual Cost / Employee presently (including fringes) | 0 |
| Avg # of Cashiers / Store presently | 0 |
| Avg Annual Cost / cashier (including fringes) | 0 |
| Avg Annual Turnover of Cashiers (%) | 0 |
| Cost of Training / new cashier | 0 |
| Avg # of Cust. Svc personnel / Store presently | 0 |
| Avg Annual Cost / Cust Svc person (including fringes) | 0 |
| Avg Annual Turnover of Customer Svc Personnel (%) | 0 |
| Cost of Training / new Customer Service Person | 0 |

### Placeholders (ask customer to estimate)

|  |  |
|---|---|
| to be determined (items customer is not comfortable estimatin | 0 |
| to be determined | 0 |
| to be determined | 0 |

### Other Retail Outlet Information

|  |  |
|---|---|
| % of customers using customer loyalty card presently | 0 |
| Avg Sales $ per cust visit of those using loyalty card | 0 |
| Avg Sales $ per cust visit of those not using loyalty card | 0 |
| Current # of transactions with human cashier error | 0 |
| Avg net cost / each human cashier error | 0 |
| Avg Annual $ 'shrinkage' per store (employee or cust. theft) | 0 |
| Cost of human errors in cash handling | 0 |
| Avg Customer checkout wait time presently | 0 |
| Ideal Avg Customer checkout wait time presently | 0 |
| % Customer walkouts due to excess wait time presently | 0 |

### Proposed Self-checkout Solution

|  |  |
|---|---|
| # of Self-checkout stations proposed | 0 |
| 1 stations systems | 0 |
| 2 stations systems | 0 |
| 4 stations systems | 0 |
| Desired Assistance in Initial Data System Integration | |
| Turnkey integration (100%) | 0 |
| Cooperative integration approach (specify %) | 0 |
| No external assistance (0%) | 0 |
| Continuing Service / Customer Support Agreement | |
| Full Service / Support Contract (100%) | 0 |
| Partial Service / Support Contract (specify %) | 0 |
| No Service / Support Agreement (0%) | 0 |

### Financial Assumptions for this Customer

|  |  |
|---|---|
| Required Return on Investment | 0 |
| Assumed Discount Rate (WACC) | 0 |
| Adjustment for Uncertainty of ROI Projections (% reduced) | 0 |
| Required Break Even Payback Period(months) | 0 |

## Include Both Upfront Investment Costs and Present Valued Ongoing Operating Costs to Calculate both a Return on Investment and Operating Profit Margin

*[Linda continues]*: "Upfront investment costs and ongoing operating costs (the present value) are included. In fact, the **Return on Investment** estimate is based upon the present value of those new investment costs. The model also calculates an **Operating Profit Margin**, which is based on the assessment of new incremental sales revenues compared with new incremental costs in use."

*[Brian]*: "It seems rather complicated, but I do have some specific questions that may help clarify things for me.

## Source of Estimates for Applying the Value-in-Use Formulas

*[Brian]*: "First of all, what if the customer can't answer some of the questions asked in the Customer Usage Profile?

"Second, it seems like the projections of new revenues and net new cost savings depend pretty much on what you call the 'Value in Use' formulas. Who came up with those formulas and how do they fit together to make projections? How do you know the customer will agree with them?

"Furthermore, does this so-called 'value-based pricing' approach consider our costs and how much profit SpeedyLane will make on the sale?

"How does the model take into consideration direct brand competitors' solutions (including their relative price) that our prospect might also be considering?

"Finally, regarding the 'attractive price' calculated by the model -- How does the framework automatically calculate that price?"

# Linda Answers to Brian's List of Questions

*[Linda]*: "Wow, those are very perceptive questions, Brian. You are a bright dude to come up with those after only a brief intro to how we build the Financial Vision. I'll give you my take with a quick and unpolished response to each of your questions, and then leave the details to those who will be running the Financial Vision Building Seminar later this spring. Let's take your questions one at a time.

## What if the customer can't answer some of the questions asked in the Customer Usage Profile?

*[Linda]*: "We have several different strategies for when a customer is unwilling or seemingly unable to answer any specific questions asked on the Customer Usage Profile. First, we have

some questioning techniques to test whether they really have no idea of the answer or are just uncomfortable making an estimate – in which case we can usually pull a reasonable estimate out of them.

"Second, we may tell them what definitive answer or informed estimate other firms have made for the particular variable. This is usually helpful in getting our current customer to make an informed estimate.

"Finally, we may just leave the variable blank for now and move it to the 'Placeholder' section you see on the bottom of the Customer Usage Profile form. After completing the Customer Usage Form, we go back to that data and test a variation of potential estimates. If a small variation in estimating a particular placeholder variable significantly changes the overall results of the model (e.g., our price and / or projected ROI), then we will ask the client more questions or do some research to solidify the estimate to the satisfaction of the customer. On the other hand, if even a large variation in estimating a particular placeholder variable brings no significant changes in the overall results of the model (e.g., our price and / or projected ROI), then we just continue with the placeholder, and may or may not eventually attempt to solidify it, depending on the customer's preference."

## Source of the Value-in-Use Formulas

*[Linda]: "Your second question was* 'who came up with those formulas and how do they fit together to make projections? How do you know the customer will agree with them?'

*[Linda]:* "We developed the formulas with multiple previous clients, refining them over time until customers believe in their validity. The formulas are all transparent to the client and we encourage questions and challenges about them. Prospects tend to ask more regarding how the formulas work together to project a value-based price and ROI that are attractive for their company.

"Below is one of our model's many illustrations of a specific formula example (cost savings, in this case), plus a summary of how all the formulas fit together to project an overall *'Net Value-In-Use'* for the client. I know that this seems, and actually is, pretty complicated. Let me just say that you'll spend more than a full day on this part of the model in your Financial Vision Building Seminar – so I'll just leave it at that for now."

## COST SAVINGS ANALYSIS (one example)

| | |
|---|---|
| **Benefit** | **Fewer Cashiers Needed** |
| **Formula** | (total cost of cashiers) * (% cost of cashiers laid off) |
| **Explanation** | Self Checkout systems allows 4 lanes to be operated by one employee instead of four, allowing the employers to eliminate some positions. Cutting two workers and moving one to customer service would still leave one worker to work the 4 self-checkout lanes. |
| **Justification** | In 8 similar previous SpeedyLane installations, 2 out of every 4 cashiers have been able to be laid off. The employee costs can be eliminated. |
| **Value Parameter for SpeedyLane** | 50% |

## Net Value in Use

| Benefits in Use | Advantage vs. Generic | | Brand Advantage |
|---|---|---|---|
| | SpeedyLane | ABC Solutions | Net Value Advantage |
| **Cost Savings** | | | |
| Fewer Cashiers Needed | $0 | $0 | $0 |
| Reduce Shrink (Employee & Customer theft) | $0 | $0 | $0 |
| Inventory carrying costs reduced by enhanced data (JIT) capabilities | $0 | $0 | $0 |
| **Revenue Enhancers** | | | |
| Better Cust. Service, Fewer Walk-outs | $0 | $0 | $0 |
| Enhanced Sales of Hi-Margin Impulse Items | $0 | $0 | $0 |
| More Customers (& more loyal customers) | $0 | $0 | $0 |
| **Total Annual Benefits in Use** | $0 | $0 | $0 |
| **Costs in Use** | | | |
| Annual Leasing Cost (if no up-front purchase) | $0 | $0 | $0 |
| More Customer Service Personnel | $0 | $0 | $0 |
| Ongoing New Maintenance Requirements | $0 | $0 | $0 |
| Ongoing Self-checkout Cashier Training | $0 | $0 | $0 |
| Scan Coordinator / Monitoring Costs | $0 | $0 | $0 |
| Ongoing Data Integration Costs | $0 | $0 | $0 |
| Continuing Custom Support Costs | $0 | $0 | $0 |
| **Total Annual Cost in Use** | $0 | $0 | $0 |
| **Net Value in Use** | $0 | $0 | $0 |
| **5 Yr PV of New Annual Costs in Use *** | $0 | $0 | $0 |

*[Brian]:* "Can't say I really understand how that all fits together. I look forward to the Financial Vision Building Seminar where we will be learning about all the intricacies of the model."

## How Does the Model Consider SpeedyLane's Costs & Profits?

*[Brian]:* "That said, how does the framework include our costs and determine SpeedyLane profits? How does it consider direct brand competitors' solutions? And how does it automatically calculate an attractive price?"

*[Linda]:* "That's a multi-part question - but let me take a shot at it. You can get more detailed answers at the Financial Vision Building Workshop you will be attending.

"Regarding SpeedyLane's costs and profits, the simple answer is that **our costs and profits are irrelevant when using Value-Based Pricing.** If we can't provide and prove that the value of our solution is significantly higher than our costs, then we'd better enhance our solution, aim at a different value segment, or get out of the business.

"Furthermore, the customer doesn't care about our costs or profits; they just care that the price they pay is significantly less than the value we can prove SpeedyLane provides.

## How the Model Considers Direct Brand Competitors

*[Linda]:* "Regarding whether we consider direct brand competitors, we do indeed – in fact that comparison provides us with our required information for pricing our solution so that the net value of our solution is clearly greater than that of our primary direct competitor.

"You also asked how we do this. This analysis starts with the formulas we reviewed earlier -- where we estimate not only *our* value-add parameters, *but also the value-add parameter for our primary brand competitor.*

"To clarify, see the example here, which is an extension of the previous Cost Savings example. (As an aside, it is important to note that a direct brand competitor's value-add parameter *on an individual item* may be better than ours, but *our overall value must be superior.* If not, we need to improve our solution or change segments to ensure that we offer superior value overall.)

| COST SAVINGS ANALYSIS (one example) | |
|---|---|
| Benefit | Fewer Cashiers Needed |
| Formula | (total cost of cashiers) * (% cost of cashiers laid off) |
| **Primary Brand Competitor (ABC Solutions)** | |
| Explanation | While ABC Solutions also offers reduced usage of cashiers, their units tend to require more help during peak use time as the software is not as user friendly. |
| Justification | In 5 previous instances with similar businesses where SpeedyLane replaced ABC Solutions, there was an additional benefit of around 10%. |
| Value Parameter for ABC | 40% |

## How We Calculate an Appropriate SpeedyLane Price

*[Linda]:* "Now let's consider how we translate all of this information into a SpeedyLane price that yields a Return on Investment (ROI)[63] and Projected Payback Period that are clearly better than those of our primary direct brand competitor. We do this based on two pieces of data:

1. Our Net Value-In-Use advantage over our primary direct brand competitor; and
2. Our primary direct brand competitor's price.

"The first number comes from the Net Value-In-Use table shown in previous pages. The second number (primary direct brand competitor's price) we typically get very willingly from our customer, because often a dominant customer negotiating tactic is to flaunt the competitor's price quote, in an effort to pressure us to reduce our price.

"We eliminate that price reduction pressure through selecting a price (using this transparent model) that provides an ROI and Projected Payback Period that are clearly superior to those of our direct brand competitor – even though our price is very often quite a bit higher than that of our competitor. Here's what the Pricing Analysis Framework looks like. This example includes some numbers in order to give you a better idea of how the model works to yield an attractive price."

## How We Calculate an Appropriate SpeedyLane Price

*[Linda]:* "Now let's consider how we translate all of this information into a SpeedyLane price that yields a Return on Investment (ROI)[64] and Projected Payback Period that are clearly better than those of our primary direct brand competitor."

## PRICING STRATEGY

| | SpeedyLane | ABC Solutions | |
|---|---|---|---|
| Annual Net Value In Use | $686,200 | $527,200 | $159,000 |
| 5 Yr PV of Value in Use Advangage (vs ABC Solutions)* | | | $602,610 |

| | SpeedyLane | ABC Solutions |
|---|---|---|
| UpFront Price | $1,259,784 | $1,200,000 |
| Other Upfront Investment Costs | $85,000 | $110,000 |
| 5 Yr PV of New Costs in Use | $229,485 | $361,187 |
| Total Investment Cost | $1,574,269 | $1,671,187 |

### Evaluating the Results

| | | SpeedyLane | ABC Solutions |
|---|---|---|---|
| Return on Investment (ROI) = | Annual NVIU vs Generic | $686,200 / $1,574,269 | $527,200 / $1,671,187 |
| | | 44% | 32% |
| Break Even Payback Period (BEPP) | In Months: | 27.5 | 38.0 |
| Operating Profit Margin (OPM) | Annual NVIU / Annual BIU | $686,200 / $788,000 | $527,200 / $664,250 |
| | | 87% | 79% |

## PRICING STRATEGY

### Value In Use Analysis

Advantage vs. Generic

| | SpeedyLane | ABC Solutions | SpeedyLane Advantage |
|---|---|---|---|
| Advantages over Gen | $686,200 | $527,200 | |
| Our Brand Advantage= | | | $159,000 |

### SpeedyLane Pricing Strategy

| | | |
|---|---|---|
| Net Value in Use Advantage | $159,000 | |
| Estimated Communications Gap | 6% | 6 |
| Value Advantage after Communications Gap* | $149,460 | |
| Pricing Strategy (% Value Added for customer | 40% | 40 |
| Price Premium over Competitor | $59,784 | |
| Competitor's Price | $1,200,000 | |
| Indifference Price | $1,349,460 | |
| Our Price | $1,259,784 | |
| Customer Incentive to Purchase | $89,676 | |
| Max Price with Required ROI | $1,646,087 | |

### Pricing Strategy Choice

Capture 40% of value: We believe that because we are a low volume industry with extremely large pricing figures, we can capture 40% of the net value in use while still leaving our customers enough incentive to purchase.

Our biggest differential advantages are in fewer cashiers, better customer service, and customer frustration. The sustainability for these categories are medium, medium, and high respectively.

Price Strategy: Skimming/Penetrating

Because our largest two advantages are only medium sustainability and not high, there is no guarantee our advantage will persistent into the future. Because of this, we would like to take as much profit as we can right now. However, we need to leave the customer ample incentive to purchase from SpeedyLane over ABC Solutions.

## Call in SpeedyLane's Financial Support Team to Help

*[Brian]:* "I'm almost sorry I asked. There's so much in there that I don't understand. This sure makes me look forward to the Financial Vision Building Seminar where we'll be learning that."

*[Linda]:* "Well, if it makes you feel any better, I don't thoroughly understand it all myself either. That's why I always call on our experts to come from headquarters for explanations and for help in developing the Financial Vision with the key financial folks in our target company. You'll be able to access that same expertise, any time you need it. Headquarters knows full well how important it is for us sales folks to develop a valid and convincing Financial Vision if we expect to continue selling our SpeedyLane solutions at a premium price."

## Critical Success Factors

*[Linda]:* "Before we are done, Brian, I want to point out one of the more important items that rolls out from building the Financial Vision – that is the set of **Critical Success Factors**. These are the factors that determine the individual **Benefits in Use** (new revenues and cost savings) and **Costs in Use Savings** that are projected to result from implementing the proposed solution. These are the set of value-add variables that drive the projected **Benefits in Use and Costs in Use** and make up part of the **Net Value in Use** exhibit reviewed earlier. We carefully monitor these for the first year or two alongside the customer in order to measure and prove that our SpeedyLane Self-checkout System is delivering on its specific promises.

"Behind each of these Value-in-Use components is a formula (such as the Cashier Cost Savings formula example in the previous few pages). In each formula, there is a value add % change (improvement) assumption (shown in red in the Cost Savings example in the previous part of the chapter). It is these specific value-added % changes that we monitor (typically on a quarterly basis) to measure the customer's progress toward reaching our promised improvements. We typically phase in the % change assumptions – depending on the individual variable.

| Benefits in Use |
|---|
| **Cost Savings** |
| Fewer Cashiers Needed<br>Reduce Shrink (Employee & Customer theft)<br>Inventory carrying costs reduced by enhanced data (JIT) capabilities |
| **Revenue Enhancers** |
| Better Cust. Service, Fewer Walk-outs<br>Enhanced Sales of Hi-Margin Impulse Items<br>More Customers (& more loyal customers) |
| **Costs in Use** |
| Annual Leasing Cost (if no up-front purchase)<br>More Customer Service Personnel<br>Ongoing New Maintenance Requirements<br>Ongoing Self-checkout Cashier Training<br>Scan Coordinator / Monitoring Costs<br>Ongoing Data Integration Costs<br>Continuing Custom Support Costs |

"Again, Bri, at the Financial Vision Building Seminar you will learn all about how to identify and use these value-add % changes to monitor results."

[Brian]: "Yikes, Linny, I think I may be in over my head. I don't know how I will ever understand all this and be able to build effective financial visions."

[Linda]: "Don't worry, if I can do it, you can certainly do it. You'll just have to give it some time and a lot of study."

# Sales Growth Secrets

## Implementing Your Account Marketing Plan: Making the Individual Sale

----

## Step 4 (of 4 Steps)
## Negotiating, Closing & Implementing the sale

---

### Step 4: *Negotiating, Closing & Implementing the Sale*

CHAPTER 55

# Prepare for
# Negotiation & Closing[65]

| Step 4 - Negotiation, Closing and Implementation | | |
|---|---|---|
| Ch | 55 | **Prepare for Final Negotiation & Closing** |
| Ch | 56 | Preparing & Using 'Stands' |
| Ch | 57 | Preparing & Using Gets & Gives Lists |
| Ch | 58 | Negotiation & Closing Conclusion |
| Ch | 59 | Example of Negotiation Dialog |
| Ch | 60 | Challenges in Implementing the Solution |
| Ch | 61 | Ensuring Effective Implementation |

*SpeedyLane's Internal planning for the final negotiation with House Depot will start in early April, after operating, transition and financial visions have been built for all key players.*

*This internal negotiation planning at SpeedyLane may take a couple of weeks in order to get all Key Players at SpeedyLane on the same page. Linda's Account Marketing Plan for HD calls for completion of this planning by mid-April.*

## SpeedyLane Prepares for Final Negotiations with House Depot (HD)

Prior to engaging House Depot (HD) in the final negotiating session, Linda, the SpeedyLane salesperson, needs to do some house cleaning and preparations back at the SpeedyLane home office. Her preliminary homework includes:

- Identifying the *'Key Concerns & Other Goals'* of all important *SpeedyLane Players* who will be affected by the prospective sale to HD or who can affect SpeedyLane solution implementation at HD;
- Agreeing internally (within SpeedyLane) upon overall *Deal 'Goals & Limits'* to evaluate the

deal on the table now and to give the SpeedyLane negotiating team objectives and limits for the final negotiations with HD;

- Agreeing on who from SpeedyLane will play what *'Role'* in the negotiation, to ensure that our SpeedyLane negotiating team coordinates its efforts in the negotiation session, while avoiding any last-minute internal conflicts;

- Fully preparing several *'Stands'* for the SpeedyLane negotiator (most likely Linda) to take in response to HD attempts to get a lower price;

- Planning, negotiating, and agreeing upon SpeedyLane's *'Gets & Gives Lists'* – which Linda and her negotiating team will use to 'expand the pie' during the negotiation itself. This will simultaneously ensure a 'win-win' final negotiated deal.

Let's take a look at these items in order to better understand them!

---

# Identify *Key Concerns & Other Goals* of Important SpeedyLane Players

Linda's first challenge in preparing for the negotiation is to identify the *'Key Concerns & Other Goals'* of all important SpeedyLane players who will be affected by the prospective sale to HD, or who can affect SpeedyLane solution implementation at HD. Meeting these goals will help ensure that the final negotiated deal does not step on any important toes inside SpeedyLane. Linda certainly doesn't want any internal conflicts to lead to a last-minute collapse of the deal, excessive delays, or other significant problems.

One of the success tests for any negotiation is whether the key concerns of all important players *in the seller company* have been met. Thus, all affected SpeedyLane players must meet prior to SpeedyLane's final negotiation with HD. This meeting will involve some internal negotiating. The goal will be to ensure a 'surprise-free' deal with HD. This deal must be thoroughly accepted by all key SpeedyLane players who will be responsible for the success of this sale and follow-up implementation. This will only occur if the key concerns of each important SpeedyLane player are met while defining the outside limits for negotiating the final deal with HD. For example, consider the *'must have'* primary concerns and other *'nice to have'* goals of some key players at SpeedyLane who will play significant roles in the prospective HD purchase and implementation.

- ***Player: Gina Wagle- SpeedyLane's VP of Marketing &Sales***
  - **Must Have - Key Concerns**
    - Needs SpeedyLane negotiating team to refuse to budge on price.
    - Needs HD to agree to serve as a reference client for SpeedyLane.
    - Needs the agreement to include an HD commitment to introduce the SpeedyLane Self-checkout System into cities nationwide.
  - **Nice to Have - Other Goals**

- Wants the SpeedyLane negotiating team to trade several of the 'gets' for 'gives' – see discussion and examples below.
- Wants HD to issue a press release with the SpeedyLane brand name both immediately after the deal is finalized and after it has been proven successful.
- Wants SpeedyLane logo and contact information displayed prominently on all SpeedyLane Self-checkout installations.
- Wants HD to agree to let acquired data be compiled into an industry-wide database.

- ## *Player: Patrick Jones, SpeedyLane's Director of Product Development*
  - **Must Have - Key Concerns**
    - Needs assurance that SpeedyLane negotiators will not promise any specified upgrades not already included in the preliminary contract with HD – i.e., resist any last minute HD demands for add-on capabilities that SpeedyLane cannot simply provide.
    - Needs assurance that SpeedyLane negotiators will not promise HD access to ANY technology still in the developmental phases at SpeedyLane.
    - Needs SpeedyLane negotiators to insist that HD will follow SpeedyLane-recommended layouts (as indicated in the preliminary contract) – to help ensure that the SpeedyLane implementation will indeed deliver the promised results.
  - **Nice to Have - Other Goals**
    - Wants HD to agree to participate in trials of new SpeedyLane self-checkout product development capabilities as they are developed.
    - Wants HD to agree to participate in brainstorming sessions, focus groups, and surveys in order to help SpeedyLane develop and test potential product enhancements over time.

- ## *Player: John Seville, SpeedyLane's IT Manager*
  - **Must Have - Key Concerns**
    - Needs HD's IT Department to agree to cooperate fully with SpeedyLane's IT Department in integrating HD's current checkout data collection and analysis system with those of the new SpeedyLane system.
    - Needs SpeedyLane negotiators to agree to not promise HD more SpeedyLane IT installment support than is currently called for in the preliminary contract. Alternatively, if additional SpeedyLane IT installment support is negotiated, then John needs SpeedyLane top management to agree (now) to promise an increase in home office SpeedyLane IT resources that is adequate to meet any expanded IT commitments to HD.
    - Needs SpeedyLane negotiators not to commit to a faster national HD implementation roll-out than is currently planned in order to minimize short-term pressures, headaches, and problems for the SpeedyLane and HD data integration teams alike.
    - Needs employees and managers at HD to attend a mandatory seminar taking place

on two Monday evenings to become educated and acquainted with the SpeedyLane technology.

- **Nice to Have - Other Goals**
  - Wants HD to agree to buy all of the required new hardware from SpeedyLane. This will reduce any potential IT adaptation requirements and facilitate smooth IT integration.
  - Wants HD and its IT Department to commit to purchasing and installing new SpeedyLane software and hardware upgrades to the system as they become available (i.e., after adequate testing, etc.).

## Agree Upon Deal Goals & Limits

Before the final negotiation with HD, the SpeedyLane negotiating team must also agree among themselves on *'deal goals and limits'*. <u>The most important point to make here is that we are setting goals and limits only on terms, NOT ON PRICE</u>. We do not need to, and we will not, give on price under any circumstance – for we and the HD Buying Committee have already committed to an attractive, acceptable price for HD. (We discussed this in the Financial Vision chapter and review it again in the 'Stands' section below.).

As indicated, however, our SpeedyLane negotiation team will allow itself some wiggle room to negotiate certain terms of the deal. The discussion of terms is likely to come up in the *'Gets & Gives'* portion of the negotiation (also discussed below). In their preliminary internal discussions, key SpeedyLane players first mutually decide on what terms can be negotiated, and then discuss and agree on specific goals and limits for each negotiable term of sale. In the example below, SpeedyLane sets goals and limits for negotiating the following two important terms:

1. Percentage of price to be paid up front (to help with SpeedyLane cash flow); and
2. Length of the service contract that is an integral part of the initial planned deal.

## Terms -- Goals and Limits

- **Reservation Deal:** Absolute minimums that our SpeedyLane negotiating team must achieve in the negotiation
  - 20% payment up front
  - 3 year contract
- **Target Deal:** Realistic, more acceptable goals for our SpeedyLane negotiating team to try to negotiate
  - 25-30% payment up front
  - 4-6 year contract
- **Opening Position:** Best Case Scenario -- Starting positions for our SpeedyLane negotiating team to propose, which leave wiggle room in compromising toward target goals
  - 40% payment up front
  - 7 year contract

## Agree on the Role for Each SpeedyLane Negotiating Team Member

Prior to the actual negotiation, the SpeedyLane team needs to agree among themselves on who will play what **_Role_** in the Negotiation. This is to help the SpeedyLane team coordinate its negotiating efforts, while avoiding any potential last minute internal conflicts. The goal is to project a thoroughly professional 'we know what we are doing' image. Among other coordinated efforts, this will include deciding on signals for breaking during the negotiations, should anyone on the SpeedyLane team become uncertain or uncomfortable with any aspect of the on-going negotiation.

# Planned Roles in the Negotiation between SpeedyLane and HD

## Our (SpeedyLane's) Point Person

### Linda Brown, *SpeedyLane Salesperson*
– Linda has been working with HD since day one. She has formed relationships with many HD employees.
– She has intimate knowledge of all the operating, transition and financial visions that have been built at HD.

## Our Support Team

### Roberto Garcia, *SpeedyLane Sales Manager*.
– Roberto is Linda's sales manager and boss.
– Roberto will be present to show respect for HD and to support Linda. In particular he wants to ensure that she does not give in to HD demands for price concessions.

### Gina Wagle, *SpeedyLane's VP of Marketing & Sales*
– Gina is there as the 'SpeedyLane big wig' to show respect for HD and to show them that they are an important prospective client.
– She is also there to authorize Linda (& SpeedyLane) to potentially make compromises in any unanticipated 'off-list' gives (& gets) that might be requested by HD in areas that neither Linda nor Roberto has the authority to make such commitments.

### Patrick Jones, *Director of Product Development*
– Patrick has thorough knowledge of the intricacies of SpeedyLane's solution for which he oversaw development.
– He is there to answer any last minute technical questions or alleviate last minute concerns about the SpeedyLane solution, its refinements over time, etc.
– Patrick has also been put in charge of *'time out rules.'*

### *John Seville, IT Manager*
– John is well informed on the data integration plan between SpeedyLane and HD.
– He is there to answer any last minute technical questions or alleviate last minute concerns about the SpeedyLane – HD data integration.

## Setting Time Out Rules

Anyone on the SpeedyLane negotiation team can signal for a time out at any time. This might be appropriate for a number of reasons. Here are some examples.

- If a couple of our own negotiating team members seem to have an open difference of opinion on any matter, SpeedyLane would rather not air the laundry in front of HD and make fools of themselves. Instead, it is much better to take a time out and resolve the difference of opinion privately before continuing.
- If an HD negotiator goes off-list with a specific, potentially doable 'Give' request, it is best not to turn it down cold. Instead, if it seems doable, take a time out to discuss its viability and to decide what SpeedyLane might receive in return.
- If any of our team members sense that someone on our team is about to violate an already agreed upon 'must have' (key interest) of a key SpeedyLane player not at the meeting, take a short time out. Then, remind all members of that specific 'must have' and other key interest areas for all important SpeedyLane players not present.
- If the discussion is simply becoming a little too heated or adversarial between SpeedyLane and HD, it is judicious to signal for a break to let things cool down.
- If at or near the end of a successful negotiation, you want to look at the remaining list of 'Gives' and together decide which would make an appropriate 'give back' to HD after negotiations are complete, call a time out. This can end negotiations on a positive note for HD, smooth out some ruffled feathers, and set the stage for a smooth launch of the implementation plan.

**The bottom line is this**: the SpeedyLane negotiating team should agree ahead of time on one or more subtle signals to take time outs as necessary in order to keep their negotiations professional and on track.

Over the next couple of chapters, we will continue our discussion of Negotiation, Closing and Implementation.

***Early April. This part of SpeedyLane's internal planning for the final negotiation with House Depot starts in Early April, with target completion date of Mid-April. (This includes preview of 'Stands' part of projected final closing at 10 am on Mon., April 30.)***

CHAPTER 56

# Negotiation, cont.
# Prepare & Use "Stands"

| Step 4 - Negotiation, Closing and Implementation | | |
|------|-----|---------------------------------------------|
| Ch | 55 | Prepare for Final Negotiation & Closing |
| **Ch** | **56** | **Preparing & Using 'Stands'** |
| Ch | 57 | Preparing & Using Gets & Gives Lists |
| Ch | 58 | Negotiation & Closing Conclusion |
| Ch | 59 | Example of Negotiation Dialog |
| Ch | 60 | Challenges in Implementing the Solution |
| Ch | 61 | Ensuring Effective Implementation |

As we saw in the last chapter, prior to engaging House Depot (HD) in the final negotiating session, Linda and SpeedyLane will need to do some preparations at the SpeedyLane home office. So far, we have reviewed that SpeedyLane needs to: identify the '***Key Concerns & Other Goals'*** of all Important SpeedyLane Players; agree internally upon overall ***Deal 'Goals & Limits;'*** and agree on which SpeedyLane team member will play which '***Role'*** in the negotiation itself. In this Chapter, we introduce '***Stands'*** and see the important role they can play in negotiations.

---

## The What & Why of 'Stands'[66]

A '***stand***' is SpeedyLane's planned response to counter any last minute request or demand from HD to reduce price. Before reviewing some examples of 'stands' (i.e., planned responses), let's consider the ***important context for 'stands.'***

## HD Has Already OK'd the Price and What It Includes.

As an integral part of cooperatively building and proving an attractive financial vision for HD, the HD financial gurus and Buying Committee have already agreed upon the SpeedyLane price and all that is included. The HD Buying Committee has, therefore, essentially pre-approved the price because, according to their calculations, the investment in the SpeedyLane solution will enable HD to surpass its minimum required, risk-adjusted ROI and Payback Period criteria. So, they are good to go with the proposed solution contents and price, even prior to any potential final negotiations.

## So, Why the Negotiations?

If HD is already satisfied with the proposed solution contents and price, why do we need 'negotiations?' Who needs the stress and potential hard feelings that can come from HD and SpeedyLane slugging it out? Well, it comes down to this: why should HD pay more than it needs to for the solution? Every dollar HD can save by going below the price 'tentatively' agreed upon, will flow directly to the bottom line and shareholders. Sooo... due diligence dictates that the HD Buying Committee, through its well-trained negotiators, should ask for a lower price, even at the last minute. Thus, the negotiation.

## Why 'Stands?'

The folks at SpeedyLane are no dummies and know that a last minute price 'squeeze' will almost certainly be requested from HD. The HD goal in this demand is to test if the originally agreed-upon price is negotiable. ***SpeedyLane has to stand firm with its price.*** Why? Because every dollar they lower their price is one less dollar added to SpeedyLane's bottom line! Nothing good comes from SpeedyLane offering their system at a lower price. As soon as SpeedyLane gives even a bit on price,

HD will then keep asking for a lower and lower price until SpeedyLane says "enough already! NO MORE!" Furthermore, the word will soon get out to other SpeedyLane customers that they are 'soft' on price, creating price pressures from all angles.

## The lesson – WE DON'T GIVE ON PRICE!
## because we don't have to! Enter 'Stands.'

*[Linda]*: "For example, here's what can happen if you DON'T take a stand and do give on price:"

## Stand Examples

As introduced earlier, a 'stand' is Linda's planned response to counter any last minute request from HD for a lower price. Let's look at several possible 'Stands' (i.e., planned responses) that Linda can take in refusing to give on price.

> ## Stand Examples
>
> **We Proved the Value' Stand**: "Your HD financial team and SpeedyLane spent considerable time cooperatively building and proving an attractive financial vision for HD. The Buying Committee has agreed to the $3.2 million price tag – knowing that this price will deliver a projected annual return of 50%, with only a two year payback period! *What has changed?*"
>
> **Delay Is Costly' Stand**: "The HD Buying Committee has confirmed that HD's current inefficient checkout system is costing you nearly $15,000 extra every day, when compared

with the proposed new SpeedyLane System. *Those losses won't stop until HD gets the new SpeedyLane system implemented. How long are you willing to put up with a $15,000 loss each and every day? Is it really worth delaying?"*

**Build More Anxiety' Stand** (by Reviewing the Pain and Vision of a Solution): "You at HD have already confirmed over and over again that you are anxious indeed to fix the inefficiencies of your current checkout system. We have seen together that adding the SpeedyLane solution can significantly reduce your checkout system costs, while simultaneously improving customer satisfaction. That's the vision and that's what the SpeedyLane solution can start delivering as soon as it is implemented. Those issues have plagued HD for some time now and have kept you from realizing your aggressive profit goals. *Without the proposed SpeedyLane system, that won't change, and those issues will still plague HD operations & financial results – continuing to disappoint top management, the Board, and shareholders alike! Let's get going now to fix these problems! Enough delays!"*

**Emphasize Broader Positives** (from Fixing the Problem) **Stand:** "We at SpeedyLane have worked with HD on diagnosing the challenges you face. You told us that addressing your efficiency and customer satisfaction problems with the proposed SpeedyLane system would set you apart from the other home improvement retail companies, yielding historic revenues and profits. *This is a proven solution, as our many reference clients have verified for you. As they all confirmed, our clients have received much, much more from the SpeedyLane solution than what they paid. The price is fair. Let's move forward!"*

---

# Dialogue – Using 'Stands' to
# Fight Off Price Concession Demands

## Setting: Preview of Final Closing, 10 a.m., Tues., April 30

*[Linda]:* "Well, it looks like we are all set. We've got all your key players at HD on board with the solution, the implementation plan, and the key success variables we will be monitoring to ensure that the SpeedyLane Self-checkout Checkout System is a success at HD. I have the contract your Buying Committee has checked off on right here. So, if you'll just sign on the bottom line, we will begin Phase I of the planned implementation next Monday."

*[Dr. Nathaniel Sinclair, HD Chief Negotiator]:* "Well, Linda, may I call you Linda?"

*[Linda]:* "Why, of course."

*[Nathaniel]:* "We are certainly impressed with your SpeedyLane solution and all the good things we've heard from some of your other clients. However, in these economically uncertain times, our top management is under severe financial pressure from our Board of Directors. So, we'd like you to lower your price. After all, I think you'd agree that $3.2 million is a lot of money – and certainly waaay, waaay more than it will cost you at SpeedyLane to provide the solution for us here at HD."

*[Linda]:* **Thought bubble** – *"Well, here we go again – I'm so glad Roberto (Linda's sales manager) anticipated this and told me how to respond."*

*[Linda to Nathan]:* "Well, Nathan, may I call you Nathan?"

*[Nathan]:* "Well, I actually favor Dr. Sinclair, but you can call me Nathaniel, if you prefer."

*[Linda]:* "OK, NaTHANiel – gee, that's a nice name!" (**Here comes Linda's 'Value Stand.'**) "Well, at any rate, as I assume you know, your financial team and SpeedyLane spent considerable time cooperatively building and proving an attractive financial vision for HD. Your own Buying Committee has agreed to the $3.2 million price tag, having calculated that the financial benefits will far exceed that price – in fact, delivering a projected 50% annual return, with only a two-year payback period! Those are your numbers – numbers we developed together! **What has changed**?"

*[Nathan]:* "Well, nothing has really changed, but your price is simply too high. We can't really be sure that your solution will deliver all of the financial benefits you have promised, so that 50% ROI could be like pie in the sky for all I know. So, we are asking for a 20% discount on the price. I assume you are aware that NAR has offered us the same solution for only $2.4 million. That's 25% less than the $3.2 million you are asking for!"

*[Linda]:* **Thought bubble** – *"Well, that 20% discount ain't gonna happen – not if I wanna keep my job and not end up on some customer service phone bank up in Alaska! Can you say, 'illogical?' I just told this guy, NaTHANiel, that we and his Buying Committee came up with the $3.2 million price tag together and that the financial benefits far exceed those projected costs!*

*"Heck, his top wigs have already agreed to this price ... OK ... Calm down Linda ol' girl, I know full well he's just squeezing me to see if he can get the blood flowing! I've just got to keep saying no, no, no – until he's confident that we won't budge one iota on price – because we don't have to! They know that we provide the best value available, even with the $3.2 million price tag!"*

*[Linda]:* "Well, Nathaniel", (**Here comes Linda's 'Value Stand,' again, and the 'Delay Is Costing You Stand'**). As I assume you know, we compared our solution with NAR's. Their projected ROI, even with the lower price, is only 25%, only half of our return, and their payback period is 4 yrs – twice as long as with our solution! Not to mention that the projected ROI from our solution is risk-adjusted, incorporating whatever uncertainty your Buying Committee said they had.

"**As your Buying Committee confirmed, your current inefficient checkout system is costing you over $15,000 every day.** Those losses won't stop until you implement the planned new SpeedyLane system. Given those numbers, I'm certain that your Buying Committee would like to get the implementation plan started right away, according to schedule. The insistence on lowering our price will simply delay the plan, because our final price is the agreed=upon $3.2 million. Your Buying Committee is happy with that price!"

*[Nathan]:* "Be that as it may, your price is simply too high."

*[Linda]:* **Thought bubble** – *"OK, a tough guy, looks like he's not gonna give up. So..., it's time for **'Plan B'** – time to move to my Gets & Gives lists."*

-----------

## Next Up: Gets & Gives

**Let's go to the next chapter to see how Linda can develop and use a 'Gets & Gives' list to transition from the somewhat confrontational 'Stands' scenario described above to a more constructive discussion.** Then, we'll also see how Linda uses her 'Gets & Gives' lists to 'expand the pie' during the negotiation itself and to ensure a final agreement where both sides will see themselves as 'winners' – i.e., a win-win result!

-----------

## Let's check up on Brian first.

Let's check and see how Brian's wardrobe is coming along.

*[Linda]:* "Hey, Brian. I want to introduce you to Gustavo. He's one of Danielle's really good friends. Danielle and I have asked him to help you with your wardrobe."

*[Gustavo]:* "Hi Brian. Hmm ... Let's see... It looks like your fashion sense is stuck at 'immature Momma's boy.'

"Desperate times call for desperate measures. I can show you a whole new world, full of dashing suits and beautiful women! What do you say?"

*[Brian]:* "I think I'm going to have to call my Mom first, to see if it's okay..."

*[Gustavo]:* (throws away Brian's cell phone) "You're coming with me, young man. **We are going to fix you up.**"

----

391

## Later—

**[Gustavo]:** "Look at you! You're a changed man. You will no doubt sweep this Lucy girl off her feet on your next date!"

**[Brian]:** "Wait 'til I show Linda!!"

*Early April. This is part of SpeedyLane's internal planning for the final negotiation with House Depot -- starting in Early April, with target completion date of Mid-April. (Includes preview of 'Gets & Gives' part of projected final closing at 10 am on Monday, April 30)*

CHAPTER 57

# Negotiation, cont. – Preparing & Using 'Gets & Gives' Lists

| Step 4 - Negotiation, Closing and Implementation | | |
|---|---|---|
| Ch | 55 | Prepare for Final Negotiation & Closing |
| Ch | 56 | Preparing & Using 'Stands' |
| **Ch** | **57** | **Preparing & Using Gets & Gives Lists** |
| Ch | 58 | Negotiation & Closing Conclusion |
| Ch | 59 | Example of Negotiation Dialog |
| Ch | 60 | Challenges in Implementing the Solution |
| Ch | 61 | Ensuring Effective Implementation |

The last items that SpeedyLane's lead negotiator, Linda, needs to prepare before entering the final negotiations with House Depot (HD) are her lists of *'Gets & Gives.'*[67]

## Why the 'Gets & Gives' Lists?

The 'Gets & Gives' lists have two purposes.

- *First*, these lists will enable SpeedyLane's lead negotiator (Linda Brown) to transition from the somewhat confrontational 'Stands' scenario described in the last chapter to a much more constructive discussion.
- *Second*, the 'Gets & Gives' lists represent an opportunity to 'expand the

pie' during the negotiation itself. This, in turn, will result in a final agreement where both sides perceive themselves as 'winners' – i.e., a win-win result!

## Transitioning from the 'Stands' Discussion

Let's start with the first purpose: transitioning to a more constructive discussion. As HD continues to squeeze for a price cut, Linda continues responding with her 'Stands.' All of the SpeedyLane stands conclude with an outright refusal to cut the already agreed upon price. Those squeezes from HD get old pretty fast and are likely to continue until Linda either 'Gets' worn out and 'gives' (making a price concession – is a real NO-NO) *or when she changes the conversation*.

The 'Gets' & 'Gives' lists offer Linda a chance to transform the whole conversation.

## The transition might go like this:

*[Nathaniel Sinclair, HD Negotiator].* Just after Linda has taken yet another stand – Nathan is still insistent that we reduce price. He says: "That's all well and good, but your price is just too high!"

*[Linda, Salesperson & SpeedyLane Lead Negotiator].* With her body language suggesting to Nathan that she may be about to give in, Linda changes the whole game, with a single comment: ***"Well, I can't do anything for you, unless you do something for me."***

*[Nathan]*: ***Thought bubble***: "Say what – what the heck is she talking about?" He responds to Linda in a somewhat bewildered fashion. "Like what?"

Here, with her simple comment (*"Well, I can't do anything for you, unless you do something for me"*), **Linda has changed the whole game, by cleverly grabbing control of the negotiation from Nathan's grasp. She now has an opportunity to make the conversation much more constructive.**

## Expanding the Pie with the 'Gets & Gives Lists'

This brings up the second purpose of the 'Gets & Gives lists: to expand the pie and to make the negotiation a win-win for both SpeedyLane and HD. *Before we look at that 'pie expansion' process, however, let's first build our 'Gets & Gives lists.'*

# Build the SpeedyLane 'Gets List'

## What are 'Gets?'

SpeedyLane's *'Gets'* are items that have <u>*high value to the seller, SpeedyLane, but low cost for the target customer, HD*</u>.

'Gets' are things that SpeedyLane wants to receive in return for potentially offering HD some of the items on SpeedyLane's *'Gives'* list (below). This is <u>***all part of the effort to 'expand the pie' so that both sides can 'win' in the negotiation***</u>.

## What should SpeedyLane put on its 'Gets list?'

Well, a good starting point is to look at the 'Must Have's' (key interests – presented earlier) of important SpeedyLane players who will be most affected by the sale.

Are some of the 'Must Haves' excluded in the original proposed contract?

Let's put those excluded 'Must Haves' on Linda's 'Gets' list. Doing so, Linda's 'Gets' list might include the following requests for HD:

- ***Become a reference client*** (like Pioneer Markets) if the implementation is successful;
- ***Run cooperative promotions and press releases*** – where SpeedyLane features HD's success in some of its ads & press releases, and HD includes prominent mention of the SpeedyLane Self-checkout System and its benefits in some of HD's ads and press releases;
- ***Make the SpeedyLane name & contact info prominently visible*** on all self-checkout lanes;
- ***Monitor and share with SpeedyLane the results of HD's key success factors*** (refer to Building Financial Vision chapter) to prove SpeedyLane has delivered on these success factors;
- ***Allow SpeedyLane to tout results of HD's key success factor improvements***, specifically citing the HD name & positive results, to help prove that SpeedyLane can deliver the successes promised;
- ***Pay 40% up front*** (opening request);
- ***Increase the contract to 7 years*** (opening request);
- ***Commit to purchasing new SpeedyLane software upgrades*** as they become available (i.e., after adequate testing, etc.) during the life of the contract;
- ***Participate in trials of new SpeedyLane self-checkout product development capabilities*** as they are developed;
- ***Participate in brainstorming sessions, focus groups, and surveys*** to help SpeedyLane develop and test potential product enhancements over time;
- ***Etc.***

**Wow, that's a long list,** with at least 10 potential 'Gets' requests. The 'Gets' examples are presented in no particular order. ***Linda and her negotiating team should prioritize these 'Gets' before asking for any of these 'Gets*****,'** since it is most unlikely that Linda will 'get all her Gets,' if you catch the drift!

---

## Build the SpeedyLane 'Gives' List

If Linda expects HD to agree to provide any of her desired 'Gets,' she better show up with a strong list of 'Gives' as well. Linda can't expect to 'get a Get' unless she is willing to 'give a Give.' ***'Gives' should be items that are of high value to the target customer, HD, of low cost to the seller, SpeedyLane, and that will help to ensure a successful implementation***.

---

### What's not to like about 'Gives' for HD?

The 'Gives' which HD receives provide value for HD, help implementation success, and cost HD little, because the only cost is in the form of low direct cost 'Gets' that HD will offer SpeedyLane.

---

### What's not to like about those same 'Gives' for SpeedyLane?

The 'Gives' SpeedyLane has to potentially offer are:

- Of high value for HD;
- Low direct cost to SpeedyLane;
- Will help implementation success; and
- Yield highly valued 'Gets' for SpeedyLane.

That is certainly a ***Win-Win***, as both parties are better off than prior to the 'Gets & Gives' add-ons to the contract.

---

### What should Linda put on her 'Gives' list?

Keep in mind, SpeedyLane 'Gives' ***should all be of high value for HD, low direct cost to SpeedyLane, and help implementation success***. Linda's 'Gives' meeting these criteria might include factors such as:

- ***Providing hardware and software upgrades at 50% discount*** for the life of the contract (worth up to $100,000 over the life of contract);
- ***Continuing web-based system training for store managers and employees***, as needed, for the life of the contract (worth $30,000 per year);
- ***Providing 24 hour call-in customer service*** for SpeedyLane hardware & software for the life of the contract (worth $20,000 per year);
- ***Having cooperative advertising and press releases*** – touting HD's efficient, customer-pleasing new checkout system both at kickoff (worth up to $50,000) and again, once success is realized (worth up to another $50,000);
- ***Providing IT help to monitor and interpret achievement of success factors*** for the life of the contract to prove SpeedyLane has delivered on success factors (worth $10,000 pcr year);

- ***Providing a faster roll out than planned in the contract*** – speeding up HD's realization of increased profits by 3 months (worth $15-$25,000);
- ***Helping to monitor HD Key Success Factors*** (refer to Building Financial Vision chapter) to prove SpeedyLane has delivered on success factors ($20,000 value);
- ***Providing software for optimizing employee / cashier scheduling*** – for maximum cashier savings without increasing wait times or compromising customer satisfaction (worth $40,000);
- ***Providing continuing store layout consultation*** (worth $10,000 per year);
- ***Giving HD access to participate in trials of all new SpeedyLane self-checkout product development capabilities*** as they are developed;
- ***Etc.***

## Include the Value of Each 'Give'

Linda should make sure to calculate and include ***a dollar value*** with the mention of each of her 'Gives' as this will reinforce the financial benefits of each 'Give.' Also remember that 'Gives' are items that Linda really doesn't mind giving because they cost SpeedyLane little and will assist System implementation. Linda is simply using the 'Gives' to barter for valuable items (to SpeedyLane) on her 'Gets' list.

# Get Before We Give!

In trying to expand the pie with her 'Gets' & 'Gives' lists, the most important thing for Linda to remember is that ***she must always Get before she Gives***.

That means that Linda must tie each 'Give' to a 'Get' – and 'get the Get' prior to 'giving the Give'! Got it! So, the conversation might go like this.

- **[Linda]:** "Well, I can't do anything for you, unless you do something for me."
- **[Nathan]:** "Like what?"
- **[Linda]:** "Well, if we have a successful implementation at HD like we fully expect, would it be possible for HD to agree to serve as a reference client for us – much like Pioneer Markets did for you?"
- **[Nathan]:** "Well, I don't know why not, but why would we want to agree to go through all that trouble? – after all, Pioneer spent an awful lot of time with us!"
- **[Linda]:** "Well, if HD could agree to that, then we would agree to make available two of our IT specialists to work with your IT Department for up to six weeks to help ensure successful integration of our two data collection and analysis systems. That's more than a $40,000 value!"
- **[Nathan]:** "Well, that sounds good. We'd be willing to commit to that as part of the contract."

  (Note, if Nathan balks at this, then Linda would specifically pull the offer (a valuable 'Give') because otherwise Nathan will simply swoop up the offer of extra IT support, while providing nothing for Linda in return. Linda would say "Well, then that offer of extra IT support is off the table."]

Assuming no balking,

*[Linda]:* "Great! Also, would it be possible for HD to agree to purchase and install all new versions of proven SpeedyLane software upgrades over the life of the contract?"

- *[Nathan]:* "Well, I'm not sure about that. What might we get in return?"

- *[Linda]:* "Well, if you would agree in the contract to purchase and install all new versions of proven SpeedyLane software upgrades over the life of the contract, we would give you the upgrades at half price for the life of the contract."

- *[Nathan]:* "Done deal. That's a good trade-off. We'd want the latest upgrades anyway to keep improving our efficiency. I'm liking the way this conversation is going!"

- *[Linda]:* "And would you, ... yada...yada...yada" – Linda continues with more requests for 'Gets' – leading to an eventual cordial closing (a more complete dialog example appears in a later chapter).

## The Gets & Gives Discussion Has Expanded the Pie

Assessing the results of the above 'Gets' & 'Gives' discussion clarifies the **second purpose of the 'Gets & Gives' list -- to 'expand the pie' for a Win-Win result**. SpeedyLane and HD have each now received more than they started with prior to the negotiation. **Importantly, this all happened without SpeedyLane having to give on price!**

Expanding the Pie with 'Gets' and 'Gives' Yields a Win-Win Result

In the next chapter we will review some principles and strategies for negotiating more effectively.

CHAPTER 58

# The Negotiation & Closing

Linda starts a negotiating lesson for Brian. [68]

*[Linda]*: "Brian, here we are going to review some of the most important principles of negotiating. If you always follow these rules, you can be a successful negotiator."

*[Brian]:* "Before you start, Linda, I should tell you that I am already a pretty skilled negotiator. For example, once in my fantasy football league, I traded Lions QB, Matt Stafford for Raider receiver Antonio Brown. I thought that was a great deal! If only Brown hadn't hurt his foot, then been traded to the Patriots, then released after one game, I might have even won my league."

*[Linda]:* "If, if, if! If's don't cut it in negotiating, Bri, as you will eventually find out. So, you might want to keep your ears open for this."

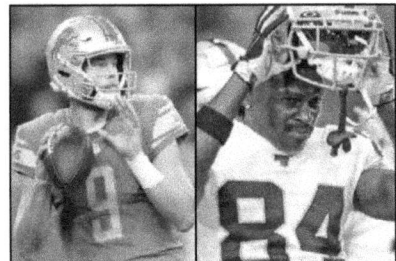

## When Is Linda Ready to Negotiate?

*[Linda to Brian]:* "Let's get going. As a starting point, you are not ready to negotiate, unless a number of pre-conditions and preliminary steps have been thoroughly addressed. These include the steps in this table. Let's review each one."

## Is it Closable?

- _X_ • **Are You Are Ready to 'Walk?'**
- _X_ • **Do You Believe You Have the Best Solution Value?**
- _X_ • **Have You Proven All Visions to All Key Internal & External Players (i.e., completed the Evaluation Plan)?**
- _X_ • **Has the Buyer Been Aware of Likely Cost for a Sufficient Period of Time?**
- _X_ • **Are You Sure You Are Negotiating with the Right Party (ies)?**
- • **Are You Are Fully Prepared?** You have:
  - _x_ • Successfully completed your intra firm negotiations
  - _x_ • Have agreed on your 'gets-gives' list
  - _x_ • Have all 'stands' prepared, and
  - _x_ • Have established who will play what role in the negotiation

## Prove We Offer the Best Value

*[Linda]:* "First off, SpeedyLane must offer the best value for House Depot (HD). Remember, value includes more than the 'naked system'. Don't bluff. If you don't 'have the goods,' then don't try to 'play the game.'

"The SpeedyLane System must offer a better value than the principle generic and brand competitors. In this case, we need to have proven that to HD -- beyond a doubt, during our vision building efforts – especially through building a solid financial vision. If that is not the case, then we are not ready to try to negotiate a final deal."

*[Brian]:* "I guess that's why I better pay special attention during that financial vision workshop next week, that's for sure!"

## Prove All Important Visions

*[Linda]:* "Next, we must have successfully completed the entire Evaluation Plan, having proved all of the most important operating, transition and financial visions to all relevant players. If any

key internal or external HD players are not yet on board, we need to hold off on final negotiations, or else we will suffer the consequences – which, in the worst case, will be a lost deal, and in the best case will be a significantly compromised final price for our solution. We obviously don't want either of those scenarios."

## Customer Must Be Aware of the Price for a Sufficient Period of Time.

*[Linda]:* "Next, as long as we don't wait until the last minute to cooperatively build the financial vision with HD's key financial players, we will have this one covered. For, in cooperatively developing and agreeing upon an attractive financial vision with the Buying Committee, the key financial players at HD will have already agreed upon and approved the price they will pay for our SpeedyLane checkout system. This agreed-upon price will provide a more than satisfactory ROI and Payback Period for HD, and they know this. We just can't spring this on HD at the last minute."

## Negotiate with the Right Folks.

*[Linda]:* "This is one that is easy to overlook. Assume we have proven all visions and that both we and HD are ready to strike the final deal. In that case, if we start the final negotiation with someone at HD who does not have the power to stamp the deal, then we are wasting time for everyone involved and that can be counterproductive. Therefore, as you will see, I will refuse to negotiate with anyone at HD who does not have the power to grant concessions and to make the purchase commitment. That is, we need to negotiate with the Buying Committee itself or with someone officially representing the committee. If HD or any target customer sends anyone else to negotiate with us, you can bet they are simply testing the waters to see if they can get us to lower our price."

*[Brian]:* "I can see how that could happen. But how do you know who does and does not have the power to grant concessions and to make the purchase commitment?"

*[Linda]:* "Hold your horses and we'll address that a little later."

## Be Fully Prepared – Including Internal SpeedyLane Agreements.

*[Linda]:* "This one should be obvious to you by now, Brian. As I've emphasized over and over again, we can't just wing it. Before trying to close, we must have successfully completed all of the preliminary steps for negotiating, as covered earlier. We must also have done our homework to get internal agreement with our SpeedyLane team on:

- '*Must Haves'* of all important SpeedyLane players;
- Overall *Deal 'Goals & Limits'* for the final agreement;
- Members of the SpeedyLane negotiating team and what *Role* will be played by each member, including agreement on who will be the lead negotiator;
- The '*Stands'* Linda will take in response to HD 'squeezes' to try to get her to lower the price;
- Our '*Gets & Gives Lists'*, which Linda will use to 'expand the pie' during the negotiation itself, while simultaneously ensuring a 'Win-Win' final negotiated deal, in which both

sides perceive themselves as a clear 'winner.'

## Finally, If We Are Not Ready to Walk, We Are Not Ready to Negotiate.

*[Linda]:* "This last one is key, Brian, and often one that new SpeedyLane team members like yourself, have a tough time fully grasping. The point is simply this. Let's do the math. If we have attended to each of the cautions above, including proving all the visions and providing all the proofs, then HD should be just as anxious to buy the SpeedyLane solution at the already agreed upon price as we are to sell it!

"We don't have to put up with the any last-minute HD negotiator squeezing us for a lower price or costly add-ons, because the deal has essentially already been agreed upon during the financial vision building process. Granting price and other concessions at the last minute will pull directly from our revenue and bottom line. That's not to mention, generating BIG TIME static from my Sales Manager and her boss, the VP of Sales (whom Top Management is now referring to as our "Chief Revenue Officer.).

"We have to be ***ready to walk***, if our target customer tries to get a better deal at the last minute. And the only way we can come into the negotiation with that mindset is if we have all our ducks in a row going in. So, if the HD negotiator asks for anything that is a net cost to SpeedyLane, we should head for the door. In nearly every situation I've experienced like that in the past, I've never gotten to the door before the target customer's negotiator backtracked.

"But keep in mind, yet again, that you'll only have the confidence to 'walk' if you know we are offering the best value available at the already agreed upon price and that we have:

- Built and proven all the visions necessary; and,
- Established an attractive, agreed-upon price through discussion with both the HD Buying Committee and SpeedyLane.

# Fundamental Principles for Linda as the Seller

If Linda, SpeedyLane's lead negotiator, keeps in mind several principles, the negotiation is much more likely to be a resounding success for all parties concerned.

## #1 Don't Give on Price.

Linda knows full well that she already offers the best solution value at her proposed price. Furthermore, the HD Buying Committee has already agreed to that price. Therefore, there is no need to give on price!

## Anticipate / Prepare for 'Squeezes' and other Buyer Strategies.

Linda must have well-practiced 'Stands' ready to go, along with a carefully prepared Gets-Gives List.

### Always Get Before She Gives.

Linda, as the seller, must draw the line first. Then, only after she resists all squeezes, Linda should change the game with the comment: "If you could do something for me, I might be able to do something for you."

### Do Not Try to Close Prematurely.

See the list of criteria above for 'When is Linda Ready to Negotiate.' For example, if Linda has not proven all the visions, she is not ready to close.

### Try for an Early Close (if all "Is It Closeable" items are completed).

Linda should include a Planned 'Early' Close in the Evaluation Plan (in the 'Pre-Proposal Review' – after all visions have been built & confirmed). If successful, this early close can help avoid the negatives that can flow from a potential 'non-optimal' negotiation.

## Get Her Ducks in a Row

Linda must have done the detailed internal SpeedyLane negotiation planning (see earlier chapter) prior to the final Negotiation with HD.

## Plan to Give a 'Throw-in' at the End of the Negotiations

Linda should be ready to close the negotiation agreement by offering one 'Give' from her Give List, without 'Getting a 'Get' from her customer. This 'Give' should be low cost to SpeedyLane, high perceived value to HD *"That's worth xxx $$"*) and be helpful in achieving a successful implementation. Such a throw-in at the end has several benefits

- It can create good will, helping to smooth over some feathers that may have been ruffled during the negotiation process itself;
- It confirms the Win-Win result, and
- It provides a good base for starting off the implementation on a positive note.

## Typical Buyer Strategies that Linda Should Anticipate and Plan for in Preparing for the Final Negotiation

| Buyers' Negotiating Strategies to Anticipate | Counter Strategies for the Seller |
|---|---|
| **Smart**. Don't underestimate buyers. They do this for a living & know all your possible strategies & tactics | **Discuss & Plan Counter Strategies Ahead of time.** See examples below for countering specific strategies. |
| **Heightened Concern over Price & Risk**. Buyers become more concerned with price and risk as final negotiation time nears | **Be Ready With Strong 'Stand' On Mutually Agreed Upon 'Value'** |
| **Buyers *try not sole source*** – so they can leverage one supplier against the other | **Try To Be 'First In'** by targeting 'not looking customers' and setting the primary buying criteria. Then prove and stand on your differential value. |
| **Early Price Pressures**. Buyer tries Price negotiation *in reverse order* - before value is on the table & before the final proposal & negotiating session | **Don't Talk Price Until Mutually Agreed Upon Value Has Been Proven.** |
| **Deadlines & Delay Tactics**. Buyers know your deadlines & will delay negotiations to put added pressure on you to give on price and other add-ons | Anticipate Delay Tactics. Try to **Avoid Negotiations When Under Intense Quota Pressure. Use Value & Other 'Stands' To Shield You From Pressures** – stick to your guns! **Bring Sales Manager Along** for enhanced pressure not to 'give' on price. |
| **Give-away, Take-away Strategy**. Buyer will lead you to believe you have the 'deal' only to take it away at last minute to put pressure on you to give more. | Anticipate Give Away - Take Away Strategy. **Don't 'Count' or Celebrate Sale Until Signed & Sealed!** |
| **Buyer Uses Sharp-penciled, Hard Nose Professional Negotiator** – someone new to you | **Don't Be Intimidated.** Stick to your Stands & Get Before Give. |

### Example of Give-away, Take-away Buyer Strategy

**The cartoon below provides an example of how a buyer can try to soften up the seller with a "Give Away – Take Away" strategy just prior to the planned final negotiation and closing.**

In this scenario, supposed 'friend' converted Power Sponsor Don Johnson, of House Depot, softens up Linda just before the impending final negotiation / closing meeting.

CHAPTER 59

# Example of Negotiation Dialog

## The Negotiation

**SpeedyLane Self-checkout Systems is the Seller**
**House Depot (HD) is the Buyer**

## Setting for the Negotiation Session

- *Scenario*: Final Proposal and signing in the board room at HD (Atlanta)
- *Players*:
    - *Seller Side*:
        - Linda Brown, SpeedyLane Salesperson
        - Patrick Jones, SpeedyLane's Director of Product Development,
        - John Seville, SpeedyLane's IT Manager
    - *Buyer Side*:
        - Cynthia Hatfield, HD CFO

- Joe Bennet, HD Director of Customer Satisfaction
- Kelly Clark, HD Director of IT
- Don Johnson, VP of Operations

- ## *Positions*:
  ### *Seller Side*:

  - **Linda Brown, SpeedyLane Salesperson:** Her primary objective is to close the sale. Currently, she has the nod from all HD players and has permission to begin the final stages of the plan. *In charge of Gets/Gives list.*
  - **Patrick Jones, Director of Product Development**: Present to address last minute concerns and questions about the quality and impact of the product. *Also, in charge of time outs during negotiation.*
  - **John Seville, IT Manager:** Present to address last minute concerns and questions in regard to implementing the new technology and its impact on HD's current system.

  ### *Buyer Side*:
  - **Cynthia Hatfield, HD's CFO:** Understands the utility which the SpeedyLane system brings to HD and wants to enjoy greater profit margins immediately. However, she is hesitant to invest in anything too quickly due to inherent risk.
  - **Don Johnson, VP of Operations (& Converted Power Sponsor)**: Needs the solution immediately to address primary pain of inefficiency in checkout. He needs to look good in front of HD's officers.
  - **Joe Bennett, Director of Customer Satisfaction**: Needs the solution to address his primary pain – lack of customer satisfaction. Wary of missed opportunities, he needs to look good in front of HD officers.
  - **Kelly Clark, Director of IT**: Needs the solution to get access to HD data reporting and security and to better train store clerks.

## *The Setting*, cont.

- SpeedyLane is preparing to enter the board room at HD.
- Linda Brown - VP of Sales, Patrick Jones – Director of Product Development, and John Seville – IT Manager hope to make the final sale of the SpeedyLane system.
- Although all the key players at HD are sold on the concept, they have yet to sign a contract.
- Signing today is critical to make SpeedyLane's numbers for this quarter and for the year in general, as demanded by SpeedyLane's Chief Financial Analyst, Jack Benson.

## Agenda / Goals of the Two Parties

- ***SpeedyLane Agenda: Sell Now while receiving Target Price***
  - Linda Brown understands that she will be confronted with vigorous efforts to cut the price. She will stick hard on price but is prepared to offer customer-valued incentives from SpeedyLane's 'give list' as needed.
- ***HD Agenda: Get Lower Price or Significant 'Freebies'***
  - As CFO, Cynthia Hartfield feels pressure to maximize overall return by bargaining down the price for SpeedyLane. However, she knows that HD cannot buy a comparable solution elsewhere. She will, therefore, push hard initially for lower price, yet has the authority to back down from her initial position to finalize the purchase. Lacking a lower price, she will at least try for some free additional valuable services from SpeedyLane.

# Negotiation Dialog Example

## Stand One – Recall the Plan

- ***[Linda Brown, SpeedyLane Sales]:*** "Okay, we have all gone over the solution, references, keys to success, and your current situation, and I think we all agree that SpeedyLane is an ideal solution for productivity problems at HD. I have a contract stating the terms that we have all agreed upon for you to read and approve. If you're satisfied, Cynthia, we can begin Phase One of implementation."
- ***[Cynthia Hartfield, House Depot CFO]:*** "We are all impressed with the solution that SpeedyLane has offered, but we can't agree on the cost of your solution. U-Scan can offer us a similar solution for 20% less. In these challenging financial times, we can't pay your price."
- ***[Linda]:*** "As you recall, our joint planning and strategy calls for implementation immediately. We agreed that your improvement of efficiency and customer satisfaction would have a significant positive influence on your revenues and costs. You even told us that these were pressing concerns which needed to be addressed ASAP. How will postponing such a solution change your situation or improve your bottom line?"

## Stand Two – Remind of the Value

- ***[Cynthia]:*** "I wouldn't be putting forth due diligence if I didn't attempt to receive the best possible price. If I can't show the board members the benefits of the solution, they may not see the benefits of employing me."
- ***[Linda]:*** "As you recall, all the financial figures we discussed with references were checked and approved by your analysts. Furthermore, we worked out all the detailed projections with your analysts, who themselves concluded that HD would reap a very

favorable ROI and an attractive payback period from implementing this solution. In that analysis, you **saw *that not implementing the proposed solution is costing you over $8,000 / day (Wasn't this previously $15,000?). What has changed?"***

---

## Stand Three – Remind of the Pain Being Addressed

- *[Cynthia]:* "I'm sorry, but your price is just too high for us. We need more proof that your self-checkout system will actually yield all the operational and financial benefits you have promised. Furthermore, our IT folks are concerned about potential delays and difficulties in trying to integrate the new checkout data system with our current system. What would you do in my situation?"
- *[Linda]:* "If you recall, you told us that your primary concerns were the inefficiencies of customer checkout and customer dissatisfaction. Those issues have plagued HD for some time now and have kept you from realizing your aggressive revenue and profit goals. *Without the proposed solution, that won't change, as those issues will continue to plague your operations & financial results."*

---

## Stand Four – Remind of the New Vision of a Solution for the Pain!

- *[Cynthia]:* "Joe and Kelly tell me that the costs here are substantial. This is a big risk for any retail hardware chain."
- *[Linda]:* "If you recall, we've worked together on diagnosing the challenges you face. You told us that addressing your efficiency and customer satisfaction problems with the proposed solution would set you apart from the other hardware companies, yielding historic revenues and profits. *This is a proven solution, as our many reference clients have told you. As they all confirmed, they have received much, much more from the SpeedyLane solution than what they paid."*

---

# Then, Change the Game – Take the Lead

---

# Get before you Give

- *[Cynthia]:* "Unfortunately, there are going to be unforeseen costs that may challenge that theory – for example, the potential IT integration problems I mentioned."
- *[Linda]: "Well, my hands are tied...I can't do anything for you unless... you can do something for me..."* (pause)

- **Here is where Linda use her *Gets/Gives list* to try to negotiate further if our client refuses to budge in demanding a lower price. With her comment (*... unless... you can do something for me...*"), Linda has likely caught Cynthia off-guard. Linda is about to try to EXPAND THE PIE for both parties (Win-Win).**

- **[Cynthia]**: "Like what?"
- **[Linda]**: "Ok, assuming a successful implementation, would HD be willing to become a reference client for SpeedyLane?"
- **[Cynthia]**: "Well, if it is a successful implementation, I guess we could consider doing that – but you would have to do something extra for us."
- **[Linda]**: "In return for agreeing to serve as a reference client, we are prepared to offer you system training for managers and employees. That's a $30,000 value! If we would commit to that, would you act as a reference client for us?"
- **[Cynthia]**: "That free training would certainly be useful to us! So, in return, we would act as a reference client for you"
- **[Linda]**: "Great, I'll get approval for that and we can get your signature and begin Phase One of implementation. Ok?"
- **[Cynthia]**: (Pause).
- **Linda senses that Cynthia is still not ready to sign, so she tries to expand the pie further for both parties.**
- **[Linda]**: "If the implementation is successful, would you consider putting the SpeedyLane name and logo clearly visible on all of your self-checkout machines?"
- **[Cynthia]**: "Well, maybe, but what would I get in return?"
- **[Linda]**: "In return, we could offer you access to Benchmarking Data which would be a valuable source of information to monitor your performance versus your primary competitors. This service is normally licensed at $25,000 a year."
- **[Cynthia]**: "That sounds tempting. I think I could approve of that tradeoff. This whole deal is starting to look better."

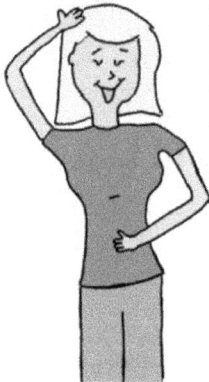

  - **[Linda]**: "Great, can we proceed further from here?"
  - **[Cynthia]**: (Pause) "That's nice but I'm still not quite comfortable signing off, given the risks I mentioned."
  - **[Linda]**: "Hmm... Again, assuming a successful implementation, as we are promising, would House Depot you be willing to issue a press release featuring your successful implementation of the new SpeedyLane checkout system?"
  - **[Cynthia]**: "Well, I can't see any harm in that, provided we get something valuable to us in return."
  - **[Linda]**: "Well, in return, we could offer you free 24-hour store manager instant call-in service at no additional charge. That service runs about $30,000 annually for our typical customer."
- **[Cynthia]**: "That sounds like an attractive trade-off! I can't see very any negatives to us to issuing such a press release."
- **[Linda]**: "Do you think that puts us in a position to move forward?"

## Deal Is Finalized

- *[Cynthia]*: "Yes, based on your concessions, I know that we would have a much better chance of success. I'm ready to sign."
- *[Linda]*: "Thank you Ms. Hartfield, WE are confident that you will be delighted with your decision, and I appreciate the careful consideration you've given the SpeedyLane system."

## Linda Finishes with a 'Give Back' – Something She Did Not Yet Give from Her Give List

- *[Linda]*: "In addition to the offer we've reviewed, including the additions we have each made, we have also included in the contract free SpeedyLane software upgrades for the two years of service. That is a $20,000 value."
- *[Cynthia]*: "Thanks, Linda! That sounds great, as it would put us in an even better position to ensure the success of this game changing new solution for us. Let's get moving on this ASAP!"

- ***Linda hands over the contract for Cynthia to sign***

## Cordial Closing

- *[Cynthia]*: (signs, contented) "We have struggled with efficiency of our checkout system for years. From all you have told us and from our reference visits and our mutual financial analysis, I am confident that our adoption and implementation of this new self-checkout System will go a long way toward solving those problems.
  - "We are excited to get started with phase one of the implementation as soon as possible."

## Assessment of the Negotiated Deal
## Was it Successful for Both Parties?

- **Win-Win**. Did both parties win (not a zero sum game)? Together, did they seek out additions and compromises that expanded the pie for both parties?
- **Key Concerns / Interests of All Parties Must Be Met**. Were the concerns of all key internal and external parties met? Yes!
- **Better than BATNA**. Does the final deal yield a result that is better than the "BATNA" (Best Alternative to Negotiated Agreement) of all parties (typical 'BATNA' will be to sell to someone else for SpeedyLane, and to continue with current inefficient checkout system for Hours Depot)? Yes!
- **Doable**. Are the transition vision (i.e., implementation plan), the operating vision, and the financial vision (i.e., with measurable financial success criteria) realistically

attainable? Yes!

- **Ethical**. Newspaper Test. Can both SpeedyLane and House Depot live with the deal under public scrutiny from its varied constituencies? Yes!

---

# Summary of Win-Win Result (2 years later)

- SpeedyLane implementation by House Depot was a huge success; implemented on time, as promised!

- ## <u>Two Years Later</u>
- The <u>*Financial Success Criteria (Keys to Success) Have Been Met*</u> & have helped HD to build on its home improvement retail reputation and leadership, largely thanks to successful implementation of the SpeedyLane Self-Checkout solution.
- *<u>Gets</u>*:
    o Product name on all modules installed
    o HD has served as Reference Client for SpeedyLane several times already
    o HD's Press Release about the successful implementation of SpeedyLane has generated 15 new Customer leads

- *<u>Gives</u>*:
    o System training for managers and employees *(worth $30,000)*
    o Benchmarking data *(worth $25,000)*
    o 24-hour customer service *(worth $30,000)*
    o A year of free upgrades *(worth $20,000)*

- House Depot and SpeedyLane both enjoyed mutual success because of SpeedyLane'
- proven abilities: ***<u>A WIN-WIN Result</u>***

CHAPTER 60

# Challenges in Implementing the Solution

*B*rian: "So, Linda, once we get through a successful negotiation and have an up-front payment, we are good to go with that client. Time for celebration!"

*[Linda]:* "Not so fast, Grasshopper! By the way, you can call me Linny, like most of my friends do."

*[Brian]:* "OK, thanks, 'Linny!'"

*[Linda]:* "But back to business. It's not time to celebrate yet - even after a successful negotiation- because there's still a major step left. And that is to implement the solution and follow-up to make sure it fulfills our promises. This implementation and follow-up process is *long, complex, and critical* to the success of any sale. Let's review each of these characteristics

to give you a better understanding and appreciation for what's involved in any successful implementation and follow-up of our self-checkout system installations.

"First of all, like I said, implementation is a *long process*, which takes months. For example, think back to when we looked at the Account Marketing Plan timeline. As you can see in the example here, the implementation and follow-up took a full four months – just as long as the selling process itself!"

*[Brian]:* "I don't see how it would take so long to implement and follow up on installing our self-checkout systems. Since you emphasized that during the Evaluation Plan, I thought we would have gotten everyone involved on board and enthusiastic about successfully implementing our system."

*[Linda]:* "That's a great observation, Bri. As you remember, we would not have even entered into the final negotiation unless we had gotten everyone involved in the implementation on board. But even with everyone at the client company excited about the new system and committed to its success because of its operating and financial benefits, the implementation is still a very *complex process* – which is why it takes so long."

## Account Marketing Plan

| Account Marketing Plan Components | Planning Phase | Convert Tgt Sponsor & Tgt Power Sponsor | Proof Management - Implementing the "Evaluation Plan" Phase / Note: Proof Mgt can be much shorter, for less complex, less costly solutions | | Implementation Phase | Follow Up Phase= > |
|---|---|---|---|---|---|---|
| **Tasks** | | January (Week #s) | February | March | April | May | June | July | August |
| **Planning Phase** | ■ | | | | | | |
| Background Research | ■ | | | | | | |
| Build Account Marketing Plan | ■ | | | | | | |
| **Convert Target Sponsor into Actual Sponsor** | | ■ | | | | | |
| Stimulate Initial Interest of Target Sponsor | | ■ | | | | | |
| 1st Sales Call | | ■ | | | | | |
| Build Operating Vision of Prospective Solution with Target Sponsor | | ■ | | | | | |
| Follow Up Letter & Reference Visit w Target Sponsor | | ■ | | | | | |
| Convert Target Power Sponsor & Build & Prove Relevant Visions for All Other Important Players | | | ■ | | | | |
| Visit & Follow Up with Target Power Sponsor | | | ■ | | | | |
| Proof Management – Design & Implement Evaluation Plan – Building & Prove Relevant Visions to All Important Players | | | ■ | | | | |
| Final Negotiation and Agreement: "The Deal" | | | | | | | |
| Implement, Monitor Results & Leverage into New Business | | | | | ■ | | |
| Implementation | | | | | ■ | | |
| Monitor Results | | | | | | ■ | |
| Leverage Success into New Business | | | | | | | ■ |
| Manage the Overall B2B Marketing Planning Process | | | | | | | |

*[Brian]:* "Complex, like how? To me it's primarily a matter of going in, pulling out some of their old cashier stations, putting in our self-checkout ones, firing up the system, and we are good to go. How complex can that be?"

*[Linda]:* "Oh, Grasshopper, don't you remember all the different folks with whom we would have built visions? These folks are in multiple different positions at House Depot (HD), with such varying responsibilities. Each one will be critical to the successful implementation of this game-changing checkout solution.

"Let's review just a few of the steps we and HD will have to go through to move from their old cashier system to a mix of cashier and self-checkout systems. For example, here's just a partial list of the many tasks involved in successfully implementing and following up on a typical

416

SpeedyLane self-checkout system installation. These steps are coordinated and completed by one of our Implementation Teams, but more on those teams later.

---

# Most Important Tasks to Be Completed for Any Successful Implementation of the SpeedyLane System

"Let's start with the customer and work back to SpeedyLane

---

## Training Customers and Cashiers to Use Self-checkout

- *Train Customers.* Set up a procedure for on-the-spot training of customers. Failure to do so may make customers frustrated upon first use and may cause them to shy away from using self-checkout.
- *Train the Customer Trainers.* Establish and teach procedures to train those who will provide the initial on-the-spot training of customers.
- *Train Cashiers.* Train selected cashiers to simultaneously manage a number of self-checkout stations.
- *Train the Cashier Trainers.* Establish procedures to train those who will provide the initial training of *Self-checkout* cashiers.
- *Set Up Cashier Support System.* Set up a system to handle foreseeable problems / challenges that the *self-checkout* cashiers are likely to face upon managing multiple checkout stations.

---

## Training Store Management to Ensure Smooth Transition to Self-checkout

- *Train Store Managers.* The full range of store managers (including Head Manager, Assistant Managers, Floor Managers, Department Managers, and Head Customer Support personnel) must be trained and prepared to manage the ongoing training of cashiers and customers. This will allow them to stimulate greater and more effective use of the store's new checkout capability. This includes in-store promotions to encourage customers to try self-checkout. It also includes ensuring that trained manpower and expertise resources are available to immediately resolve any initial or ongoing self-checkout snafus.
- *Refine product tags & ID codes.* Product tags and ID codes become more important with self-checkout, because they demand enhanced store attention to ensuring the proper ID coding of all feasible products.
- *Supporting Self-checkout for non-standard items.* This could mean different vegetables for a food store or different size individual nuts and bolts for a home improvement store. The *Self-checkout* software must have clear instructions for self-checkout of such non-standard items.

## Training Store Management

- **Train Store Managers to Methodically Assign Displaced Cashiers to Enhance Customer Experience and Satisfaction** – using strategies such as moving displaced cashiers to capacities such as:
- Store greeters, key department support, expanded store roaming customer support, more creative and active in-store merchandising roles, more timely re-stocking positions, and improved customer service desk support.

## Designing and Implementing New Data Capture and Data Integration Capabilities

- Integrating new *Self-checkout* station data with traditional cashier station data in the individual store
- Capturing and integrating new *Self-checkout* station data from multiple stores into the client's current centralized database
- Interfacing captured *Self-checkout* data with ACNielsen, Retail Data Systems, Retail Data Services, and other outsourced data analysis services currently used by the new customer

## Physical Installation of New Self-checkout Units

- Deciding which current traditional cashier checkout stations to remove
- Deciding where to put the new self-checkout units
- If more than one self-checkout configuration is being installed, deciding where to put each type of self-checkout unit
- Physical removal of old cashier checkout stations
- Disposal or sale of replaced traditional cashier checkout station units
- Physical installation of new self-checkout units
- Testing of each new self-checkout unit upon installation
- Programming each new self-checkout unit to interface with stores' product / ID codes and database

## Managing Production, Inventory, and Innovations of New Self-checkout Units

- Interfacing production planning with anticipated sales
- Keeping optimal inventory of different styles and sizes of self-checkout units on hand. Here, optimal refers to having enough on hand or being assembled for timely response to committed sales, but not too many that will lead to excess inventory or accumulating inventory of soon-to-be out of date units
- Keeping physical product innovations up to date with (social media) indicated evolving customer demands / requests and expectations
- In-plant testing of units prior to shipping

- Transportation planning – getting units to designated customer store locations
- Keeping self-checkout unit built-in software capabilities up to date with (social media) indicated, evolving customer demands / requests and expectations

# Developing & Implementing Controls to Monitor Performance and Key Success Factors

## Monitoring Performance

Monitoring initial use of self-checkout systems to identify and immediately address any initial challenges, whether they may be failures or inconsistencies in:

- Any physical parts of the Self-checkout hardware;
- Any dimension of the software built into each unit;
- Extracting and / or integrating the data captured by individual self-checkout units into a single store's overall database; or
- Extracting and / or integrating the data captured from individual stores into the client's overall centralized database.

## Monitoring Key Success Factors.

Comparing data gathered on key performance indicators with specific objectives set with the client when developing the financial vision. This would typically include weekly, monthly, and quarterly:

### Customer Measures

- Customer use of self-checkout as percent of overall checkout totals
- Average time per checkout for all customers
- Customer satisfaction with self-checkout
- Customer satisfaction with customer service overall store experience – for all stores
- Customer satisfaction with overall store experience – for all stores
- Number of customers versus a controlled sample of stores without self-checkout

### Costs -- versus a controlled sample of stores without self-checkout

- Overall cashier costs
- Overall manpower costs
- Losses due to inaccuracies, dishonesty, or outright pilferage

### Revenues -- versus a controlled sample of stores without self-checkout

- Overall revenue / trends
- Average margin of overall sales (reflecting projected increase in sales of high

margin impulse items)

**Bottom Line Financial Performance**

- Return on investment – tracked quarterly – monitored versus goal
- Break Even Payback Period – monitored versus goal

*[Linda]:* "And that's just a few of the different tasks. The ***Implementation Plan itself includes more than 200 tasks*** to coordinate and implement for each new client."

---

# Implementation Teams

*[Brian]:* "OK, I see what you mean. That sure is a lot of stuff to do. Do you, I mean, do we, in the Sales Department have to coordinate all this?"

*[Linda]:* "No way, thank heavens. In fact, ***we have six formal Implementation Teams*** led by six Implementation Managers who do that.

"Even a mere glimpse at the list of tasks above that are necessary for a successful implementation should open your eyes to the complexity of the challenge. Organization and superior management, coordination, balancing, and motivational skills are all required to implement the system. After all, we sales folks will have made specific promises and commitments to our customers in terms of scope and quality, meeting a set timetable, and sticking to a fixed resource budget. If successful completion of all required implementation tasks is not carried out on time and on budget, we have egg on our face as sales professionals.

"***And now, with the emergence of social media***, it does not take long for horror stories of any failure on SpeedyLane's part in any dimension of our promised implementation to get out to the public. That includes any failure in promised scope/quality, failure to meet planned timeline, and / or failure to accomplish successful implementation on budget. Failure in any of these areas can be made known to the public immediately and can create a public relations and marketing nightmare for us.

"So, you see, successful implementation is really ***an absolutely critical dimension of our selling process and a critical determinant of our long-term SpeedyLane image and success.***"

*[Brian]:* "Yikes! I can see how important it is for us in sales to thoroughly understand everything involved in the implementation process. I would guess we would then have to also proactively interface with our implementation team before committing to a specific implementation scope, timetable, and budget. I can't understand how I could possibly learn about all these implementation steps and challenges, so I don't make any mistakes by over-promising to a client. I keep thinking of our National Sales Manager - Catherine- and her directive to 'under-promise and over-deliver' with each new client."

*[Linda]:* "Fortunately, our Implementation Managers and teams are real pro's and work with us to keep from over-promising on scope, timetable, or budget for any sale we make.

"While you'll be going through this material with incredibly thorough training later on this month, I think it's worthwhile to give you a quick overview right now of some of the processes and tools our implementation managers and their teams use to do their jobs more effectively. That way, you can think about it a bit and be prepared to ask some better questions when it's time for your formal training."

--------

The next chapter provides an overview of some of the key processes and tools the SpeedyLane Implementation Teams use to ensure effective, on-time, and on-budget implementations.

CHAPTER 61

# Ensuring Effective Implementation

This chapter provides an overview of some of the key processes and tools that the SpeedyLane Implementation Teams use to ensure effective, on-time, on-budget implementations.

## A Step-by-Step Formal Project Management System

*[Linda]:* "Like I was saying, Brian, we use ***a formal Project Management Process*** to ensure the efficiency and timeliness of our implementations (i.e., manufacturing, customizing, delivering, installing, data integrating, training, and other required tasks). We do this to use our implementation resources (manpower, expertise, financial, manufacturing capacities, and the like) efficiently, while meeting our completion time commitments to our new customers.

*[Brian]:* "That makes sense. So, what is involved in this Project Management Process applied by our Implementation Teams?"

*[Linda]:* "Our Project Management Process approach includes several steps.

## Identify the Tasks

1. "First, we identify the long list of ***tasks*** that must be completed for any SpeedyLane self-checkout system implementation to be successful. You already saw a partial list of those 200+ tasks, so no need to review those again."

## Order the Tasks

2. "Second, we then ***order the tasks*** identified in step one. Here we consider each task independently and ask, "What other task or tasks need to be completed before this specific job can be tackled?" Using the simple example of our self-checkout stations, we recognize:

   - The stations can't be **installed** in retail outlets before they have been delivered;
   - The stations can't be **delivered** until they have been manufactured;
   - The stations can't be **manufactured** until we know the specific number and types of stations for each retail outlet; and
   - We can't **determine the specific number and types of stations** for each retail outlet until we properly scale the solution to the particular customer's situation and needs.

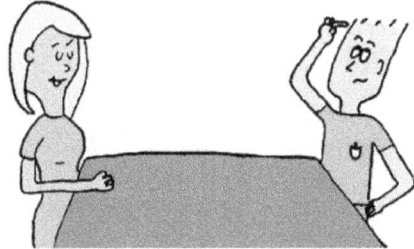

## Summarize the Tasks & Order in a PERT chart

"We summarize this ordering process with a ***PERT (Program Evaluation and Review Technique) chart***[69]. I'll show you an example in a minute. Note that multiple independent tasks can be undertaken simultaneously. But whether or not they are implemented simultaneously depends upon:

- The resources required (e.g., manpower, facilities, expertise, or finances) for implementation;
- The resources currently available for implementation (in-house or potential outsourced resources for specific tasks – I'll cover outsourcing in a moment); and
- Any time constraints we project and commit to with any specific customer.

## Estimate the Time Required to Complete Each Task

3. "Next, we estimate the ***time that each task will take*** from start to completion.

   Steps 2 & 3 are summarized in a ***Gantt Chart.***[70] I'll show you an example of that, too, in just a moment. This chart helps us estimate how long the project will take from start to finish. The Gantt chart assumes many independent tasks are carried on simultaneously – which is the key to minimizing total implementation time.

## Finally, Identify the "Critical Path"

4. "Finally, we carefully monitor any tasks on the '**_Critical Path_**'. The Critical Path identifies specific jobs that must stay on schedule in order to meet the projected completion date for the entire implementation. If any task on the critical path is not completed on schedule, the final projected completion date for the whole project will be pushed back. When a task on the Critical Path is potentially delayed, we either shift internal resources or access outside manpower, expertise, or finances to keep that task on schedule. By doing so, we stay on schedule to meet our promised implementation deadline."

*[Brian]:* "Yikes, again! I sure am glad we in sales don't have to do all that."

*[Linda]:* "We don't have to do it, yes, **_but we do have to understand it_**. It's important that we realize the complexity of the process and don't underestimate completion dates when talking with our new customers. Oftentimes, it can be very tempting to promise a customer a shorter completion time than possible, especially when a customer keeps pressing for a faster implementation time.

"So, here's a bit longer description of each of the steps, except the first one - the lists of implementation tasks - which we have already covered.

## Step 1. Identify _Tasks Required_ for any SpeedyLane Self-checkout Implementation

This was already discussed in the last chapter.

## Step 2. _Ordering_ the Tasks

*[Linda]:* "Once we identify all the tasks necessary for implementation, we next **order all those required implementation tasks**. In this process, we consider each task independently and ask, "What other task or tasks must be completed before this specific task can be tackled?" We summarize this ordering process with a **PERT chart** (Program Evaluation and Review Technique - See exhibit for an example). **A timing estimate is not included** in this ordering process but will be added in Step 3.

"In order **to reduce implementation time**, it is important to identify and simultaneously undertake tasks (as resources allow) that are not interdependent. For example, early installation of a sample checkout station would allow for cashier training programs to begin well before the full inventory of stations slated for a retail outlet are even manufactured. Also, data integration challenges between SpeedyLane checkout software and the customer's software can be identified and addressed prior to full-scale checkout installation. Simultaneously undertaking and completing multiple implementation tasks shortens the overall projected and actual total implementation time.

"During particularly busy periods, when many systems have been sold over a short period of time, limited availability of SpeedyLane implementation resources (manpower, expertise, finances, manufacturing capacities, etc.) can hinder us from executing independent tasks simultaneously. In such cases, we need to be conservative in making our 'time to completion' promises and, when in jeopardy of missing a deadline, we often secure outside resources in order to stay on schedule.

"This **_next diagram_** shows an example of a PERT chart ordering required tasks."

"Now brace yourself, Brian, because the Exhibit below (**_next page_**) is the actual PERT Chart that the Implementation Coordinating Team staff at headquarters has developed and uses for our SpeedyLane implementations for each new sale we make!"

*[Brian]:* "Are you kidding me? I almost wish you hadn't shown me that! It hurts my brain just to think about all that went into developing that diagram! Do we have to communicate that to our customers when we are talking about implementation?"

*[Linda]:* "It hurts my head too, to be honest. And, no, fortunately for us, they reduce it to a much simpler chart to use when we are talking with customers – one that is similar to the chart we use to summarize our Account Marketing Plan – but I'll show you that in a minute."

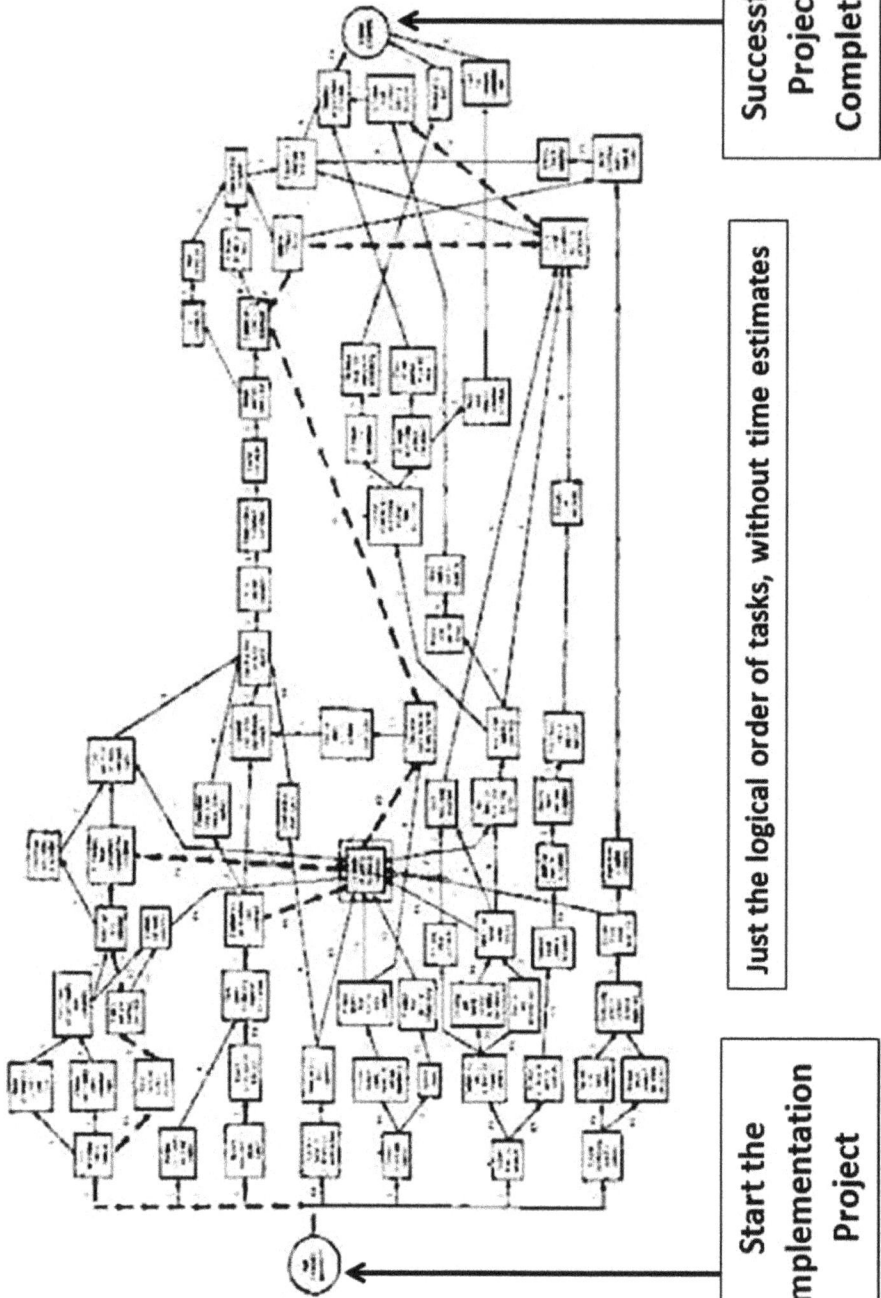

*Ordering Tasks Required*

A PERT Chart Example of a Complex Project like Self-checkout Implementation

Successful Project Completion

Just the logical order of tasks, without time estimates

Start the Implementation Project

## Step 3. Estimate the Time that Each Task Will Take

*[Linda]:* "This next step helps reduce the complex PERT Chart to a 'Gantt Chart,' which is much easier to interpret. For that conversion, our SpeedyLane Implementation Coordinating Team carefully estimates several different time dimensions for each implementation task. As we look at this more closely, it will become clear why several time estimates are needed."

## Dimensionalizing Each Implementation Task

*[Linda]:* "For each step in the self-checkout implementation process, the Implementation Coordinating team identifies a number of different variables. Most of these are time related and include the following:

- **Task Description and Responsibility**. This includes a brief description of the implementation task as well as who will be responsible for completing that particular job.
- **Earliest Start Date**. This is a specific date, but is also interdependent on other tasks, because most tasks cannot start until other specific tasks have been completed. For example, self-checkout units cannot be shipped to store locations unless they have first been assembled.
- **Duration**. This is the estimated time (in days or weeks) a specific task will take to complete. By moving around implementation manpower, expertise, and/or financial resources - adding them or pulling them from other tasks or other implementation projects - the time can be compacted (if on 'critical path') or expanded (if not on critical path). There will be more on 'Critical Path' strategies in Step 4, below;
- **Earliest Finish**. This is the minimum amount of time the task could take if implementation resources were re-aligned to speed task completion (without compromising task quality).
- **Latest Start**. This is the latest possible time the task can be started without ultimately extending the total implementation time from start to finish."
- **Latest Finish**. This is the latest possible time the task can be finished without ultimately extending the total implementation time from start to finish.

## Float (or 'Slack Time')

*[Linda]:* "The 'Float,' or slack time, is the amount of time that a project task can be delayed without causing a delay in the whole project. Positive slack would indicate ahead of schedule; negative slack would indicate behind schedule; and zero slack would indicate on schedule.

"This information (from Steps 2 & 3) is then taken and summarized in a *Gantt Chart* – as in the following the Exhibit. This Gantt chart integrates the ordering (Step 2 within "Dimensionalizing Implementation Tasks") and the duration of each task (part of Step 3 of "Dimensionalizing Implementation Tasks") of all implementation tasks. This chart enables us to estimate how long the whole project will take from beginning to end. Note that many of the independent tasks are carried out simultaneously. This is essential for minimizing the total implementation time from start to finish.

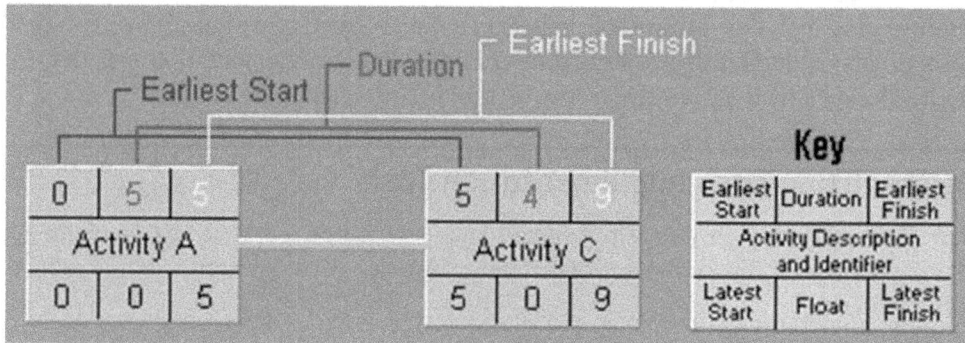

"Finally, in the next step, step 1, we carefully monitor all tasks on the 'Critical Path' (see below) in order to meet our implementation completion deadline."

*[Brian]:* "Linny! This is a bit over-wheming for me. Do I have to know all these steps?"

*[Linda]:* "No, that's what the implementation teams are for. We do indeed have a well organized, practiced process for implementing the SpeedyLane Self-Checkout System in a well-practiced efficient manner. You never know when one of a target client's key players might ask about that – often a concern prior to committing to a purchase. After several sales, you'll be able to follow and see the efficiency of our implementation teams in action and be able to address prospective buyer concerns regarding effective, timely implementaiton."

*[Brian]:* "Well, that's a relief! I was afraid that I'd have to be able to explain this all to my first prospective client – and there's no way... "

*[Linda]:* "No problem, Bri. It will all become second nature after a few operating periods and successful sales and implementations. Now, let's move on to review Step 4."

## Step 4. Monitoring the *Critical Path*

"We do have some degree of control over how long the entire implementation will take from start to finish. We can try to minimize this total implementation time by starting each new task immediately after all preliminary required jobs for the specific task have been completed.

"At any given time, one or several tasks are always 'holding up the show' or are 'on the Critical Path,' as it's referred to in formal Project Management. This means that any delay in the starting time or end time for the critical task(s) will delay the projected completion date for the entire implementation – which we certainly do not want to occur.

"Therefore, in order to control the total implementation time, we specifically identify and carefully monitor the execution of all tasks on the Critical Path. To avoid pushing out the completion date beyond the date promised to our customer, we can shift resources - sometimes outsourcing specific Critical Path task components - in the effort to ensure that every task on the Critical Path is completed on time or as projected."

---

**PERT Chart of SpeedyLane Self-checkout Implementations Project[71]**

# Red Signifies the Critical Path

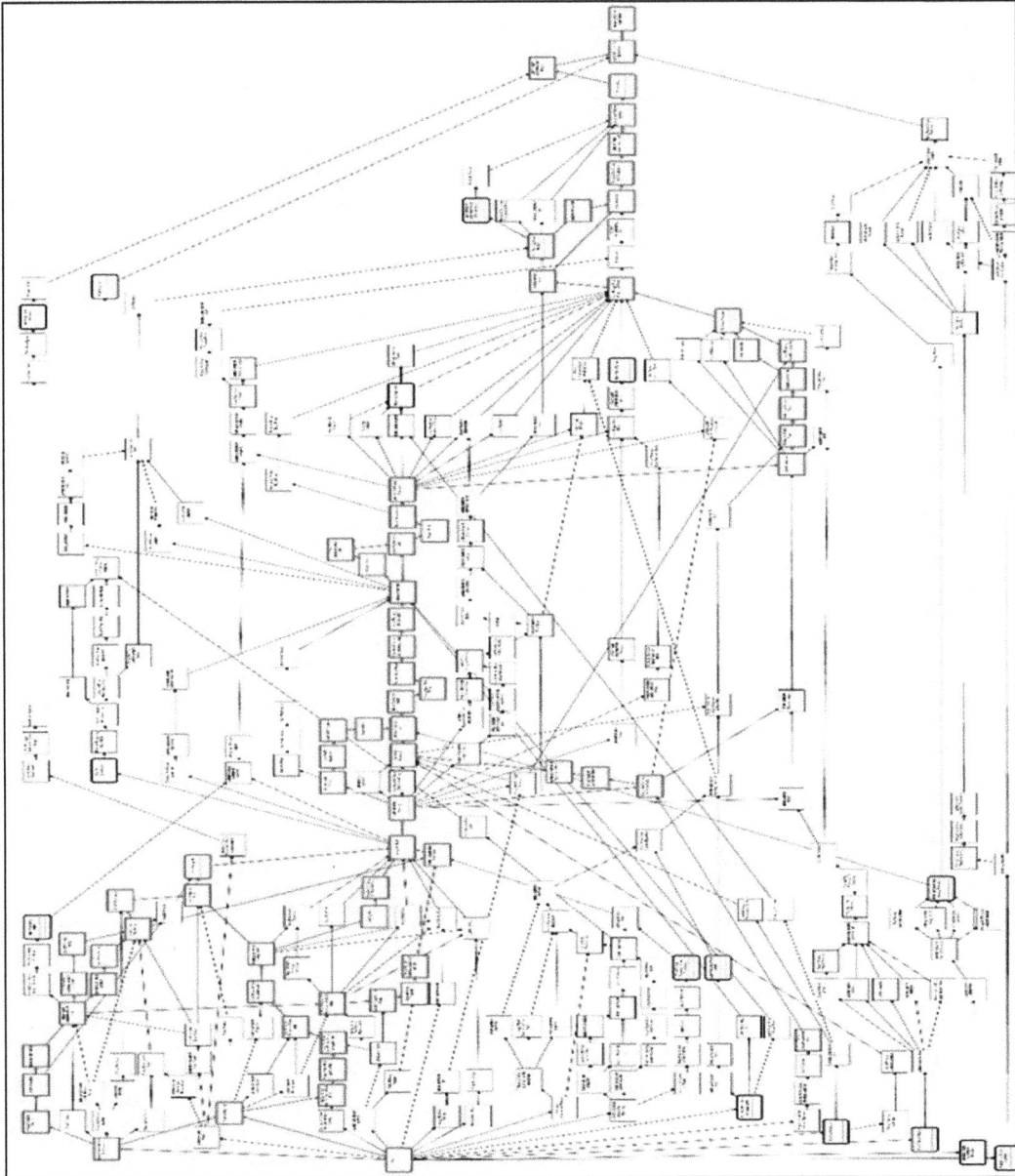

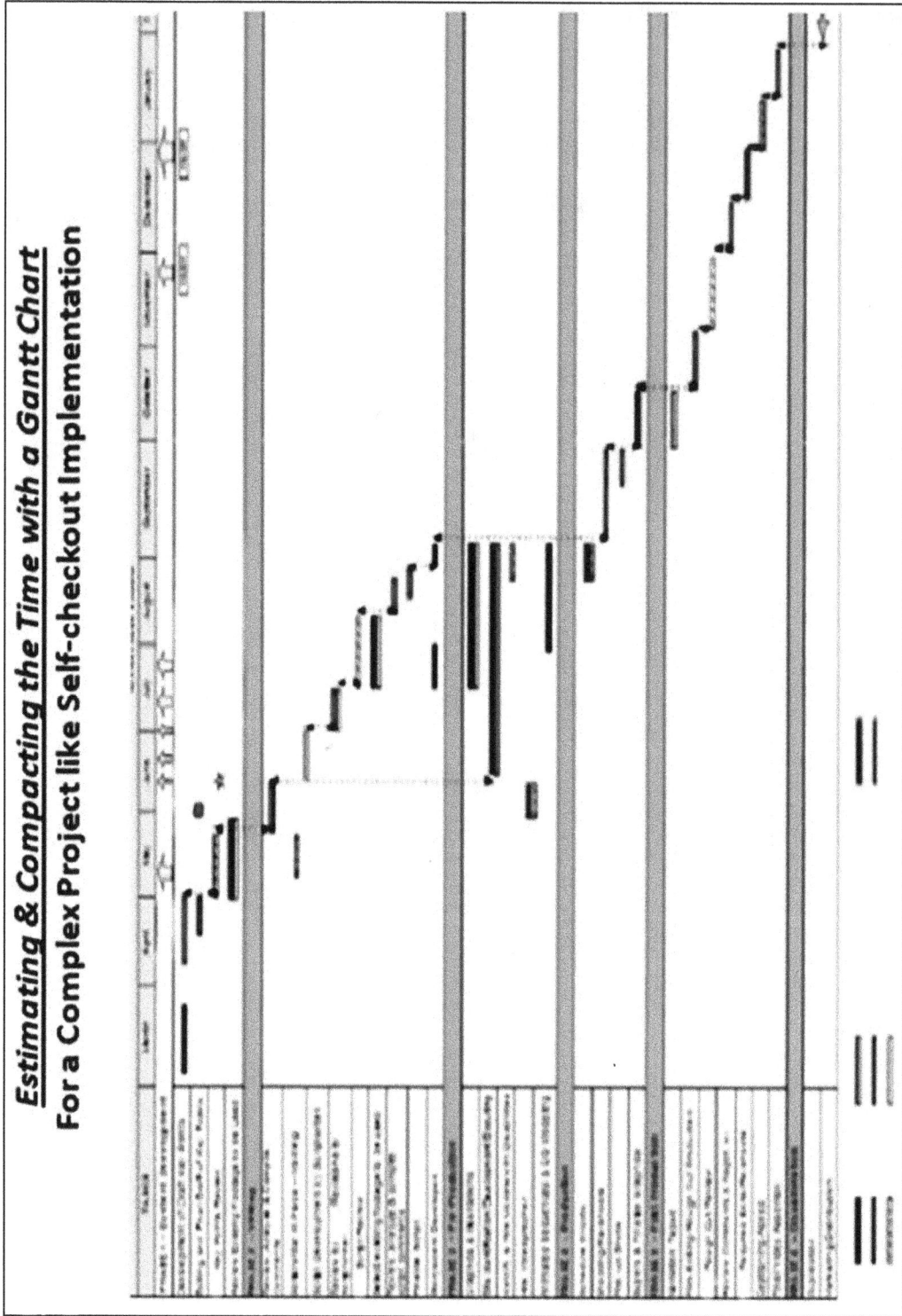

*Estimating & Compacting the Time with a Gantt Chart For a Complex Project like Self-checkout Implementation*

# SpeedyLane Outsources
# Some Important Implementation Steps

## SpeedyLane's Areas of Expertise and Specialization.

*[Linda]:* "In order to focus our resources on areas where we have proven expertise, we at SpeedyLane carry out many implementation steps ourselves – focusing our internal expertise, manpower and other resources on areas such as:

- **Engineering** – designing multiple self-service configurations called for by our customer base;
- **Self-Checkout Software** -- developing and continually refining the complex and dynamic software required to both maximize self-checkout dependability and productivity and to integrate self-checkout data seamlessly with customers' data systems;
- **Assembly** -- assembling virtually all of its self-checkout stations in its three assembly plants in the USA – Atlanta, Chicago, and Las Vegas;
- **Training** – developing and offering continual training programs for the most effective use of self-checkout stations by store-level customers' cashiers and store management, and corporate level IT and marketing departments;
- **Physical installation** – maintains specialized installation expertise and an installation workforce shared by all of SpeedyLane implementation teams. This workforce installs the physical units and uses their close connection with company software teams back at headquarters to link data from the new self-checkout systems with each store's data network. SpeedyLane does this to help ensure 'no problem' installation; and
- **Servicing** – servicing installed units to ensure continuous trouble-free performance."

*[Linda]:* "Note that these are only some of the items mentioned in the steps to be executed for any successful SpeedyLane implementation."

## Outsourced Areas of Expertise and Specialization

*[Linda]:* "On the other hand, we at SpeedyLane choose to outsource selected critical steps in order to implement systems more quickly and more economically without compromising quality. By outsourcing, SpeedyLane can focus its internal energies and resources on areas of its special expertise (which were mentioned above). Among the more important functions that we typically outsource are:

- **Component Manufacturing** – while SpeedyLane designs all of the details of all of its self-checkout units in house, it partners with several different companies that have and maintain state of the art manufacturing facilities and capabilities to meet SpeedyLane's demanding performance specifications; and
- **Delivery** – SpeedyLane partners with DHL for on-time delivery of specified self-checkout units to each customer's individual stores. To do this most efficiently, DHL is fully partnered with SpeedyLane and has an office and a manager located permanently in each of SpeedyLane's three assembly plants here in the USA (Atlanta, Chicago, and Las Vegas). Each DHL office has complete access to SpeedyLane sales and implementation data and coordinates directly with the Implementation Management and Implementation Teams in its relevant geographic area.

"In order to avoid promising an unrealistic total implementation time, we project a realistic -- not necessarily minimum -- possible time for completing each task on the critical path. We make such estimates based upon our past experience (using a longest possible, shortest possible and most likely time estimate scenario)."

# Sales Growth Secrets

## Part 4: *Ensuring Continuous Sales Growth*

### *Sales Growth Secrets Book Summary & Conclusions*

CHAPTER 62

# Meet Catherine Russell, SpeedyLane National Sales Manager

| Ensuring Continuous Sales Growth | | |
|---|---|---|
| Ch | 62 | **Meet Catherine Russell, SpeedyLane National Sales Manager** |
| Ch | 63 | Catherine Introduces SpeedyLane's Sales Management System |
| Ch | 64 | Monitoring Each Selling Effort of Each Salesperson |
| Ch | 65 | Monitoring All Selling Efforts of One Salesperson |
| Ch | 66 | Monitoring the Performance of the Whole Sales Team |
| Ch | 67 | Strategies for Increasing Opportunities in the Pipeline |
| Ch | 68 | Strategies for Increasing the Avg Size of Each Opportunity |
| Ch | 69 | Strategies for Improving Closing Rates |
| Ch | 70 | Sales Growth Secrets Book Summary and Conclusions |

**Full name:** Catherine Russell

### Education:

- Graduated from Loyola Academy, Chicago. 4.00 GPA, co-valedictorian with her twin sister, Ellie. Illinois State Cross Country Champion in her sophomore and senior years, while sister Ellie won the other two years.

- **Bachelor's degree in marketing** from the University of Notre Dame, Class of 20xx. 3.83 GPA. Multiple volunteer activities. Social VP for Marketing Club. President of the Midwest Chapter of the Turtle Club. Made and sold chocolate & peanut butter cookies to classmates. These cookies were ultimately so successful that 'Catherine's Cookies' became a favorite fare in all the ND dorms and financed Catherine's and Ellie's fully involved college social life – including four academic years without a single miss of 'socially-mandatory' Wednesday night visit to Finney's and a Thursday late night at the 'Feve' night club.

## Personal / Romantic Interest:

• Now a forever-young '29,' she is determined to remain single until she can somehow land one of her favorite Country Western singers.

• Once had a three-year love affair with CW singer Kenny Chesney, although Kenny didn't know about it. For these three years she sang herself to sleep most nights to the tune of *You Save Me*.

• Broke up with Kenny (it was her idea), when she won a backstage pass to a Brad Paisley concert, fell in love with him instantly and even got to shake his hand. Refused to wash that hand for six months!

• More recently, she is Internet hounding a new love interest – the 'gorgeous' Tim Riggins from Friday Night Lights. Checks his Facebook page at least 15 times a day, hoping he will acknowledge just one of the daily love letters she sends his way.

## Employment Background:

• Interned in Marketing Department at Jim Beam and is credited with single-handedly developing JB's ultra-successful 'Skinny Girl' line of light liquor concoctions targeted specifically for the under 30 female segment.

• For her first three years out of college, was a star sales trainer for SPI out of Charlotte, NC -- the creators of the Solution Selling System.

• Hired away from SPI by SpeedyLane, after she'd given a week-long sales seminar to the SpeedyLane Regional Sales Management team.

• Started with SpeedyLane as the Southwest Regional Sales Manager, headquartered out of Austin, TX. Austin is her favorite city and where she hopes to eventually settle down once she lands one of her country singing idols or, of course, the gorgeous Tim Riggins.

• Primary editor for the *Sales Growth Secrets* book you are now reading.

• Multiple mentoring positions throughout high school and college, capitalizing on her empathetic, soft-hearted concern and feelings for anyone disadvantaged.

## Current Position & Company:
- National Sales Manager for SpeedyLane for the past 5 years. Tops her intimate knowledge of systematic selling with legendary enthusiasm, personality, and motivational skills. Is credited with playing a crucial role in spurring continuous sales growth at SpeedyLane ever since she took the reins as National Sales Manager.
- Her constant smile and contagious commitment to fun are both epitomized by her continuing role as President of the Midwest Chapter of the Turtle Club. Catherine is also a member of the International Board of that prestigious organization.

## Physical Appearance:
- Has converted her long, ruler straight blond hair from college into a variety of more sophisticated auburn hairdo's
- Ultra-trim – svelte even -- reflecting her commitment to a healthy lifestyle.
- Turns heads wherever she travels

## Nickname:
- 'Rine,' because her twin sister, Ellie, still can't pronounce the full name 'Catherine,' even after all these years!

## Wardrobe:
- At home, she favors lowbrow jeans, tank tops, sweats, shorts, and flip-flops.
- At work, it's a totally different story. There, she always successfully projects an ultra-professional image. In fact, Catherine's style & wardrobe at work rivals the class and elegance of Audrey Hepburn. Her absolute favorite look includes classic black tailored pants, peep-toe heels, and a sleek bun. Milly style dresses fill her closet, and she is never found at work or on the go without a quilted Chanel purse over her shoulder. Quite a contrast from her 'at home' look.
- Her size 8aaaa ultra narrow feet cause all sorts of challenges. Her shoes, from her running shoes to her high-end heels, are all custom-made – costing her a small fortune. Lately, she has taken to buying 8aa's off the shelf and stuffing them with cotton to keep them from falling off.

## Hobbies:
- **Getting Taller** – Hangs upside down for 30 minutes each morning, prior to her run every day. Her goal is to try to get as tall as her twin sister Ellie, who used to tower over her by three inches. The strategy seems to be working, as Catherine now finds herself but one inch shorter than Ellie and will soon be able to dump the one inch lifts she wears whenever in Ellie's company. When in grammar school, she and Ellie regularly played 'twin shifts,' covering for each other when convenient. That all ended in 8th grade when Ellie grew those extra three inches.

- **Running**. Still a competitive runner. Age group champion in distances from 10K to marathons. Runs a minimum of six miles per day – more typically twice that on the weekend. Has a room in her high-end condo dedicated to nothing but her 300+ trophies. Friends call it her 'hero' room.
- **Dog Catching**. She loves dogs, especially big ones that jump up on you, lick your face, roll over to be tickled, and the like. Volunteers one evening a month after work to help the local dogcatcher and spends another evening at the Pet Rescue Shelter.
- **Cooking**. Loves to cook – mostly organic health foods, consistent with her near-fanatical concern over maintaining her sleek, trim look. Submits to chocoholic and peanut butter addictions each Friday evening – always topped off with a pint or two of Guinness Stout -- which partially explains why she doubles her running mileage on Saturdays. Then it's the weekly pig-out each Saturday night with sister Ellie and other friends at one of their several favorite Italian restaurants – which explains her extra miles on the road each Sunday.
- **Learning and Speaking Italian**. Nearly fluent in Italian, having spent more than a year in study abroad programs in Italy. Dreams in Italian and sometimes lapses into Italian at work without being aware of it. Colleagues are both bemused and amused.

## Vehicle:

- Classy electric Italian Alfa Romeo, reflecting her love of all things Italian as well as her commitment to environmentally friendly practices in every facet of her life. Keeps an unloaded deer-hunting rifle up in the back window to serve as a reminder to move back one day to her beloved Austin, TX.

*Flashback: Approximately one month after Brian started working with Linda, his Sales Mentor at SpeedyLane. February, 20xx.*

CHAPTER 63

# Catherine Introduces Brian to SpeedyLane's Sales Management System

| Ensuring Continuous Sales Growth | | |
|---|---|---|
| Ch | 62 | Meet Catherine Russell, SpeedyLane National Sales Manager |
| **Ch** | **63** | **Catherine Introduces SpeedyLane's Sales Management System** |
| Ch | 64 | Monitoring Each Selling Effort of Each Salesperson |
| Ch | 65 | Monitoring All Selling Efforts of One Salesperson |
| Ch | 66 | Monitoring the Performance of the Whole Sales Team |
| Ch | 67 | Strategies for Increasing Opportunities in the Pipeline |
| Ch | 68 | Strategies for Increasing the Avg Size of Each Opportunity |
| Ch | 69 | Strategies for Improving Closing Rates |
| Ch | 70 | Sales Growth Secrets Book Summary and Conclusions |

*L*inda: "Brian, I'd like you to meet Catherine Russell. As you know, she's our National Sales Manager."

*[Brian]*: "Great to finally meet you, Ms. Russell. Linda has told me all about you!"

*[Catherine]*: "Well, for starters, we go by first names around here, so please call me Catherine, or even use my nickname, Rine, if you prefer. What exactly has my old friend Linny told you about me?"

*[Brian]*: "Well, for one thing, she told me that everyone here at SpeedyLane refers to you as the 'Growth Queen' because they so admire the steady sales growth that SpeedyLane has experienced since you took over as National Sales Manager five years ago."

*[Catherine]*: "I've heard that one before. I think it's kind of funny, especially since I just happen to have been in the right place at the right time to help us experience that growth."

*[Linda]*: "Don't believe her, Bri. I've been on the sales team since before Rine arrived, and let me tell you, it's like night versus day since she took over. She has almost single-handedly gotten all of the Regional Sales Managers and their sales folks on the same page by using the systematic approach she introduced to us upon her arrival at SpeedyLane.

"Our top level management hired her immediately after she had given a week-long sales seminar to our Regional Sales Management team. At the time, she was a trainer for SPI out of Charlotte – the creators of the Solution Selling System. Our management was extremely impressed with the systematic approach she taught us, and was also excited about her enthusiasm, personality, and the motivational skills that she brought to the table. She can really get a team moving! I think everyone in the company recognizes the critical leading role she has played in our turnaround over these past eight years."

*[Catherine]*: "That's high praise coming from one of our very top sales folks, so I'll accept it, but not without deflecting most of the credit to our dedicated sales team – from our Sales Managers to our super folks like Linny.

"But, okay, enough of this mutual admiration gibberish. Linny says you wanted to know how we manage sales to ensure steady, profitable growth, which we have proven we can do successfully. Well, it should be no surprise to you that it all starts with the individual sales professionals doing their job each and every day to continuously identify and then systematically and tirelessly pursue new sales opportunities. They do that using the step-by-step system that Linny has been teaching you since you arrived.

"We are strong believers in learning by doing. This is why we are so committed to thoroughly mentoring new members of our sales team like you so they can hit the ground running when they're finally out on their own. Linny tells me that you are a curious and fast learner, so no doubt you'll be out on your own with your own sales territory in no time."

*[Brian]*: "I hope so, anyway. I can't wait! But I'm still learning so much every day from Linda that I'm afraid it will be a while before I'm ready to get out on my own."

*[Catherine]*: "You might be surprised. We'll actually be having you work with some smaller accounts before you know it. Kind of a trial by fire if you will."

*[Brian]*: "Yikes, I hope I'm ready and don't screw up. That would not be a good way to start!"

*[Linda]*: "Don't worry, Bri. I won't put you out there until I think you are prepared. Plus, I'll be accompanying you on your first few customer visits. I'll be looking over your shoulder every step of the way and I'll offer my help if you need it."

*[Brian]*: "Whew! Glad to hear that!"

*[Catherine]*: "Oh, I am sure you will do great, Brian. Success may not come right away, but you are obviously a fast learner and, just as importantly, you seem very willing to learn – which is why our HR team liked you during your original screening at Bucknell."

"But now, back to the business at hand. My role today is to introduce you to the Sales Management System[72] that overlays our sales folks' individual selling efforts. SpeedyLane executives and I strongly believe that without a detailed Sales Management system, our overall sales growth would be nowhere near as steady, aggressive, and profitable as it is today. I'm not saying that to boast, but rather to emphasize how committed we are to both the Solution Selling System you're currently learning and the Sales Management System overlay that I'll be introducing to you today.

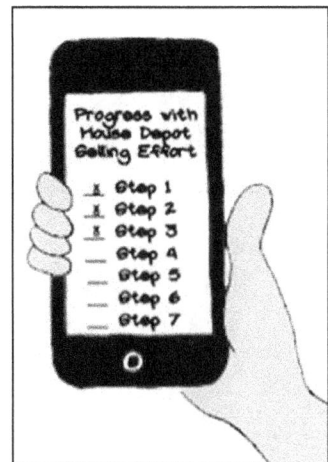

"In starting, I want to emphasize that I'll only be giving you a brief overview. After you begin selling on your own, your Regional Sales Manager, Roberto, will go over the details with you many times, which will give you the chance to ask questions and better understand it.

"If you think you'd like to get into Sales Management eventually, then you'd have to really comprehend all the specific details. But if you don't think Sales Management is right for you, you won't necessarily have to fully understand it all. To be honest, most of our sales folks – even Linny here – never do quite grasp all the intricacies of the system. And that's fine, as long as they trust and work closely with their Sales Managers and 'press the buttons' recommended."

*[Brian]*: "Got it! I have to tell you, I am really up for trying to learn as much about this Sales Management System as I can. I like to understand the 'big picture.'"

*[Catherine]*: "OK, then, here it goes. I'd like to start by asking you what Linny has told you so far."

*[Brian]*: "Not much really. I just see her using her iPhone after nearly every step she takes with a customer – whether it's a visit or even just a phone call. She tells me that whatever information she inputs goes up into the cloud and then is entered into some sort of SpeedyLane Sales Automation System. Beyond that, it's all been pretty much a mystery to me. When I asked Linda if she could tell me more about this system, she said you could do a much better job of explaining it. She also wanted me to spend a little time with you, since you are my 'Big Boss!' So here we are!"

*[Catherine]*: "Well, I like to think of us as a team, rather than me being your so-called 'Big Boss,' as you put it. You just happen to be reporting to your Regional Sales Manager, Roberto, who, in turn, reports to me. As Linny knows, I like to spend a little personal time with each of our new sales reps as they get started. It helps me to put a face on the various reports I will regularly receive from the field once you begin selling on your own."

*[Catherine changes gears and continues]*:

"The 'Sales Automation System,' as you refer to it, is more aptly described as our '**Sales Management System**'."[73]

============
Back to check on Linda and her good friend Danielle (of Pioneer Markets). **Setting: Linda and Danielle chatting after their weekly racquetball game**.

[Linda]: "Say, Danielle, did you have a good time on your visit to Gustavo in Tampa last weekend?"

[Danielle]: "The best time, Linny! He even taught me some Italian!"

*Flashback – Approximately one month after Brian started working with Linda, his Sales Mentor at SpeedyLane. February, 20xx. The conversation (Catherine, Brian & Linda) continues.*

CHAPTER 64

---

# Monitoring Each Selling Effort of Each Salesperson

| Ensuring Continuous Sales Growth | | |
|------|------|---------------------------------------------------------|
| Ch | 62 | Meet Catherine Russell, SpeedyLane National Sales Manager |
| Ch | 63 | Catherine Introduces SpeedyLane's Sales Management System |
| **Ch** | **64** | **Monitoring Each Selling Effort of Each Salesperson** |
| Ch | 65 | Monitoring All Selling Efforts of One Salesperson |
| Ch | 66 | Monitoring the Performance of the Whole Sales Team |
| Ch | 67 | Strategies for Increasing Opportunities in the Pipeline |
| Ch | 68 | Strategies for Increasing the Avg Size of Each Opportunity |
| Ch | 69 | Strategies for Improving Closing Rates |
| Ch | 70 | Sales Growth Secrets Book Summary and Conclusions |

---

## Monitoring a Single Selling Effort of One Salesperson using the *Opportunity Analysis Form*

Picking up the conversation of Catherine, Brian, and Linda from last chapter ........

*[Catherine to Brian]*: Given what you've experienced from Linny's input and explanations thus far, do you have any specific questions about how this system works?"

*[Brian]*: "Tons, actually. I'm not even sure where to begin. Perhaps you could start by telling me just what happens when Linda, or I, or any other salesperson punches in a progress report on

an individual sales effort. For example, we have a sales effort going on with House Depot right now. It seems to be going well, but I'm not entirely sure."

[*Catherine*]: "Well, Linny, let's check it out on the computer and you can tell me about it. Then I'll have a better perspective for answering Brian's question."

"OK, viewing the computer screen, the form we're looking at here is what we call an '**Opportunity Analysis Form**.'[74] It summarizes and updates the current stage of an individual selling effort. This is Linny's *Opportunity Analysis Form* for her House Depot account."

## Opportunity Analysis Form

| Region | South East | |
|---|---|---|
| **Regional Sales Manager** | Roberto Garza | |
| **Sales Person** | Linda Brown | |

| % Probability | Step # | Activity | House Depot Acct |
|---|---|---|---|
| 5% | 1 | Identify legitimate leads in the Target Market Segment | 1/8/2012 |
| 10% | 2 | Contact and Arrange for Face to Face Meeting with Target Sponsor | 1/12/2012 |
| 15% | 3 | Build initial operating vision with Target Sponsor | 1/15/2012 |
| 20% | 4 | Convert Target Sponsor – with reference visit | 1/22/2012 |
| 30% | 5 | Access Target Power Sponsor & build operating & financial vision | 2/2/2012 |
| 40% | 6 | Convert Target Power Sponsor – with reference visit – thus gaining access to buying committee and other players above & below money line needing vision creation (operating, transition or financial visions) | |
| 60% | 7 | Scale and agree on breadth & depth of the solution – in the process building Financial Vision & agreeing on base price | |
| 80% | 8 | Simultaneously build remaining Operating & Transition Visions for the solution | |
| 90% | 9 | Negotiate the Final Deal -- final terms + final gets & gives | |
| 100% | 10 | Sign Deal & start Implementation | |
| | | **Projected Size ($$) of each Opportunity** | $3,200,000 |
| | date 5-Feb | **Size x Probability** | $960,000 |

[*Catherine continues*]: "Linny tells me that she currently has eight selling efforts underway. That would be pretty typical for all of our sales folks. Now in this particular *Opportunity Analysis*

*Form,* we only see her selling effort for her House Depot account. It looks like that effort is moving along nicely. She started with a lead from the Home Improvement Convention in Las Vegas in early January, and now, in early February, she's already through 'Step 5,' after completing a successful vision building effort with her Target Power Sponsor. That's pretty fast progress that tells me Linda's all over this opportunity."

----------

*[Brian]:* "Hey, Catherine, can we back up a bit?"

*[Catherine]:* "Sure, what's up?"

*[Brian]:* "Well now that I see how important it is for Roberto to closely monitor each of his salesperson's progress on each account – like Linda with her House Depot account - I realize that this information must be pretty accurate, or else your whole sales projection thing will fall apart and be pretty meaningless. What's prevents a salesperson from being overly optimistic and reporting progress on an account when no progress has actually occurred?"

*[Catherine]:* "That's a great question. What did Linny call you before – 'Grasshopper?' I'm going to have my eye on you over time – you seem to have the makings of a future member of Sales Management.

-----

"At any rate, sure, a salesperson can report bogus progress on an account, and it actually does happen on occasion. The accuracy and effectiveness of our whole Sales Management System depends on truthful reporting by our individual sales folks. So, if a salesperson like Linda missed her sales quota numbers for a couple of operating periods, because she was overly optimistic and attempted to mislead her Regional Sales Manager, she would receive a warning. She would then be expected to acknowledge her over-optimism, shape up and become more realistic, or else she'd be sent packing.

## Milestone Worksheet

"We also have a safeguard in place to help cut back on that potential problem. It's a detailed version of the *Opportunity Analysis Form* that each salesperson is expected to keep on each account. We call this a '***Milestone Worksheet***.'[75] Let's look at Linny's for the House Depot account."

"As you can see, this form includes many more details for each step that Linny will take to capture a sale. For example, Linny would only report progress on the relevant *Opportunity Analysis Form* for a target customer when she reaches each of the 'boxed-in steps' (e.g., 'Potential Sponsor Identified'). At any time, however, her boss, Roberto, can also view her *Milestone*

*Worksheet* for each client as well. You'd be surprised how this cuts down on 'overly optimistic' projections by our sales folks. Does that answer your question?"

## Milestone Worksheet for Each Target Customer

| Your Firm's Selling Activities and Customer Evidence (highlighted) | Probability % and Milestone | Yield % |
|---|---|---|
| ☐ In assigned territory <br> ☐ Meets marketing criteria <br> ☐ Potential sponsor Identified | 0% | |
| | Lead | 10%, |
| ☐ Pain admitted by Sponsor <br> ☐ Sponsor has a buying vision <br> ☐ Sponsor agreed to explore <br> ☐ Access to Power negotiated <br> ☐ Sponsor communication agreed upon | 10% | |
| | Opportunity qualified | 20% |
| ☐ Access to Power Person <br> ☐ Pain admitted by Power Person <br> ☐ Power Person has a buying vision <br> ☐ Power Person agreed to explore <br> ☐ Evaluation Plan proposed <br> ☐ Evaluation Plan agreed upon | 20% | |
| | Executive sponsorship verified | 40% |
| ☐ Evaluation Plan underway <br> ☐ Preliminary solution agreed upon | 40% | |
| | Solution proposed | 60% |
| ☐ Evaluation Plan completed <br> ☐ Pre-proposal review conducted <br> ☐ Asked for the business <br> ☐ Proposal issued, decision due <br> ☐ Verbal approval received | 60% | |
| | Solution validated | 80% |
| ☐ Contract negotiation in progress <br> ☐ Signed documents | 80% | |
| | YOU win | 100% |
| ☐ Update prospect database | 100% | |
| | Deployment in progress | |

[Brian]: "Makes good sense. No wonder you are so confident in accurately projecting overall SpeedyLane sales even while you have so many individual selling efforts in the works."

[Catherine]: "You are right there! It took a long time to adopt this 'selling process' framework to best fit our specific market solution of self-checkout systems. But now that we've finalized it, all of our new sales folks, like you right now, go through in-depth training to build their own selling and reporting skills. It's the real key factor behind our long term, steady, profitable growth – and behind my job security, I might add."

[Brian]: "Well, I can sure see that!"

---------

# Opportunity Synthesis Form

*[Brian]:* "Getting back to Linda's ***Opportunity Analysis Form*** for House Depot, what does the $960,000 on the bottom of the form mean?"

*[Catherine]*: "Based on our previous experience and our initial profile of House Depot, we estimated that if Linny is successful with this selling effort, it will generate a SpeedyLane sale of about $3.2 million. Since we reached the end of the sponsor step (Step 3), based on our experience, we believe she has a 30% chance of winning this particular deal. We call this 30% our 'win odds.' We will not 'count' any individual target deal, such as this one for $3.2 million, until it is actually won. So, we really don't forecast revenue from individual selling efforts.

"That said, we do forecast in aggregate, from a collection of opportunities. For example, let's say that my regional sales manager, Roberto, had 10 deals worth $10 million (potential total) that have reached the market 'sponsor complete' stage (i.e., through step 3, with 30% win odds). Then Roberto would project a yield of 30% x $10 Million = $3 million for step 3. He then does the same thing for all other opportunities at each step level and adds together the projected yield numbers for every step in order to project overall revenue for the relevant operating period. Then, depending on the resulting overall projection, Roberto may or may not need to initiate actions to ensure he hits his overall number."

*[Brian]:* "Oh, I get it. That means Linda is doing great so far this year, right?"

*[Catherine]*: "Maybe yes, maybe no. To assess Linny's overall performance to date for this year, we have to consolidate her *Opportunity Analysis Forms* for all of her current accounts. We add up her progress on all her current opportunities together, and the result that we get is important. We assess her overall progress with all of her accounts with what we call an ***'Opportunities Synthesis Form.'*** Excuse all the lingo – but we try to develop self-explanatory names for each form. So as this form's name suggests, here we synthesize all of Linny's current selling efforts."

We'll pick up the conversation about the ***Opportunity Synthesis Form*** in the next chapter.

=============

## *In the meantime, …*

*[Catherine side comment to Brian]*: "Hey, Brian, by the way, that's a nice suit – very impressive. Linny didn't tell me you were such a snappy dresser."

(Of course, this was after Danielle's boyfriend, Gustavo, took Brian out on the town and had him spend a small fortune on an Armani suit with all the trimmings. Brian smiles slyly as Linda elbows him in the ribs with a wide grin on her face.)

*[Brian]*: "Oh thanks, I'm kind of new to the fancy clothes and stuff, but Linda has been helping me out."

*Flashback – Approximately one month after Brian started working with Linda, his Sales Mentor at SpeedyLane. February, 20xx. The conversation of Catherine, Brian, and Linda continues.*

CHAPTER 65

# Monitoring All Selling Efforts of One Salesperson

| **Ensuring Continuous Sales Growth** | | |
|------|-----|------------------------------------------------|
| Ch | 62 | Meet Catherine Russell, SpeedyLane National Sales Manager |
| Ch | 63 | Catherine Introduces SpeedyLane's Sales Management System |
| Ch | 64 | Monitoring Each Selling Effort of Each Salesperson |
| **Ch** | **65** | **Monitoring All Selling Efforts of One Salesperson** |
| Ch | 66 | Monitoring the Performance of the Whole Sales Team |
| Ch | 67 | Strategies for Increasing Opportunities in the Pipeline |
| Ch | 68 | Strategies for Increasing the Avg Size of Each Opportunity |
| Ch | 69 | Strategies for Improving Closing Rates |
| Ch | 70 | Sales Growth Secrets Book Summary and Conclusions |

## Monitoring All Selling Efforts of One Salesperson with the *Opportunity Synthesis Form*

Picking up the conversation of Catherine, Brian, and Linda regarding the *Opportunity Synthesis Form* from the last chapter....

[*Catherine*]: "... To assess Linny's overall performance to date for the year, we have to consolidate her *Opportunity Analysis Forms* for all of her current accounts. What's important is the overall result we determine when we add together her progress on all of her current opportunities taken together. We do that with what we call the '*Opportunity Synthesis Form*.'[76]

Let's take a look at Linny's current *Opportunities Synthesis Form* and I'll show you how we interpret it. Hope that's OK with you, Linny."

*[Linda]:* "Well, of course," *Linda says with a smile.* "Especially since I'm doing pretty well this year after a couple of last minute crash and burn accounts I blew near the end of last year."

*[Catherine]:* "Well, I wasn't going to remind you of that. As you know, we were all disappointed when that happened. But anyway, let's see how you are doing this year."

Catherine pulls up and takes a moment to study and interpret Linda's current *Opportunity Synthesis Form* (see exhibit).

*[Catherine]:* "Ah Ha, no wonder you are smiling, Linny."

*[Brian]:* "Please tell me what you see -- because all I see is a bunch of confusing numbers and Xs."

*[Catherine]:* "Let's have Linny take a crack at explaining it."

*[Linda]:* "Ah, thanks, but no thanks," *says Linda, frowning noticeably at the perplexity of even giving thought to the matter. She's just not a numbers person and is well aware of that weakness!*

"All I know is what Roberto, my Sales Manager, tells me, and he said, 'you have a nice surplus right now Linda.' So, I am good to go. You guys can do the number crunching. You know I never could figure out the gyrations in that spreadsheet opportunity consolidation form, or whatever you call it. That's why I keep telling you I'm happy in sales and don't need to get into Sales Management."

*[Catherine]:* "Kind of figured that, Linny. I was just testing the waters again. I'll be glad to handle it."

*[Catherine continues]:* "OK, Brian, here it goes. The important numbers Roberto and all the other Regional Sales Managers and I look at are down at the bottom of the table -- namely:[77]

- *Projected Size of Each Opportunity;*
- *Failed Opportunities* and *Total Opportunities Remaining;*
- *Sales Goal for Mid-Year;*
- *Probability x (times) Opportunity Size;*
- *Booked Sales;* and
- *Total Projected Sales*.

"Let's take a look at each of these. First of all, look at the ***Projected Size of Each Opportunity***.

# Opportunity Synthesis Form

**Region:** South East
**Regional Sales Manager:** Roberto Garza
**Sales Person:** Linda Brown

**Jan 1-June 30, 20xx (1st 6 mos of 20XX)**

**Linda Brown's Ongoing Selling Efforts**

| % Probability | Step # | | Activity | 1 | 2 | House Depot | 4 | 5 | 6 | 7 | 8 | |
|---|---|---|---|---|---|---|---|---|---|---|---|---|
| | | | | 10/1/2011 | 11/15/2011 | 1/8/2012 | 12/5/2011 | 1/8/2012 | 1/10/2012 | 11/15/2011 | 1/28/2012 | |
| 10% | 1 | Lead | Identify legitimate leads in the Target Market Segment | x | x | x | x | x | x | x | x | |
| 10% | 2 | | Arrange for Face to Face Meeting with Target Sponsor | x | x | x | x | x | x | | | |
| 15% | 3 | | Build initial operating vision with Target Sponsor | x | x | x | x | x | x | | | |
| 20% | 4 | Sponsor | Convert Target Sponsor - with reference visit | x | x | 2/1/20XX | x | failed | 2/1/20XX | | | |
| 30% | 5 | | Access Target Power Sponsor & build operating & financial vision | x | x | | x | | | | | |
| 40% | 6 | Power Sponsor | Convert Target Power Sponsor - with reference visit - thus gaining access to buying committee and other players vision (operating, transition or financial visions) | x | x | | 2/1/20XX | | | | | |
| 60% | 7 | | Scale and agree on breadth & depth of the solution - in the process building Financial Vision & agreeing on base price | x | x | | | | | | | |
| 80% | 8 | All Visions Built | Simultaneously build remaining Operating & Transition Visions for the solution | x | 2/1/20XX | | | | | | | |
| 90% | 9 | Ready to Negotiate | Negotiate the Final Terms + final gets & gives | x | | | | | | | | |
| 100% | 10 | Closed | Sign Deal & start Implementation | 1/15/2012 | | | | | | | | |
| | | | Projected Size ($$) of each Opportunity | | $2,000,000 | $3,200,000 | $400,000 | $3,300,000 | $1,500,000 | $800,000 | $3,800,000 | $15,000,000 |
| | | | Failed Opportunities | | | | | $3,300,000 | | | | $3,300,000 |
| | | | Total Opportunities Remaining | | | | | | | | | $11,700,000 |
| | | | Probability (based on Step Achieved to date) | | 80% | 20% | 40% | 0% | 20% | 10% | 10% | |
| | | | Size x Probability | | $1,600,000 | $640,000 | $160,000 | $0 | $300,000 | $80,000 | $380,000 | $3,160,000 |
| | | | Booked sale | $3,500,000 | | | | $0 | | | | $3,500,000 |

**date 5-Feb**

| | | |
|---|---|---|
| Quota for period | Linda's Goal For The Year, goal for 1st 6 Mos = 50% of that = $5,000,000 | $5,000,000 |
| Progress Toward Quota | Linda's Progress & Projection To Date | $3,500,000 + $3,160,000 = $6,660,000 |
| Projected Gap or Surplus for this Period | Projected Gap or Surplus for this 6 mo Period | $6,660,000 - $5,000,000 = ($1,660,000) |

**Assessment to Date**

Significant Shortfall
Some shortfall
About at Goal
Some surplus
Significant surplus  x

## Projected Size of Each Opportunity.

When Linny got her 'hot lead' for House Depot at the Home Improvement Convention in January, Roberto and Linny got together and did a little research on House Depot, ultimately discovering that HD had roughly 200 retail outlets. Using that information coupled with previous experience, they ball-parked the size of the prospective House Depot sale at $3.2 million. So, if you add that estimate to the other seven opportunities on Linny's *Opportunity Synthesis Form,* your total result equals $15 million.

## Failed Opportunities and Total Opportunities Remaining

"Next up, let's look at **Failed Opportunities** and **Total Opportunities Remaining** data. Linny's opportunity #5 failed when she couldn't convert the Target Sponsor in Selling Step #4. I don't know specifically what happened – it could have been any number of things – but I am sure Linny discussed it with her boss, Roberto. None of our sales folks will likely ever convert 100% of their opportunities in a given year. It's part of the landscape. At any rate, subtracting this $3.3 million lost opportunity gives us **Total Opportunities Remaining**. In this case, Linny's *Total Opportunities Remaining* equal the $15 million minus $3.3 million, yielding $11.7 million as the total. Are you following me, Brian?"

*[Brian]*: "Yea, pretty much, but what if Linda discovers and follows up on some new leads this year? Where do they fit?"

## Sales Goal for Mid-Year

*[Catherine]*: "Well, each new lead pursued would call for a new *Opportunity Analysis Form* and would also be shown in this *Opportunity Synthesis Form.* We expect that to happen, because if it doesn't, it is very unlikely that Linny will make her $5 mil **Sales Goal for Mid-Year**, which you can also see on her *Opportunity Synthesis Form.* In fact, as you'll see in a bit, one of the real keys to steady growth from every one of our sales folks is to keep the 'Pipeline' filled with new leads, just like you asked about!

## Probability x Opportunity Size

"The next critical number is labeled '**Probability x Opportunity Size.**' The probability of Linny realizing each sales opportunity is determined by checking the current selling process stage for each opportunity, and then referring to column 1, which contains the related likelihood or probability of realizing that particular final sale. Multiplying the probability times the size for each opportunity yields a projected sales number for Linny for mid-year. Adding these up in the form we have here suggests a total of $3.1 million in projected sales for Linny for this current 6-month period.

---

## Booked Sales

"Next comes '**Booked Sales**.' One of the reasons Linny is smiling today is because she had a great jumpstart this year, booking a $3.5 million deal a couple weeks ago in January. That is 70% of her quota for the first 6 months of this year and 35% of her quota for the entire year. No wonder she's so happy."

*[Brian]:* "Wow, I remember a couple weeks ago when you told me you closed a big deal, Linda, but I had no idea ... No wonder you took us all out to dinner that night! I am really happy for you!"

*[Linda]*: "Well, shucks, Bri, that's nice of you! I'm sure you'll do the same when your first big deal comes through – maybe even before our operating period quota deadline on June 30. That would set you up for a solid first year at SpeedyLane! I guess we'll see."

========

# An Important Aside on the Length of the Selling Process

*[Catherine]*: "Well, like I was saying, Linny started working on that deal way back in October of last year. This is a good time to mention the importance of the '**length of the selling process**' for SpeedyLane Self-checkout systems. Historically, the average length of time it takes for a SpeedyLane salesperson to convert a hot lead into a 'booked deal' is four months. This means that Linny had better have enough in her Pipeline four months prior to the end of each operating period. More specifically, these dates are Feb 28 for the first six-month operating period ending June 30, and August 30 for the second six-month operating period ending December 31. This highlights the importance of Linda continually adding new leads to her Pipeline and, thus, to her *Opportunity Synthesis Form*.

========

---

## Total Projected Sales

"At any rate, Linny's booked sale total of $3.5 million is added to the $3.1 million in projected sales for her this current 6 month period based on the opportunities still in her pipeline. This yields $6.6 million for Linny's '**total projected sales**' for this operating period ending June 30. This means that she is in great shape for this operating period, given her sales goal of $5 million.

"If she were not on or ahead of her six-month goal, then she and Roberto would try to implement some of the strategies that I'll review with you, Brian, a little later (in the next chapters). These strategies are designed to provide better balance for Linny's pipeline, in order to help ensure that she can meet her sales goals each six-month period, year after year. Like I said, we'll talk more about these strategies in a little bit."

-------

[Linda]: "How's your head? Is it spinning as much as mine? Now I am guessing you are starting to understand why I've opted out of the Sales Management track!"

[Catherine]: "I know this is getting a little complicated, Brian, but we need to assess every bit of data and make all of these projections if we hope to avoid revenue and profit growth disappointments at the end of each operating period.

"Are you at least kind of understanding this, Brian?"

[Brian]: "Yea, pretty much anyway. I think I'm closer to 'getting it' now. Is that about it for this Sales Management analysis stuff?"

[Catherine]: "Not by a long shot. We still have two additional important forms to talk about:[78]

1. ***Sales Team Gap Analysis Form*** – which consolidates the Opportunity Syntheses Forms of the entire sales team for each Regional Manager; and the

2. ***Strategy Analysis Form*** – which identifies alternative ways to address any Sales / Revenue Gap that may be revealed in any region's *Sales Team Gap Analysis Forms*.

[Brian]: "Yikes, Linda! Now I'm REALLY starting to see why you've decided not to get into Sales Management! I can't believe all of these numbers that are being thrown at us!"

----

[Linda]: "Hey Bri, how's your head? Is it spinning as much as mine

[Brian]: "You've got that right, Bri. Does anyone have some Tylenol?"

[Catherine]: "Guys! Guys! Hey, this isn't exactly rocket science! You're scaring Brian off, Linny. I'd like to think that maybe after a few years earning his stripes on the sales team, he'd consider an upward move to Sales Management -- if such an opportunity were to become available."

*Flashback – Approximately one month after Brian started working with Linda, his Sales Mentor at SpeedyLane. February, 20xx. The Sales Management conversation of Catherine, Brian, and Linda continues*....

CHAPTER 66

# Monitoring the Performance of the Whole Sales Team

| **Ensuring Continuous Sales Growth** | | |
|---|---|---|
| Ch | 62 | Meet Catherine Russell, SpeedyLane National Sales Manager |
| Ch | 63 | Catherine Introduces SpeedyLane's Sales Management System |
| Ch | 64 | Monitoring Each Selling Effort of Each Salesperson |
| Ch | 65 | Monitoring All Selling Efforts of One Salesperson |
| **Ch** | **66** | **Monitoring the Performance of the Whole Sales Team** |
| Ch | 67 | Strategies for Increasing Opportunities in the Pipeline |
| Ch | 68 | Strategies for Increasing the Avg Size of Each Opportunity |
| Ch | 69 | Strategies for Improving Closing Rates |
| Ch | 70 | Sales Growth Secrets Book Summary and Conclusions |

Catherine finished the last chapter by mentioning two additional important forms to talk about:
1. The ***Sales Team Gap Analysis Form (this chapter)***; and
2. The ***Strategy Analysis Form (next chapter)***.

## Monitoring the Performance of the Whole Sales Team using the *Sales Team Gap Analysis Form*

*[Catherine, continuing]*: "Ok. Now, where was I? Oh yeah, the **Sales Team Gap Analysis Form**. [79] This form shows Roberto and me how his whole sales team is doing so far in this operating period. Let's look at it together.

"First of all, note the heavy black line across the middle of the form. The data on top is simply a summary of the detailed data below the black line. The analysis down there is just like the analysis done on Linny's Opportunity Synthesis Form that we previously reviewed. The only difference is that it collects and **summarizes all of the Opportunity Synthesis Forms from Roberto's entire sales team**.

"For example, if you look across the page for 'Brown' (that is, Linny), you see the same data that we just reviewed on Linny's Opportunity Synthesis Form. It shows that Linny has already closed $3.5 million this period and is projected to close another $3.16 million, for a total projection of $6.66 million. With this projection, she would surpass her $5 million quota by a healthy margin of $1.66 Mil.

*[Brian]*: "Again, way to go Linny!"

*[Linda]*: "Well, thanks! I just hope I can keep up that pace for the whole year!"

*[Catherine]*: "I hope so too! Now, Brian, any questions so far?"

*[Brian]*: "It all seems logical enough. I guess the key to understanding this form is to first understand the **Opportunity Synthesis Form** for Linny and each of the other individual sales folks."

*[Catherine]*: "That's exactly right. Now, moving on, the **Sales Team Gap Analysis Form** also tells me that Roberto's overall team so far in this six-month period has achieved $10.8 million of its $25 million goal. It projects additional sales of $17.65 million, which would yield an overall projection of $28.45 million (which is $3.45 million over the goal). It's this summary data that appears on the top of the form that most interests both Roberto and me. In this case, it shows that Roberto and the Southeast region are doing pretty well. That's what Roberto and I like to see!

---

## Some Over Quota

"Quite naturally, not all of Roberto's sales folks are doing equally well. For example, Sam Grant is doing great, with projected sales of $8.23 million, which is $3.23 million over his goal. Linny and Chris Davis are also doing well as both are more than 30% over their quotas.

---

## Some Under Quota

"Cynthia Burke and Rob Casini, on the other hand, have not been nearly as successful so far this operating period. Roberto and I will be exploring those situations to see if we can do anything to help turn around those two. We are only five weeks into the six-month period and the average sales cycle is only four months, which means it is not too late to help the stragglers improve their numbers. We need to make immediate changes though, since there are fewer than five months left in this operating period."

*[Brian]*: "What do you mean 'make immediate changes?' What can you actually do about it with such little slack time? It sounds like you all would have to act this month if they are going to have any chance of reaching their numbers."

*[Catherine]*: "That's very observant, Brian, and specifically why we have the last form, the **Strategy Analysis Form**. This last form helps to identify alternative ways to address any Sales Gaps that are revealed and analyzed in the **Sales Team Gap Analysis Form** for any of our different regions. We'll consider that next."

## Sales Team Gap Analysis

**Region:** South East  
**Regional Sales Manager:** Roberto Garza  
**Current Date:** 2/1/xx  
**Average Sell Time:** 4 months  
Jan 1-June 30, 20xx (1st 6 mos of 20XX)

| Sales Rep Name | Reps' 6 mos Quota | Semi-Year Revenue Closed (out of) | Still Need to Close | Projected to Close (Likely Additional) | Projected Overall | Projected Surplus or (Gap) |
|---|---|---|---|---|---|---|
| Brown | $5,000 | $3,500 | $1,500 | $3,160 | $6,660 | $1,660 |
| Burke | $5,000 | $1,000 | $4,000 | $3,380 | $4,380 | ($620) |
| Casini | $5,000 | $0 | $5,000 | $2,560 | $2,560 | ($2,440) |
| Davis | $5,000 | $2,300 | $2,700 | $4,320 | $6,620 | $1,620 |
| Grant | $5,000 | $4,000 | $1,000 | $4,230 | $8,230 | $3,230 |
| Totals | $25,000 | $10,800 | $14,200 | $17,650 | $28,450 | $3,450 |

**Current Projection for this region**

|  | Yes | No | Amount |
|---|---|---|---|
| Gap |  | x |  |
| Surplus | x |  | $3,450 |

### Closed — 100%

| Sales Rep Name | # | Amount | Probability | Projected in Close |
|---|---|---|---|---|
| Brown | 1 | $3,500 | x |  |
| Burke | 1 | $1,000 | x |  |
| Casini | 0 | $0 | x |  |
| Davis | 1 | $2,300 | x |  |
| Grant | 2 | $4,000 | x |  |
| Totals |  | $10,800 |  |  |

### Ready to Negotiate — 90%

| Sales Rep Name | # | Size | Probability | Projected in Close |
|---|---|---|---|---|
| Brown | 0 | 0 | 90% | $0 |
| Burke | 1 | $900 | 90% | $810 |
| Casini | 0 | $0 | 90% | $0 |
| Davis | 1 | $2,300 | 90% | $2,070 |
| Grant | 0 | $0 | 90% | $0 |
| Totals |  | $3,200 |  | $2,880 |

### All Visions Built — 80%

| Sales Rep Name | # | Size | Probability | Projected in Close |
|---|---|---|---|---|
| Brown | 1 | $2,000 | 80% | $1,600 |
| Burke | 1 | $800 | 80% | $640 |
| Casini | 2 | $1,800 | 80% | $1,440 |
| Davis | 0 | $0 | 80% | $0 |
| Grant | 1 | $2,800 | 80% | $2,240 |
| Totals |  | $7,400 |  | $5,920 |

### Converted Power Sponsor — 40%

| Sales Rep Name | # | Size | Probability | Projected in Close |
|---|---|---|---|---|
| Brown | 1 | $400 | 40% | $160 |
| Burke | 1 | $2,200 | 40% | $880 |
| Casini | 1 | $1,000 | 40% | $400 |
| Davis | 1 | $2,300 | 40% | $920 |
| Grant | 2 | $3,600 | 40% | $1,440 |
| Totals |  | $9,500 |  | $3,800 |

### Converted Sponsor — 20%

| Sales Rep Name | # | Size | Probability | Projected in Close |
|---|---|---|---|---|
| Brown | 1 | $4,700 | 20% | $940 |
| Burke | 2 | $1,400 | 20% | $280 |
| Casini | 1 | $1,600 | 20% | $320 |
| Davis | 1 | $2,300 | 20% | $460 |
| Grant | 0 | $0 | 20% | $0 |
| Totals |  | $10,000 |  | $2,000 |

### Active Leads — 10%

| Sales Rep Name | # | Size | Probability | Projected in Close |
|---|---|---|---|---|
| Brown | 3 | $4,600 | 10% | $460 |
| Burke | 3 | $7,700 | 10% | $770 |
| Casini | 2 | $4,000 | 10% | $400 |
| Davis | 4 | $8,700 | 10% | $870 |
| Grant | 3 | $5,500 | 10% | $550 |
| Totals |  | $30,500 |  | $3,050 |

### Total Projected to Closes & Close Rates (Likely Additional Yield)

| Sales Rep Name | Projected to Close | Opportunity Size | close rate now projected |
|---|---|---|---|
| Brown | $3,160 | $11,700 | 27.0% |
| Burke | $3,380 | $13,000 | 26.0% |
| Casini | $2,560 | $8,400 | 30.5% |
| Davis | $4,320 | $15,600 | 27.7% |
| Grant | $4,230 | $11,900 | 35.5% |
| Totals | $17,650 | $60,600 | 29.1% |

## *Meanwhile ...*
### Let's check on Brian's relationship with Lucy.

[Linda]: "Brian, did you call Lucy for another date?"

[Brian]: "No, but she called me. We are going out tonight! I think she might like me...maybe?"

[Linda]: "Well, do you like her?"

[Brian]: "I don't know. It's a little too early for me to think about that."

[Linda]: "For what it's worth, she already told me that she really likes you!"

**Brian's _thought bubble_:**

*Flashback – Approximately one month after Brian started working with Linda, his Sales Mentor at SpeedyLane. February, 20xx. Catherine, Brian, and Linda continue their conversation regarding SpeedyLane's Sales Management system.*

CHAPTER 67

# Strategies to Increase the Number of Opportunities in the Pipeline

| Ensuring Continuous Sales Growth | | |
|---|---|---|
| Ch | 62 | Meet Catherine Russell, SpeedyLane National Sales Manager |
| Ch | 63 | Catherine Introduces SpeedyLane's Sales Management System |
| Ch | 64 | Monitoring Each Selling Effort of Each Salesperson |
| Ch | 65 | Monitoring All Selling Efforts of One Salesperson |
| Ch | 66 | Monitoring the Performance of the Whole Sales Team |
| **Ch** | **67** | **Strategies for Increasing Opportunities in the Pipeline** |
| Ch | 68 | Strategies for Increasing the Avg Size of Each Opportunity |
| Ch | 69 | Strategies for Improving Closing Rates |
| Ch | 70 | Sales Growth Secrets Book Summary and Conclusions |

Picking up the conversation of Catherine, Brian, and Linda from last chapter .........

[*Catherine*]: "Like I was saying, Brian, we still have another form to review. By the way, I'm happy to tell you that this is the last form we use to try to ensure that we meet our national sales target and grow virtually every single year!"

## Strategy Analysis Form

[*Catherine*]: "We call this final form the **Strategy Analysis Form**. [80] This form helps to identify alternative ways to address any sales gaps that are revealed in the **Sales Team Gap Analysis Form** for any of our regions. This form comes into play when any Regional Sales Manager projects a sales gap rather than a surplus for a specific operating period.

| Region | | | North East |
|---|---|---|---|
| Regional Sales Manager | | | Tom Cooper |
| **Strategy Analysis Form** | | | |
| How much in new leads would be needed | | | |
| Projected Gap (if any) | | Close Rate for New Leads | | New Leads Needed |
| ($9,140) | | 10.0% | = | ($91,400) |
| How much current opportunities have to increase | | | |
| Projected to Close | | Total in Pipeline Now | | Close Rate Now Projected |
| $12,360 | / | $49,300 | = | 25.1% |
| Projected Gap (if any) | | Close Rate Now | | New Opportunities |
| $9,140 | / | 25.1% | = | $36,456 |
| Close rate needed for opportunities now in the | | | |
| New Sales Needed | | Total in Pipeline Now | | Close Rate Needed |
| $21,500 | / | $49,300 | = | 43.6% |

"It is easiest to explain the form using an example. Let's look at the Northeast region, where our Regional Sales Manager, Tom Cooper, has been having all sorts of trouble. His region underperformed the last two operating periods and is struggling again this period.

"As you can see in this *Sales Analysis Form,* Tom and his sales team are projected to be roughly $9.14 million short of their $25.0 million target for this operating period. This is more than a 35% shortfall and is unacceptable from any point of view – but especially mine since this inferior performance will poorly reflect on my own performance as National Sales Manager as well.

"So, the question becomes 'can we fix this situation in the five months we still have left in this operating period?'. We have several potential strategies for turning around the current disappointing sales projection for the Northeast region. These strategies include:

1. **Identifying and More Aggressively Pursuing Selected, Large Opportunities;**
2. **Improving the Number and Balance of Opportunities in the Pipeline (i.e., Active leads);**
3. **Increasing the Size of Opportunities Now in the Pipeline;** and

4. **Improving the Closing Rates (or 'Win Rates') for opportunities now in the pipeline.**

"Of course, these are not mutually exclusive opportunities. That means that Tom and his team can use a combination of these strategies to try to reach their $25.0 million goal for this operating period."

*[Catherine, continuing]*: "Now, Brian, rather than me continuing to yap about how Tom and I assess these alternative potential strategies, what strategy or combination of strategies do you think Tom and his team should try?"

*[Brian]:* "I have no idea. The numbers in the ***Strategy Analysis Form*** seem like a foreign language to me right now. But I'm guessing for starters that it might help to compare some of the data from Tom's region to similar data from Roberto's region or another region where no sales gap is projected."

*[Catherine]*: "That's a fairly good answer, Bri! And, as you will see in a moment, we'll do just that as we try to figure out what may or may not be realistic strategies for Tom's Northeast region. Let's start with a drill down on each of those four alternative potential strategies. We want to see if we can come up with some recommendations for Tom and his sales team to attempt to close the rather large sales gap projected for their region this period."

## 1. Strategies for Identifying and More Aggressively Pursuing Selected, Large Opportunities

*[Catherine]*: "The first strategy involves reallocating regional and national selling resources and expertise. We would implement this strategy in order to try to improve the chances of closing on any particularly large opportunities that any of Tom's sales folks may already be working on. For example, let's say we spot a large opportunity where a salesperson is hung up on trying to develop an attractive financial vision. We have a lot of expertise on that here in the home office that we can use proactively to help in building that financial vision.

"Alternatively, if they're lacking large active opportunities in the current pipeline, we might help and encourage Tom and his team to aggressively seek out new, particularly large opportunities to add as active leads. These new opportunities might be added over the next month -- or even over the next two months – if Tom and his team could reduce the selling cycle on these large opportunities from the typical four months to, say, three months.

The bottom line goal of this strategy is to refocus selling resources and expertise in order to improve the close rate on larger opportunities. We will consider this further when we discuss 'improving close rates' as a specific strategy in a little bit."

## 2. Strategies for Improving the Number and Balance of Opportunities in the Pipeline (i.e., Active leads)

*[Catherine continues]*: "We at headquarters work closely with the Regional Managers to try to keep the pipelines in all regions both 'full' and 'balanced.' The Regional Managers, in turn, are responsible for doling out and managing available opportunities among their sales teams, specifically trying to keep each salesperson's pipeline "healthy" - which we define as being both full and balanced. Despite these efforts, any region can at times experience a simple ***shortage***

*in the number of opportunities in its pipeline or can experience an out-of-balance pipeline.*"

[Brian]: "What do you mean by an 'out-of-balance pipeline'?

[Catherine]: "If Regional Managers and their sales teams are not pursuing new leads **on a regular basis**, some pipelines can get out-of-balance, which means there are too few opportunities at different developmental stages of the selling cycle. This lack of balance results in significant fluctuations in sales that can wreak havoc with our overall corporate effort to have steady sales growth period after period, without significant sales peaks and valleys."

[Brian]: "I think I get it. If you don't let opportunities build up at any particular stage of the selling process and keep new active leads coming into the pipeline at a steady rate, then ultimate sales 'wins' are likely to be more constant from one operating period to the next. Is that about right?"

[Catherine]: "Couldn't have said it better!"

---

## Improving the Number of Active leads

[Catherine, continuing]: "I wanted to get back to how we at headquarters help feed the pipelines on a regular basis. We do that by systematically analyzing industry trade data for new pipeline opportunities. Then we complement that by continually generating other new leads through active promotion campaigns, which include initiatives such as:

- Aggressive use of Social Media;
- Advertisements in trade journals, magazines, newspapers, as well as in captive media such as TV and radio;
- Trade show participation, demonstrations, etc.;
- Internet ads and promotional web sites;
- Direct e-mail and snail mail campaigns;
- On-site seminars featuring demonstrations;
- Demonstrations in key cities that allow retailers to try the self-checkout experience themselves; and
- Development of network contacts through reference client retailers.

"Of course, both Regional Managers and their individual sales folks are also required to spend a certain amount of time each week searching out new potential opportunities and making cold calls to nurture such opportunities. How much time each Regional Manager and salesperson is expected to spend on these activities is dependent on the current balance of the relevant region's or individual salesperson's pipeline. Regional Managers are responsible for making sure that individual sales folks do indeed help in this critical lead generation activity – just as I continually encourage all Regional Managers to do the same.

"Our corporate-wide ongoing sales training initiatives and 'targeted sales coaching' – which I'll cover in a moment – are directed primarily at increasing our closing rates. This coaching includes regular seminars and communications to help both Regional Managers and their sales folks to learn and develop more effective ways to both identify new potential opportunities and to turn them into active leads – particularly leveraging our forward-looking social media programs and strategies.

"In addition to using our dedicated, three-person training staff here in the home office to accomplish this task, we also use selected Regional Managers and individual sales folks in our training initiatives. For example, Linda's Regional Manager, Roberto, has proven to be very effective at both uncovering new potential opportunities and converting them into active leads. So, we use Roberto as a regular presenter in both our online sales training and in our national sales meetings when we discuss active lead generation."

## North East — Tom Cooper

**Region:** North East
**Regional Sales Manager:** Tom Cooper

### Strategy Analysis Form

**How much in new leads would be needed**

| Projected Gap (if any) | | Close Rate for New Leads | | New Leads Needed |
|---|---|---|---|---|
| ($9,140) | / | 10.0% | = | ($91,400) |

**How much current opportunities have to increase**

| Projected to Close | | Total in Pipeline Now | | Close Rate Now Projected |
|---|---|---|---|---|
| $12,360 | / | $49,300 | = | 25.1% |

| Projected Gap (if any) | | Close Rate Now | | New Opportunities Needed |
|---|---|---|---|---|
| $9,140 | / | 25.1% | = | $36,456 |

**Close rate needed for opportunities now in the**

| New Sales Needed | | Total in Pipeline Now | | Close Rate Needed |
|---|---|---|---|---|
| $21,500 | / | $49,300 | = | 43.6% |

## South East — Roberto Garza

**Region:** South East
**Regional Sales Manager:** Roberto Garza

### Strategy Analysis Form

**How much in new leads would be needed**

| Projected Gap (if any) | | Close Rate for New Leads | | New Leads Needed |
|---|---|---|---|---|
| $0 | | 10.0% | = | $0 |

**How much current opportunities have to increase**

| Projected to Close | | Total in Pipeline Now | | Close Rate Now Projected |
|---|---|---|---|---|
| $17,650 | / | $60,600 | = | 29.1% |

| Projected Gap (if any) | | Close Rate Now | | New Opportunities Needed |
|---|---|---|---|---|
| ($3,450) | / | 29.1% | = | ($11,845) |

**Close rate needed for opportunities now in the**

| New Sales Needed | | Total in Pipeline Now | | Close Rate Needed |
|---|---|---|---|---|
| $14,200 | / | $60,600 | = | 23.4% |

## Does the Northeast Region Have Enough Opportunities in its Pipeline?

"Now, back to the question regarding whether Tom and his Northeast sales team have enough opportunities in their pipeline. This is when a comparison between the Northeast region and other regions can come in handy. For example, let's compare the **Sales Analysis Forms** for Tom's and Roberto's regions. This comparison shows that as of 2/1/xx, Tom's region has $49.3 million in its pipeline while Roberto's Southeast Region has slightly over $60.0 million in its pipeline. This means that Tom's team is actively pursuing opportunities that are worth 20% less than Roberto's team. That's a red flag for me and alerts me that I need to work with Tom to figure out exactly why that has happened before we even consider a possibly remedy."

*[Brian]:* "I'm curious to see whether you can remedy it or not, and if you can, how you would go about doing it."

*[Catherine]*: "All in due time, Bri. I'll tell you right now though, I have my doubts about whether Tom and I can come up with a strategy that will close such a large 'opportunity gap.' The fact that we have a typical four-month selling cycle is part of the challenge. The four-month selling cycle means that, since we are already a month into this six-month selling cycle, we would have only one month to add enough new opportunities that might close the sales gap by 6/30/xx.

"That said, we at headquarters may be able to help by immediately sending some new leads Tom's way. Doing this might help Tom and his sales team to at least *start* addressing the current shortage of opportunities in their pipeline, but it would have to be combined with additional strategic initiatives as well.

"Related to this, another one of our big concerns here at headquarters is to avoid depleting our list of cold, inactive leads, lest we stimulate sales this period, only to find even worse opportunity shortages next period and beyond. So, even if we do send a raft of new, cold leads Tom's way, we would also strongly encourage Tom and his sales force to be more proactive in their own efforts to both develop and convert more inactive leads into active leads over the next month."

*[Catherine, continuing]*: "Let's do a drill down on the number of new opportunities the Northeast region would actually need to close their projected sales gap. Brian, looking at Tom's **Strategy Analysis Form** for his region, how much in new active leads do you think Tom and his team would need in order to close their projected $9.14 million sales gap?"

*[Brian]*: "Well, looking at Tom's ***Strategy Analysis Form,*** it shows that only 10% of new active leads actually turn into sales. So, to close the $9.14 million sales gap, as shown in the ***Strategy Analysis Form*** for the Northeast, Tom's team would need $91.4 million in new active leads – or ten times his current sales gap."

*[Catherine]*: "Right on, Bri! Now do you think Tom's team can add that $91.4 million in leads?"

*[Brian]*: "Looking at the form again, I see they only have $49.3 million in their active pipeline right now, so I would think that adding $91.4 million more would be a really stiff order, especially since they would have to add all those leads within the next 30 days!"

*[Catherine]*: "Right you are! In fact, while adding new active leads over the next 30 days might help, there's no way they could possibly add the required 91.4 million in that time."

---

## 3. Strategies to Increase the Average Size of Opportunities in the Pipeline

*[Catherine]*: "This takes us to the next potential strategy, which is to attempt to increase the size of opportunities currently in the pipeline – a portion of which are projected to close by 6/30/xx."

We look at that in the next chapter.

*Flashback – Approximately one month after Brian started working with Linda, his Sales Mentor at SpeedyLane. February, 20xx. The conversation regarding SpeedyLane's Sales Management System continues.*

CHAPTER 68

---

# Strategies to Increase the Average Opportunity Size

| **Ensuring Continuous Sales Growth** | | |
|---|---|---|
| Ch | 62 | Meet Catherine Russell, SpeedyLane National Sales Manager |
| Ch | 63 | Catherine Introduces SpeedyLane's Sales Management System |
| Ch | 64 | Monitoring Each Selling Effort of Each Salesperson |
| Ch | 65 | Monitoring All Selling Efforts of One Salesperson |
| Ch | 66 | Monitoring the Performance of the Whole Sales Team |
| Ch | 67 | Strategies for Increasing Opportunities in the Pipeline |
| **Ch** | **68** | **Strategies for Increasing the Avg Size of Each Opportunity** |
| Ch | 69 | Strategies for Improving Closing Rates |
| Ch | 70 | Sales Growth Secrets Book Summary and Conclusions |

Catherine has been educating Brian about potential strategies for turning around the current disappointing sales projection for Tom Cooper's Northeast region. These strategies include two covered in the last chapter:

1. **Identifying and More Aggressively Pursuing Selected, Large Opportunities;**
2. **Improving the Number and Balance of Opportunities in the Pipeline (i.e., Active Leads);**

In this chapter, we address the third strategy:

3. **Increasing the Average Size of Opportunities Now in the Pipeline; and**

Then, in the next chapter, we will address the fourth potential strategy:

4. Improving the **Closing Rates** (or 'Win Rates') for opportunities now in the pipeline.

## Strategies to Increase the
## Average Size of Opportunities in the Pipeline

*[Catherine]*: "This takes us to the next potential strategy – attempting to **_increase the size of opportunities already in the pipeline_**. [81] This strategy consists of **up-selling and cross-selling**. For example, we take an opportunity already in the pipeline and try to add additional self-service checkout hardware, software, or supporting services.

| Region | | | | North East |
|---|---|---|---|---|
| **Regional Sales Manager** | | | | Tom Cooper |
| **Strategy Analysis Form** | | | | |
| **How much in new leads would be needed** | | | | |
| Projected Gap (if any) | | conversion rate for new | | new Leads Needed |
| ($9,140) | | 10% | = | ($91,400) |
| **How much current opportunities have to increase** | | | | |
| projected to close | | total in pipeline now | | close rate now projected |
| $12,360 | / | $49,300 | = | 25.1% |
| **Projected Gap** | | conversion rate now | | new opportunities needed |
| $9,140 | / | 25.1% | = | $36,456 |
| **Close rate needed for opportunities now in the pipeline** | | | | |
| **new sales needed** | | **total in pipeline** | | **Close Rate Needed** |
| $21,500 | / | $49,300 | = | 43.6% |

"We have a number of tools available to help our Regional Sales Managers like Tom up-sell and cross-sell. For instance, we will suggest that Tom and his sales team access our online SpeedyLane **training videos** focused specifically on up-selling and cross-selling. We also host live **seminars** and provide **one-on-one training sessions** at our annual sales convention. Tom should insist that his sales folks attend these next January – even though it will be too late to help with Tom's immediate opportunity size problem.

"An additional important resource at his team's disposal is our current national sales force itself – with roughly 50 sales team members. Among these, we have identified a half dozen who have proven themselves over time to be highly effective at increasing opportunity size during the selling process through up-selling or cross-selling. In fact, Linda here is on that short list. This falls under our '***Targeted Coaching Program***,' which I will discuss in more detail later.

"Linny, perhaps you could introduce Brian to how our targeted coaching works - specifically concentrating on up-selling and cross-selling in this case."

[*Linda*]: "Let me take a shot at it. This is how it works. Since I am on Catherine's 'Hot List' for up-selling and cross-selling, I've taped a session on those topics for our web-site -- which is available 24/7 for any of our sales folks. In my video, I focus on describing specific examples of how I've been able to increase opportunity size throughout the selling cycle by up-selling and cross-selling. I've also given a seminar on this topic each of the past few years at our annual sales convention in January. It's a really fun part of my job.

"In addition, and I think this is the most helpful part, a couple of times a month I'll get a request from a Regional Sales Manager to talk to one or more of his or her salespeople. This typically happens after the manager has reviewed a series of his sales team's ***Opportunity Synthesis Forms*** and ***Sales Gap Analysis Forms*** over several periods and has identified one or more sales folks who have succeeded at improving average opportunity size during the selling cycle.

"I really enjoy this part of my job because it gives me an opportunity to get to know many of our other sales folks, and I can tell that they really appreciate the help I give them."

[*Catherine*]: "Good summary, Linda. So, do you get the idea, Bri?"

[*Brian*]: "It's great to hear that you really work as a team and support each other so much. I wasn't expecting that, but I'll surely make use of it!"

[*Catherine*]: "So, getting down to specifics, and again looking at Tom's ***Strategy Analysis Form***, how much would Tom and his team have to increase the average size of opportunities already in their pipeline in order to close his projected $9.14 million gap for this six-month period?"

[*Brian*]: "Um... I don't think I see the answer to that in Tom's ***Strategy Analysis Form***."

[*Catherine*]: "Well, let's review what we already know from his ***Sales Team Gap Analysis*** and his ***Strategy Analysis Form*** for the Northeast region. We know that his sales goal is $25 million, of which he has already closed on $3.5 million. This leaves $21.5 million yet to be captured. They currently have $49.3 million in their pipeline with a projected 25.1% win ratio. This generates projected sales of $12.36 million, which, as we know, is $9.14 million short of their goal. So, let's see if you can take it from there."

*[Brian]:* "OK, I'll play your game. But doubt I'll get it right. Let's see, 25.1% of "X" has to equal $21.5 million. So, that's 21.5/.251. Using my handy iPhone, that equals a potential of $85.66 million required in the pipeline. That means Tom's team would have to beef up the total current size of $49.3 million opportunities by over $36 million in order to reach the required $85.66 million. That would be an increase of 85.66/49.30, let's see, that's 73.4% in the average size of opportunities now in the pipeline! So, he'd have to increase the average size of each opportunity now in his pipeline by 73.4%! Yikes, that's a lot!"

*[Linda]:* "Holy cats, Brian, where did you learn all that stuff? What are you, some sort of brainiac?"

*[Brian]:* "Hold your horses, Linda, I don't even know if I'm right."

*[Catherine]:* "I have to say, Bri, you are right on with your analysis as well as with your '*Yikes, that's a lot*' conclusion. Increasing the average size of opportunities currently in the pipeline by 73% is a 'pipe-dream' and is not going to happen. It would take a miracle for Tom's team to up-sell and cross-sell current opportunities projected at $49.3 million by over $36 million to reach their goal of $85.6 million. Like I said, that is just not going to happen."

*[Brian]:* "What about combining those two strategies – increasing the number and average size of opportunities in the pipeline?"

*[Catherine]:* "That's a good, logical thought, Brian, but it would be a tall order to close the huge 35%+ sales gap of $9.14 million, even by increasing both the number and average size of opportunities in Tom's pipeline. They just have such a huge projected sales shortfall."

"That brings up the next potential strategy we will discuss, which is to **Improve the Close Rate**" (we'll consider this in the next chapter).

*Flashback – Approximately one month after Brian started working with Linda, his Sales Mentor at SpeedyLane. February, 20xx. Catherine, Brian, and Linda continue their conversation regarding SpeedyLane's Sales Management system.*

CHAPTER 69

# Strategies to Improve Closing Rates

| Ensuring Continuous Sales Growth | | |
|---|---|---|
| Ch | 62 | Meet Catherine Russell, SpeedyLane National Sales Manager |
| Ch | 63 | Catherine Introduces SpeedyLane's Sales Management System |
| Ch | 64 | Monitoring Each Selling Effort of Each Salesperson |
| Ch | 65 | Monitoring All Selling Efforts of One Salesperson |
| Ch | 66 | Monitoring the Performance of the Whole Sales Team |
| Ch | 67 | Strategies for Increasing Opportunities in the Pipeline |
| Ch | 68 | Strategies for Increasing the Avg Size of Each Opportunity |
| **Ch** | **69** | **Strategies for Improving Closing Rates** |
| Ch | **70** | Sales Growth Secrets Book Summary and Conclusions |

Picking up the conversation of Catherine, Brian, and Linda from last chapter ........

[Catherine]: "This brings us to the next potential strategy -- '**Improving Closing Rates**.' Let's consider this possible strategy for Tom and his sales team."

[Brian]: "Sounds good – I'm with ya!"

## Strategies to Improve Closing Rates[82]

[Catherine]: "To start, let's compare the closing rates of the Southeast and Northeast regions. The two **Strategy Analysis Forms** show a projected 25.1% closing rate for Tom's Northeast region versus a 29.1% closing rate for Roberto's Southeast region.

"Now, Linda, what do the two **Strategy Analysis Forms** tell us about increasing Tom's closing rate as a potential strategy? Remember, Tom and his sales team need $9.14 million in additional sales in order to close their projected sales gap for this operating period."

**Region** South East

**Regional Sales Manager** Roberto Garza

## Strategy Analysis Form

### How much in new leads would be needed

| Projected Gap (if any) | | Close Rate for New Leads | | New Leads Needed |
|---|---|---|---|---|
| $0 | / | 10.0% | = | $0 |

### How much current opportunities have to increase

| Projected to Close | | Total in Pipeline Now | | Close Rate Now Projected |
|---|---|---|---|---|
| $17,650 | / | $60,600 | = | 29.1% |

| Projected Gap (if any) | | Close Rate Now | | New Opportunities Needed |
|---|---|---|---|---|
| ($3,450) | / | 29.1% | = | ($11,845) |

### Close rate needed for opportunities now in the

| New Sales Needed | | Total in Pipeline Now | | Close Rate Needed |
|---|---|---|---|---|
| $14,200 | / | $60,600 | = | 23.4% |

---

**Region** North East

**Regional Sales Manager** Tom Cooper

## Strategy Analysis Form

### How much in new leads would be needed

| Projected Gap (if any) | | Close Rate for New Leads | | New Leads Needed |
|---|---|---|---|---|
| ($9,140) | / | 10.0% | = | ($91,400) |

### How much current opportunities have to increase

| Projected to Close | | Total in Pipeline Now | | Close Rate Now Projected |
|---|---|---|---|---|
| $12,360 | / | $49,300 | = | 25.1% |

| Projected Gap (if any) | | Close Rate Now | | New Opportunities Needed |
|---|---|---|---|---|
| $9,140 | / | 25.1% | = | $36,456 |

### Close rate needed for opportunities now in the

| New Sales Needed | | Total in Pipeline Now | | Close Rate Needed |
|---|---|---|---|---|
| $21,500 | / | $49,300 | = | 43.6% |

*[Linda]*: "You got me! You know this analysis stuff is not my strong suit. Brian, what do you think?"

*[Brian]*: "Well, let's see if I can get this. Tom's **Strategy Analysis Form** shows that his team needs $21.5 million more in sales. But he is currently projected to get only $12.36 million in additional sales. We also see that he has $49.3 million in his pipeline. So, I guess the first question is how much Tom's team would have to increase their current closing rate -- from the now projected 25.1% -- in order to get the additional $21.5 million still needed to reach their quota for the period. So, given $49.3 million in the pipeline and the need of $21.5 million to reach the goal, that is 21.5 over 49.3, which equals a required closing rate of, ah, let me see (*using his iPhone again*) 43.6%.

"Do you think they could do that, Catherine?"

*[Catherine]*: "Negatory. Your numbers are correct, but we've never had any region during any operating period have a closing rate of over 40%. In fact, we generally regard 30% as a solid closing rate.

"But, increasing the closing rate could at least help Tom and his team move closer to their $25.0 million sales goal -- especially if combined with the strategies considered earlier for increasing the sales opportunities in the pipeline."

*[Brian]*: "That all sounds good, but if they could improve their closing rate, why aren't they already doing it?"

*[Catherine]*: "Another good question, Bri! This is where our **Targeted Coaching Program** comes in."

## Using Targeted Coaching to Improve Closing Rates

*[Catherine continues]*: "The most important goal of our **Targeted Coaching Program** is to help individual sales folks improve their Closing or 'Win' Rates. We ask each Regional Manager to constantly monitor each salesperson's pipeline. The purpose is to spot when help is needed to keep an individual selling effort moving forward. An even more important purpose is to watch for tendencies of specific sales folks who may get hung up on particular stages of the selling cycle with multiple target customers. Regional Managers are on the lookout for hang-ups in **these particular stages of the selling cycle**:

1. **Stimulating Interest** -- lead development & first contact – turning leads into active leads;
2. **First Sales Call to Target Sponsor**
   a. **Getting Target Sponsor to admit pain** -- bringing to the foreground the Target Sponsor's most pressing operating issues;
   b. **Vision Building with Target Sponsor** -- cooperatively building the Target Sponsor's vision of your differentiated solution as a resolution to his or her most pressing process issues;
3. **Converting the Target Sponsor** [through reference visit(s)] and then **gaining access to the Target Power Sponsor**;
4. **First Meeting with Target Power Sponsor**

    a. **Getting Target Power Sponsor to admit pain** -- bringing to the foreground the Power Sponsor's most pressing operational & related financial issues;

    b. **Vision Building with Target Power Sponsor** -- cooperatively building the Target Power Sponsor's vision of your differentiated solution as a resolution to his or her most pressing operational and related financial issues;

5. **Proof Management** – Building all operating, transition, and financial visions for all remaining important internal and external players;

6. **Reaching Agreement on Nature of the Solution** -- exact dimensions, price, and criteria for monitoring successful implementation; and

7. **Negotiating the Final Deal**.

8. **Timely Implementation**;

9. **Follow-up monitoring of success criteria**;

10. **Leveraging successes into new opportunities** with this client and other clients.

"By monitoring and studying each salesperson's ***Opportunity Synthesis Form,*** *which we reviewed earlier*, the Regional Manager can spot when a salesperson is stuck on a particular stage of the selling cycle with individual target customers. The manager can then question the salesperson regarding the particular hang-up and see if there might be a way to help the salesperson over this hurdle and hopefully move the selling effort forward.

"As suggested, however, an even more important purpose for carefully monitoring each salesperson's ***Opportunity Synthesis Form*** is to keep an eye out for tendencies of specific sales folks to get hung up on particular stages of the selling cycle with multiple target customers. When that happens, it's time to take advantage of the ***Targeted Coaching Program***.

"You recall, Brian, we mentioned this program earlier when we were discussing how Linda regularly helps others to up-sell and cross-sell in order to increase the size of opportunities in the pipeline. Like I said before, Targeted Coaching tips are available online from Headquarters for each stage of the selling process. And we have also identified specific regional managers and sales folks who have excellent track records in moving through each selling stage. For example, Linda here is also among those who are frequently called upon by Regional Managers to talk with individual salespersons who are having trouble converting the Target Sponsor into an actual sponsor.

"Linda, why don't you tell Brian how that works?"

*[Linda]*: "Well, I guess I have developed a fairly good reputation for converting Target Sponsors since I've been asked to give a seminar on it at our annual sales meeting for the last several years. Similar to how I can help with up-selling and cross-selling, I'll get a request from a Regional Sales Manager a couple times a month to talk with one or more specific salespeople in his or her region. This happens when they have reviewed their sales team's ***Opportunity Synthesis Forms*** and have identified one or more sales folks who are obviously having trouble successfully converting Target Sponsors. I really enjoy this aspect of my job, because it gives me an opportunity to get to know many of our other sales folks, and I can tell that they really appreciate my help."

*[Brian]*: "Well, what do you actually say to them when you try to help them out?"

*[Linda]*: "Well, I'll start by talking in depth with them, usually asking for an example of a failed effort to convert a Target Sponsor. As I listen, I am on the lookout to determine exactly where the hang-up usually occurs. For example, converting the Target Sponsor involves:

- Getting pain admitted;
- Building a buying vision;
- Getting agreement to explore our solution;
- Negotiating access to power; and then, finally,
- Getting the Target Sponsor to introduce him/herself to the relevant Target Power Sponsor after a successful reference visit(s).

"A specific salesperson's problem could be in a single one of these areas or it may lie in multiple areas. The most typical problems I usually discover include:

- Jumping into vision building without getting pain clearly admitted;
- Steering the person too much during vision building and not recognizing the importance of letting the Target Sponsor self-conclude. This is a biggie that I run into all the time; and
- Outright suggesting that we have a solution for all their problems. This is another common mistake and a real turnoff for many Target Sponsors.

"Once I feel that I've identified their specific problem or problems, I talk them through another example in which the process was done correctly. Through leading them though a successful process, I try to get them to self-discover the difference and why the approach I describe ended in success and why theirs did not. It's actually kind of funny, because when talking with them, I essentially apply the same 'self-discovery principle' that we encourage them to use when vision building with their target customer – that is, using the nine block approach that we discussed earlier."

*[Brian]*: "That sounds cool. It must be very satisfying to help out like this and to meet many of your colleagues in the process."

*[Linda]*: "It sure is. And there's another big benefit as well. While I might have learned well when it comes to converting Target Sponsors, when I first began here at SpeedyLane, I was horrible at building convincing financial visions. Also, I was no good at running negotiations effectively. I attended some in-house seminars in both areas and utilized our online resources designed to reinforce the training we go through in each of these areas. But I found the most help I received was from individual colleagues who were superior in each of these areas. They helped me immensely with my approach and my confidence in building financial visions and in negotiating more effectively. So, it's really a 'you scratch my back – I'll scratch yours' kind of thing. It's highly effective."

*[Catherine]*: "Great summary, Linda! You explained it better than I could!"

--------------------

*[Catherine continues]*: "Well, Brian, that wraps up our meeting. I hope you got a better understanding about how the Regional Sales Managers and I manage our overall sales force's selling efforts in order to ensure profitable growth year after year."

*Flashback – Approximately one month after Brian started working with Linda, his Sales Mentor at SpeedyLane. February, 20xx. The conversation of Catherine, Brian, and Linda continues.*

CHAPTER 70

---

# Sales Growth Secrets Book Summary and Conclusions - Lessons Learned

| **Ensuring Continuous Sales Growth** | | |
|------|------|---------------------------------------------------------|
| Ch | 62 | Meet Catherine Russell, SpeedyLane National Sales Manager |
| Ch | 63 | Catherine Introduces Brian to the Sales Management System |
| Ch | 64 | Monitoring Each Selling Effort of Each Salesperson |
| Ch | 65 | Monitoring All Selling Efforts of One Salesperson |
| Ch | 66 | Monitoring the Performance of the Whole Sales Team |
| Ch | 67 | Strategies for Increasing Opportunities in the Pipeline |
| Ch | 68 | Strategies for Increasing the Avg Size of Pipeline Opportunities |
| Ch | 69 | Strategies for Improving Closing Rates |
| **Ch** | **70** | **Sales Growth Secrets Summary and Conclusions - Lessons Learned** |

Picking up the conversation of Catherine, Brian, and Linda from last chapter .........

   *[Brian]*: "Catherine, if you had to narrow it down, what do you think are the most important factors enabling the steady, profitable growth you've been able to achieve at SpeedyLane?"

   *[Catherine]*: "Well, at the risk of repeating myself, I'd say these are the key points."

- We at the home office are constantly doing research to monitor the dynamic needs of our target segments and customers as well as our competitors' strategies.
- We overtly recognize that we need to maintain significant, dynamic, sustainable advantages over both our primary generic competitors and brand competitors. This pertains especially to the extensive, dynamic range of services that we develop to surround and support our basic self-checkout solution technologies.
- Our entire sales force uses exactly the same step-by-step selling approach. This enables us to identify and proactively address specific weaknesses – particularly sales pipeline imbalances – before they potentially cause sales gaps in any operating period.
- As you saw today, we have a lock step process for systematically assessing and projecting the health of our sales pipelines for individual salespersons, for individual regions, and nationally for the company as a whole. Again, this is enabled by our entire sales force using the exact same step-by-step selling process.
- Last but not least, as we just discussed, we have an effective cooperative process in place for on-the-fly training of individual salespersons in order to help each person continually improve his or her effectiveness in each step of the selling process."

---

## A 'Master Selling Approach' Drives the Growth Plan

**In closing the book, it is worth emphasizing a section from an earlier chapter -- A 'Master Selling Approach' Drives the Growth Plan**

*[Catherine continues]*: "I can't emphasize enough that successful companies use a single, refined selling process for their entire sales teams. The whole team must understand and use the same process. The process has been refined and adapted for the specific solutions that our particular company is selling. The whole sales team contributes to improving the system over time and participates regularly in training themselves and new members of the sales team on all dimensions of the system.

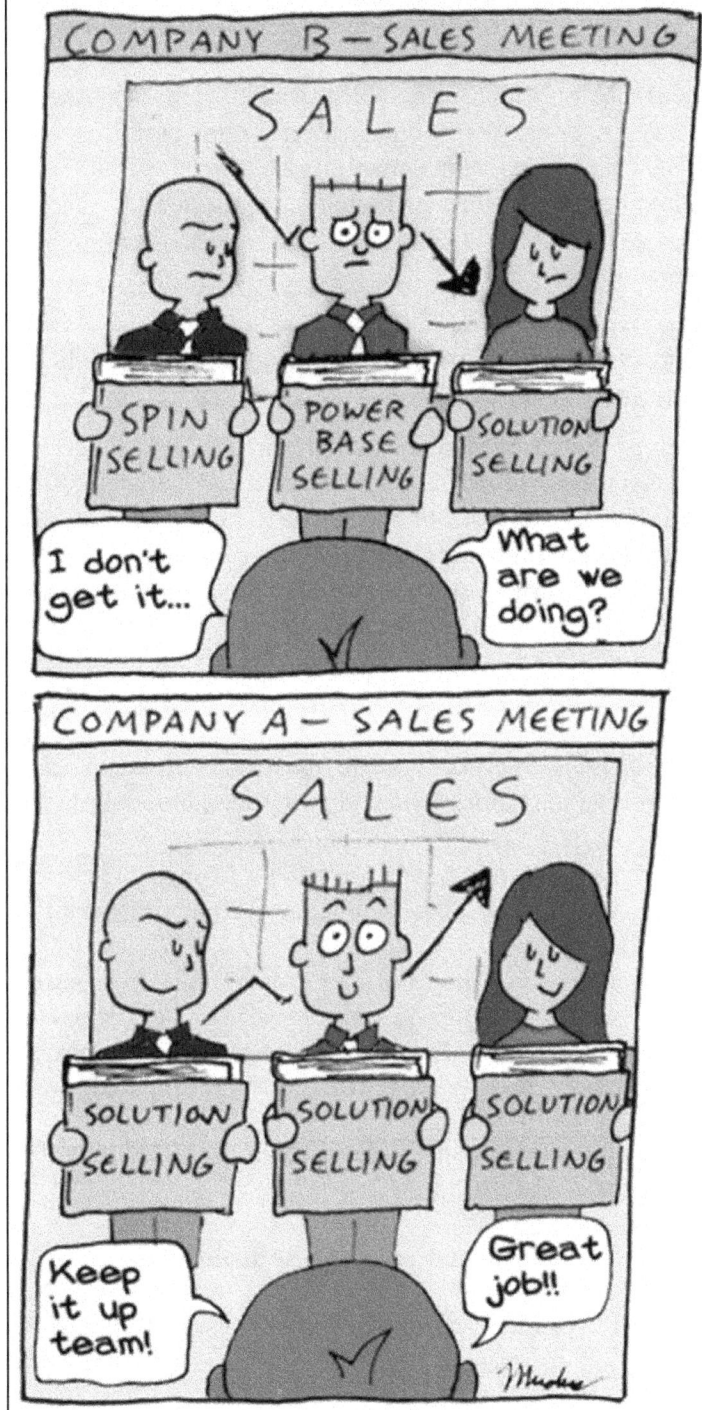

## Improving Close Ratios on Individual Accounts

Using a single, detailed selling process – regardless of which specific system is used -- has multiple benefits. The ***first set of benefits*** focuses on achieving improved close ratios on individual accounts for the whole sales team by:

- Enabling sales rookies (with considerable live mentoring) to hit the ground running;
- Helping grizzled old veterans to enhance their sales performance, once they can be convinced to buy into the system (sometimes a challenging task -- as you know!);
- Helping solid sales force performers become super performers; and
- Even helping those who are already sales superstars to generate even better sales and profit growth numbers.

## Helping Sales Supervisors and Marketing Managers at All Levels to Reach the Company's Overall Sales Growth Goals

The ***second set of benefits*** answers the prayers of sales supervisors, such as Sales Managers, Sales Directors, VPs of Sales, Marketing Directors, Marketing Managers, and the VP of Marketing or CMO. Reaping the relevant benefits for sales supervisors depends upon:

- A rigid commitment to **the *exact* same selling process** by the entire sales force; and
- Overlaying the process with technology-enabled live reports from sales folks in the field. These reports are timely updates on progress made (or not made) on every single important sales effort underway.

The benefits provided are listed below. Sales supervisors at all levels now have potential quantitative bases for:

- More accurately projecting operating period results *during each operating period*, rather than awaiting sometimes good and sometimes disappointing numbers at the end of the quarter;
- Stepping in with coaching aids *during the quarter* in order to help individual sales folks who may be stuck in any step of the selling process with important prospective clients; and
- Knowing ahead of time when the 'sales hopper' is getting thin at any place – from the top to the bottom – and interceding in order to generate more new prospects (via new solutions, new uses, new target segments, or simply more innovative and aggressive prospecting) and to stimulate selective sales efforts already underway.

***Done properly, this can ensure steady, long term, profitable sales growth for the company – the Business Growth Secret's goal!"***

---

*[Brian]*: "Thanks, Catherine! This sure makes sense to me!

"And thanks so much to you too, Linda, for all the help and insights you have provided for me going over this whole selling process. I just hope that someday I can be as successful as you."

## Bottom Line

We have seen that steady, long-term, profitable growth is driven by a 'Master Selling Approach' for individual accounts. That is critical because it frames the entire growth planning process, as detailed in this Sales Growth Secrets book. A company can't expect to grow unless its sales team can consistently convert target customers into actual customers. In this last section we have shown how ongoing, singular sales efforts and successes fit into a larger framework that overlays marketing and sales success. Such a framework can help to ensure that any company has continued success in profitably selling to customer after customer.

# Sales Growth Secrets Glossary

# Sales Growth Secrets Glossary

**BATNA (Best Alternative to Negotiated Agreement):** Final negotiations must yield a result that is better than this.

**Best Overall Solution:** The solution that has the highest overall net value for the target customer. A company's overall market solution includes a core product or service surrounded by a bundle of auxiliary attributes and related benefits.

**Billable Event:** A step in the evaluation plan that must be paid for by the target customer. By ensuring the target customer has some "skin in the game," we can move forward in the selling process with increased confidence of making a sale.

**Brand Advantages:** Unique and sustainable advantages that set your solution apart from your brand competition.

**Brand Competitor:** Specific competitor that directly competes with your solution.

**Building Rapport:** It is important to develop a personal relationship with your clients. Potential customers should be treated as more than just business. However, be sure to make sure you have the appropriate balance of personal conversation and business conversation.

**Buying Committee:** This is a collective group of executives and managers who will make the ultimate decision on whether or not to adopt a new solution. We refer to these individuals as "above the money line."

**C-Level Players:** Chief executives including but not limited to: Chief Executive Officer, Chief Financial Officer, Chief Marketing Officer, Chief Operating Officer, etc. These executives are considered to be 'above the money line'.

**Can Do Transition Players:** Individuals who, despite envisioned disadvantages for them in the short term, will reap long-term benefits from the proposed new solution.

**Can't Do Transition Players**: Folks who would have to expend effort to help successfully implement the proposed new solution, but who would typically not reap any long-term net benefits from the new solution.

**Closing Statement:** Used at the end of a face-to-face meeting. Reviews the conversation with the Key Internal or External Player and looks ahead to later steps of the selling effort, such as accessing the Target Power Sponsor.

**Cold Call:** A sales call to someone that the sales representative has never met before.

**Commodity Drift:** Commodity Drift is the gradual but continuous shift in power from suppliers to buyers over time for virtually any market solution. The market shifts from attractive, unique, and highly differentiated core solutions with high profit margins to lower priced, heavily frilled, and higher cost solutions with lower-profit margins. Marketing's goal is to slow commodity drift.

**Compact Reference Story:** When initially telling a reference story to a Target Sponsor, we present a version of our reference story that focuses on only a few of the operational benefits of our solution.

**Company Experts**: Experts who monitor the pulse of target customers and primary competitors.

**Convert**: The process by which a relevant internal or external player self-concludes that a particular solution will be right for him.

**Converted Power Sponsor:** The target power sponsor becomes a converted power sponsor when he/she joins the sales representative on the selling team. They are now on-board with the solution.

**Converted Sponsor:** The target sponsor becomes a converted sponsor when he/she admits pain and that this pain can be solved by your key advantages. They are now willing to take you to the target power sponsor.

**Core (or Naked) Solution:** An unbundled, basic solution without any frills, add-ons, extra services, etc.,

**Critical Success Criteria:** Metrics used to determine the achievement level of a product implementation. Data is collected on the most important determinants of success, including Return on Investment, Payback Period, etc.

**Deal Goals and Limits:** What you hope to garner from a negotiation, and the maximum amount of something that you are willing to give up.

**Direct Probing Questions:** More specific, targeted questions that are used as a last resort to get various issues acknowledged by the target customer.

**Educational Approach:** Used instead of a traditional selling approach, firms constantly monitor online consumer behavior to stay as up to date as possible.

**Enlightened Leaders:** Individuals who know the pitfalls of static market solutions in dynamic markets. They provide dynamic market solutions that respond to ever-changing customer expectations as well as to increasingly threatening competitive initiatives.

**Envelope Method:** The envelope method consists of cashing your check each month (or week), paying all fixed monthly or weekly bills, divvying up the remaining proceeds into separate envelopes for identified, budgeted items (food, babysitter, entertainment, automobile expenses, household maintenance, etc.) – and then pulling money out of envelopes as expenses occur. Finally, and inevitably, as the next payday approaches, you start raiding any envelopes with money remaining to cover items for which you 'somehow' find an empty envelope.

**Extend and Control Questions:** Used in the second row of the 9-Block. These are used to influence the Internal and External Players' search for Reasons, Impacts, and Capabilities.

**External Players:** Individuals outside of the target company who can either affect or will be affected by the prospective adoption and implementation of our proposed solution.

**Final Evaluation Plan:** The proposed evaluation plan will be reviewed by the buying committee and adjusted to their liking. By making these slight modifications, the sponsor and the rest of the buying committee feel that they 'own' the evaluation plan.

**Financial Benefit:** Monetary benefit that is realized from implementation of a key advantage or capability.

**Financial Players:** Those who will construct a detailed cost and revenue model with the sales representative. Ultimately, they determine whether or not the proposed investment will meet the company's (buyer's) required, risk adjusted return on investment (ROI) and projected payback period.

**Financial Vision:** Proves that the solution makes financial sense as promised.

**First Face-to-Face Meeting:** The initial interaction between the sales representative and the target sponsor. The goal of this meeting is to get the target sponsor enthused about the solution.

**Flexible Market Solution:** The ability to add potential enhancements to your core solution in order to customize the solution based on customer needs (quality & innovation, customer relationship, cost efficiency, etc.).

**Follow-up Letter to Target Sponsor:** Sent to the Target Sponsor after the first face-to-face meeting. It contains summary highlights of the meeting and a proposal for a visit to a reference client as a way to prove that your company can indeed deliver the promised capabilities for the target customer.

**Follow-up Letter to Target Power Sponsor:** Sent to the Target Power Sponsor after you are introduced by the Target Sponsor. It summarizes the meeting and proposes an evaluation plan.

**Generic Advantages:** The general advantages of your market solution.

**Generic Competitor**: Non-specific competition, i.e., in-house or do-it-yourself solutions.

**Gets & Gives List:** A list of opportunities to expand the pie during negotiations. 'Gets' are items that are of high value to you but low cost to the target customer. 'Gives' are items that are low cost to you but high value to the target customer.

**Getting Pain Admitted:** During the initial face-to-face meeting, the seller's goal is to unearth the target sponsor's latent pain. The seller needs to take the target sponsor from latent pain to pain so that they realize they need the capabilities that your solution can provide.

**Go/No-Go Opportunities:** Events worked into the Evaluation Plan that require a joint decision by the seller and target customer to proceed with the remainder of the Evaluation Plan.

**Indirect Probing Questions:** Straightforward questions that ask for facts from the target sponsor. These inquisitions are non-accusatory and non-threatening.

**Inevitable Price Question:** Early in the selling process someone in the customer company is going to ask, "How much would this cost us?" or some variation thereof. This is given that 'feared high cost' is one of the reasons why the relevant solution hasn't been considered seriously before. There are planned ways to respond to this without giving an actual number.

**Informed Buyer:** In the current age of social media and increased information transparency, the average consumer is more knowledgeable about industries, products, and solutions than ever before.

**Internal Players**: Individuals in the target company who can either affect or will be affected by the prospective adoption and implementation of our proposed solution.

**Key Advantage Links Summary Sheet:** Diagram used to demonstrate the connection of the primary financial issues to the primary operating issues, to the causes of the primary operating issues, and to the capabilities needed to resolve each cause, thus providing the desired operating and related financial benefits.

**Key Advantages:** Important generic differentiators, for which one's company's solution has a clear, sustainable advantage over would-be primary brand competitors or generic competitors.

**Key Concerns and Other Goals:** The objectives of all of the individuals entering into a negotiation.

**Lead:** A potential customer who expresses any direct or indirect interest in your solution or product. A lead turns a would-be cold call into a warm call.

**Light Usage:** Amount of a market solution that a customer uses over a fixed period of time – whether it be one-time per day, per week, per month, or per year.

**Light Users:** Segment that is currently using a solution but not to its full potential. Light users can be converted into 'full' or heavy users with a targeted marketing program.

**Looking Customer**: Firms or businesses that are already considering (i.e., 'looking for') a new generic alternative to their traditional way of doing things.

**Master Reference Story:** Previous success story of another client used to stimulate interest with the Target Sponsor that includes all of the relevant issues, advantages, and benefits.

**Master Selling Plan:** Detailed strategy for systematically building all the visions required to ensure the successful acquisition and implementation of the proposed market solution.

**Money Line:** Executives with direct financial responsibility are above the money line.

**Nine Block Vision Processing Model®:** Tool used by the sales representative to help the Target Sponsor (Target Power Sponsor) self-conclude that your company has a solution that can solve their primary operating issue (primary financial issue).

**Non-Users:** Potential customers who are currently using some sort of generic substitute for the market solution of interest. Non-users are typically using older, more traditional 'generic alternatives' to the proposed new solution.

**Not-Looking Customer:** Firms or businesses that have not considered your solution and are currently satisfied with their way of doing things. They may not be looking because they are too busy, have had a bad previous experience, have heard ugly rumors, are unaware of alternatives, or have no interest in innovation.

**Open Questions:** Used in the first row of the 9-Block to search for input from the Internal and External Players.

**Operating Benefit:** Positive outcome that is projected to flow from each prospective new generic advantage/capability.

**Operating Issue:** Problem the Target Customer is facing that can be addressed by a prospective new generic advantage/capability.

**Operating Players:** People whose day-to-day operating responsibilities would be affected by the adoption and implementation of the proposed new way solution.

**Operating Vision:** Vision that proves that the solution will work as promised.

**Overall Market Solution:** See Flexible Market Solution.

**Prepared Script:** Rehearsed statement for introducing our self, our company, and our solution to a Target Sponsor. Its purpose is to give the sales team a template for trying to start a fruitful conversation with the Target Sponsor.

**Pre-proposal Review:** Opportunity for the sales representative and the buying committee to confirm that the operating, transition, and financial visions have all been built to the satisfaction of the Top Management Buying Committee's requirements.

**Price Umbrella:** Resisting lowering prices to help all firms in the industry maintain relatively high profit margins for as long as possible. A leading company can do this without compromising its own sales and market share because its image as an industry innovator and leader is itself a highly valued, sustainable differentiator for many target customers.

**Primary Financial Issue:** Main financial issue that is being caused by the primary operating issue.

**Primary Operating Issue:** Main operating issue that is causing the primary financial issue. The market solution aims to solve this problem for the target customer.

**Primary Target Power Sponsor:** Individual who you believe will make the best Target Power Sponsor.

**Primary Target Sponsor:** Individual who you believe would make the best Target Sponsor.

**Pro-active Commodity Drift Strategies**: Attempt to delay commodity drift for <u>current</u> market solutions and <u>current</u> target customers.

**Probing Questions:** Designed to stimulate the target sponsor to think about, admit, and potentially discuss the various operating issues that are addressed by our solution.

**Proposed Evaluation Plan:** Vehicle for building and proving all visions. It serves to thoroughly convince all important internal and external players in the target customer of the market solution.

**Reaction Threshold:** The price at which a company's 'loyal customers' will decide to re-evaluate their brand purchase habits.

**Re-active Commodity Drift Strategies**: Attempt to salvage profitable growth where significant commodity drift has <u>already occurred</u>.

**Reference Visit:** A trip where the sales representative takes the target sponsor to demonstrate how the seller's proposed solution has been successfully implemented at another company.

**Role:** Job of an individual taking part in a negotiation.

**Sales Superstar ('Rainmaker'):** Salesman that is prepared, has enlightened leaders, teams with company experts, has intimate knowledge of solution selling and outsells everyone else, or nearly everyone else in the company. Sales superstars are made, not born.

**Secondary Target Power Sponsor:** Back-up Target Power Sponsor option in case the initially targeted party selection does not work out.

**Secondary Target Sponsor:** Back-up Target Sponsor option in case the initially targeted party selection does not work out.

**Segment Choice Criteria:** Attributes that make one segment more attractive than another. They include size, growth potential, profitability, availability, sustainability, and communicability.

**Segmentation Map:** Diagram that helps you to break down the market into subsets to determine what segment to target.

**Segmentation:** Process which involves breaking down the market into subsets (segments) to determine where we have the best chance for success.

**Self-Discovery:** Idea that people tend to believe what they conclude for themselves – especially when they are talking with strangers. The salesperson should spend more time asking than telling -- so that the prospective customer can draw conclusions for themselves.

**Social Marketing Advisor:** A company employee who is a master of the social media domain and uses Internet applications to enhance a company's marketing initiatives.

**Social Media:** The Internet-based applications that allow for users to generate and exchange material.

**Social Media Dashboard:** Website where a company can receive a constant stream of information from a variety of social media sources.

**Stand:** Planned response to counter any last minute request or demand from the target customer to reduce price.

**Summary and Confirm Questions:** Used in the third row of the 9-Block. Simply summarize and confirm what the Internal or External Player has said.

**Sustainable Advantages:** Features that can be added to a market solution to stimulate growth without compromising profits. These advantages are unique differentiators that cannot be quickly or easily duplicated by primary competitors and are of high value to customers.

**Target Power Sponsor / Buyer:** Usually the Target Sponsor's boss. This player is above the 'money line' ("purse string power") and is concerned as much with the financial benefits as he or she is with the operating benefits of the proposed solution.

**Target Sponsor:** Person in the target customer company who will most directly benefit on a day-to-day basis from the operating benefits promised by the proposed new solution.

**Test for Power:** A question designed to find out who handles the purse strings for the potential purchase commitment by the target customer.

**Throw-in:** A give that is offered to the target customer at the end of the negotiations. This creates good will, confirms the Win-Win result, and provides a good base for getting implementation off to a good start.

**Time Out Rules:** Guidelines created for negotiation sessions in order to signal to others on your team that you need a break to discuss an issue privately.

**Transition Players:** Players such as the legal staff, human resource personnel, IT folks, etc. who are less directly affected by prospective adoption of the new solution. These people can still exert considerable influence on both the adoption and implementation of the solution.

**Transition Vision:** Vision that proves that the solution can be successfully implemented as promised.

**Trusted Advisor:** An individual or Internet forum that demonstrates sophisticated knowledge in a particular industry, product, or service -- without mention of a company affiliation.

**Unaffiliated expert:** Marketing strategy where firms respond to and interact with customers while appearing highly knowledgeable and helpful without pitching their brand.

**Unsustainable Advantages:** Costly new features and services added for customers that can be quickly and easily duplicated by competitors.

**Value Focus:** Emphasizing the dimension(s) of your market solution that your target customer is willing to pay for.

**Warm Call:** Sales call to someone that the sales representative has met with/spoken to previously.

**What Business Are You In?** The set of fundamental needs your company is trying to address or 'solve' with its current primary product or service.

**Win-Win Result:** Outcome where you and the target customer both walk away with improved situations.

# Notes/References

1 Spencer Stuart Study 2006 - cited in Fast Company, 6/07

2 Francis Goh, "10 Companies that Failed to Innovate Resulting in Business Failure" https://www.collectivecampus.io/blog/10-companies-that-were-too-slow-to-respond-to-change

3 Ibid.

4 https://money.cnn.com/2011/11/10/pf/walmart_black_friday/index.htm

5 Adapted from Anderson, J., and J. Narus, Business Market Management, Prentice Hall, (1st Edition).

6 While a variation is presented here, the Commodity Drift concept flows from: V. K. Rangan and G.T Bowman, "Beating the Commodity Magnet," Industrial Marketing Management, 21: 215-222.

7 Anderson, J., and J. Narus. Business Market Management: Understanding, Creating and Delivering Value. (1st edition), Prentice Hall.

8 Anderson, J., and J. Narus. Business Market Management: Understanding, Creating and Delivering Value. (1st edition), Prentice Hall.

9 Weber, John A., "Illusions of Marketing Planners," Psychology and Marketing, Vol. 18, no. 6, 527-563.

10 Refer to later chapter on Social Marketing Strategies

11 In deference to the too oft frustrated 'Lion faithful,' it is certainly possible, but remains to be seen, whether Mathew Stafford, the #1 overall pick by Detroit in 2009, will become a 'great quarterback.' This will depend upon the performance of other high draft picks by the Detroit in more recent years, the effectiveness of the revolving coaching team, and the extent to which the Lion's improve their win percentage over the years.

-----

12 Wikipedia

13 'Not Looking' concept and terminology comes from Solution Selling® - SPI, Charlotte, NC.

14 As reviewed in an earlier chapter, in more mature segments, existing light users as well as current non-users may constitute significant and worthwhile growth opportunities. The principles considered in this chapter, therefore, are also applicable for attacking 'light user' and 'light usage' segments in more mature markets, as well as non-users in immature segments (which is the focus here).

-----

15 Target Sponsor & Power Sponsor terminology and framework is adapted here from the Solution Selling® system.

-----

16 This concept and diagram comes from Solution Selling®.

17 Many, if not most, companies do not use the value-based pricing approach suggested here and described more thoroughly in a later book in this Book. Note, the traditional Solution Selling®' approach does not use this approach.

18 Primary source for this section is: Gillin, P and E. Schwartzman, Social Marketing to the Business Customer, NY: Wiley, 250 p.

19 Source for this section is: http://socialmediab2b.com/2012/06/b2b-linkedin-generate-leads-company-page/

20 Primary source: http://roarlocal.com/services/social-media-marketing/

21Source: Financial Times.

22https://www.oberlo.com/statistics/how-many-people-use-social-media#

23 https://dustinstout.com/social-media-statistics/

24 https://www.statista.com/statistics/272014/global-social-networks-ranked-by-number-of-users/

25https://www.statista.com/statistics/259379/social-media-platforms-used-by-marketers-worldwide/#:~:text=Facebook%20remains%20the%20most%20important,the%20B2B%20and%20B2C%20spectrum.

26https://www.statista.com/statistics/259379/social-media-platforms-used-by-marketers-worldwide/#:~:text=Facebook%20remains%20the%20most%20important,the%20B2B%20and%20B2C%20spectrum.

27 Ibid.

28Source for this section is: http://socialmediab2b.com/2012/06/b2b-linkedin-generate-leads-company-page/

29 https://thelinkedinman.com/linkedin-kills-products-services-tab/

30Many of these ideas for Prospecting come from Solution Selling®

31https://www.statista.com/statistics/259379/social-media-platforms-used-by-marketers-worldwide/#:~:text=Facebook%20remains%20the%20most%20important,the%20B2B%20and%20B2C%20spectrum.

32For background, see http://gigaom.com/2013/03/16/why-google-killed-off-google-reader-it-was-self-defense/; and, for alternatives, see http://www.newstatesman.com/sci-tech/2013/03/what-should-i-use-instead-google-reader

33 The primary source for the summaries below is directly from Dustin Stout website at: https://dustinstout.com/social-media-statistics/. For detailed, expanded data on Social Media & Marketing, consult Statistica.com sources such as https://www.statista.com/statistics/272014/global-social-networks-ranked-by-number-of-users/. For expanded discussions of using social media for marketing, see some of the many related publications from Hootsuite, such as https://www.hootsuite.com/solutions/social-marketing

-----

34Most of the material on warm and cold call scripts comes Solution Selling®

35http://smallbusiness.chron.com/face-to-face-communication-business-2832.html

36 These percentage 'chances' may vary from one market solution to another, for different size purchase opportunities, etc. The specific percentages are calculated from a database of previous sales successes and failures for a specific market solution.

37 Terminology and framework for the first sales call come from Solution Selling®

38 In some countries, other than the USA, small talk itself may be a much more critical part of the selling process – with the prospective buyer using small talk to size the salesperson up from different angles, to determine whether or not to 'trust' the salesperson, prior to entertaining any detailed conversation about the prospective solution.

39 No Pain, No Gain concept and diagram from Solution Selling®

40 9 Block Vision Building concept, process and diagrams come from Solution Selling®

41 Terminology & framework in this chapter come from Solution Selling®

42 Terminology & framework in this chapter come from Solution Selling®

43 Terminology & framework in this chapter come from Solution Selling®

44 If Roger's response is 'no,' or 'no thanks,' then Linda has failed somewhere along the way in the earlier parts of the vision building process and is most likely going to be an unhappy camper heading out the door in short order. In such an instance, Linda should, sooner rather than later, consult her sales manager and / or sales colleagues, review with them exactly how she handled Phases I & II of the vision building effort with Roger (previous two chapters), and get their opinion on where she failed – hopefully remedying such oversights in her future vision building efforts with new target customers.

45 In traditional Solution Selling terminology, a 'Converted Sponsor' is referred to as an 'Actual Sponsor.'

46 But what if Roger hedged or said no? In that case, Linda could have a real problem. It would be time to assess where she messed up in her vision building effort with Roger and time to try to rebuild his anxiety. She may even have to give up on Roger and seek out our secondary Target Sponsor at HD if she can't get Roger on her side. This would mean starting all over with her whole sales effort for HD. Not ideal, but worth the effort, instead of giving up and heading to the next target customer!

47 These percentage 'chance' once through any stage of the selling process may vary from one market solution to another, for different size purchase opportunities, etc. The specific percentages are calculated from a database of previous sales successes and failures for a specific market solution.

48 Terminology & framework in this chapter come from Solution Selling®

49 Terminology & framework in this chapter come from Solution Selling®

50 The terminology & the framework in this book on 'Converting the Target Power Sponsor' are adapted from Solution Selling®

51 Note: Linda would also include ny additional required capabilities that Roger may have mentioned – whether or not SpeedyLane currently has those specific additional capabilities.

52 Terminology & framework in this chapter come from Solution Selling®

53 Terminology & framework in this chapter come from Solution Selling®

54 Evaluation Plan framework comes from Solution Selling®

55 Terminology & framework here come from Solution Selling®

56 Terminology & framework here come from Solution Selling®

57 If Don is particularly excited about the prospective positive transformation of HD's checkout system, he may elect to invite additional key players at HD (e.g., important members of the Top Management Buying Committee) to make the reference visit to Pioneer Markets with him – to broaden the questions asked of Pioneer's key players.

58 This, as well as the other parts of building the financial vision can be somewhat complex and we only touch on them in this book (see later chapter, 'Building Financial Vision.). Details on how to conduct the audit, to build the Financial Vision, project ROI and Payback period, and to set Key Financial Success Criteria will be included on the 'Sales Growth Secrets' website.

59 Vision Building framework comes from Solution Selling®

60 Most of the terminology & the framework in this chapter come from Solution Selling®. In Solution Selling® terminology, building a transition vision is typically referred to as 'making the transition sale.'

61 In Solution Selling® terminology, building a financial vision is typically referred to as 'making the financial sale.'

62 For readers interested in building and using the menu-driven Excel model described in this chapter, we will be providing a detailed Excel tutorial on website: BusinessGrowthSecrets.com

63 Note, where SpeedyLane leases, rather than sells the units to a customer, the relevant percentage to look at when comparing our solution with that of our direct brand competitor is the promised annual Operating Profit Margin on the net new sales generated, rather than ROI.

64 Note, where SpeedyLane leases, rather than sells the units to a customer, the relevant percentage to look at when comparing our solution with that of our direct brand competitor is the promised annual Operating Profit Margin on the net new sales generated, rather than ROI.

65 Some of the terminology & the framework in this chapter come from Solution Selling®

66 Some of the terminology & framework in this chapter come from Solution Selling®

67 Some of the terminology & framework in this chapter come from Solution Selling®

68 Some of the terminology & framework in this chapter come from Solution Selling®

69 https://www.projectmanager.com/training/create-a-pert-chart

70 https://venngage.com/blog/gantt-chart-example/

71 https://www.projectmanager.com/training/create-a-pert-chart

72 Many of the concepts and some parts of the framework in this chapter and in several of the next several chapters on Sales Management come from Solution Selling®

73 From Solution Selling®

74 Many of the concepts and some parts of the framework in this chapter and in several of the other chapters on Sales Management come from Solution Selling®

75 From Solution Selling®. These milestone percentages may vary from one market solution to another, for different size purchase opportunities, etc. The specific percentages are calculated from a database of previous sales successes and failures for a specific market solution. The traditional win odds used by Solution Selling are 10, 25 (SPONSOR), 50 (POWER AND PLAN), 75, 90 AND 100%.

76 Many of the concepts and some parts of the framework in this chapter and several of the other chapters on Sales Management come from Solution Selling®

77 from Solution Selling®

78 from Solution Selling®

79 Many of the concepts and some parts of the framework in this chapter on Sales Management come from Solution Selling®

80 Many of the concepts and some parts of the framework in this chapter on Sales Management come from Solution Selling®

81 Many of the concepts and some parts of the framework in this chapter on Sales Management come from Solution Selling®

82 Many of the concepts and some parts of the framework in this chapter on Sales Management come from Solution Selling®

www.ingramcontent.com/pod-product-compliance
Lightning Source LLC
Chambersburg PA
CBHW082121210326
41599CB00031B/5837